JFK AND THE END OF AMERICA

INSIDE THE ALLEN DULLES/LBJ PLOT THAT KILLED KENNEDY

TIM FLEMING

Strategic Book Publishing and Rights Co.

Strategic Book Publishing and Rights Co., LLC
USA | Singapore
www.sbpra.com

For information about special discounts for bulk purchases, please contact Strategic Book Publishing and Rights Co., LLC Special Sales, at bookorder@sbpra.net.

ISBN: 978-1-948260-08-4

In Memory of John Fitzgerald Fleming
(1965–2015)

CONTENTS

PROLOGUE

Recent polls indicate that the number of Americans who believe that President John F. Kennedy was murdered as a result of a conspiracy is about 65%. This is remarkable, considering the mammoth efforts made by media and government in this country to convince us otherwise. Somehow, against the tide of endless propaganda spewed at us for a half-century, and in spite of the deaths of the majority of Americans who had first-hand memories of November 22, 1963, the truth (or at least the rejection of the lie that Lee Harvey Oswald alone killed JFK), for the most part, has survived the passing of time and generations. As Kevin Costner (playing New Orleans district attorney Jim Garrison) predicted in the movie *JFK*, it has taken word of mouth and an almost underground network of researchers to preserve some semblance of historical accuracy concerning how and why the 35th President died.

Why have those in power tried so mightily to keep the truth from us? Because truth is a dangerous thing. Because knowledge is power, and an informed electorate is a dangerous electorate. If the citizenry of a nation knows its true history, that citizenry is much more likely to throw out the bums who have lied to them, suppressed them, and manipulated them. That's why it is important to keep the truth alive, now more than ever, because American democracy is teetering on the brink of extinction. Some even say it is already dead. Historian, author, and former military intelligence officer Colonel Fletcher Prouty wrote that, "At no time in the history of mankind has the general public been so misled and so betrayed as it has been by the work of the propaganda merchants of this century and their 'historians.'"[1]

How did this happen? How did Jefferson's great experiment turn into a for-profit enterprise ruled by a secret oligarchy which considers itself above the laws of the land? The roots of this evil "shadow government" can be traced back to the robber barons of the late 19th century whose obscene wealth led to restraint of trade and excessive control over the economic engine called capitalism. After the government forced the Rockefeller family to break up its Standard Oil monopoly, it dawned on the ruling class that American politicians needed to be bought in order for democracy, capitalism's natural enemy, to be subverted. This is not to say that American robber barons invented political corruption, but they refined it enough to usher in a lucrative age of perfidy.

With the invention of the automobile, oil became the black gold of the United States. A new class of millionaires (mostly in the wild west of Texas) was born, and these wildcatters used their wealth to sabotage democracy in new ways. Politicians like Lyndon Johnson became their wholly owned subsidiaries and were sent to Washington to procure government contracts and to legislate corporate welfare in the form of oil depletion allowances.

Rampant cheating and free-wheeling stock market speculation caused the crash that brought a temporary end to the oligarchy's reign. Oh, they survived fine. Their millions were safely stashed when the economy collapsed in the 1930s. But their scam was exposed to the rest of us knaves, and we elected a quasi-socialist, Franklin Roosevelt, to protect us from the bastards' ruthless ways. Then the war came along. America won, and the economic engine started humming again. A vibrant middle class burgeoned. The common man had enough money to now do what previously only the privileged could do—buy a home, own a couple of cars, get an education, have free time, perhaps even ponder the utility of the American political system and our way of government.

It is hard to believe now, but collectivist ideologies—for instance, communism and democratic socialism—were once active and impactful political movements in this country. They had their own public membership, national conventions, and candidates for office. But after World War II, rich American aristocrats, having seen the power accorded communist Russia in the new world order, became terrified that collectivist ideas would take root in America, just as they had in post-World War I Russia. The Russian Revolution had scared American plutocrats to death. The overthrow of a closed ruling class like the tsars, despots or not, made communism a terrifying ideology to American patricians. It was an ideology that needed to be vanquished; capitalists feared the unwashed hordes might come for them with pitchforks and lanterns. The American ruling class (now known as the 1% who own 98% of all the country's abundance) didn't want to lose its vast wealth and power to some populist uprising, so they took steps to squash the left-wing both privately and publicly, at home and abroad. The public witch trials, better known as the House Un-American Activities hearings, served their purpose by humiliating and destroying liberals, thus sending the message to Americans at large: mind your place, think only government-approved thoughts, and support the status quo lest you be subpoenaed, harassed, excoriated, ostracized and ruined.

These unconstitutional and immoral hearings served the ruling class well, but there were also threats abroad with which to deal. The Red Menace was expanding across the globe. And not just in Europe and the Middle East. In the western hemisphere, third world countries like Guatemala and Cuba, vital to American business interests, turned to leftist leaders in the 1950s amid the unrest over right-wing corruption and oppression. To squash the international communist movement after World War II, America's wealthiest individuals and corporations needed more than Joe McCarthy, a hack, alcoholic junior Senator from Wisconsin. They needed the Central Intelligence Agency.

An outgrowth of the Office of Strategic Services (a capable and necessary wartime agency), the Central Intelligence Agency was officially created in 1947. President Harry Truman signed it into existence and regretted it ever after. Originally chartered to spy on foreign nations, the CIA became an insidiously evil force in domestic policy and decision-making. Accountable to no entity, not even the president, and subject to no oversight, the CIA and its secretive leaders ran roughshod over the Constitution and the country's long-standing democratic principles. Among its covert atrocities were granting safe haven in America to Nazi war criminals, the drugging and brainwashing of innocent civilians, spying on student demonstrators and war protestors, infiltration and subversion of the free press, and the murder of its own commander-in-chief.

In the pages that follow, these atrocities will be enumerated, and evidence to support these assertions laid out. But beyond the details of the CIA's misdeeds is an uglier truth that, hopefully, will elucidate the broader sweep of the dismantling of American democracy. For if you think we live in an open and free democracy, you are mistaken. For the last 70 years, the CIA and its minions have had free reign to erode our form of governance, and what's left is an empty shell of a system resembling a burned-out building nearly destroyed by an inferno. We can still see the framework, but inside is nothing but a rotted-out remnant of what once was. It is not an oversimplification to say that the CIA is largely responsible for this; even so, it had plenty of help from its complicit, cowardly, greedy, frightened, fascist collaborators. Each time a person refused to stand up to the CIA, each time someone lied, or killed, or assisted it in any way, American democracy was eroded just a bit. And in the end, Edmund Burke's prophecy came to pass for the United States, "All that is necessary for the triumph of evil is for good men to do nothing."

The CIA's greatest triumph of evil occurred on November 22, 1963. The how, why, and who of the event will be delineated in the pages that follow. There is new evidence to assess; more importantly, there are new connections to illuminate and new assumptions to make. Only through the determined courage of a small army of researchers has the truth been kept alive. Most have specialized in limited areas of the assassination. Rightly so, because the plot that took JFK's life is broad in scope. It encompasses the medical evidence, the ballistics, the witnesses, the films and photographs, the CIA, the FBI, Texas businessmen, and Lyndon Johnson. Lee Harvey Oswald's pitiful and manipulated life alone is worth a hundred books. It is almost an overwhelming prospect to synthesize all this information into a logical and concise narrative—of what happened in Dallas, why it happened, how it was covered up, and, most importantly, who was behind it.

Yet that's what this book attempts to do; in the end it will fall short of presenting an exhaustive, in-depth rendition of all facets of the plot. That is an impossible task. But at least the reader, by book's end, will have an overview of the wherefores, the who, the how, the what, and the why of it all. The "why," in its most rudimentary form, is put forth in Prouty's book, *JFK: The CIA, Vietnam And The Plot To Assassinate John F. Kennedy*: "…the enormous dollar potential of the Vietnam War to the great military-industrial complex… [made] it necessary for them, to bring about this coup…"[2] This is, of course, an oversimplification. Kennedy's enemies were not confined to the Pentagon and its contractors. Without question, the generals who surrounded him—reactionary, old-school warriors like Lyman Lemnitzer, Curtis LeMay, and Arleigh Burke—believed he was a coward and a traitor. But Kennedy made other deadly foes in the backrooms of Washington, the boardrooms of Texas, the inner sanctums of Wall Street, and the lairs of Mafia dons. They hated his youth, his charisma, his nuanced way of dealing with the communist bloc. They hated his foreign policy. They hated his brother for prosecuting gangsters. They hated it when he stood up to them like no other president had. When they killed him they took over America.

What tied the plotters together and unified them in their purpose were two men: Allen Dulles and Lyndon Johnson. While many may have wanted Kennedy dead, Dulles and Johnson, above all others, had the means and the bloodthirstiness to get the job done. Dulles's beloved CIA, from which he had been deposed by Kennedy, faced extensive reforms or possibly extinction in a second Kennedy term. Johnson, on the verge of imprisonment for corruption, would have had his political career destroyed if not for Dallas. Between the two of them, they gathered a small army of Judases. An elaborate scheme was concocted. Little was left to chance. Contingencies were covered. In the end, all power accrued to them. They controlled all avenues of inquiry. The truth was vanquished. Dissent was discouraged through violent and subtle methods. The official lie survives today. No mainstream media outlet or establishment journalist dares to challenge the lie, lest their careers be torpedoed.

Why does 11/22/63 still have resonance today and forever? Because we can draw a straight line from Dallas to the political, economic, and cultural morass we face today. The plotters won, and the vision they had for America came to pass. We and our government are controlled by a privileged, secretive few for their own benefit. And America no longer works for the vast majority of its citizens. The people are angry; they know somehow they have been duped or left behind. In their blind rage, though, they do stupid things like elect a malevolent circus clown/con artist/narcissist. Perhaps Donald Trump's crude, naked rapaciousness appealed to some; at least we know that he has no qualms about using public office to enrich himself, as opposed to more polished politicians who feign rectitude. The irony is, incensed by government lies, we elected the world's biggest liar. Taken in again, with mendacity all around us, it is easy to give up on the Republic. Still, the truth is not beyond our grasp, and that starts with the truth of 11/22/63, the day America began its slow descent into the abyss. And the truth is what really frightens the ruling class that the CIA and its secret cabal created.

Chapter 1

The Plotters

"Ye shall know the truth, and the
truth shall set you free."
--inscription in the lobby of
CIA headquarters

"Ye shall know the truth if ye are
me and the President."[1]
--Allen Dulles

A college professor friend of mine, now deceased, with whom I shared much of what's to follow in these chapters, said something to me before he died that stunned me then and which I share with you here: "America is a hoax, a Ponzi scheme run to victimize its citizens. For all its bluster about freedom and democracy, it is, at its core, a fraudulent enterprise run by and for a few powerful, wealthy elites."

I knew how much it pained my friend to say that. He once loved his country enough to fight fascism in World War II and proudly wear the medals which his country had bestowed upon him for so doing. He returned home to attend college on the GI Bill, got married, raised a family, bought a home in the suburbs, and voted for Ike twice. Then the '60s came, and the age of college campus unrest dawned. My professor friend, at first, was appalled by his students' disrespect for the nation he loved. Slowly, though, over time he himself came to question the country's leaders and motives. He was

1

an inquisitive man, not one to blindly accept government pronouncements and propaganda. One of the things he most loved about his country was the freedom to think for one's self. He devoured books on the topics of Vietnam, Watergate, the assassinations, Iran/Contra, the Savings-and-Loans scandal in the '80s, 9/11, and the Wall Street bailouts. Gradually the ugly truth of America's hidden history turned him away from the myth of America he once cherished. The last e-mail he wrote me contains the pain of his disillusionment: "America is nothing more than a for-profit enterprise. If you are rich, America works quite well. If you are not, you are just another sucker lured by the promise of a dying Constitution and a decaying political system."

It is hard to accept such a depressing reality. And it begs the question: Why don't we do something about it? Because it is much easier to throw up our hands in despair and live our lives in quiet surrender. What can we really do? Barely half of us even bother to vote; elections are rigged and stolen anyway. We are no match for the well-armed few who control the levers of power. As Americans disengage from democracy and civilized Socratic debate, conditions become conducive for tyranny. Andrew Sullivan, writing for *New York* magazine, claims America has never been more ready for a fascist takeover. Though his intent is to warn Americans about Fuhrer Donald Trump, his evocation applies to the takeover of the country by any person or entity with the ruthlessness and power to do so. "Neo-fascist movements do not advance gradually by persuasion; they first transform the terms of the debate, create a new movement based on untrammeled emotion, take over existing institutions, and then ruthlessly exploit events."[2] This is a perfect description of how a secret domestic cabal can subvert democracy.

How did it get this way? How did the hopeful, united country my professor friend grew up in become the regressive plutocracy of 21st century America? After World War II, extremism in all forms faded. Eventually the McCarthy hearings and the Red Scare were exposed as intrusions on our liberty to speak freely and associate with whom we pleased. We elected a president who, having seen the brutality of fascism in World War II, was determined to advance the causes of peace and democracy at home and abroad. Eisenhower embraced moderate policies and social support programs. He once wrote to his brother that, "Should any political party attempt to abolish social security, unemployment insurance, and eliminate labor laws and farm programs, you would not hear of that party again in our political history. There is a tiny splinter group, of course, that believes you can do these things. Among them are H. L. Hunt (you possibly know his background), a few other Texas oil millionaires, and an occasional politician or business man from other areas. Their number is negligible and they are stupid."[3]

Ike, who today would be considered a moderate Democrat, served two peaceful terms. America temporarily abandoned war. A vibrant middle class developed. Old racist paradigms of the South were challenged by Brown v. Board of Education and Little Rock. A new era seemed at hand as a young president was elected in 1960. But underneath the dreamy veneer was a sinister force at work consolidating its power and scheming to subvert democracy for its own malignant purposes.

What Americans did not know was that Eisenhower made a Faustian bargain with his Secretary of State, John Foster Dulles, and his Director of Central Intelligence, Allen Dulles. In exchange for staying out of a shooting war, of which Eisenhower had seen enough, the Dulleses were given carte blanche to fight communism through hardline diplomacy and covert intelligence means. This was an enormous amount of power to be held by one family, and the brothers fought dirty. Rather than quell our enemies, they heightened tensions and created worldwide animosity for American imperialism. Ike kept us out of a hot war, but we paid an enormous price for the "peaceful" era between Korea and Vietnam. Foster and Allen were hard at work, stealing democracy from the masses and creating a fraternity of supreme patricians. The tumor that had invaded the American system in the 1940s metastasized in the 1950s and killed its host in the 1960s. The Dulleses oversaw the death, and, in so doing, they secretly transformed America into a permanent war state, one which needs constant enemies, real or imagined, to advance the cause of unfettered profit-making for an elite few at the expense of all the rest of the world.

An unprecedented military armaments and defense industry expansion took place in 1950s America, in large part because the Dulles brothers and their cronies were determined to scare America into acquiescing to the need for this expansion. Foster Dulles, burning with the righteousness of American imperialism, exacerbated the Cold War with his hardline policies. Allen Dulles, the master spy who used the CIA to overthrow sovereign governments and suppress domestic democracy, used his power to create immense profits for his corporate clients. The two, in effect, ran the country for their own means, and helped to create an elite class of corporate overlords that still dominates American politics and governance today.

As head of the omnipotent CIA, Dulles placed assets in all walks of American life—the military, the media, education, private industry, and all facets of government. Without identifying themselves as such, CIA agents infiltrated these organizations to influence policy and practices, and report on possible subversives. It amounted to nothing less than a secret government run by the CIA. Author James Douglass, in his book *JFK and the Unspeakable*, described it this way: "…when Kennedy became president…the CIA had placed a secret team of its own employees through the entire U.S. government."[4]

In addition to their formidable government positions, the Dulleses had deep and long-standing connections to the richest men in America through their law firm, Sullivan and Cromwell. The firm's client list included Standard Oil, General Electric, United Fruit,

Ford, DuPont, Chase Manhattan Bank, IBM, and U.S. Steel. These companies profited handsomely from their association with Allen Dulles and his intelligence network. When American corporate interests were threatened, at home or abroad, Dulles used his vast network of spies, paramilitary personnel, media contacts and foreign intelligence assets to come to the rescue.

Before and during World War II, Dulles actively schemed to protect his clients' business interests in Germany. He went so far as to subvert FDR's policies and U.S. interests to keep Nazi money flowing to Standard Oil and General Motors. According to author David Talbot, "Dulles...enjoyed a professional and social familiarity with many members of the Third Reich elite...and shared many of these men's postwar goals."[5] Namely, to turn America into a quasi-fascist state. Or as Mussolini referred to it, "the merger of state and corporate power."

Despite their treachery, Dulles and his cronies were never made to publicly account for suborning democracy. Their ever-flexible morality and cunning political instincts prevented them from ever being caught on the losing side of a cataclysmic event. When it was clear that the Nazis were going to lose the war, Dulles and company presented themselves as patriots who exalted in the Third Reich's demise; yet, all the while they were surreptitiously smuggling Nazi scientists, doctors and spies (war criminals all) into the United States.

By the time Foster Dulles died in 1959, Allen Dulles had already accumulated enough powerful allies to enforce his will on America without his brother's help. By turning over foreign and domestic policy to them, Ike basically abdicated the power of the presidency. In exchange for no American boots on the ground in a hot war, the Dulleses were allowed to overthrow left-leaning governments around the globe through covert operations that resulted in few or no American casualties. In essence, the President gave the Dulleses a blank foreign policy check. At times, however, Eisenhower was so startled by the Dulles brothers' brazen machinations that he was forced to step in. In 1954 Foster Dulles "brought up the possibility of using nuclear weapons…on China [which] would kill twelve to fourteen million civilians."[6] Ike was aghast at Dulles's callous proposal of bringing the world to the brink of World War III. Without oversight, the CIA was secretly preserving a fascist movement we thought we had conquered in World War II. And in the middle of the 20th century, unbeknownst to all but a few Americans, a great war was taking place between the forces of good (democratic pluralism) and the forces of evil (repressive despotism). President Kennedy, who evolved from conventional Cold Warrior to peace proponent in his thousand days in office, carried on an internal war with his own national security state and America's military monolith, what Eisenhower called the "military-industrial complex." Kennedy resolved to end American involvement in southeast Asia (limited as it was), much to the dismay of the Pentagon. He also sought rapprochement with the Soviet Union in order to end the Cold War rather than try to win it in a cataclysmic nuclear exchange (the unthinkable strategy promoted by his military advisors). Living in peaceful coexistence with the communist world was an earth-shatteringly radical idea in 1963. And it put a target on JFK's back. It infuriated the military-intelligence state; for without the communist threat (real or imagined), there was no need for its existence. There would be no need for a secret, unaccountable, out-of-control intelligence apparatus or a massive arms build-up that greased the war-for-profit engine of America.

The decisive blow in the war occurred in Dallas, November 22, 1963. The forces of evil won. Kennedy's dream of a permanent peace state was killed; a permanent war state was born. Since that day in Dallas we have constantly been at war or under the threat of war; we have been victimized by terror or cowed by the threat of it. We have been at the mercy of a military-industrial complex which has enriched defense contractors, debauched our democracy, and killed historical truth.

It is now, for all honest and serious investigators at the first part of the 21st century, beyond dispute that a secret cabal—composed of disaffected CIA personnel, including their criminal underworld assets, a vast network of covert operatives, and their corporate bene-factors; military chiefs; key Secret Service agents; and Lyndon John-son and his nefarious associates—arranged for the murder of President John F. Kennedy. The circumstantial, eyewitness and physical evidence overwhelmingly supports this assertion. All who profess otherwise are either disinformationists, propagandists, media lackeys or bureaucratic obstructionists. In other words, any-one who claims Oswald alone did the deed is either severely deluded or is lying for a purpose. And by "purpose" I mean to protect one-self, hide a secret agenda, or preserve one's status. No one who is unbiased, uncoerced or unencumbered by fear can conclude any-thing other than that an elaborate, well-coordinated and highly sophisticated conspiracy brought down the leader of the free world in 1963.

This does not mean that the CIA as a whole was in on the con-spiracy. It certainly was not. Rather, a parallel, renegade spy agency run by Allen Dulles in exile in the early 1960s was the culprit. This secret cabal was composed of former and current CIA operatives, but was not beholden to the normal restraints of everyday CIA activities. Then again, the agency as a whole had never been sub-jected to rigorous scrutiny by the legislative, executive or judicial branches of the government. It has always been a government unto itself, and in the early 1960s one of its evil tentacles pulled off a coup d'etat. America has never been the same.

To be sure, Dulles's secret cabal could not and did not execute JFK on its own. It needed the cooperation, willing or otherwise, of the Pentagon's hierarchy (namely, the Joint Chiefs of Staff), pivotal personnel of the Secret Service, elements of the criminal under-world, Texas oil billionaires' financing, and, most importantly, the new President, Lyndon Johnson. After the fact, the cover-up required the cooperation of a compromised and lethargic national media, as well as a CIA/Mafia killing machine with the means and access to rub out key witnesses and troublemakers.

The Dulles cabal had the power and the contacts to persuade all these entities to do its bidding. In some cases, no persuasion was necessary, for President Kennedy had amassed a formidable list of enemies. Military warmongers, Wall Street power brokers, wealthy oilmen, captains of industry, deadly Mafioso, and his own vice president had all come to loathe JFK and his administration. And this lethal mix had the wherewithal, the motive, and the smug audacity to kill a president and get away with it.

But it was Dulles and Johnson who, more than anyone else, sanctioned and propelled the plot. Dulles, a Cold War intelligence icon, had been fired by Kennedy after the Bay of Pigs fiasco in April of 1961. And Dulles was not a man who lightly endured such disgrace. Johnson, in the fall of 1963, was perilously close to facing criminal prosecution for corruption. Spurred on by Bobby Kennedy, who despised Johnson, eastern journalists were running stories of Johnson's kickback schemes and government contracts fraud. LBJ had become a political liability for Kennedy, who told his secretary shortly before Dallas that Johnson would not be his running mate in the 1964 election.[7]

Massively egocentric and extremely powerful in 1950s Washington politics, Dulles and Johnson were not men to passively endure humiliation from a man they considered a presidential impostor. In their eyes, Kennedy was too young and inexperienced, and, more to the point, too incorruptible to hold high office. Ruthless and cynical, Dulles and Johnson viewed governance as nothing more than a power grab; all that mattered was attaining power; it didn't matter how. They were also kindred spirits in foreign policy—America should exert its will and dominance over the rest of the world, whether through covert subterfuge or outright military might.

Johnson's influence was so great that "by the end of 1958," writes author Barr McClellan, "Johnson was de facto president and the most powerful man in America."[8] While this is an exaggeration (one must remember that McClellan's son was George W. Bush's press secretary, and so Barr McClellan was invested in obscuring the Bush family's secret ties to Allen Dulles and the CIA), it is not far from the truth. Only two other men in America had the contacts, influence and "clients" that Johnson had—the Dulles brothers. And when John Foster Dulles died in 1959, it could reasonably be argued that no other men so highly placed in the U.S. government were mightier than Lyndon Johnson and Allen Dulles. Together they had more impressive sponsors and assets—in finance, big oil, media, the military and the three branches of government—than any other two public servants. They shared many of these assets; their paths crossed at big oil and military contractors many times over.

Most significantly, for the purposes of this narrative, all involved, directly or indirectly, in the murder of JFK, and the cover-up after the fact, can be tied to either Johnson or Dulles. In many cases the perpetrators and actions can be tied to both men. And it is difficult to overstate the vast connections that each man had. They reached into the highest echelons of private and public influence. And both Johnson and Dulles had an army of willing underlings at their command.

As Senate majority leader Johnson controlled nearly all legislation and government appropriations. As head of the CIA Dulles controlled not only the flow of information to and from allies and enemies of the state, but also commanded a secret coalition of corporate, paramilitary, media, and intelligence personnel which formed no less than a hidden government. Both men had committed high crimes and treasonous acts in their climb to the top, and each had the resources and experience to conceal their crimes. Despite violating virtually every law of the land and each dictate of the Constitution, they entered the 1960s with their reputations virtually intact. One was readying himself for the Presidency; the other was busy pursuing a New World Order by installing quasi-fascist states around the world.

Then, within a matter of a few months, their almost unlimited power came to an abrupt end with the nomination and election of one man: Jack Kennedy. By late 1961 Johnson and Dulles were suddenly nonentities and persona non grata on the domestic and international stage. Johnson was reduced to a political afterthought by the irrelevance of the vice-presidency, and Dulles was out as head of the CIA. Both were relieved of their previous status by JFK. For Johnson and Dulles, men of huge egos and appetites unaccustomed to ceding authority to anyone in their spheres, it was a shocking and humiliating comedown. One they would not countenance for long.

Johnson and Dulles also shared deeply conservative political convictions. In Dulles these beliefs were long-standing and undeniable; Johnson, on the other hand, at least on the surface, seems to be one of the most liberal presidents the nation has ever had. However, prior to becoming president, Johnson was a rock-ribbed right-winger. As majority leader in the Senate he stood with the racist southern caucus and consistently blocked any and all consequential civil-rights legislation. He regularly used derogatory terms in referring to African-Americans, and in the 1950s and early '60s he did not speak out in defense of civil rights. When he became president he finally pushed through significant bills to help black people, only after years of impeding Kennedy's attempts at getting similar legislation through Congress. Johnson, as vice-president, could have twisted arms, bent elbows, and swapped favors with his old pals in the Senate and the House, but he was saving the acclaim for himself, for the day when he knew he would become president and could take credit for being an enlightened leader. When he finally did sign the Voting Rights Act into law, Johnson declared, "I'll have them niggers voting Democratic for the next two hundred years."[9]

Johnson cemented the black vote for himself when he signed the Civil Rights Act of 1964 into law. In the audience that day was Bobby Kennedy, who was conspicuous by his lack of enthusiasm for the LBJ ceremony. As all others present leapt to give the President a standing ovation, Bobby sat somberly unmoved. He knew, as did all astute observers, that it was the memory of his dead brother which impelled lawmakers to accede to their better angels and do the right thing. Johnson had given lip service to JFK's memory in his first address to Congress after JFK's assassination. But by 1964 LBJ was taking all the credit. He was not about to do something that was good for the country unless there was something in it for him. As Johnson biographer Robert Caro put it, Johnson exercised power "...not to improve the lives of others, but to manipulate and dominate them."[10]

At the same time as he was advancing the cause of black Americans, he was supporting right-wing causes and laying the groundwork for an unnecessary war.

Johnson effectively blocked all attempts to reduce the oil depletion allowance, an expensive government giveaway to big oil companies. Big oil and Lying Lyndon had always had a cozy relationship; Johnson was beholden to men like D.H. Byrd, H.L. Hunt, Clint Murchison and Sid Richardson—Dallas millionaires who financed Johnson's political career. He was more beholden to big oil than any of his other constituencies, and his legislative agenda reflected that. His Senate record includes anti-union and pro-business stances, and a proclivity for granting huge defense contracts to his Texas cronies.

In gratitude for the support of the Texas right wing, Johnson awarded them lucrative defense contracts once the Vietnam War was in full swing. Giving the people butter and bullets, all the while making himself more powerful and admired, was Johnson's way of feeding his huge need to be loved. In psychological terms he would be described as a classic narcissist—one who exaggerates his own self-importance while having a lack of empathy for others. All his life Johnson was callous, vain and envious, with an overwhelming need for power, prestige and wealth. Most of all, he needed to be worshipped unconditionally by the masses; when they turned on him during the Vietnam War, he felt betrayed and became enraged. For the sycophants with whom he surrounded himself, he was a monster. Some of those close to him came to see him as dangerously unstable.

Johnson might have been the only man in the world whom Dulles legitimately feared. Dulles knew that LBJ had not and would not practice restraint with immense power. If Dulles were to plot JFK's murder without Johnson's assent and compliance, Dulles would always have the fear of Johnson using his newfound power of the presidency to come after Dulles and his co-conspirators. Hence, Dulles needed Johnson to be on board with the planned coup in 1963. As it turned out, Johnson had no reason to object to the plot; in fact, he stood to gain more from the death of JFK than any one human being on the planet. What is more, it may well have been Johnson who first approached Dulles with the idea of a coup. For without question, Johnson had neither the sophistication nor the experience to pull off the intricate and well-disguised covert operation required to kill a president and get away with it. It's apparent, then, that Johnson and Dulles needed one another to successfully execute a coup d'etat. Indeed, one could not have done it without the other's acquiescence. And the supposition that they partnered to kill JFK is more than just conjecture. The CIA's fingerprints are all over the murder, and Johnson's killer's fingerprints were literally found at the crime scene. Combine this with the fact that both men had ample motive to want JFK dead, and it becomes evident that both Johnson and Dulles should have been prime suspects.

After the assassination, the two men warily circled one another.

Johnson kept constant tabs on the progress of the Warren Commission, and the shadow of Dulles's renegade CIA always loomed over Johnson. According to the memos of Paul Rothermel, ex-FBI man and head of security for Dallas oil billionaire H.L. Hunt, "Lyndon Johnson [was] mortally afraid of being assassinated and does not trust the Secret Service...and has ordered the FBI to be present everywhere he goes..."[11] This might have been a figment of Johnson's enormous paranoia, for the guilty plotters knew better than to turn on one another for fear of mutual destruction. Then again, Johnson saw first-hand in Dallas what the CIA and the Secret Service were capable of, and he surely never fully trusted the CIA.

With JFK's death, Johnson achieved his life-long obsession of becoming president, he stayed out of prison by quashing congressional investigations into his shady business dealings, and, by becoming the most powerful man in the free world, he was able to cover up his involvement in the crime of the century. By killing JFK, he had also neutralized his hated enemy Bobby Kennedy, who was powerless without the backing of his brother. With JFK out of the way, no longer did Johnson have to worry about the Kennedys, who "...were out to ruin [Johnson] completely by making him look like a crook."[12]

Dulles also reaped immense benefits from the death of JFK. His vision of a world dominated by an elite cadre of plutocrats was restored. His beloved CIA was preserved; without meddling from the Kennedys, the agency's illegal and unconstitutional operations flourished, and its power over American and international policy became more dominant than ever. The Cold War, which JFK wanted to end, became hotter than ever. Dulles's clients and assets were enriched by war and the expansion of American imperialism. The largest impediment to Dulles's quasi-Fascist America had been surgically removed. It was sweet revenge for his bitter ouster after the Bay of Pigs. As Dulles once told magazine editor Willie Morris, "That little Kennedy, he thought he was a god."[13]

Upon Kennedy's death, the two titans of American governance were restored to positions of such power that they were beyond any prosecution. One man stacked the investigatory commission with men he could easily control, and the other man became the de facto head of that fraudulent commission. It is hard to bring killers to justice when the killers are the ones conducting the murder investigation.

Ruthless Men

The Dulles brothers grew up in the kind of noblesse-oblige family that believed it owned America and was only leasing it to the rest of us, for a steep price of course. Their patrician roots, religious fervor, and political leanings can be traced back to the first of their forebears to set foot on American soil. Joseph Dulles, fleeing anti-Protestant persecution in Ireland, came to America in 1778. A smug sermonizer, Joseph failed to heed God's humane passages and became a slave-holding plantation owner in South Carolina. He made a fortune off slave labor, enough to afford elite educations for his sons. They, in turn, used their advantages to grant their own children and grandchildren entrée into the privileged sanctuaries of America in the Gilded Age.

Allen and Foster's father, Allen Macy Dulles, married into the wealthy and prestigious John Foster Watson family in the 1890s. Watson was a rabid Republican activist who was appointed to diplomatic posts by Presidents Grant, Hayes and Garfield. In 1892 another Republican, Benjamin Harrison, made him Secretary of State. Secretary Watson's most noteworthy accomplishment was to assist white settlers in overthrowing Queen Liliuokalani's monarchy in Hawaii (not yet a state). Essentially labeling the natives as stupid and lazy, Watson became the first American secretary of state to overthrow a foreign government.[14]

Deeply rooted, then, in Allen Dulles's family tree are the sentiments and ideologies that he would use to advance his own agenda in the 20th century: an aversion to Catholicism; fanatical American imperialism; the superiority of the white Protestant male; right-wing politics; the entitlement of the upper class; arrogant self-righteousness; the power that comes from covert intelligence operations; and the benefit of overthrowing unwanted governments. In short, it was Allen Dulles's ancestral design and manifest destiny to manipulate world events for the benefit of a small group of elite capitalists.

And that's exactly what he and his brother did in the 1950s. Allen, as Director of the Central Intelligence Agency, and Foster, as Secretary of State, controlled the reins of covert and overt foreign policy. It was and is the only time in American history that brothers owned such a monopoly. British double agent Kim Philby, who knew quite well the dubious methods employed by the Dulles brothers, said that, "John Foster Dulles needed communism the way that Puritans needed sin."[15] What Philby meant by that is the Dulles brothers considered the fight against communism a religious crusade, no less than a global battle between good and evil.

Self-avowed Calvinists, the Dulleses saw no shades of gray in international politics, diplomacy and espionage. Strangely though, the struggle was not an altruistic one; it was purely selfish. They were willing to sacrifice American lives and values to enrich themselves and their cronies. In a perverse way, they were willing to destroy America in order to protect it. Communism was evil because it presented a dire threat to Dulleses' patrician privilege, not because it threatened democracy. The Dulleses had little use for democracy. They preferred right-wing totalitarian regimes where suppression of the masses and suspension of free speech and elections were the norm. Human rights and civil liberties were not principles to be embraced and nurtured; in fact, such democratic ideals were a threat to the Dulleses. Free and open societies, where accountability and representation are the bylaws, are anathema to the advancement of a small privileged class bent on hoarding all the power and resources for itself. Accordingly, Allen Dulles used whatever means were at his disposal to crush democracy and communism around the globe. He would sanction any black op, regardless of the fallout; raise money by any nefarious means to fund all necessary operations; tolerate, even condone, any human casualties; and bring down any sovereign government, even duly elected ones, to achieve his means. He and his loyal subordinates would routinely lie, cheat, steal, and murder. Their mania bordered on psychosis. So much so, that it is not beyond reason to question their mental health. At the very least, they were megalomaniacs with god complexes. Drunk with power and bound by no laws, they were a scourge on civilized societies everywhere.

But Allen was not content to play god with the rest of the world; he also meddled in domestic affairs even though such actions were expressly forbidden by the CIA's charter. His agency's insidious operations included:

MK-ULTRA, a brainwashing experiment gone wild. Innocent American citizens were dosed with psychedelic drugs and subjected to unspeakable torture in an attempt to see if human thought and behavior could be controlled.

Operation Paperclip gave safe haven to Nazi war criminals; they joined our intelligence apparatus, our rocket science programs, our defense industry, and our medical research agencies. They lived and worked among us, and were accorded a protected status unworthy of their murderous backgrounds.

For pure sleaze, *Operation Climax* topped them all. It used prostitutes to lure unsuspecting citizens into compromising situations for drug experimentation.

But perhaps the most sublimely diabolical perversion of democracy was *Operation Mockingbird*. Mockingbird subverted the free press in America. Journalists were induced by the CIA to spread agency propaganda and lies, or to just ignore agency atrocities. This operation, begun in earnest after World War II, was particularly crucial to the plotters in their plan to murder Jack Kennedy. Without open and honest investigative journalism, there was no way for Americans to get the truth of how and why the assassination took place, and, more importantly, who was responsible. There was no one to hold corrupt officials at the highest levels of government responsible for their treasonous acts.

These dirty programs were just a few of the illicit and terrifying projects dreamed up by Dulles and his cronies in the name of national security. It is now clear they were unconcerned about national security; they were concerned only about the security of their self-interests. Not even presidents could control them. According to David Talbot, "Dulles undermined or betrayed every president he served."[16] Allen and his CIA thrived under Truman and Eisenhower, but in the early 1960s they encountered a President with the courage to stand up to them. Soon enough, Dulles and Kennedy were waging a secret and cataclysmic war over the direction the country was headed.

In steering America away from the paranoia and danger of the Cold War, Kennedy courted many deadly enemies. Among them was his own Vice-President Lyndon Johnson, who, by 1963, was a desperate man trying to save his political life and fortune. His criminal schemes were being exposed, and the word in Washington was JFK was dumping him as a running mate in 1964. As ruthless and Machiavellian as Allen Dulles, LBJ was capable of anything to preserve his own self-interests.

Unlike the Dulleses, Johnson was born into modest and rural circumstances. He grew up in the Texas Hill Country where only the barest of life's essentials could be found. He began displaying unruly and repulsive behavior when he was very young. When he was just five years old, his grandmother Ruth Ament Huffman Baines predicted he would wind up in prison.[17] Rumors persist that Lyndon, as an adolescent, had sexual intercourse with Ruth.[18] Whether this is true or not, it is a fact that, early on, Johnson displayed severe anti-social tendencies. It is possible his mental defects can be traced to his unusual relationship with his parents. His father, Sam, was a politician and was away on state government business in Austin for long stretches. During these absences, his mother Rebekah invited her young son into her bed. Upon Sam's return, young Lyndon would be shunned by Rebekah. Perhaps out of shame or revulsion, she would not speak to her son for days at a time.[19] The psychological damage caused to a boy who was treated this way by his own mother is certainly profound; at the very least he would grow up deeply conflicted and insecure.

There is little doubt, then, that Johnson suffered from mental and psychological defects. Today psychologists would diagnose him with a borderline personality disorder. Some who knew him were convinced he was a sociopath. He learned as a child never to suffer lightly a slight or an insult. He lashed out when reprimanded or emotionally injured, and he learned to play the victim to his advantage. According to author Jeff Shesol, "LBJ's self-pity was bottomless."[20]

Lyndon had little concern for his fellow human beings. He was unstable and often showed signs of manic-depression. He could be cruel without remorse. He carried deep and lasting grudges against his political rivals. His paranoia was rampant; like Nixon he saw enemies everywhere. Johnson had few real friends, and he came to be despised by the men and women who served under him. George Reedy, a White House aide, once described him as "...one of the nastiest, most insufferable, sadistic SOBs that ever lived."[21] Still, he could be charming and gracious when it served his purposes. As an aspiring politician, Johnson ingratiated himself with power brokers who could advance his career. He could be polite and obsequious to rich businessmen looking for a corrupt lawmaker. At the same time, he liked to portray himself as a folksy commoner from the Hill Country for the benefit of his voting constituents.

He was chameleon-like in his approach to politics. Coming of age in volatile political times, especially for the Democratic party which was ruptured by a conservative-southern/liberal-northern split, Johnson managed to appear conservative to those who demanded he be conservative and a Texas moderate to assuage liberals. He campaigned for the Senate as a populist, pro-FDR candidate, but he accepted millions from right-wing oil oligarchs. As president he excoriated his 1964 opponent Goldwater for his hawkishness, and then a few months after the election thrust America headlong into its most senseless and disastrous war to date. A war from which he profited mightily. What JFK said of Johnson, just one day before the tragedy in Dallas, was true: "The man was incapable of telling the truth."[22] He pretended to be all things to all people in order to get what he wanted for himself. Those who got in his way were destroyed.

In sum, LBJ was a monster, likely suffering from mental illness, capable of anything, including murder, to win his lifelong prize— the presidency. Once he got there, he enriched himself and his business cronies who had propelled his rise to the top.

Johnson had a lifelong fear of dying young and penniless like his father had, and he was determined not to succumb to the same fate; thus, as a young congressman in Washington, he plotted ceaselessly to attain the riches that had eluded his father. As Johnson's biographer Robert Caro puts it, "[Johnson] talked repeatedly about... working in poorly paid or humiliating jobs" when the day came that he would be forced to step down from public office.[23] Johnson expected his lofty position in Congress to be worth something. He wasn't in the game to perform a noble public service; he was in it, first and foremost, to line his pockets and secure a nest egg for himself. To that end, he courted the friendship and financial favors of rich businessmen who had the means to fund his political ascent and make him rich enough to assuage his deep fear of destitution. One of the business cronies he wooed was George Brown of Brown & Root. Yes, that Brown & Root. The company that has made obscene fortunes off government war contracts. The company that once consolidated with Dick Cheney's Halliburton. The company that dredged Cam Ranh Bay and built air bases and other military infrastructure during the Vietnam War, the war that was escalated by President Johnson once his predecessor was out of the way.

According to Caro, Brown & Root "…became, thanks to Johnson, an industrial colossus" in shipbuilding and oil pipelines.[24] Brown and his brother Herman made untold billions from government contracts arranged by Johnson. No telling how much Lyndon took for himself in the form of kickbacks, campaign funds and slush money. But we do know he was overheard, less than an hour after Jack Kennedy was murdered, saying, "Oh, I gotta get rid of my goddamn Halliburton stock."[25]

The Brown brothers were not the only businessmen for whom Johnson served as government contract procurer. David Harold Byrd was another beneficiary of LBJ largesse. Byrd was a Dallas businessman and oil tycoon with some powerful connections in Texas and the Pentagon. He was a personal friend of JFK's Air Force Chief of Staff, Curtis LeMay. Nicknamed "Bombs Away," LeMay was a virulent right-wing war hawk who butted heads with JFK over Cuba, Russia, and nuclear policy. Byrd shared LeMay's right-wing views and made no secret of his hate for the Kennedys. After JFK's assassination, Byrd's company, Ling-Temco-Vought was awarded a large government contract, with LBJ's help, to build the A-7 Corsair II plane. This is significant because Byrd was no ordinary Dallas millionaire. He founded, at General LeMay's request, the Louisiana Civil Air Patrol, of which a young Lee Harvey Oswald (as well as several other shady characters connected to the Kennedy assassination) was a member. Byrd also owned the Texas School Book Depository building, where Oswald was employed on November 22, 1963. The fact that Byrd was closely connected to men who had motive to kill Kennedy, and that his organizations provided employment for the President's accused assassin, should have raised red flags for the Warren Commission. But exploring the possibility that Oswald was moved around like an oblivious dupe in a tragic game would have damaged the commission's primary purpose—to hang the assassination on him and him alone. So naturally the commission did not question Byrd. Conveniently he left Dallas in November 1963 for a two-month African safari.

Somehow Byrd has escaped closer scrutiny by assassination investigators, even though he was associated with many known Kennedy haters in Texas. He belonged to the Dallas Petroleum Club whose members included not only Texas oil millionaires like H.L. Hunt, Sid Richardson, and Clint Murchison, but also CIA and political operatives like George DeMohrenschildt (Oswald's friend and handler in Dallas), David Atlee Phillips, and George H.W. Bush (yes, he was CIA before he became head of the Agency in 1976). Byrd also belonged to a right-wing cabal of businessmen and Texas politicians called the Suite 8F Group. Their members included LBJ benefactors George and Herman Brown, John Connally, and LBJ himself.

Byrd's business and political activities expose a nexus through which passed key players in Kennedy's murder. In fact, his connections are so extensive that one must be incredibly naïve or deluded to dismiss Byrd's suspicious acquaintances as coincidences. The Civil Air Patrol, itself, was a breeding ground for CIA recruitment, and many CAP trainees went on to play significant roles in executing and covering up JFK's death. And the mere fact that Byrd and the designated patsy can be connected at two points in time and two different cities is beyond any innocent explanation.

The connection to Byrd is just one of many ways LBJ was tied to corporate titans and military contractors. For decades in Washington Johnson was a fearsome fixture in America's military-industrial complex. A man of big appetites and few scruples, LBJ enriched himself in the mania of Cold War militarism. He had no qualms accepting bribes and kickbacks. His style was brutal, and his "horse trading" ways were legendary. Back-room deals and unholy partnerships were his way of doing business as a leader in the U.S. Senate. If someone stood in his way, he did not hesitate to use blackmail against his enemy. And there is plenty of evidence that he even resorted to murder when all else failed.

Johnson began his career in the rough-and-tumble world of Texas politics. Nicknamed Lying Lyndon by opponents and allies alike, Johnson ascended to power by stealing elections, bribing officials, and using a hit man to wipe out political enemies when necessary. He surrounded himself with a coterie of dirty lawyers, crooked judges and compliant bagmen to achieve his ends.

The only reason Johnson ascended to the Senate was that he stole the 1948 Democratic primary in Texas. How LBJ pulled this off is a part of Texas political lore. One of his hatchet men, lawyer Don Thomas, a partner in Johnson's legal firm—Clark, Matthews, Thomas, Harris & Denius—personally stuffed the ballot box in tiny Alice, Texas, to swing the razor-thin election to Johnson. Rushing to complete the task before the voting deadline, Thomas, according to author Barr McClellan, "...started adding names of the dead...[and] voted more names than were on the precinct list as qualified voters."[26] The final tally for the precinct was a laughably lopsided 202 votes for Johnson and none for his opponent Coke Stevenson. It became known as the infamous "Ballot Box 13" scandal, and it swung the election for Johnson.

Stevenson was certain he and the citizens of Texas had been defrauded; the results were challenged, and a hearing was scheduled. But another cunning Johnson lawyer, Ed Clark, prevailed on a Johnson judge to issue an injunction prohibiting any examination of Ballot Box 13. When Stevenson's appeal went all the way to the Supreme Court and the U.S. Senate, the contents of Ballot Box 13 suddenly disappeared and many of the witnesses to the fraud vanished.

Years later one Sam Smithwick, a deputy sheriff in the county where the election was stolen, came forward to say he knew where the missing Ballot Box 13 could be found. Unfortunately Smithwick was in a Texas prison for murder at the time, and could not get his hands on the proof unless he was released. (He had been convicted of murdering one of Johnson's political opponents a couple years prior, but the horrors of Huntsville prison had converted him to the anti-Johnson camp.) According to Barr McClellan, who was once an associate in the crooked Johnson law firm of Clark, Thomas, et al, Johnson made sure Smithwick never got out of prison alive. Smithwick "...was strangely hanged by the neck at the side of his bunk with his knees on the ground."[27] It was ruled a suicide, but the Texas governor at the time, Allen Shivers, "...was convinced Johnson was behind it."[28]

Johnson has been associated with many other murders in Texas, some of which were carried out by his assassin of choice: a man named Malcolm "Mac" Wallace. A stocky, dark-skinned fellow who was as brilliant as he was disturbed, Wallace first came into Johnson's sphere as a student at the University of Texas at Austin. Wallace was president of his class, and upon graduation he got a government job in Washington. A natural rabble-rouser with a short fuse, Wallace acquired a reputation for participating in subversive activities. His excessive drinking got him arrested for public drunkenness, and soon he would ask for Johnson's assistance with legal matters. Johnson kept a safe distance from Wallace; at the same time, he recognized the usefulness of having a volatile man like Wallace to perform unsavory tasks for him.

Wallace's private life was a series of sordid affairs. He and his wife became entangled in illicit love nests with Josepha Johnson, Lyndon's sister, and a golf pro named Douglas Kinser. On October 22, 1951, Wallace walked into a pitch-and-putt golf course where Kinser worked and shot him dead. Months later Wallace stood trial and was convicted of murder. To the shock of everyone in Austin he was given a five-year suspended sentence and was set free the very day the trial ended. Keen observers of Austin politics and justice suspected that Lyndon Johnson had somehow played a role in Wallace's light sentence. Later it was revealed that Wallace's lawyer and the presiding judge were Johnson cronies. There were also allegations of jury tampering.

Wallace, on orders from Johnson who closely monitored the trial, did not present a single defense witness, nor did he take the stand in his own behalf. Fearing that lurid family secrets and Josepha's promiscuous lifestyle would be revealed, Johnson knew he could not risk Wallace being cross-examined. In return for Wallace's silence, Johnson rigged the trial to arrange for Wallace's absurdly light sentence. From then on, Wallace was beholden to Johnson. Proving he was capable of murder, Wallace became Johnson's go-to guy when a political foe needed to "disappear."

Johnson moved Wallace around like a deadly chessboard piece, waiting for the moment when violent action was needed. According to Barr McClellan, "Johnson arranged for Wallace to take a job with Luscombe Aircraft which soon became part of Ling-Temco-Vought."[29] LTV's principal shareholder was the aforementioned D.H. Byrd. In 1961 Wallace was assigned to a branch office of Ling Electronics, a division of LTV, in California. He needed a security clearance to work for LTV, since it was a government contractor. Despite his criminal record, Wallace obtained clearance with Johnson's assistance.

Wallace would periodically disappear from his job, to perform "services" for Johnson. One such incident occurred in 1961 when an agriculture official named Henry Marshall was found shot to death in a Texas field. (It has been alleged that Johnson somehow convinced the county coroner to rule Marshall's death a suicide, even though Marshall's body was riddled with five bullet holes.) Marshall was about to expose Johnson's cotton allotment kickback scheme involving convicted swindler Billie Sol Estes. On the surface, it may seem far-fetched that Johnson was involved in such high-level and blatant illegalities, but, according to authors Glen Sample and Mark Collom, Estes kept "tape recordings…of LBJ, Cliff Carter (a close political consultant), and himself discussing illegal cotton allotment schemes. These recordings were made with Cliff Carter's knowledge as a means of Carter and Estes protecting themselves should LBJ order their deaths."[30] Johnson and Estes made millions from the scheme, and Marshall proved incorruptible when he found out about it. Wallace was sent to do the hit, and Marshall's death was ruled a suicide despite the fact that Marshall had been shot five times. An inquiring journalist might have wondered how a man committing suicide could have shot himself five times, but apparently Texas had no such reporters under Johnson's watch.

This pattern of killing political opponents recurred throughout Johnson's career. With the help of his corrupt allies, especially Ed Clark and his team of lawyers, Johnson was able to deftly cover his tracks. To this day, many LBJ historians refuse to acknowledge or research Johnson's bloody past, despite the fact that there is plenty of evidence of it, much of it provided by one of Johnson's bag men and payoff artists: Estes.

It wasn't until long after LBJ died, that Estes finally came clean about his criminal ties with the 36th President. In 1984 his lawyer Douglas Caddy wrote a letter on Estes's behalf to the U.S. Justice Department accusing Johnson of ordering the murders of several people, including Henry Marshall, Douglas Kinser, Josepha Johnson (LBJ's own sister), and "President J.F. Kennedy."[31] Caddy's letter further states that, "Mr. Estes is willing to testify that LBJ ordered these killings, and that he transmitted his orders through Cliff Carter to [Malcolm]Mac Wallace, who executed the murders."[32] These facts have been conveniently ignored by Johnson biographers; Robert Caro, Doris Kearns Goodwin, and Robert Dallek have nothing to say on these matters. Nor do they acknowledge the statements of LBJ's long-time lover, Madeleine Brown, who asserted that she was present at a "kill Kennedy" party in Clint Murchison's home near Dallas on the night before the JFK assassination. Murchison was supposedly throwing a fete honoring J. Edgar Hoover, when Lyndon Johnson suddenly appeared and hurried into a secret meeting with Hoover, H.L. Hunt, Clyde Tolson (Hoover's FBI deputy and lover), John McCloy (former CEO of Chase Manhattan Bank and Warren Commission member), and George Brown (of Brown & Root) among others.

Many researchers have dismissed Brown's claims, and she seems to have varied the attendees of the meeting over the years. But independent corroboration of Brown's claims comes from Murchison's servant, cook and chauffeur. May Newman, a Murchison family servant, was told by the family chauffeur that there had been a gathering at the "big house," the luxurious Murchison residence near Dallas on the evening before the assassination of JFK, at which J. Edgar Hoover and others were present. The chauffeur drove Hoover to and from the airport, and was angry that Hoover had not tipped him. Newman stated that the Murchison family cook, Beulah Mae Holman, also verified Hoover's presence at the big party.[33]

Murchison and Hoover had been acquainted for years. Hoover would often vacation, free of charge, at Murchison's Del Charro Hotel in southern California, where he received celebrity treatment and mingled with gangsters, oilmen and politicians. It should not come as a shock, then, to imagine Hoover showing up at Murchison's home in Texas. After JFK was killed, claims Newman, "The mood in the Murchison family home was very joyous and happy for a whole week…like champagne and caviar flowed every day."[34]

No high-profile historian has investigated Brown's or Newman's assertions. It is as if they never existed; there is no mention of either woman in any of Caro's volumes. They are also ignored by Goodwin and Dallek, even though there is little doubt that Brown had an illegitimate son by Johnson. There is also now no question that

Johnson was financially supported by and beholden to Dallas oil billionaires like Murchison, Hunt and Byrd, and that these men, together, had plenty of reasons to want Kennedy dead. They had motive and the financial means to do the job. And when Kennedy came to Dallas, opportunity presented itself.

Why would LBJ's biographers ignore his culpability? Apparently Johnson's bullying, lying and arm-twisting extended to those who would write of his legacy and protect his reputation. Johnson was a master of falsifying history—his own and the nation's. This, as much as any other factor, is the reason his role in JFK's assassination has remained so well hidden from the public. He used close associates, allies, lovers, subordinates, reporters and family members to distort the truth. Lying was second nature to him, and he never missed a chance to cover up his indiscretions or polish his outsized image. Johnson would often plant the seeds of misinformation with aides and sycophants, knowing full well those filthy seeds would later bear rancid fruit, palatable to the gullible but nothing more than rotten produce to those who now know better. For this reason, assassination author Philip Nelson writes that, "...practically all the Johnson biographies...have distorted the real history of the Johnson administration."[35]

Goodwin's biographies of Johnson need to be read with a good bit of skepticism because there is reason to believe that she and LBJ had a romantic relationship. The rumor circulated widely among academics, journalists and the political realm of Washington in the early 1970s. Even Goodwin's fellow students at Harvard were under the impression that she was LBJ's lover; Goodwin confirmed the rumors in a candid interview with *Washington Post* reporters Richard Harwood and Haynes Johnson.[36] After Johnson's death, Goodwin admitted to reporter Sally Quinn that Johnson had not only made sexual advances but had asked for her hand in marriage.[37] Johnson's courtship of Goodwin is now seen as his attempt to manipulate a budding historian into presenting a sanitized version of Johnson's life and presidency. Goodwin apparently complied because there is little or no reference to Johnson's sordid character and numerous crimes in her books. Nonetheless, she is regularly booked on TV talk shows and political roundtables which seek her commentary as a legitimate presidential historian. Too bad she has barely heard of Bobby Baker.

Baker, once the Senate majority secretary under Johnson, was another of Johnson's partners in crime. He was the bagman for LBJ's payoffs and bribes; legislative influence was the product he was selling, and he used liquor, prostitutes and blackmail to get his way. His ties to Johnson were being investigated by Congress and national reporters just before JFK was killed. On the morning of November 22, 1963, *Life* magazine was preparing to do an in-depth story on the Johnson/Baker corruption scandal, and in Washington the Senate rules committee was scheduled to hear testimony on the same matter.

Much of the evidence implicating Johnson was provided by the Kennedys who wanted Johnson off the 1964 presidential ticket. Bobby Kennedy fed damning information on Johnson to his media sources, and declared that it was open season on the Vice-President. Although they publicly denied they were dropping him, the Kennedys were out to ruin Johnson. Faced with the end of his political career and a potential jail sentence, Johnson knew there was but one thing to do.

Once the job was done, LBJ reversed Kennedy's policy on Vietnam, and America was never the same again. Idealism, diplomacy and disarmament were replaced by bullets, bombs and war profiteering. An unbiased examination of Johnson's life reveals that whatever altruism he possessed was pitilessly surpassed at all stages of his political life by his avarice. It is now believed he left office with a personal fortune of $25 million, the 1960s equivalent of approximately a quarter of a billion dollars in today's money.[38] And this figure might be low. His vast array of government-graft schemes were, of necessity, largely surreptitious; cash payoffs were immune to record-keeping.

In exchange for amassing his obscene wealth, Johnson owed the men who had helped put him in office; they had a big payoff coming: Vietnam and the money to be made from the bloodlust of America's hawkish weapons makers. But the cost was dear—a nation torn apart and the dismantling of the presidency Johnson had lusted after all his life. As Nelson puts it, "LBJ thought he could create a nice manageable war…on the other side of the world…to ensure that many of his friends, and himself, would become even richer."[39]

CHAPTER 2

Motive, Means, and Opportunity

"Who controls the present controls the past."
—George Orwell, 1984[1]

The plot that took Jack Kennedy's life was a complex covert operation, utilizing many layers of deception and replete with slick operatives experienced in misdirection, disguise and tradecraft. The scope and breadth of the operation was beyond the capabilities of Lyndon Johnson alone, whose previous murders had been crude, rushed actions usually riddled with mistakes and mishaps. (Henry Marshall's "suicide" was the most glaring example.) Johnson and his henchmen had neither the sophistication nor the resources to pull off the enormous task of killing JFK and disguising it. This is not to say that Johnson did not play significant hands-on roles in the plot. He did. He and his political prodigy John Connally lured JFK to Dallas; Johnson also provided one of the assassins, re-directed the parade route, delayed Air Force One's departure from Dallas, and appointed a fraudulent investigatory body after the fact. But Johnson was not the mastermind; he had neither the patience nor the artfulness for such a tangled operation.

No, the plot had all the earmarks of a covert intelligence operation, designed to kill JFK in a camouflage of misdirection and mystery; and then forever suppress the truth of the murder through the diabolical contrivance of altering the prime medical evidence—JFK's corpse. The only organization in America capable of such subterfuge in 1963 was the Central Intelligence Agency—Kennedy's bitter nemesis.

Those who are in the Oswald-did-it-alone camp ("lone-nutters" is the derisive term used by the JFK research community), dying breed though they are, assert that the CIA had no call to kill Kennedy. They cite cordial relations between the two, even after Dulles and his deputies were fired in 1961. But the CIA has always been expert at hiding its true intentions. When asked about Kennedy's death in the days after Dallas, Dulles publicly had kind words for the martyred President. Privately, however, he despised JFK. Dulles had been humiliated by his dismissal after the Bay of Pigs, and he had never forgiven Kennedy for the public disgrace he suffered.

It is an undeniable fact that during his Presidency, Kennedy was privately at war with his intelligence and national security people. Behind closed doors the CIA and the military chiefs expressed dismay at JFK's policies, and often would take actions to subvert his handling of the Cold War, Vietnam and nuclear disarmament. Historians and political commentators who deny this reality are either oblivious to the facts or they are intentional disinformationists. Even in exile, Allen Dulles commanded the loyalty of key high-level CIA operatives such as Richard Helms, Cord Meyer, William Harvey, David Atlee Phillips, James Jesus Angleton and E. Howard Hunt. These Dulles loyalists were active in undermining the Kennedy presidency right up until his death, by disobeying his explicit orders regarding his administration's directives on Cuba, the Soviet Union, Laos, Vietnam, Indonesia and Latin America.

Even though he began his Administration as a Cold Warrior, with an inaugural address full of rigid, nationalist rhetoric, Kennedy, humbled by the hard lessons learned from the Bay of Pigs and the Cuban Missile Crisis, tried to calm the mounting tension with the Soviets and actually turned his back on the advice of his intelligence and military advisors. He came to understand just how dangerous the CIA and the generals were; by the end of his days, he knew he was surrounded by traitors. It is not known if he grasped

the full extent of the precariousness of his position, but he acknowledged on several occasions that he was aware of the dangers of his
peace initiatives. According to author James Douglass, "…JFK was
keenly conscious of the peril of a military coup d'etat."[2] After reading *Seven Days In May*, a popular novel about a fictional overthrow
of a U.S. President, Kennedy said, "It could happen in this country…and I know a couple [military commanders] who might wish
they could."[3] And it wasn't just the military and his own Vice-President who wanted JFK dead; his most dire enemy was the CIA, and
the CIA was everywhere.

As stated previously, under Dulles's reign the CIA surreptitiously
amassed an army of agents who infiltrated many sectors of American life. The goal was to misinform, or just bypass altogether, the
citizenry, in order to advance the agenda of an elite and secretive
group determined to make the country its own by any means necessary, including assassination. Author Fletcher Prouty, who served
during the Cold War as Air Force and Defense Department liaison
to the CIA for military support of covert operations, called this
group "The Secret Team." The team "…consists of security-cleared
individuals in and out of government who receive secret intelligence
gathered by the CIA…[and whose power] is enhanced by the cult
of the gun."[4]

The Dulles army became so broad and powerful that feeding the
citizenry lies to advance its agenda became easy. Prouty writes, "It
is quite often difficult to tell exactly who many of these men are…
some may wear a uniform and the rank of general and really be
with the CIA."[5] But its reach goes far beyond the military. It has a
"…vast intragovernmental undercover infrastructure…[such as]
investment houses, universities, and the news media."[6]

The implications of this are enormous. It means we as Americans
have lived in an alternate reality since the inception of the CIA. The
events which have shaped the country since World War II have
secret causes and consequences beyond our comprehension. People

we did not elect, and some we did, changed our world behind our backs. They occupy, without acknowledging their secret missions, prominent positions which affect the course and success or failure of democracy. Indeed, democracy is often the enemy. When the CIA controlled the levers of influence; the truth became muddled. Keeping citizens in the dark benefited those with illegitimate power. In the time of Dulles, Americans were largely unaware of the truth. What was real and what was not real was determined by Dulles and his men. Under such conditions, the uninformed come to believe an alternative history of the country, an official, and twisted, version of events. Like sheep, they are easily led to the slaughter.

Over many decades, the CIA has engineered events about which the public at large has many misconceptions or knows little at all. The 1953 CIA overthrow of Iranian Prime Minister Mohammad Mossadegh, who nationalized the lucrative Iranian oil industry and thus threatened British and U.S. petroleum profits, had far-reaching ramifications for America. A quarter of a century on, during the Iranian Hostage Crisis, few Americans understood that its own government was responsible for creating the intense Iranian hostility which led to the crisis. When the CIA, after deposing Mossadegh, installed the Shah, Mohammed Reza Pahlavi, it ushered in a repressive, corrupt regime despised by the majority of Iranians. The 1979 revolt forced the Shah to flee, and Iranians took U.S. embassy workers hostage. The knee-jerk reaction in America, fueled by right-wing nationalism, was to downplay or ignore the CIA's role in creating the extreme anti-American hostility which ignited the crisis.

Other cataclysmic events, instigated, and then denied in whole or part by the CIA, include the 1954 overthrow of Guatemala's Jacobo Arbenz as retaliation for nationalizing the lands owned by United Fruit Company (on whose board sat Allen Dulles); the 1961 assassination of Patrice Lumumba, the first democratically elected leader of the Congo; the 1960 downing of a U-2 spy plane over Russia, which undercut Eisenhower's peace summit with Kruschev;

the Bay of Pigs; the assassinations of the 1960s in America; the Pentagon Papers; Watergate, which led to Nixon's resignation; Iran/Contra and the Savings and Loans scandals of the 1980s; and the Iraq wars.

Even the power of the U.S. presidency could not contain the CIA in the second half of the 20th century. Kennedy, more than his predecessors or successors, was determined to do something about it but faced resistance to his initiatives on many fronts. After the Bay of Pigs and the Cuban Missile Crisis, Kennedy wanted to avoid another confrontation with Castro and Kruschev. But according to Douglass, "From Cuba to Vietnam, the CIA was systematically undermining Kennedy's peace initiatives and antagonizing Kruschev."[7] A violent anti-Castro group of Cuban exiles called Alpha 66, under the direction of the CIA's David Atlee Phillips and E. Howard Hunt, "repeatedly attacked Soviet ships in Cuban waters…to publicly embarrass Kennedy and force him to move against Castro."[8] In Vietnam, CIA operatives disrupted Kennedy's plans for peaceful resolution by killing Buddhist demonstrators in Hue, inciting the North with imperialist rhetoric, and assassinating Ngo Dinh Diem, president of South Vietnam. Even Kennedy's own hand-picked ambassador to Vietnam, Henry Cabot Lodge, ignored the President's communiques, countermanded policy, and violated protocol. Lodge, the CIA and the State Department were guilty of nothing less than insurrection.

Kennedy knew he was surrounded by enemies and at one point declared that he wanted to "splinter the CIA into a thousand pieces and scatter it to the wind."[9] He was not able to accomplish the task in his thousand days, but he did reduce the CIA's budget; this move had a backfire effect, however, in that it forced the agency to fund its secretive operations by conducting illegal activities like drug running. The agency was determined to resist all efforts by Kennedy to rein it in.

The visceral reaction to JFK's refusal to commit U.S. military forces to salvage the Bay of Pigs operation is evident in the writings of key officers involved. David Atlee Phillips wrote of being sick and drunk with anger.[10] Howard Hunt accused Kennedy of betraying "Cuban patriots" and humiliating the U.S. in the eyes of the world; out of the Bay of Pigs, Hunt claimed, "grew the Berlin Wall, the missile crisis, guerilla warfare throughout Latin America and Africa, and our Dominican Republic intervention."[11] Dulles acolytes were apoplectic after he was fired by JFK. They saw the move as an attempt by Kennedy to lay the blame for the Bay of Pigs fiasco at the CIA's feet. From then on, the President and the intelligence agency were mortal enemies.

Kennedy also made enemies of Texas oil barons who were closely connected to both Johnson and Dulles. In January 1963 JFK proposed a plan to revise the oil industry's depletion allowance and overhaul the code on oil profits. The reforms if enacted would have cost the oilmen close to $300 million in annual profits. H.L. Hunt called the reform "criminal offenses"; JFK, in turn, criticized Hunt for using his tax breaks to subsidize ultra-right causes.[12] Hunt often boasted he was the richest man in the world and could do any damn thing he pleased. Financing a hit on a sitting president, and using his immense financial and political influence to help cover it up, would have been within the realm of possibility for the richest man in the world. From all accounts, Hunt had a god complex and felt that it was his right and duty to secretly control the destiny of America. He wrote a lunatic work of fiction he titled *Alpaca*, in which he advocated that the ideal form of government would be one in which only a handful of the wealthiest men held all the power. This is the very definition of fascism.

The interests of Texas oil and the CIA converged in Dallas. The city was home to several organizations which provided the opportunity for CIA operatives and oilmen to exchange ideas, share political leanings, and commiserate about their shared hatred of President Kennedy. The Dallas Council on World Affairs and the

Crusade For a Free Europe, both ostensibly CIA proprietary organizations, included among its members oilmen (Murchison, Byrd
and Hunt), the CIA's George DeMohrenschildt (Oswald's handler
in Dallas) and George H.W. Bush. (Bush and DeMohrenschildt
had other close ties which will be discussed later.) Also members
were Abraham Zapruder, whose infamous film captured JFK's murder, and Sarah Hughes who swore in LBJ aboard Air Force One on
November 22, 1963. The Dallas Petroleum Club included the CIA's
David Phillips, Bush and DeMohrenschildt. Was treason fomented
in these exclusive clubs? We have no definitive proof; however, the
intersection and commingling of such ardent Kennedy haters makes
one wonder if deadly plans took shape there. Certainly the clubs
provided convenient cover for men of like minds to convene and
consider sedition if they so chose.

If the CIA had the motive, it certainly had the means and the
opportunity to kill JFK. It was quite experienced in overthrowing
governments, and it had a vast network of secret programs and
assets upon which to draw. Perhaps the most blatant proof of CIA
involvement in the assassination is Lee Harvey Oswald's role as the
fall guy. It is now beyond dispute that Oswald was a CIA asset.
According to Walt Brown, author of *Treachery in Dallas*, "To believe
the denials of a CIA-Oswald link, we must overlook the names of
Spas T. Raikin, George DeMohrenschildt, David Ferrie, Guy Banister, and Clay Shaw, CIA operatives whose paths often bisected
Oswald's."[13]

Oswald's Circle of Friends
In the mid-1970s The House Select Committee on Assassinations
found that James Angleton, CIA counterintelligence chief, opened
a 201 file on Oswald as far back as 1960. A 201 file is the agency's
means by which to profile an asset or employee with personality
traits, background and prospective usefulness as a covert operative.
Oswald's CIA file was numbered 39-61981.[14] The reason it was

initiated by Angleton is that the CIA counterintelligence division ran the false defector program.[15] This accounts for Oswald's mysterious journey to Russia. Despite his public proclamations at the time, his defection was not genuine; he was a double agent acting on behalf of the U.S. government. Little did he know that the CIA was probably creating a false legend to paint him as a communist sympathizer. So while Oswald was trying the fool the Russians (the Russians saw right through the defection ruse, and may have fed him false information), the CIA was playing a trick on Oswald. There is no evidence that Oswald provided any useful intelligence to the CIA during his time in Russia. His primary purpose seems to have been to meet and marry Marina Prusakova, the niece of a high Russian official, Ilya Prusakova, who worked at the Ministry of Internal Affairs.

Oswald's CIA connection explains why, upon his return to the United States, he was neither detained nor interrogated by State Department officials, despite the fact that he had just a few years before proclaimed himself a Marxist. At the height of the Cold War one would expect such an avowed anti-American as Oswald to be treated as suspicious, if not immediately imprisoned or deported as a traitor, after returning from the Soviet Union with a bride whose family had ties to high-ranking communist officials. In fact, quite the opposite occurred. On April 13, 1961, four days before the Bay of Pigs, the State Department informed the U.S. embassy in Moscow that Oswald was to be issued a passport for his return to America. The memo was signed by none other than JFK's own Secretary of State, Dean Rusk, with the instructions that the embassy thoroughly question Oswald before granting passage to the U.S. This may or may not have been done. Rusk also advised that for security reasons the embassy should not mail Oswald's passport to him.[16] One might reasonably wonder why the Secretary of State would intervene on behalf of a nobody-defector like Oswald in the first place, and why he would advise that Oswald's passport be delivered

to him in person. Did Rusk suspect that Oswald was working for
the CIA as a double agent and that his mail might be monitored by
the Russians? If so, this raises serious questions as to Rusk's state of
mind when, two years later, the President for whom he worked was
assassinated by, according to early reports, Lee Harvey Oswald.
How much did Rusk know? Why had he intervened on Oswald's
behalf? It is noteworthy that Rusk never publicly admitted to being
aware of Oswald prior to 11/22/63.

Despite Rusk's intervention, Oswald was not able to make it
back to the United States for another year. When he finally arrived
in June of 1962, he was met by one Spas T. Raikin, a representative
of the Traveler's Aid Society, who had suspicious links to the FBI,
military intelligence and hard-core anti-communist groups.[17] With
Raikins's help, Oswald zipped through customs, got a loan from his
brother Robert for airfare to Fort Worth, and resumed his life as an
American. But it was hardly a normal existence. For a guy who
spent years in communist Russia when it was considered the evil
empire, especially in the southern regions of the U.S., Oswald, for
the last 17 months of his life, did some rather remarkable things
and worked for some unusual employers in the American South.
And it was his CIA-connected friends who got him the work.

George DeMohrenschildt, an intrepid presence in the sordid
tale of JFK's murder, immediately befriended Oswald upon Lee's
arrival in Dallas. Given the backgrounds of the two men, there is
no innocent explanation for why DeMohrenschildt would strike
up a sudden friendship with Oswald. They were miles apart in
education, social status and worldliness. DeMohrenschildt was
educated, sophisticated and connected to the country's elite eastern
families and Texas oil barons. He had a degree in geology and often
worked as a consultant for oil companies. His nephew roomed
with George H.W. Bush at Andover, an elite prep boarding school.
Incredibly enough, DeMohrenschildt also knew the Bouviers,
Jackie Kennedy's family. It is even reported that Jackie referred to

him as Uncle George.

To be succinct, there is nothing Oswald and DeMohrenschildt had in common except that they had both once lived in Russia and could speak the language fluently, and they were both employed by the CIA. Oswald looked up to DeMohrenschildt as the kind of smooth, debonair character he could never be; DeMohrenschildt knew this and used Oswald like a piece on a chessboard, building his pro-communist legend by controlling Lee's movements and behavior. At the same time, DeMohrenschildt procured a defense-related job for Oswald. This created a contradiction in Oswald's persona—publicly a communist but privately a military-industrial-complex insider—which still confuses researchers. What was the CIA really up to? Perhaps it thought that the American people would never be curious enough to delve into the conundrum of Oswald—a person now synonymous with inscrutability.

In 1962 Oswald went to work for Jaggers-Chiles-Stovall which did government contract work in the area of military mapping and photography. One of JCS's contractual obligations was to place captions, arrows and notations on sensitive security photos includ-ing the U-2 reconnaissance of Cuba during the Missile Crisis in October of 1962. The job required a security clearance which Oswald, despite defecting to the Soviet Union just three years prior, easily obtained. A JCS co-worker suspected Oswald of being a gov-ernment agent.[18]

It was during this time that Oswald, according to the Warren Commission and the House Select Committee on Assassinations, tried to kill General Edwin Walker, a John Birch Society member who had been dismissed from his command by JFK in 1961 for propagandizing his troops with extreme right-wing rhetoric. On April 10, 1963, someone fired a shot into the Dallas home of Walker, who maintained that the attempt on his life was a con-spiracy; nonetheless, the House Select Committee on Assassina-tions blamed Oswald alone. Using neutron activation analysis, it

concluded that the bullet recovered from Walker's house "was probably a Mannlicher-Carcano bullet."[19] In other words, it matched
the weapon which Oswald had acquired by mail order. For some
reason, Oswald felt compelled to purchase an inferior rifle (one the
Italian army criticized as the weapon which couldn't shoot straight)
through the mail, despite the fact that he could have walked into
any gun shop in Texas and purchased any other rifle (and any other
rifle would have been better). (The purpose of the mail order seems
to have been to create a paper trail by which to later incriminate
Oswald.)

Disputing the definitiveness of the HSCA assertion on the identification of the Walker bullet is the testimony of Robert A. Frazier,
an FBI ballistics expert who was "unable to reach a conclusion" on
whether or not the Walker bullet matched the Mannlicher-Carcano
rifle found on the sixth floor of the Texas School Book Depository
on November 22. Warren Report records indicate Marina Oswald
testified that Lee admitted shooting at Walker and regretted missing
him; a note Lee left Marina that night also implicates him.[20] But all
of Marina's testimony would later come under scrutiny; prior to her
appearances before the Commission she was coached, prodded and
threatened with deportation if she did not depict her husband as a
crazed killer.

Whether or not Oswald shot at Walker, there are problems for
those who want to depict Oswald as a deranged and efficient killer.
If Oswald did try to kill Walker, he failed miserably. The attempt
was poorly planned and hastily executed. More importantly, he
missed his target. He was a poor marksman using an inferior
weapon. On the other hand, if Oswald did not shoot at Walker it
proves that he was being set up to appear as if he were a man
capable of violence against prominent figures to address some
political grievance. But even this frame-up fails to explain why
Oswald would shoot at a proto-fascist like Walker, and then also
be motivated to shoot at Walker's opposite, JFK, a left-of-center

President who condemned Walker's politics. In short, the Walker incident does not provide any explanation as to why Oswald would want to shoot Kennedy. According to DeMohrenschildt and others, Oswald admired and respected JFK. That conundrum left the Warren Commission with only one rationale—Oswald had a deep inferiority complex, borne of the frustration of being beaten down by the inconsequence of his life; by killing the President he would become the center of the world's attention, thus compensating for his profound inadequacies. If this was the case, why did Oswald not take credit for the murder of JFK? Why did he not admit to murdering the leader of the free world, instead of loudly proclaiming his innocence when he was apprehended and charged with the assassination?

Oswald worked at JCS until April 1963, when he left for New Orleans where his activities became increasingly suspicious. He worked for the Reily Coffee Company, a CIA proprietary organization which was located in the heart of the intelligence community in New Orleans. It was there that Oswald was filmed handing out pro-Castro leaflets in a staged demonstration. There was a phony scuffle in which Oswald engaged with several anti-Castro protestors, an incident designed to raise Oswald's profile as a communist agitator. The problem was, the leaflets contained an address, 544 Camp Street, which was affiliated with right-wing, *anti-Castro* activists involved in covert paramilitary operations against Cuba.

It was also in April 1963 that DeMohrenschildt wrote a letter to Lyndon Johnson's office in Washington, requesting the opportunity to meet with the Vice-President. On April 18, 1963, LBJ aide, Walter Jenkins promptly wrote a perfunctory reply. Five days later, LBJ's military aide, Colonel Howard Burriss, wrote to Jenkins "… suggesting that LBJ be kept informed to the maximum extent possible in as many areas as possible…*that he be more nearly prepared to assume the reins of government in case he is called upon to do so* (emphasis added)."[21] For a high-ranking aide to Johnson to make such a statement just seven months before Johnson *did* assume the reins of government is stunning. Why would Johnson and his military staff even be considering such an unthinkable contingency, unless, of course, they had foreknowledge of events which would unfold in November 1963? This was not just whimsical, off-the-cuff daydreaming on the part of Johnson's aide; this was a pointed, purposeful statement to someone very close to the man who would become the accused assassin of Johnson's predecessor.

Apparently Johnson and his military staff were so interested in what DeMohrenschildt had to tell them that they actually met in person with Oswald's good friend. According to researcher Martin Shackelford, Burriss, and possibly Johnson, saw DeMohrenschildt in Washington on April 26, 1963, and Johnson definitely met with him on May 20 of that year.[22]

The letters and meetings may, of themselves, have been a mini-covert operation meant to compromise Johnson. Perhaps the CIA wanted to create a record of a connection between DeMohrenschildt and Johnson for later use if the agency needed to remind its co-conspirator that when he ascended to the presidency that it had the goods on him. An insurance policy, if you will, against the immense power Johnson would have in just a few months.

Then again, DeMohrenschildt's mission might have been a straightforward update on the manipulation of the patsy. Either way, it is just another indication of the key role DeMohrenschildt played, wittingly or unwittingly, in the plot to frame Oswald for the murder of JFK.

Meanwhile, Oswald was dismissed, supposedly for poor performance, from JCS, and, as he had many times previously in his short life, he took off on a strange odyssey without having any firm prospects and without revealing what he was really up to. Therein lay the truth of his secret missions. He was doing intelligence work, and one can discern hidden meanings by following Oswald and his timeline. He left for New Orleans on April 24, 1963. On that same day an article appeared in the Dallas newspapers in which Lyndon Johnson was quoted as saying that President Kennedy would visit Dallas some time in 1963. In the same week, a pregnant Marina Oswald and her small child moved into Ruth Paine's house in Irving. (More on Paine later.)

Oswald's mundane job at Reily Coffee was merely a cover for his other activities which included intelligence work and political intrigue. Reily was located next door to U.S. government office buildings and parking garages. This meant that Oswald had easy access to FBI, CIA and Naval intelligence agents who would be entering and leaving their places of employment. In addition, Oswald was often seen at 544 Camp Street, the offices of Guy Banister, an ex-FBI man who was deeply involved in coordinating anti-Castro Cuban political and paramilitary activities, activities which had been expressly forbidden by President Kennedy.[23] All the while, the public Oswald was posing as a pro-Castro activist. Aside from the highly visible Fair Play for Cuba leaflet ruckus, Oswald also went on a New Orleans radio show in August to debate Carlos Bringuier, of the anti-Castro community. The pattern of Oswald's behavior is quite evident in retrospect: while conducting his pro-Castro activities, he quite demonstrably drew attention to himself with his antics; meanwhile, in private, he associated with virulently anti-Castro agents in a very low-key manner. This, in CIA terms, is called "sheep dipping," the process of making an asset appear to be one thing while he is really another. In other words, Oswald had alternate identities to cloak his true purposes. He was becoming immersed, as publisher Kris Millegan put it, "...in an officially sanctioned covert arena where one's inventive legend becomes entry into a netherworld of intrigue, compartmentalization, secret operations and contrived situations."[24] This is another sure sign that Oswald's activities were not of his own design. He was being "run" by his intelligence-agency handlers.

It was in New Orleans in the summer of 1963 that Oswald, away from his expectant wife and small child, fell in love with a cancer researcher named Judyth Vary. By all accounts, Vary (now known as Judyth Vary Baker) in the early 1960s was a brilliant young science student. At the age of 18 she received offers to advance her career and education from all over the country. She accepted an invitation to work in the area of cancer research for the Ochsner Clinic in New Orleans. According to some, this research was poached by the CIA. In the Foreword to Baker's book, *Me & Lee*, Edward T. Haslam writes, "Judyth and Lee had been part of an effort to use cancer-causing viruses as a biological weapon… intended to kill Fidel Castro."[25]

Alton Ochsner, founder of the clinic, was a rabid right-winger with an intense hatred of communism, just the kind of man the CIA was prone to recruit during the Cold War. Ochsner's research in cancer causes and cures was groundbreaking, so much so that, according to Baker, the clinic was on the verge of wiping out cancer. Instead the CIA perverted the breakthrough into a deadly weapon intended for our enemies. (Some JFK researchers believe that Jack Ruby, among other assassination figures, was killed by cancer cell injections, but there is scant proof of this.)

Haslam also claims that "60 Minutes researched [Vary-Baker's story] …and their producer Don Hewitt called it 'the biggest story of our times.'"[26] Not surprisingly, CBS never aired the story. It chose instead to air a fluff piece about what a hero Secret Service agent Clint Hill was, and how he had suffered years of depression and survivor's guilt over not saving Jack Kennedy's life in Dallas. The *60 Minutes* piece, with Mike Wallace as the interviewer, mentioned nothing of Secret Service drinking and carousing until 4 a.m. the night before the assassination; and, of course, there was no mention of Hill's lucrative new book-writing career, made up of safe, sanitized observations on Dallas. Hill also made no reference to JFK's wounds (he had an unobstructed view of the President's head while riding in the back seat on the way to Parkland). Wallace was either ignorant of the salient facts of the assassination, or he carefully steered away from dangerous areas of inquiry. Thus, *60 Minutes* viewers did not hear that Hill saw an exit wound at the back of the President's head (exactly the one that Dallas doctors described) which indicated a shot from the front; nor did they hear that William Greer, Kennedy's limo driver, slowed the car to a complete stop and pointed a gun directly at Hill as he jumped onto the back of the car (more on this in a later chapter).

Vary-Baker's book, *Me & Lee*, makes several other sensational claims. Among them that she and Lee carried on a love affair during his time in New Orleans, and that Lee was privy to the work she was doing for the Ochsner clinic. Incredibly this was not the Vary family's first brush with classified government work. Vary-Baker's father, Donald Vary, was an electrical engineer who worked on the Redstone rocket, the first U.S. nuclear ballistic missile. The rocket got its name from Redstone Arsenal in Huntsville, Alabama, where famed Nazi rocket scientist Wernher Von Braun developed the technology for the Apollo and Gemini space programs. In the kind of circular, wildly improbable connections one makes when unearthing the truth of the Kennedy assassination, there is a circuitous trail which leads from Redstone and Von Braun straight back to the CIA, Allen Dulles and Oswald.

The CIA's Nazis

One of Hitler's fair-haired boys, Von Braun was a genius scientist who had invented the V-rockets for the Third Reich during World War II. The development of the V-2 technology, achieved in collaboration with his fellow Nazi scientist, Walter Dornberger, nearly turned the tide of World War II, and, had it been perfected sooner, might have brought about a Nazi victory. An example of the V-2's devastating impact came on December 16, 1944, when a rocket smashed into an Antwerp movie theater and killed 567 civilians. (Dornberger was so bloodthirsty that he literally wept with joy at

V-2 rocket launches.)[27] That night, Von Braun and Dornberger were honored with the Knight's Cross, one of Hitler's highest honors. So fearsome was the V-2 that Dwight Eisenhower admitted that its existence earlier in '44 might have made the Allied invasion of Europe impossible.[28]

Von Braun and Dornberger, built the rockets at the Mittelwerk factory in Nordhausen with slave laborers. The laborers were imported from Nazi concentration camps and were literally worked to death. They were neither fed nor sheltered properly, and untold thousands simply died on the job. Von Braun and Dornberger would have been tried as war criminals had they not been protected by American intelligence operatives. After the war, they were secretly smuggled into the United States as part of Operation Paper-clip. Operation Paperclip was an Allen Dulles scheme, in conjunc-tion with the super-secretive JIOA (Joint Intelligence Objectives Agency) which was dedicated to sidestepping political landmines and international law to give Nazi scientists safe haven in America. It was no easy task for JIOA to get Von Braun to America. He had been an SS-Sturmbannfuhrer sponsored by Heinrich Himmler.[29] Likewise, Dornberger was well-known by the Allies as a war crimi-nal. But with Dulles's help, Von Braun's and Dornberger's status in The Third Reich was "decontaminated."

Dulles implemented Operation Paperclip while working for the OSS (forerunner of the CIA) in an attempt to beat the Russians to cutting-edge technology that would provide military and sci-entific advantages in the coming Cold War. According to Profes-sor Paul Cutter, "Dulles...assimilated Nazi scientists into the American establishment by obscuring their histories and short circuiting efforts to bring their true stories to light."[30] On Dulles's orders, Paperclip Nazis avoided the war crimes trials conducted in Germany and, instead, had their war records sanitized or "de-Nazified"; they were given new lives and lucrative jobs in the U.S., and they blended into American culture. They were debriefed and "re-trained" at Fort Bliss, and most were placed into defense, intelligence and science jobs in the Deep South, where their Nazi ideologies—racial purity and segregation of the races—were already embedded in the culture. Being surrounded by those of like minds made it much easier for the Nazis to accept and be accepted by their neighbors. Their funny accents were overlooked because the Nazis had security clearances and well-paying government or defense-contract jobs. Most importantly, they were white.

Dulles and His Paines

While Von Braun was placed in Alabama, Dornberger got a war-industry job. In the early 1950s he was placed with Bell Aircraft in Buffalo to work on the X-1 and X-2 rocket planes.[31] Later he was transferred to Bell Helicopter in Dallas/Fort Worth where he worked closely with Michael Paine, husband of Ruth Paine—the same Ruth Paine who took into her Dallas-area home Lee Harvey Oswald's wife and children while Lee was in New Orleans. As it so happened, Ruth Paine's mother-in-law, Ruth Forbes Paine, was best friends with Mary Bancroft, one of Allen Dulles's mistresses. During World War II, when Dulles was overseeing espionage activity in Bern, Switzerland, he hired Bancroft (a Beacon Hill patrician, descended from C.W. Barron, publisher of *The Wall Street Journal*) to write political analysis.[32] Bancroft and Dulles began a passionate, long-lasting affair, one of many that Dulles, a compulsive womanizer, would have in his lifetime. As the consummate spymaster, he used people—even lovers—for his own devious ends. Reportedly he told Bancroft, "We can let the work cover the romance, and the romance cover the work."[33]

It was Bancroft who introduced Dulles to the Paine family. The Paines were a quirky bunch. They were from old New England Quaker descent, and their politics leaned towards socialism, but they were ardently anti-communist. In today's America this would be unfathomable; however, there was once in this country a segment of the far left which was just as rabidly anti-communist as the right-wing was. According to David Talbot, "George Lyman Paine Jr. and Ruth Forbes Paine were the kind of odd ducks that [Bancroft] liked collecting—quirky offspring of prominent New England heritage."[34] But when Dulles entered the picture the attraction became more than just eccentricity.

Dulles was always on the lookout for recruits who would have entrée into areas of American life he felt needed close scrutiny. The left always presented problems because of their penchant for anarchy and their deep resentment of the injustices and ruthlessness of capitalists and the American right. Dulles had his American corporate interests to look out for, and any information he could gather on the forces which threatened them was a valuable commodity. The Paines, because of their vast wealth (they owned their own island off Cape Cod) and their left-wing sensibilities, were vulnerable targets for a predator like Dulles. And they shared a common snobbishness about their entitlement. In a March 1964 letter to Dulles, Bancroft wrote that the Paine and Forbes families were "... the kind of people who still believe today that the U.S. is their invention on lease to all the rest of us."[35]

After the assassination of JFK, Dulles and Bancroft exchanged a series of letters which were probably designed to minimize the Dulles-Paine-Oswald connection as just one fantastic coincidence. Dulles even remarked how conspiracy theorists, if they knew of the connection, would be feverishly suspicious. Without question the two were intimately acquainted with this spycraft technique while entwined in Switzerland. As a writer of political cover stories, Bancroft had been well-trained by her lover. The ruse wasn't necessary, of course, because Dulles was busy steering the Warren Commission away from areas that would implicate himself or his cohorts in the assassination. Still, the coincidence of the de-facto head of the Warren Commission having a direct connection to the landlady of the accused assassin's family is so fantastic that one must make a

giant leap into the sea of denial to pass this off as completely innocent. Nevertheless, Ruth Paine, as of this writing still alive, claims
it is an innocent coincidence. She denies her own family's considerable CIA ties, and she sees nothing sinister about her family's relationship with Allen Dulles.

But the circumstances of Paine's life belie her own vehement
protestations of innocence. Ruth's sister, Sylvia Hoke, worked for
the CIA at its Langley headquarters, and Ruth visited Sylvia in
September 1963.[36] The timing of the visit, just two months before
the Kennedy assassination, is suspicious because it puts Paine in
close proximity to the organization for which her friend Lee Oswald
was working. There's more. Sylvia's husband, John, and Ruth's
father, William Hyde, also worked for a CIA proprietary organization, the Agency for International Development. If all this is not
enough to cast doubt on Ruth Paine's guiltlessness, consider this: it
was Paine who got Oswald his job at the Texas School Book Depository upon her return from visiting her CIA sister. And there is
reason to believe (despite Paine's denials to the Warren Commission) that she neglected to tell Oswald about a better paying job
offered to Lee.

At the suggestion of a neighbor, on October 14, 1963, Paine
phoned the Texas School Book Depository and was told there was
a job opening. She informed Oswald, and Oswald was interviewed
the following day and started working there on October 16, 1963.[37]
But according to James Douglass, on the day before Oswald began
work at the TSBD, "Robert Adams of the Texas Employment Commission phoned the Paine residence with a much better job prospect for Oswald...as a baggage or cargo handler at Trans Texas
Airways, for a salary $100 per month higher than that offered by
the TSBD."[38] This salary discrepancy so aroused Warren Commission staffer David Slawson that he wrote a memo to WC attorneys
which, in part, read, "...Oswald may have had a non-economic
reason for taking the job at the TSBD."[39] Slawson might have

thought he discovered Oswald's malice aforethought, but there were two serious problems with his presumption: one) Oswald had no way of knowing that his new place of employment would put him in position to kill Kennedy; the motorcade route had not yet been announced and was unknown to the public at the time Oswald accepted the TSBD job; two) apparently Slawson was unaware that Paine had never even mentioned the TTA job offer to Oswald. Thus, the Warren Commission never considered the fact that perhaps Oswald was the designated CIA patsy and could not accept a better paying job because his presence was needed at the TSBD on the day, just five weeks later, when JFK's motorcade would pass right in front of the building. The Commission also overlooked, or neglected, this salient fact: the neighbor who supposedly called to tell Paine about the opening at the TSBD, one Linnie Mae Randle, denied to the Warren Commission that she ever knew of any such job.[40]

Paine would not have been in a position to decline non-TSBD job offers for Oswald if she and her husband had not stopped living together right around the time that the Oswalds themselves took up separate residences. It is yet another convenient coincidence that Michael and Ruth Paine were estranged by 1963. This gave Marina and the kids living space, and Lee the opportunity to visit them in suburban Irving on weekends, which he did regularly. (During the work week, Oswald typically stayed at his boarding house on Beckley Street in Dallas.) As JFK researcher Barbra LaMonica put it, "The Paines...insured the continued separation of Lee and Marina..." so that Lee would have "...no witnesses to his activities or associates...leading up to the assassination..." and the Paine residence "...provided storage space for evidence that would be used against Oswald."[41] Namely, the Mannlicher-Carcano rifle, which both Michael and Ruth claimed was hidden in the Paines' garage. This was an important piece of information to provide authorities in the frame-up of Oswald. When law enforcement personnel searched Paine's garage shortly after the assassination, they did not find the Mannlicher-Carcano, but they did find a Minox spy camera; it was the type of camera that would be in the possession of only those involved in intelligence activities.[42] The camera was the size of a cigarette lighter and was not available to the general public.

Another important reason for removing Michael from the Paine household in Irving was to hide even more revealing links between the Paines, Oswald, Dulles and the CIA. In yet another suspicious coincidence, Michael Paine in 1963 was working at Bell Helicopter in Fort Worth alongside ex-Nazi rocket scientist Walter Dornberger. Any honest examination of Dornberger's time in the U.S. leads straight back to the CIA's Operation Paperclip; surely, Dulles wanted to avoid that connection. If Michael Paine had lived with his wife at the time of the assassination, his employment situation would have come under greater scrutiny. And close examination of Michael Paine's background reveals a lot about the way in which the CIA helped make fortunes for the military-industrial complex during Vietnam.

The Paine family history with commercial and military helicopters dates back to before the Korean War. Paine's stepfather, Arthur Young, of Paoli, Pennsylvania, invented the first commercial helicopter, the 47-A, or MASH helicopter. The patent was bought by Bell Aviation, and Bell sold the helicopter for military uses around the world. Bell was also involved in political king-making. According to author Robert Bryce, "Lyndon Johnson had enjoyed a long and profitable relationship with the company…Bell had provided money for Johnson's 1948 election campaign…and free use of a 47-B helicopter."[43] It was Johnson who encouraged Bell to move its headquarters and production facilities to Texas and join the super-secretive and powerful Suite 8F Group.[44]

By the late 1950s, however, due to the lack of America's military involvement on foreign soil, Bell was, according to CIA expert and Pentagon insider Fletcher Prouty, "…near bankruptcy when the

First National Bank of Boston approached the CIA about developing helicopter usage for Indochina."[45] The problem was JFK planned to withdraw from Vietnam and to significantly reduce the military's budget. In March 1963 Kennedy proposed cutting "52 military installations in 25 states, [and] 21 overseas bases."[46] But when JFK was killed and Johnson ramped up the Vietnam War, Bell was contracted to build over 10,000 "Hueys" and made a fortune, over $600 million by one estimate.[47] It was during this period that Michael Paine was employed as an engineer by Bell.

Clearly then, the Paines' connections to Bell and Arthur Young are worth a closer look. During her long, meandering trip in the summer of 1963, Ruth Paine paid a visit to Young in Paoli. It was from there that she wrote a letter to Marina Oswald at the Oswalds' residence on Magazine Street in New Orleans (Marina had rejoined Lee there). Ruth requested that Marina come live at the Paine residence in Dallas while Marina awaited the birth of her child. Ruth offered to pick up Marina on the way back from her eastern trip, and suggested that Marina reply to her in care of Arthur Young's address in Pennsylvania.[48]

Paine and Marina set up house in Irving just a couple months before the assassination. The timing is more than coincidental; it gave Lee Harvey Oswald a residence to visit and store things separate from his rooming house in Dallas. Paine's residence was a place where the homeowner could easily help frame the patsy by planting evidence or making insinuations about his intentions. When Paine directed Oswald to the Texas School Book Depository his fate was sealed. Afterwards, the Paines seemed to know full well the implications of their association with the Oswalds. Within hours of the assassination, a male voice was overheard on a phone call placed to Ruth's residence saying that Oswald didn't kill Kennedy but that "we both know who did."[49]

If the Paines' role was to help set up the patsy in a CIA-controlled plot, the above facts do nothing to refute that. Despite this,

JFK and the End of America

Ruth Paine denies any accountability. As of this writing, she is living in a Quaker retirement community in northern California. Her "estranged" husband Michael is living in the same community.

The Warren Commission, understandably, did little to investigate this dangerous territory. Rather, commissioners either ignored, or were steered away from, evidence and testimony that pointed toward a conspiracy. Dulles was particularly adroit at this.

Given his above connections with the major players in the drama, Dulles should have made a full disclosure of his relationships with Bancroft, Dornberger, the Paines, and, by extension, the Oswald family. If these relationships were innocent, there would be no reason for not disclosing them. But Dulles kept his secrets, and did not recuse himself from investigating the murder of a president he despised and whose supposed killer had tangible, albeit indirect, links to Dulles himself. This failure to expose his own compromised status as an unbiased and objective investigator should have made Dulles a prime suspect in the murder of the century. Instead, he became one of the dominant forces on the Commission as it pushed forward to a faulty conclusion.

The other Commission members may have suspected they were being led astray, but they put up only half-hearted fights in the face of the powerful entities on whom they relied for facts—the CIA and the FBI. Had the members known of Dulles's secret past, they might have been less pliable and more resistant to the whitewash job with which they are now forever associated. But in 1963 the hideous malevolence of the CIA's covert operations was largely unknown. Programs like ZR-RIFLE, an assassination team run by a deranged drunkard named William Harvey, from whose department may have come one or more of the assassins in Dealey Plaza, would have given Commissioners pause had they known of them. Operation Northwoods, a false flag operation proposed by the CIA's Edward Lansdale and the Joint Chiefs, and rejected by JFK in 1962; Operation Mockingbird, the subversion of the free press in America (which will be discussed in a later chapter); Operation MK-ULTRA, a mind control program dedicated to developing Manchurian Candidate killers; the CIA overthrow of governments around the globe—from Guatemala to Iran, and the Congo to South Vietnam; and the many CIA attempts to kill Castro, or "whack out the Beard," were largely unknown to the Commissioners and their staff members.

CHAPTER 3

Signs of Intelligence Life

"It was common knowledge
in the Tokyo CIA station that
Oswald worked for the agency."[1]
—Jim Wilcott,
CIA Finance Officer

Oswald's mysterious and covert activities for the duration of his short adult life can only be understood if seen through the prism of his CIA connections. From his early days as David Ferrie's cadet in the Civil Air Patrol, through the time he spent at the Atsugi Air Base; from his false defection to Russia and his unfathomably unfettered repatriation, through his secretive activities in New Orleans and Dallas, Oswald was being moved around like a pawn in a perplexing game. He was, at once, the patriotic marine and the communist sympathizer who was nicknamed "Oswaldovitch" by his fellow soldiers; he was a defector who hated America, but who could not wait to return to his native land; he was a Marxist in New Orleans who associated with virulently rabid anti-Castroites; he loved Kennedy, but he went around Dallas telling everyone he would like to shoot Kennedy. These wild inconsistencies and contradictions indicate that Oswald's handlers wanted his legend to be flexible enough to conform to any contingency. But it also duped Oswald into believing that he was the con artist in a crooked game, when, in fact, he was the one being suckered. While he thought he was infiltrating a New Orleans plot (supposedly hatched by Ferrie and

Shaw) against JFK, he was really being lured into a bigger and darker scheme in which he was the mark. All along, his CIA "shepherds" were really wolves; their goal was to devour him, not protect him.

His CIA recruitment began in the Louisiana Civil Air Patrol, which turned out to be a grooming school for many nefarious characters who would later play roles in JFK's assassination. CAP was originally formed, according to its own website, in 1946 as a "benevolent, nonprofit organization."[2] The Louisiana branch of CAP was founded shortly thereafter by LBJ crony David Harold Byrd. Byrd liked to be photographed in his Air Force Colonel's uniform, a rank bestowed upon him by none other than his close friend General Curtis (Bombs Away) LeMay, virulent Kennedy hater and Air Force Chief of Staff under same. During the Cuban Missile Crisis, it was LeMay who was infuriated about Kennedy's resistance to invading Cuba, an event we now know would have ignited World War III and likely a nuclear conflagration. An ardent warmonger who firebombed Tokyo and selected the atomic bomb sites of Nagasaki and Hiroshima during World War II, LeMay fumed, "Those goddamn Kennedys are going to destroy this country if we don't do something about them."[3]

Byrd and LeMay made the LCAP look like a unit of weekend flyboys to outsiders, just an excuse to make Byrd a colonel and to have an auxiliary pilot training presence in the South. This was a cover though. U.S. military intelligence and the CIA used the cover to train and recruit pilots to make surreptitious flights into the Caribbean and beyond for weapons trading, support for paramilitary operations, and drug running (later Air America). Sitting on the Gulf Coast, with easy access to Cuba, Latin America and South America, Louisiana was a logical base of operations. In an era when fear of the spread of communism was pervasive, the CIA needed pilots and mercenaries for its covert operations in The Third World. Overthrowing leftist leaders like Guatemala's Arbenz required quick movement of manpower and materials. Byrd was doing his patriotic bit.

Later, of course, Byrd provided Oswald with another employment opportunity—at the Texas School Book Depository building. This is yet another incredible coincidence which "lone- nutters" must explain away: Byrd, a Texas oil millionaire, defense contractor, and LBJ benefactor, provided the first and last places of employment for Oswald. Dismissing the improbability of such an innocent accident, one is left to conclude only this: Byrd's organizations were used as fronts for intelligence reasons, and Oswald was being moved around by unseen forces as part of covert operations. Think of it, JFK's supposed assassin fires from a building owned by the same man to whose air patrol unit he was attached as a cadet nearly a decade earlier. And Byrd neither admitted to, nor was questioned about, this suspicious happenstance. If he had been questioned by the Warren Commission, he likely would have invoked plausible deniability. He unknowingly provided the facilities for intelligence operations, while keeping a safe distance from the action. But Byrd's acquaintances make this argument moot. He belonged to the Dallas Petroleum Club and the Dallas Council on Foreign Relations; he had intelligence connections on the Dallas police force; he was a close business associate of Neil Mallon of Dresser Industries (Mallon's importance is detailed later); and he was an Air Force insider with powerful friends in the Pentagon.

In his biography, written 15 years after Kennedy's murder, Byrd makes no mention of his dubious place in history as the owner of the building from which the President was supposedly shot. However, he does devote many paragraphs to denouncing the socialist policies of the federal government and oil industry regulation, a typical refrain of Texas millionaires who at the time were fearful that JFK would abolish the oil depletion allowance which amounted to a handout for the rich. Oil-drenched Dallas patricians felt America belonged to them; they had no problem letting others wallow in squalor while they ruined the environment with their rapacious greed.

Byrd writes that he "…was the victim of an antitrust suit brought by the federal government against booming Ling-Temco-Vought, in which [he]…was a heavy stockholder."[4] Byrd was one of the original investors in Temco Aircraft. In 1961 Temco absorbed Chance Vought, an aircraft manufacturer with defense industry ties. This prompted the Justice Department suit which, according to Byrd, "…set off a knee-jerk reaction…which claimed we were getting too big."[5] Byrd does not mention the Kennedys by name, but the head of the Justice Department at the time was Robert Kennedy, Attorney General of the United States. LTV stock plunged as the suit was adjudicated, and Byrd's finances "…were strained to the limit" by it.[6]

Byrd's fortunes enjoyed a big upswing, however, after Kennedy was killed. LBJ, one of the men Byrd "…could go to at any time that I wanted action,"[7] made LTV immensely profitable again by ramping up the Vietnam War and throwing defense contracts to Byrd's company. Perhaps this was Byrd's reward from the plotters for lending his enterprises to the covert actions which culminated in JFK's death.

Byrd's LCAP

The ideal candidates for CIA recruitment were young, impressionable, adventuresome patriots seeking a life of daring and stealth. In the alternative, they were outcasts and misfits, willing to commit abnormal or questionable acts without hesitation. Consequently, an unusually high number of LCAP cadets became psychopathic killers, CIA pilots or gullible, low-level fall guys. Besides Oswald, a startling number of LCAP graduates were either tangentially or directly connected to the JFK hit. Among them were: Charles Rogers, a CIA pilot who murdered his parents in Houston in 1965 and who was photographed in Dealey Plaza on November 22, 1963; Barry Seal a CIA pilot who ran drugs and weapons for the agency; James Bath, a close associate of the Bush family and another pilot with a criminal background; and John Liggett, who became an infamous mortician and body reconstructionist with ties to organized crimes and U.S. intelligence. Scrutinizing Liggett's movements on the weekend of Kennedy's assassination is crucial to understanding the critical role he played in covering up the medical evidence that has made the murder so hard to solve a half-century on. His tale is astonishing and will be discussed at length in another chapter.

In order to facilitate its recruitment of LCAP members, the CIA needed mesmeric leaders who had sway over young men. It found one such person in David Ferrie, a defrocked priest, a skilled pilot, a hypnotist and a pedophile. Oswald was probably directed to Ferrie and LCAP by Dutz Murret, Oswald's bookmaking uncle who worked for New Orleans crime boss Carlos Marcello. Ferrie worked for Marcello as a pilot. When Marcello was deported as an undesirable by Bobby Kennedy's Justice Department in 1961, Ferrie flew a private plane to Guatemala, picked up the gangland boss, and flew him back home. Ferrie fancied himself an expert pilot, and loved flying secret missions for the Mafia and the CIA. In LCAP he insisted on being called Captain Ferrie, and despite his weird appearance (he wore an orange wig and painted-on eyebrows) his trainees were apparently defenseless against his hypnotic powers. He kept in touch with his cadets even after they graduated. He reconnected with Oswald in New Orleans in 1963, and he occasionally showed up in Dallas at the home of John Liggett in the mid-1960s.

Ferrie taught his prized pupils some of the tricks of spycraft. And while most LCAP alums tried to maintain their covers after joining the CIA, Barry Seal was flamboyantly and unabashedly open about his occupation. His remarkable life is well-chronicled in Daniel Hopsicker's book *Barry And The Boys*. Seal was entrusted by the CIA to fly drugs out of southeast Asia, Central America and South America; guns in and out of trouble spots all over the globe; and operatives to secret CIA missions. He was a rogue narcotics trafficker, a fast-talking, cocky Special Forces veteran, and a DEA informant who worked both sides of the law. He was well acquainted with Oswald, with whom he met "…at least three times a week in David Ferrie's quasi-military outfit…Oswald epitomized the unit. He was extremely bright, and spoke Spanish and some Russian."[8]

On November 22, 1963, shortly after JFK was assassinated, Dallas citizens who lived next to Red Bird Airport, a small facility just eight miles south of Love Field where Air Force One landed that day, called police to complain about the loud revving of an airplane engine which muffled the sounds of their TVs as they tried to listen to reports of the tragic events in their city that day. The offensive plane, described as a green-and-white Comanche, much like the one owned and flown by Barry Seal, was oddly parked on the grass near the airport fence.[9] About 1 p.m., right around the time Kennedy was declared dead, the plane took off. From his position in the control tower, air traffic controller Louis Gaudin could see several men standing near the plane as well as one or more pilots in the plane. Gaudin "grew so suspicious…that when the plane took off… he asked the pilot…which way the plane was heading."[10] The pilot replied "south," and then promptly turned the plane in a northerly direction towards Love Field, where the plane landed a few minutes later. Gaudin later identified one of the pilots as David Ferrie.[11] Hopsicker believes he knows the identity of the other pilot. In *Barry & The Boys*, he writes, "We believe Seal did indeed fly that 'getaway' plane out of Dallas…a gunrunner to Cuba, a veteran of the Bay of Pigs, and a CIA pilot, [Seal] should have been a prime suspect…[but] was never questioned."[12]

More evidence of CIA activity at Red Bird at the time of the assassination comes from Wayne January, owner of American Aviation, a company which rented out small airplanes. January sold a DC-3 to a Cuban pilot who bought it on behalf of an Air Force colonel who worked for Houston Air Center, a CIA front organization.[13] For days leading up to the assassination, January and the Cuban pilot worked together as mechanics preparing the DC-3 for flight. During the course of their work, the Cuban shared some stunning news with January. "Wayne, they are going to kill your President...[and] they are going to kill Robert Kennedy and any other Kennedy who gets in that position."[14]

January dismissed the Cuban's assertions, until November 22 when January got the reports of Kennedy's assassination. The Cuban pilot told him, "It's all going to happen just like I told you."[15]

January was interviewed by the FBI, but, fearing for his life and the safety of his family, he did not mention the story of the CIA purchase of his plane and the statements of the Cuban pilot. January kept his story to himself for decades until he finally opened up to researcher Matthew Smith. Smith showed January a doctored FBI document which assailed January's credibility. This prompted January to open up about the suspicious DC-3 sale.[16]

The FBI document in question was a report made by January of having seen Lee Harvey Oswald, or someone who looked like Oswald, as one of a group of mysterious people who, two days before the assassination, tried to rent a Cessna 310 which they said they needed for a flight to Mexico on Friday, November 22.[17] But the real Oswald was at work in the Texas School Book Depository on November 20. How could the man at Red Bird Airport trying to rent a plane for a possible post-assassination escape be anything but an Oswald impostor? This necessitated a fraudulent pre-dating of January's report. To January's shock, the FBI report claimed that he had made his identification in July 1963, four months before the incident actually happened.[18] This is just one of many examples of how federal agencies employed a phony Oswald to frame, in advance and after the fact, the real Oswald for the murder of JFK, and then tried desperately to cover up the "two-Oswald ruse."

The Red Bird incidents have even broader implications though. They are indicative of how all-encompassing CIA involvement in the crime was. Preparation and planning were intricate and precise, but also flawed. The perfect crime would have required complete silence from the conspirators and more judicious use of the Oswald double. But in a plot of such magnitude and complexity perfection was not possible. That's why the plotters had to resort to such drastic measures in the cover-up phase. The Red Bird slip-ups were only a few of the mistakes that needed to be wiped away.

It's no surprise that Red Bird was a hub of furtive CIA activity leading up to and on the day of the assassination. The plotters needed planes to fly out agency assets—assassins, clean-up crews, and perhaps even cover-up artists who accompanied the dead President's body back to Washington—who had been on the ground in Dallas that day. Given LCAP's notorious reputation for training pilots and other covert agents, it should have been logical that investigators look into the backgrounds of CAP grads. However, the House Select Committee on Assassinations discovered that most of the squadron's records had been "stolen" in late 1960, about the time Kennedy was elected President.[19]

Oswald's Double Life

While great effort was made to disassociate Oswald from the CIA, we today have an abundance of evidence to indicate he was not only employed by the agency but that he was being set up by the agency. All along Oswald's journeys, CIA "shepherds" accompanied him. In LCAP it was David Ferrie. In Dallas it was DeMohrenschildt. In New Orleans it was David Ferrie, Clay Shaw, ex-FBI agent Guy Banister, and a rat's nest of violent anti-Castro Cubans, in whose company Oswald was often seen. Ruth Paine watched over Oswald's family in Irving; she later implicated Oswald as the assassin. David Atlee Phillips, a high-ranking CIA officer, met with Oswald. Even while in the Marine Corps and Russia, Oswald was apparently under orders from the CIA.

Oswald joined the Marines after completing his stint with LCAP. His Marine Corps commander, John Donovan, described Oswald as "a wise guy, troublemaker, officer baiter, revolter against author-ity."[20] Oswald often spoke to his fellow marines of his affection for the Soviet Union and Marxist philosophies, yet his assignment gave him access to highly classified items—"secret radio frequencies, call signs and codes which were compromised…at the time of his defec-tion."[21] It seems quite peculiar that, at the height of the Cold War, a Marxist was loudly, obnoxiously, and without fear of repercussion espousing his political views while in the United States Marine Corps. Oswald's fellow Marines were naturally put off by him; they viewed him as an oddball who was somehow protected by the higher-ups. Despite this, Oswald was court-martialed twice for infractions which had nothing to do with his insurrectionist poli-tics. Not only was he not kicked out of the Marines, he was assigned to a top-secret American installation in Japan. While securing intel-ligence assignments, Oswald also cemented his legend as a com-munist agitator.

As part of his Marine Corps service, Oswald was assigned to Atsugi Air Base. According to Edward Jay Epstein, "Atsugi wasn't simply an Air Force defense base; it was a CIA base. And the CIA program at that base involved one of America's most secret and important reconnaissance missions, the U-2 spy plane."[22] The U-2 could fly at heights that were beyond Soviet radar capabilities, and thus the plane could conduct valuable espionage missions without detection by the Russians. Until May 1, 1960, that is, when an American U-2 piloted by Gary Powers was shot down over Soviet air space. How did the Russians gather the intelligence to know when and where the U-2 was flying? Some have speculated that Oswald could have supplied this information to the Soviets when he defected. Oswald was a radio communications operator at Atsugi and certainly would have had "access to highly sophisticated mate-rials."[23]

But there is some question as to whether it was the real Lee Har-vey Oswald who was assigned to Atsugi in the first place. (For some, this conundrum has never been satisfactorily resolved; even now one wonders, "Who was the real Oswald, and who was the fake?") A fellow Marine claims the Oswald he knew bore no resemblance to the Oswald arrested in Dallas on November 22, 1963. This was one of the first of many Oswald impostor scenarios [like the Red Bird Airport Oswald impostor previously mentioned), as reported by scores of witnesses who knew Oswald (or his double) and remembered him (or his double) quite vividly. Richard Bullock served with Oswald at Atsugi, and came to know him rather well. Bullock was fully acquainted with Oswald's physical appearance, and the guy he saw shot down by Jack Ruby on November 24, 1963, was not the "Atsugi Oswald." Bullock claimed that the Oswald he saw on TV after the JFK assassination looked "nothing like…the man I knew…the 'Ozzie' I knew in the marines [was] two or three inches taller, 40 pounds heavier…and wore thick glasses."[24]

Bullock was not called to testify to the Warren Commission, but Oswald's commander John Donovan was. When the WC counsel refused to question Donovan about Oswald's classified work in the Marines, Donovan was aghast. "Don't you want to know about the U-2?" Donovan asked.[25] The reply was thanks, but no thanks. Commissioners, perhaps briefed by their WC superior Dulles, were careful to avoid areas of connection between Oswald and the CIA.

The U-2 incident sabotaged the Eisenhower-Kruschev peace summit scheduled for later that spring, and there was only one agency with the means and motive for such treachery: the CIA. A peace pact with the Soviets would not have been in the agency's interests. According to Fletcher Prouty, "…probably…Eisenhower did not know that the U-2 had been dispatched…[he] had come within two weeks of a lasting and hopeful peace."[26] Three and a half years later, JFK had a similar dream shot down.

Oswald's enigmatic adventures continued upon his release from the Marines. The ease with which he made it to Russia screams CIA involvement. In late 1959 he traveled by ship from New Orleans to

Europe. He traveled across Europe to Finland, and left from Finland for Moscow on October 15. In Russia he hired a private tour guide, Rimma Shirokova, who provided him with deluxe class tourist service. Where did Oswald get the money for this long, luxurious trip? His financial records indicate he had a mere $200 in the bank when he left New Orleans,[27] yet the journey cost him more than $200. Oswald's CIA pay records are classified, but we know from his paymaster, Jim Wilcott (see quote at beginning of chapter), that Oswald was indeed drawing funds from the CIA. He was most likely being funded by the false defector program which was run by an Allen Dulles surrogate, James Jesus Angleton, whose name is often invoked in connection with JFK's murder.

At first, the Soviets rejected Oswald's request for political asylum. The KGB, for good reason, was suspicious of Oswald's real intentions. But to show his genuine desire to stay in Russia, Oswald took drastic measures with an apparent suicide attempt. He slashed his wrists, but doctors who examined him determined that the wounds were superficial and called it a "show attempt."[28]

Oswald was allowed to stay in the country long enough to meet and marry Marina Prusakova, who was the niece of a prominent officer in the Soviet Ministry of Internal Affairs. Lee and Marina married in 1961, but soon grew disenchanted with life in the Soviet Union. By June 1962 they moved to the least likely place on the planet one would expect a Marxist, an American defector, and a Soviet émigré to reside—Dallas, Texas, once the national headquarters of the Ku Klux Klan. In 1962 Dallas was a hotbed of right-wing zealots and anti-Soviet sentiment. Its leading citizen, the self-proclaimed richest man in the world, oilman H.L. Hunt, publicly ranted against the communist leanings of the city and country he loved. He funded a quasi-fascist radio program called "Life Line." He belonged to the First Baptist Church of Dallas, whose pastor declared that, "Communism is a denial of god...communism is like a kingdom of darkness presided over by a prince of evil...the greatest challenge the Christian faith has ever faced."[29]

Texans may have thought of the Kennedys and the federal government as the epicenter of northern liberalism and communist appeasement. But there were those in Washington who were just as rabidly right-wing as any Texas extremist. Men like Allen Dulles, Curtis LeMay and J. Edgar Hoover hated the Kennedys and their policies just as rabidly. One Dallasite who was not oblivious to the Washington enmity for JFK was Hunt. He was plugged into Washington politics, and he was quite familiar with the players who were planning the President's demise. Hunt knew D.H. Byrd and LeMay, personally and professionally. Hunt himself was LBJ's ardent supporter at the Los Angeles nominating convention in 1960, and he knew of Johnson's lust for the presidency. As corruptible, crooked and ruthless as any politician who ever lived, Johnson would have gladly bent over backwards to please Hunt and would have joined in any scheme, no matter how pernicious, to keep Hunt's support. Each knew the mood of Dallas in the early 1960s, and each knew Dallas would be the perfect place to ambush Kennedy while risking the least amount of exposure. Many Dallas cops were members of the John Birch Society, and the town's leaders belonged to fringe radical organizations like the Dallas Citizens Council. These groups seethed with hostility towards JFK.

On the face of it, then, it would seem that a leftist like Oswald would not be safe in such a rabidly anti-communist place, but, as in every other stage of his adult life, he was somehow protected by a shadowy cabal of intelligence operatives. In Dallas it was the white Russian community; one of its members, the loquacious and erudite George DeMohrenschildt, took the introverted and unrefined Oswald under his wing.

The Man Who Knew Everyone
DeMohrenschildt, in many ways, was the most intrepid and incredible figure in the entire assassination scenario. He was connected,

directly and indirectly, to almost all players involved, including Jackie Kennedy. It is almost as comical as it is astounding that Lee Harvey Oswald's best friend in Dallas was acquainted with the wife of Oswald's supposed victim. Coincidence theorists no doubt consign it to the long, seemingly endless, list of coincidences surrounding Kennedy's murder, but given DeMohrenschildt's extensive trafficking in CIA, oil, politics, and Eastern elite and Texas social circles, perhaps we should not be surprised at all.

DeMohrenschildt was a man whose life reads like a character in a bad spy novel. He was a dapper, well-spoken, multilingual raconteur who ran in upper-class circles, but also descended (or condescended) to befriend an uneducated, lower-class malcontent in Oswald. Born of Russian royalty, DeMohrenschildt and his family fled Russia after the Revolution. George arrived in America with a deep resentment of communism and a determination to recreate the type of privileged existence his forebears had enjoyed. DeMohrenschildt joined his brother Dimitri in New York in 1938. Dimitri, a staunch anti-communist himself, was an OSS agent and one of the founders of the CIA's propaganda outlet, Radio Free Europe.

George eventually obtained an advanced degree in geology, with a specialty in underground exploration for oil. This specialty brought him in contact with a wide spectrum of oilmen and petroleum adventurers. He worked for Pantipec Oil, a company owned by William F. Buckley's family, and Shell Oil in Houston. According to author John Craig, DeMohrenschildt "became a friend of many prominent wildcatter oilmen, including John Mecom, Sr., of Houston and H.L. Hunt of Dallas."[30] A Dutch journalist with CIA ties named Willem Oltmans once told HSCA counsel Robert Tanenbaum that DeMohrenschildt knew Hunt for 20 years and attended parties at Hunt's mansion.[31] DeMohrenschildt was a member of various right-wing organizations in Dallas—the Dallas Petroleum Club, the Dallas Council on World Affairs, and the Texas Crusade for Freedom among them—where he mingled with

Hunt; oil barons Clint Murchison and Sid Richardson; CIA asset Earle Cabell (Dallas mayor and brother of Dulles's CIA deputy Charles Cabell); ultra-right publisher of the *Dallas Morning News*, Ted Dealey, for whose ancestors the Dallas plaza where JFK was killed was named; and Neil Mallon, intimate of the George Bush family. David Talbot calls the Dallas Petroleum Club "…a hotbed of anti-Kennedy ferment, whose leading members…were tied to Dulles, Lyndon Johnson, and J. Edgar Hoover."[32] If a plot to kill Kennedy were hatched by these like-minded titans of American industry, politics, intelligence and government, it had a great chance to succeed because this small group of men had more wealth and power than the rest of the country combined. They controlled law enforcement, government, information and oil (the lack of which could have paralyzed the country); these men had a death grip on America, and they could have successfully executed and covered up the assassination of a sitting U.S. president. Dulles's deadly network of assassins could do the deed, and wipe out any uncooperative witnesses after the fact; Hoover could use his FBI to squash real evidence and create fake evidence to frame the patsy; Johnson, as the murdered president's successor, could appoint a whitewash commission to cover the plotters' tracks; and Texas oil barons could supply unlimited funds to finance the plot's expenses—hiring killers, pilots, clean-up crews and other operatives, and bribing officials as necessary. It was convenient cover for these men to meet under the guise of conducting the business of petroleum boards, civic councils or citizens' committees. And Dallas was at the heart of it all.

Zapruder Profits
Also a member of the Dallas Council on World Affairs was Abraham Zapruder, recorder of the now-infamous film of the JFK assassination which has become the most analyzed home movie in the history of the world. The film, which was locked away from public view for

12 years, clearly shows the impact of a bullet, fired from the President's front right, violently snapping his head to the left and rear. A human head struck by a bullet from a high-powered rifle moves in the direction of the bullet, not towards the origin of the shot. Unless all laws of physics were suspended in Dealey Plaza during the assassination, this is a clear indication that the fatal shot was not fired from the Texas School Book Depository. And this, then, means that a conspiracy took the life of the 35th President; for all investigators, pro-conspiracy and lone-nutters alike, agree that Oswald was in the Book Depository, to the right *rear* of the President, during the shooting. Therefore, he could not have fired the fatal shot from the right-front of the motorcade.

It was essential that the plotters keep this damning film from perusal by the American public, and the man who stepped up to purchase it from Zapruder for an exorbitant price was none other than Henry Luce who had extensive ties to Allen Dulles and the CIA. The owner of *Time* and *Life* magazines, Luce was "…a Skull and Bones colleague of Prescott Bush (George H.W.'s father) and a devotee of intelligence—whose wife, Clare Booth Luce had personally funded efforts to overthrow Castro."[33] Zapruder was paid $150,000 (the equivalent of nearly $1 million in today's money), but lied to the Warren Commission about the sum. When questioned by Wesley Liebeler, Zapruder said he was paid "$25,000… and I have given it to the Firemen's and Policemen's Funds."[34] Among all the photographers and filmmakers in Dealey Plaza, Zapruder was the only one who profited so handsomely from the death of JFK. In 1999 the U.S. government turned over $16 million, plus interest, to the Zapruder family.

To the uninformed, Zapruder's presence in the ideal location on a pedestal on Elm Street is no surprise. He he was an avowed Kennedy lover and naturally wanted to see the President pass by. Zapruder's secretary, Marilyn Sitzman, said, "He talked about [JFK] all the time, admired his politics."[35] But that didn't stop him from making a tidy profit off the sale of the film mere hours after the assassination. Forrest Sorrels, Secret Service agent in charge of the Dallas field office, reported to Washington that Zapruder "…agreed to furnish me with a copy of this film with the understanding that it was strictly for the official use of the Secret Service…as he expected to sell the film for as high a price as he could get for it."[36] C.D. Jackson, publisher of *Life* magazine, quickly dispatched his representative, Richard Stolley, to Dallas to pay Zapruder a small fortune for the print rights to his movie. It is important to note here that Jackson was a close associate of Allen Dulles and a willing participant in Operation Mockingbird, the CIA's program to control the American press.

Zapruder may have had an even more direct contact with Allen Dulles just prior to the Kennedy assassination. Using the excuse of promoting his newly-penned book, *The Craft Of Intelligence*, Dulles made a trip to Dallas in October 1963, and he spoke of the Red Menace to a rapt audience at a meeting of the Dallas Council on World Affairs.[37] One wonders if Abraham Zapruder was in the audience that night. For Dulles, the trip to Dallas was a special occasion; according to author Russ Baker, "…[Dulles] appears to have made no book-related appearances outside the Washington-New York corridor except for Dallas."[38]

Zapruder had other interesting connections with CIA assets. He worked at Nardis, a Dallas fashion designer and manufacturer, with Jeanne de LeGon who became the fourth wife of George DeMohrenschildt. The man who took the most famous film of JFK's murder was closely acquainted with the accused assassin's best friend in 1962. This is yet another wild coincidence which lone-nutters have to explain away in order to justify their Oswald-did-it-alone dreamscape.

Bush, Mallon, Dulles, Dresser and the CIA

Despite his protestations, George H.W. Bush worked for the CIA long before he became its director in the mid-1970s. There is evidence that Bush was recruited by Allen Dulles prior to the Bay of Pigs because Bush had oil interests in Cuba and would naturally be sympathetic to the cause of overthrowing Castro. Two of the ships involved in the operation were named the Barbara and the Houston, the latter the name of Bush's wife and the former the name of his home city. The invasion operation itself bore the CIA codename Zapata, the same name as Bush's oil company. Nevertheless, Bush has always denied his involvement with the CIA prior to his becoming Director of the CIA, but as author Russell Bowen puts it, "Of course, Bush has a duty to deny being in the CIA [prior to 1976]. The CIA is a secret organization. No one ever admits to being a member."[39]

Bush may well have been involved in Cuban espionage as early as 1959. He helped organize anti-Castro resistance among bitter Cuban refugees shortly after Batiste was ousted in 1959. According to Bowen, Bush worked with "…Felix Rodriguez and other anti-Castro Cubans…there are records in the files of Rodriguez…that expose Bush's role…in the Bay of Pigs invasion."[40] This is significant because Felix Rodriguez participated in several notorious CIA operations over the next three decades. He was a leader of the militant Operation 40 and Brigade 2506 organizations, where he worked with CIA operatives David Atlee Phillips, E. Howard Hunt and Frank Sturgis (names which repeatedly surface in the JFK assassination); he headed the secret team which hunted down and killed revolutionary Che Guevera in 1967; he participated in Operation Phoenix, the ruthless CIA assassination program; and he has documented ties to his old pal G.H.W. Bush in the Savings & Loan scandals of the 1980s.

There were those who were convinced that Allen Dulles was using Bush as a piece of leverage or a counterweight against Bush's father Prescott, who was a member of the Senate Oversight Committee responsible for monitoring the CIA's practices.[41] With his own son as a covert operative, Prescott was likely to overlook agency malfeasance. Intelligence insider William Corson believed that George lived in fear of his intimidating, austere father, and "George's insecurities were clay to someone like Dulles."[42]

Prescott Bush had many business interests prior to successfully running for the U.S. Senate. One of them was Dresser Industries. Dresser was involved in the manufacture and sale of products needed for drilling in the oil business. The business expanded as World War II approached, and it began procuring government defense contracts. Bush appointed a close family friend, Neil Mallon, to be president of Dresser, and the firm moved to Dallas after the war to be closer to the military-industrial complex it served. According to author Russ Baker, "Dresser was well-known in the right circles as providing handy cover to CIA operatives."[43] Enter George H.W. Bush who was hired by Dresser after graduating from Yale. Dresser and the CIA had a history of hiring Skull-and-Bones members who knew how to keep a secret and promote the self-interests of one another.

As head of Dresser, Mallon helped gather the richest and most influential of Dallas citizens to form the elite and ultra-conservative Dallas Council on World Affairs. Oil men, bankers, politicians, military officers and CIA operatives dotted the membership roster. Included was one Robert G. Storey, who became liaison between the Warren Commission and Texas Law Enforcement in 1964.[44] The organization was almost exclusively composed of WASP males, but one notable exception was Abraham Zapruder. How did Zapruder wind up with an unlikely seat at the table of the DCOWA with the high-powered WASPs? Perhaps it was through his link to Tom Slick, whose airline company distributed Nardis products all over the country. Slick was "a Dresser Industries board member and good friend of Prescott Bush."[45] Mallon and the others may have liked the idea of having a Jew or two on the DCOWA in case the day came to assign some dirty work to someone who was not really part of the inner circle. Like Jack Ruby, Zapruder might have been sucked up in history's maelstrom without full knowledge of the consequences.

These links come full circle with George DeMohrenschildt whose nephew, Edward Gordon Hooker, roomed with George H.W. Bush at Andover in their youths. Their eastern prep-school ties aside, Bush and DeMohrenschildt, were connected as oil entrepreneurs and CIA operatives in Texas and the Caribbean in the early 1960s. And many years after the assassination, when Bush was CIA Director and the House Select Committee on Assassinations sought to question DeMohrenschildt about his involvement with Oswald, the paths of the two Georges crossed again in a tragic way. DeMorhenschildt, as detailed in a later chapter, was found shot to death after writing a letter to Bush about his relationship with Oswald and its importance in the assassination.

Given these nefarious connections, DeMohrenschildt should have been under intense scrutiny by the Warren Commission, but, with Allen Dulles's deft direction, DeMohrenschildt was treated as a harmless eccentric who just happened to bump into Oswald while traveling in the White Russian circles in Dallas. But the way in which DeMohrenschildt and Oswald met is hardly innocent. Author Russ Baker suggests that Allen Dulles might have arranged it through the CIA's Dallas office. Agent J. Walton Moore, assigned to the Domestic Contacts Division of the CIA, approached DeMohrenschildt with the idea that Oswald, when he returned from his assignment in Russia, would need to be shepherded into the Dallas right-wing Russian community. When Oswald found his way home in 1962, Moore's office notified DeMohrenschildt of Oswald's Fort Worth address, and DeMohrenschildt took it from there.[46]

The Oswalds were poor, friendless, and in need of financial assistance. George and Jeanne DeMohrenschildt were their saviors. The DeMohrenschildts invited the Oswalds to parties, took them to doctors' appointments, found them housing, and arranged jobs for Lee.

Zapruder and the Motorcade

As important as the Zapruder film is, it is not the infallible historical record one might imagine. There is ample cause to suspect that the film has been doctored by the CIA (clarified in a later chapter), and that Zapruder's presence in the Plaza that day was no accident. It is a historical fact that Zapruder was the only person, in a plaza full of people with cameras, who recorded the assassination from the north side of Elm Street from where the fatal shot was likely fired. Since JFK was seated on the right side of the limousine (the north side of the car as it traveled west on Elm Street), Zapruder had the best view of the President as he was shot. All other bystanders' camera angles—Mary Moorman's, Robert Hughes's, Charles Bronson's, Phil Willis's, and Beverly Oliver's to name just a few—were somewhat obstructed views from the south side of Elm Street. Even professional photographer James Altgens' photo, taken from in front and to the left of the limo, is somewhat obstructed by the limo's windshield. Altgens originally intended to photograph the motorcade from the overpass overlooking Elm Street atop the Triple Underpass, but he was forced to leave this position by Dallas police officers J.W. Foster and J.C. White (presumably authentic cops).[47] He gravitated to a position, like all other photographers except one, on the south side of Elm. The only clear sightline to the damage caused by the kill shot to JFK's head was through Zapruder's Bell & Howell 8mm camera. I do not believe this is an accident; I do not believe the plotters would have left this to chance. Of course, it is possible that Zapruder wound up standing on a pergola's pedestal (despite having vertigo) on the north side of Elm purely by chance. However, it would have been a very fortuitous accident for the plotters to have access to the one completely unobstructed view of the President as he is shot, filmed by one of their own who, rather than making it a public record, sold it to a Skull-and-Bonesman who locked it away for 12 years. And after 50 years of investigating the assassination I have become quite suspect of excessively fortunate happenstances that have favored the plotters' execution and cover-up of the murder.

Zapruder has been deceased for many decades, but his daughter, Myrna Hauser, spoke for him when she was interviewed several years ago. "Well, he had no special secret motivation or special information," she indignantly declared. "He read it [that the motorcade would travel down Elm Street] in the paper."[48] Hauser was quite miffed that anyone would even ask her an innocent question about her father's activities on November 22. The fact that she felt compelled to even address the possibility that her father would have prior knowledge from a covert source (a fellow DCOWA member?) of the motorcade's unlikely turn onto Elm Street is strange in and of itself.

If Zapruder did indeed read of the motorcade's route in the local newspapers, he must have picked the one day when the correct route was published. The Tuesday November 19 editions of the *Dallas Morning News* and the *Dallas Times-Herald* "for the first time…published the route of the presidential motorcade "[49] including the jagged turns onto Houston and then Elm from Main; other route diagrams contained no such drastic turns off Main Street. Other editions of the *Morning News* in the days leading up to November 22 incorrectly depicted the route, eliminating the zig-zag turns onto Houston and Elm altogether.[50] This raises the question: how did anyone know that the motorcade was going to pass in front of the Texas School Book Depository if the correct route was so underpublished? This underpublication, if intentional, served a dual purpose for the plotters—1) it kept the eyewitnesses to the crime at a minimum; 2) if Oswald was to be the accused assassin, he needed at least one notice that his target was going to pass in front of his place of employment on November 22. In other words, the plotters had to account for the patsy's foreknowledge of opportunity to kill the President without publicizing the coming event too much.

But the one-time-only advance notice of the motorcade route presents serious incongruities for those who insist Oswald acted alone. If Oswald did not know of the parade route prior to November 19, then he could not have been planning the murder of JFK for months, perhaps years, as is suggested by some Warren Commission defenders. It makes no sense for someone to plan a murder if he has no opportunity to commit the act. Put another way, Oswald had no idea his target was going to pass right in front of his workplace until three days before the assassination; thus, any suggestion of long-range foreplanning on Oswald's part is pure nonsense. Unless, of course, he was getting inside information from someone that President Kennedy would indeed pass right in front of the TSBD. And this, of itself, would indicate an inside job concocted by government agents and powerful insiders, for those are the only people who knew the actual parade route months in advance. Lone-nutters want to have it both ways—an Oswald who plans the President's assassination far in advance, ostensibly with his magical powers to predict the President's movements seven months in the future, but not an Oswald who gets his information from secret plotters.

Oswald the Psychic

If we assume that Oswald had no knowledge of the President's motorcade route until he read about it in the Dallas newspapers on November 19, then his mail-order purchase of a Mannlicher-Carcano rifle was not done with the intention of killing Kennedy. For not in his wildest dreams could Oswald have imagined, when he purchased his rifle in the spring of 1963, that his target, poorly protected and driven at a dangerously slow speed would, eight months later, pass right below his workplace window and momentarily come to a complete stop in an open car, on a sunny day, as if out of some assassin's daydream.

Same thing for Oswald's trip to Mexico City: his motive for contacting KGB assassination agents at the Soviet embassy could not have been to receive his assignment to kill Kennedy, as the CIA would have liked us to believe. The list of people who, in early October, knew Kennedy's motorcade route in Dallas eight weeks hence certainly did not extend to Russian embassy employees.

Oswald's lack of knowledge of opportunity (one of the three classic murder elements—motive, means and opportunity—investigators assess when looking for the murderer) also negates the "framing" effect of the fake (as will be explained in detail later, there was an Oswald impostor running around Dallas) Oswald's actions in the weeks leading up to the assassination. For instance, two target-practice incidents, meant to lay a trail of guilt prior to the fact, can now be viewed as bungling attempts by the plotters to incriminate the real Oswald. At least twice in the fall of 1963 a man who looked like Oswald needed help sighting a weapon at a Dallas rifle range. Malcolm Price gave him that assistance, but then the Oswald lookalike used the weapon to shoot at the target of Garland Slack. Slack and "Oswald" argued, and Slack naturally remembered the incident when he saw Oswald on TV after the assassination. Price also recalls fixing "Oswald's" sight on September 28, at a time when Oswald was supposed to be in Mexico City.[51] At one of these rifle range incidents, "Oswald" was overheard to say, "I thought I was shooting at that son-of-a-bitch Kennedy."[52]

Another incident occurred in October 1963 in the presence of Mrs. Lovell Penn. Mrs. Penn heard shots being fired on her property. She saw a man who looked like Oswald accompanied by a Latino, and ordered them off her property. The men left behind a 6.5 Mannlicher-Carcano shell which Mrs. Penn kept and turned over to the FBI after the assassination. She informed the FBI that the man who had fired the shot looked like the Oswald she had seen on TV. The FBI claimed the shell did not match Oswald's rifle and dropped the whole matter.[53] This seems odd, given the fact that the federal government was heavily invested in finding evidence that would inculpate Oswald. A shell matching the murder weapon found in the TSBD should have done the trick, but the other (real?) Oswald was elsewhere that day. And hiding the "two Oswalds" scenario was more important than using a stray shell to frame him.

By attempting to frame Oswald, the plotters outwitted themselves. Besides the fact that the Oswald impersonator(s) always seemed to show up in places and at times that conflicted with the real Oswald's whereabouts, the plotters neglected to account for the fact that Oswald had no prior knowledge of opportunity when he was "practicing to kill Kennedy." Oswald was either the biggest fool in the world for drawing public attention to his violent enmity towards a man he had no reason to suspect would ever be in his target sights, or he was the luckiest assassin in the history of the world. For weeks he practiced a kill that, according to the Warren Commission and all lone-nutters, he had no way of knowing would be available to him. Miraculously, though, one day, just out of the blue, the opportunity opened up before him. The incredible coincidence of the President's motorcade passing right in front of Oswald's workplace makes Oswald seem like a psychic. Or, perhaps, it was no coincidence at all.

This raises the question: If Oswald did know of the motorcade route months in advance of November 22, who would have told him and why? It seems dangerous for the plotters, if they were attempting to frame Oswald, to have let him in on the motorcade arrangements months in advance of the event. Wouldn't they have feared that their patsy would smell a rat? On the other hand, if Oswald's intelligence handlers wanted him to believe that his placement in the Book Depository building was helping them to somehow *foil* an assassination attempt, they might have trusted him with this knowledge without revealing the true nature of his role in the tragedy. There is some evidence of Oswald trying to forewarn authorities about the assassination. On November 17 someone sent a telex to FBI offices claiming that a militant revolutionary group was going to assassinate President Kennedy on his trip to Dallas; some believe that Oswald was the source of the telex.[54] If this is so, then there would have been a basis for Oswald having some fore-knowledge of the assassination, but there is no evidence that he knew the exact motorcade route prior to November 19, 1963.

In addition to lacking the opportunity for long-range planning, Oswald had no motive to kill the President. By all accounts he admired Kennedy. It was only after the fact that he suddenly became a Kennedy hater, and only after lone-nutters realized their flawed theory of the crime needed some Oswald "incentivization" to make it plausible. The problem was, the real Oswald had never said a cross word about JFK. This is not to say that the real Oswald knew nothing of Kennedy's impending visit and had no intelligence assignment to carry out on 11/22/63, but the known facts of his actions and words leading up to the event are more indicative of his being set up as an intelligence patsy than they are of his lone guilt.

The scarcity of information about the deadly turns of the Dallas motorcade, prior to the event, extended to the President's body-guards. Clint Hill now admits that, "For most of us, this [was] our first time to Dallas…the streets, the buildings, the geography, [were] completely unfamiliar."[55] This raises many disturbing questions. If the parade route was completely foreign to the people trusted to protect the President, how could they be expected to perform their jobs efficiently? In addition, it is standard procedure for advance security to check buildings along any presidential motorcade route prior to the parade. This was obviously not done. Film footage from that day shows open windows on the upper floors of tall buildings as the limousine slowly moves along the "canyon" of downtown Dallas. Any of these vantage points would have provided a potential assassin a rifle sightline. Woefully unprepared Secret Service agents, several of whom were hungover and sleep-deprived, found themselves in a motorcade where, as Hill puts it, they literally had "no idea what's around the corner."[56]

This means that the Secret Service and everyone else in the motorcade were entirely dependent on following the cars in front of them to show them the way. They all followed the pilot car which led them into the death trap that was Dealey Plaza. This pilot car, which preceded JFK's limousine by just a few blocks, was driven by Dallas Deputy Police Chief George Lumpkin; riding in the car with him was Lieutenant Colonel George Whitmeyer. Both of these men were members of the 488th Military Intelligence Reserve unit in Dallas. This unit was founded by a man named Jack Crichton in 1956, and he served in the unit until 1967. Crichton was connected, both personally and professionally, with George H.W. Bush, George DeMohrenschildt and D. H. Byrd. Crichton was Bush's running mate on the Republican ticket in the 1964 Texas elections for governor and U.S. Senator respectively. According to author Fabian Escalante, the two men also had CIA and oil interests in common. Referring to the Bay of Pigs invasion, Escalante writes, "…Richard Nixon was the Cuban case officer and had assembled… [a] group of businessmen headed by George Bush…and Jack Crichton, both Texas oilmen, to gather the necessary funds."[57] Crichton and Byrd were connected to each other and to DeMohrenschildt "through oil business dealings."[58] And all of these people were well acquainted with Allen Dulles.

The pilot car stopped only once during the motorcade; Lumpkin got out of the car and briefly spoke to a policeman who was handling traffic at the corner of Elm and Houston, very near the Texas School Book Depository. What did Lumpkin say to the traffic officer? We can only speculate. Perhaps it was an innocent coincidence that Lumpkin was concerned with traffic at the very intersection where moments later the death car would make its final turn into the kill zone. Or perhaps, something more sinister was afoot. The one thing the conspirators could not have happen was civilian traffic being allowed onto Houston or Elm streets just before the presidential limousine arrived. Lumpkin may have been reminding his subordinate that under no circumstances was any traffic to interfere with the motorcade procession.

Crichton, who got his start in intelligence work with the OSS during World War II, may or may not have been directly involved in the selection of the pilot car occupants, but he was certainly responsible for selecting an interpreter for Marina Oswald. Shortly after the assassination, Crichton put Ilya Mamantov in touch with the Dallas police who needed to question the Russian-speaking wife of the accused assassin. Mamantov, a rabidly right-wing anti-communist, according to Russ Baker, "…embellished Marina's comments to establish in no uncertain terms that the 'leftist' Lee Harvey Oswald had been the lone gunman."[59] Marina struggled with English and probably had no idea how deeply Mamantov was burying her husband with police investigators and the media. Subsequently, she was turned over to the Secret Service and was kept in "protective custody" for three months without the aid of legal counsel or advice of family members. "Let's face it," writes Harold Weisberg, "she was sweated and threatened. The Secret Service told her that if she wanted to stay in this country…she had better cooperate."[60]

Before his death, Crichton slipped up and revealed the close association between his Army Intelligence unit and the Dallas Police Department. Nearly half of the members in his 488th intelligence unit were Dallas police officers.[61] For this reason, the Dallas police and the members of the 488th should have been investigated by the Warren Commission. Of course, they were not; the close ties that Crichton had with powerful interests in Dallas insured that he would be immune from scrutiny. His close friendship with George Bush alone guaranteed that Allen Dulles, de facto head of the Warren Commission, would never allow Crichton to be subjected to examination.

The Media Go to Sleep

Americans would have a clearer understanding of the complex and sinister connections of the men who devised JFK's demise if the press had done its job. But the disgraceful legacy of journalistic neglect in covering the assassination has made getting at the truth a tedious and demoralizing endeavor.

It has been said of the fourth estate that it is the only thing that stands between democracy and tyranny. A free and objective press is necessary to expose corruption, wrongdoing, and evil in the halls of power, whether that be the government, the military, private industry, organized crime, or wherever injustice and oppression reside. Without a free press we are at the mercy of those who seize power for their own secret and selfish purposes. If this is so, then the fourth estate has failed us miserably; for if, as is the contention of this work, a vast conspiracy involving Allen Dulles's renegade CIA, Lyndon Johnson, members of the Joint Chiefs, Texas oilmen, elements of organized crime, and certain Secret Service agents took the life of JFK, such a conspiracy has gone undetected by the mainstream "free press" in America. In fact, the conspiracy has been aided and abetted by misinformation disseminated through journalistic outlets.

This was the whole point of Allen Dulles's infiltration of the journalism profession—once noble and proud, now a neutered and sanitized corporate confederacy—to transform it from democracy's guardian to an agent for democracy's undoing. It is an insidious truth that Dulles and his Mockingbird agents subverted the free press for their own despicable means, and this transformation, more than anything else, has prevented us from getting at the ultimate truth of the Kennedy assassination.

Dulles believed that journalism was a perfect cover for secret operatives to obtain intelligence, suppress the true nature of CIA operations, rebuke negative publicity attached to the agency, plant false information when necessary, or print glowing propaganda about the agency's activities. According to reporter Carl Bernstein, Dulles "...sought to establish a recruiting-and-cover capability within America's most prestigious journalistic institutions...among the executives who lent their cooperation were William Paley [of CBS], Arthur Hays Sulzberger of the *New York Times*, and Henry Luce of Time, Inc."[62] For years, "Luce's personal emissary to the CIA was C.D. Jackson...[who] approved specific arrangements for providing CIA employees with *Time-Life* cover."[63]

So much for honest, reliable journalism in 1963. Rather than serving the genuine truth, the American press was serving the CIA's version of the truth. All reporting of the Kennedy assassination by the mainstream media, even to this day, must be judged through the distorted lens provided by CIA collaborators. There are those who wonder how and why the whole truth of the Kennedy assassination has never been broadcast or published in mainstream media outlets; the unholy alliance between the CIA and American journalism answers that question. If the criminals control the press, it is unlikely the truth of the crime will be divulged.

Thus the Zapruder film was locked away by C.D. Jackson, and Americans were left to wonder what it really showed. Even the Warren Commission refused to examine the film; when Commission attorney J. Lee Rankin was asked why the film had not been subpoenaed, he replied that it was "private property,"[64] a flimsy excuse if ever there was one. The Commission had the power to subpoena any document or person it wished.

Without the ability to peruse the Zapruder film, the public relied on journalists and government agencies to reveal its contents. The first reporter to widely spread misinformation about its contents was William Paley's own employee, a young and eager Dan Rather. Within a day or two of the assassination, Rather aired many inaccuracies when describing to millions of American people what Zapruder had filmed, including the following: 1) Falsehood: the President's limo was *proceeded* by only one other car containing

Secret Service agents; <u>Truth</u>: the Secret Service agents' car *followed* the President's car and the pilot car and lead car contained various intelligence and police officials. 2) <u>Falsehood</u>: when shot in the head, JFK lurched *forward* with considerable violence; <u>Truth</u>: Kennedy's head snapped back and to the left when struck. 3) <u>Falsehood</u>: Mrs. Kennedy was trying to get herself out of harm's way by climbing onto the back of the trunk; <u>Truth</u>: Jackie was reaching for a piece of the President's skull which had blown out to the back and left, indicating a shot from the right front. Each of these lies, whether delivered with the deliberate cunning of a Mockingbird asset or not, served the plotters' purposes well. If the pilot car were erased from history, the story of the suspicious characters in it would evade public scrutiny; if Kennedy's head moved dramatically and suddenly forward upon being hit, it would indicate a shot from above and behind, implicating Oswald; if Mrs. Kennedy had abandoned her husband in an instinctive move to protect herself, why couldn't all of America abandon the search for the truth of his death; and if there were no skull fragment blowing out to the left rear of the trunk, the evidence for a right-front shooter would be diminished. In Rather's defense, early information and reports were sketchy, garbled and sometimes contradictory, and his misinterpretation of the Zapruder film might have been an innocent mistake. But it is clear, now, to anyone who has ever viewed the film that Kennedy's head does not move violently forward; it snaps violently backwards and to his left. How could Rather have made such a mistake?

The blunder did not hurt Rather's career; in fact, he catapulted to the top of the journalistic heap at CBS. All along, he has been an ardent defender of the Warren Commission. He and Walter Cronkite co-anchored a CBS special in 1967 called "CBS News Extra: November 22 and The Warren Report." (It pre-empted "Mr. Ed," the show about a talking horse; in retrospect, a talking horse was more credible than the information Cronkite and Rather provided.)

The special opens with a view from the sixth floor window of a car turning onto Elm Street in Dealey Plaza. A voiceover, accompanied by string music to add profundity, says, "You are watching an official re-enactment of the murder of John F. Kennedy, filmed from the window where the alleged assassin crouched."[65] One minute into this supposed objective journalistic endeavor, we are led to believe Oswald was guilty.

CBS compromised any honest investigation when it consulted with Allen Dulles before and after the program. Dulles was allowed to inspect the transcripts and was said to have had some minor objections to the content. This was Dulles's shrewd way of letting CBS think it actually had some independence while still controlling what was broadcast. In the end, the CIA had nothing to fear. William Small, the network's news director at the time, exchanged a series of letters with Dulles in which Dulles "...commended Small for a job well done."[66] Such was the broadcast media's obsequious subservience to Dulles and the CIA. Fact finding lost out to the secret state's official version of the assassination. As a result, a false history of America was created; one that is still deeply embedded in the mythology of this country's past.

Rather and Cronkite, and their ilk, were willing accomplices in this fraud. Why did they do it? Were they just blissfully unaware of the genuine truth? Did they gullibly swallow whole what was fed to them by the plotters? Or were they just ambitious men, consumed with the prestige and influence their mere faces and voices transmitted, and unwilling to surrender their lofty positions by actually challenging the men who really ran the country? Whatever their motives, it is hard to believe that they did not recognize the Warren Report for what it really was—an implausible fairy tale concocted by flawed men to cover up the ugliest political crime in American history. But instead of summoning the courage to face that ugly truth, CBS and all the other Mockingbird assets chose the path of least resistance. The CIA's Frank Wisner once bragged that

Operation Mockingbird was like his own personal Wurlitzer: he could play any tune on it he wanted, and America would follow along. And consider these chilling declarations from Dulles's successors—William Colby (CIA Director from 1973-76): "The CIA owns everyone of any significance in the major media"[67]; William Casey (DCIA from 1981-87): "We'll know our disinformation program is complete when everything the American public believes is false."[68]

Even that giant of the television medium, Walter Cronkite, was not immune to corruptive influences. As a fellow Texan (Cronkite spent his youth in Houston), Cronkite had an affinity for Lyndon Johnson. Johnson "treated him more like a second cousin than a fourth-estate adversary."[69] Cronkite's boss at CBS, Frank Stanton, was a close friend of Johnson's. According to Cronkite's biographer Douglas Brinkley, "[LBJ] hoping to exert control over CBS...would routinely call Stanton to grouse about on-air content...[and] whenever LBJ went to New York, Stanton would fete him with limousines, cocktails, and coffee...to keep him happy."[70]

Cronkite was also linked to Allen Dulles. In 1976 an ABC News reporter named Sam Jaffe claimed that he had seen Cronkite's name at the top of the list of journalists who worked for the CIA. Jaffe also confirmed that Cronkite had received a briefing from Dulles as part of his normal duties. When Cronkite learned of Jaffe's allegations, "...the anchorman sprang into damage control mode, traveling from New York City to Langley, Virginia, to confront George H.W. Bush [then CIA Director]... Cronkite demanded the list of news people who had actually been CIA agents."[71] Bush refused to release it, but later the CIA "confirmed that...CBS correspondents had worked for the agency."[72] Beyond Cronkite's understandable consternation at having his journalistic reputation compromised, it is revelatory to note here that a list of CIA journalist assets apparently DID exist. And George Bush, head of the CIA, kept it secret. Cronkite did not deny being a CIA asset, nor did he seek a disavowal of his collaboration with the agency from George Bush. Instead, Cronkite sought to verify that he was only one of many newsmen who had worked for the CIA, as if public knowledge of such common practice would legitimize it. It speaks to the power of Operation Mockingbird. If the CIA had ensnared Cronkite, the number one television journalist of the 1960s, what newsman was immune to the agency's insidious influence?

For his part, Rather might have also served causes other than journalistic integrity. He was one of LBJ's favored reporters. By Rather's own admission, Johnson would sometimes send considerate notes to Rather and his family when the reporter was called on to work extra hours on the White House beat. Perhaps there was a kinship between the two men because they were both Texas natives. Whatever the reason, Johnson apparently wooed Rather like he wooed others for his own purposes—to cement his legacy and steer the public away from his darker deeds. To his credit, Rather did not give Johnson a pass on Vietnam. CBS's laudable reporting on the war helped expose it for what it really was—an ugly, imperialist aggression against yellow people engaged in a civil war (halfway around the globe) which posed no threat to us. War-profiteering cronies of Johnson and Dulles got very rich from it; otherwise, it was totally worthless and completely unnecessary.

But CBS and the other networks would not come near the most dangerous truth of the turbulent '60s: who really killed Kennedy? In his biography, Rather raises one of the most common arguments among lone-nutters when he writes, "If shots had come from the grassy knoll…those bullets had to have gone somewhere. But where? No one has ever found any hard evidence documenting where those shots might have landed."[73] Maybe if Rather had done a more thorough job of investigative journalism he would have come across the possibility that the bullets and bullet fragments which struck JFK were removed from his body before it arrived at

Bethesda. Rather was oblivious to, or ignored, these incontrovertible facts: someone removed JFK's body from the expensive Dallas casket (or never placed him in this casket) and put it into a cheap shipping casket before it arrived in Washington; someone altered his wounds and removed bullets prior to the autopsy; Bethesda medical personnel said that JFK's body arrived before the ambulance supposedly containing his body did, meaning that the Dallas casket offloaded at Andrews Air Force base was either empty or contained a fake corpse.

Perhaps Rather's malpractice can be explained by his stunning promotion after Dallas. He was assigned to cover the new president, LBJ, as chief White House correspondent.[74] And in 1981, he ascended to the position which all talking heads lust after—anchor of the evening news. He sat in that chair at CBS for almost a quarter of a century.

Picking on Cronkite and Rather is somewhat unfair, for all the big-name TV "journalists" of their era, including Huntley, Brinkley, Brokaw, Jennings (a known Kennedy hater), and others got it wrong too. As recently as 2013, on the 50th anniversary of the assassination, Brian Williams hosted an NBC program on which Brokaw and Rather both affirmed that they were satisfied that Oswald, and no others, had killed JFK.

Media complicity in the JFK cover-up can also be attributed to the intelligence backgrounds of many of the giants in print journalism. Ben Bradlee and Bob Woodward took on intelligence assignments in their military careers. One of Bradlee's closest childhood friends was Richard Helms who became director of the CIA in late 1960s. On the surface Bradlee had the resume of a solid liberal, but others thought he was infiltrating leftist causes. After World War II, Bradlee joined the ACLU, but Deborah Davis writes, "This job, so out of character for the young patriot, may or may not have been an intelligence assignment."[75] Subsequently, Bradlee took a job with the U.S. Informational and Educational Exchange, widely suspected of being a CIA affiliate which disseminated propaganda materials during the Cold War. In 1952 he carried out a CIA assignment in Paris, reportedly meeting there with Allen Dulles, to examine documents relating to the Rosenberg spy case.[76] According to author Peter Janney, "In the Cold War era, many journalists considered cooperation with the CIA a kind of patriotic duty... [and] Bradlee was referred to as one of the [CIA's] men."[77] When he became editor of the prestigious *Washington Post*, Bradlee ran in elite circles in Georgetown; he socialized with the CIA's Allen Dulles, James Angleton and Wistar Janney. Bradlee and his wife Tony also became fast friends with Jack and Jackie Kennedy.

The CIA was even part of Bradlee's family. His brother-in-law was Cord Meyer, one of the CIA's Operation Mockingbird directors. During the Red Scare of the 1950s, Meyer was suspected of being a communist sympathizer and was called to testify by Joe McCarthy. This was the beginning of the end of McCarthy's reign of terror. CBS unleashed its attack dog, Ed Murrow, on him.

At first, William Paley, president of CBS and good friend of Allen Dulles, tried to stifle Murrow. But when McCarthy began attacking prominent CIA assets, Paley okayed Murrow editorials which exposed McCarthy for the right-wing tyrant he was. McCarthy soon found out who had the real power over politics and the media in America: the CIA.

As for Bradlee, until the day he died he denied any conspiracy in the murder of his good friend Jack Kennedy. The *Washington Post* may have zealously and relentlessly pursued the Watergate scandal and Nixon's corruption, but it wanted nothing to do with the Kennedy assassination. As researcher James DiEugenio put it, "Why didn't [Bradlee] do anything while the House Select Committee on Assassinations was reopening [his] friend's murder case?"[78] Whatever friendship Bradlee shared with JFK, it seems Bradlee had little concern for Kennedy's death and legacy. He refused to use the massive influence of his newspaper to investigate the truth of the assassination. In his superficial and misleading book, *Conversations With Kennedy*, Bradlee denigrates the presidency of his old pal. (Bradlee had the gall to call out JFK for interfering in a sovereign state's affairs; imagine the hypocrisy of a CIA asset claiming the high ground in a discussion of a foreign nation's sovereignty.[79]) Maybe Bradlee was just following the edict of his boss Katharine Graham, publisher of the *Post* and friend of Lyndon Johnson, who said, "There are some things the general public does not need to know and shouldn't."[80] The CIA could not have said it any better.

Yet another journalist who failed history was Richard Dudman, Washington correspondent for the *St. Louis Post-Dispatch*. A dogged and respected reporter, Dudman, at first, was on the trail of the truth with his early dispatches from Dallas. On November 23,1963, he reported that: Oswald was denied legal representation and repeatedly insisted that he did not shoot Kennedy; Oswald's fingerprints were not found on the alleged murder weapon; no witnesses saw Oswald fire a weapon from the Book Depository; and the Dallas doctors saw an *entrance* [emphasis added] wound to the front of the President's throat and an exit wound at the rear of his head.[81] On November 25 Dudman wrote that Ruby's execution of Oswald "…stamped a seal of permanent doubt on the assassination."[82] On November 27 Dudman let the world know that Secret Service agents had custody of Marina Oswald and were speaking to her through a Russian interpreter.[83] (The interpreter was provided by George Bush's intelligence pal, Jack Crichton.) And just nine days after the assassination, Dudman filed perhaps the most stunning news report to come out of Dallas. Through persistent fact-finding and tireless work he came up with some conspiratorial morsels in an article entitled, "Uncertainties Remain Despite Police View Of Kennedy Death."[84] Much of what Dudman discovered has formed the basis for dismantling the official government version of the crime. He did not mince words when he wrote: "At the time of the shooting, the President's open automobile was moving almost directly away from the window from which the shots were thought to have been fired...[yet] Dr. McClelland [Parkland ER physician] told the Post-Dispatch, '[the throat wound] certainly did look like an entrance wound'...[Parkland doctors] are familiar with bullet wounds. We see them every day...The question that suggests itself is, 'How could the president have been shot in the front from the back?'"[85] That question lingers today; more than any other evidence in JFK's murder, the medical evidence points to conspiracy. Dudman went so far as to imply possible locations in Dealey Plaza for multiple shooters.

But just when Dudman seemed to be on the verge of cracking the case wide open with his diligent and honest reporting, his dispatches stopped. Was he silenced by higher-ups, or did he just lose interest? Some clues come from a letter he wrote to this author many years later. Dudman dismissed all conspiracy theories in the JFK case because they "violate a rule of logic called Occam's Razor."[86] Occam's Razor, in a nutshell, says that one should accept the simplest explanation when presented with conflicting evidence. I wrote back to Dudman that, when it comes to the JFK assassination, the simplest explanation is that the President was murdered as a result of a conspiracy. To believe that Oswald acted alone required that one accept improbable, if not impossible, explanations for how Oswald pulled off the murder with a defective rifle in less time than it took a sharpshooter to re-enact the shots. I threw Dudman's own words back in his face: How was JFK shot in the front from behind? I reminded him that his own reporting disclosed that the Dallas doctors had observed completely different wounds on the dead President than did the Bethesda doctors.

I never heard back from Dudman. But just a month later, he wrote a remarkable article which appeared in the *St. Louis Post-Dispatch*; one that might explain Dudman's about-face on the Kennedy assassination. It concerned one Richard Bissell, a high CIA official, with whom, it turns out, Dudman was a close friend. Dudman lived next door to Bissell in Washington, and later moved to a small town in Maine where Bissell maintained a home. Bissell had been appointed Deputy Director of Plans under Allen Dulles in the late 1950s, and by 1960 he was busy planning the Bay of Pigs invasion. When the invasion failed, JFK took the blame, but privately he seethed that the CIA had deceived him. In a 1961 purge, Dulles, Bissell and Charles Cabell (another CIA operative) were fired by Kennedy. Dudman's article, an homage to Bissell and his CIA career, steers clear of Bissell's animosity towards Kennedy, but it is well-known that the CIA was furious with the President for not providing air cover that would have prevented the Cuban invasion from becoming a miserable failure and embarrassment. Instead, wrote Dudman, "Bissell blames the Joint Chiefs of Staff for not objecting to the plan, Congress for not scrapping it, and himself for overconfidence."[87] To blame the generals and congressmen for one's own faulty plans is an outrageous shifting of the blame for the disaster. There is now much support for the contention that Dulles and Bissell, fully aware that the invasion had no chance of success, were laying a trap for Kennedy. Under Eisenhower, the CIA was in total command of foreign policy, and it was teaching a lesson to the new, inexperienced president: go along with the program or you will be at our mercy. The CIA did not anticipate Kennedy's fierce independence and self-reliant intellect, qualities which he put to good use to save the world from a nuclear holocaust just 18 months after the Bay of Pigs.

Dudman admits to having a ringside seat at big CIA events. He was on the ground in Guatemala for the overthrow of Arbenz. He covered the U-2 spy plane crash over Russia. He visited training camps in Central America prior to the Bay of Pigs. From his window next door to the Bissell residence, he witnessed titans of industry, like Lockheed's Kelly Johnson and Polaroid's Edwin Land, enter and leave Bissell's home. He was in Dallas when Kennedy was shot.

Yet his mainstream reporting never quite uncovered the CIA's true intentions and culpability in these matters. Perhaps he was blinded by his proximity to Bissell. The two went on picnics together. They sailed together to Maine. They were close friends for nearly 40 years.[88] It is not hard to imagine that Bissell was able to co-opt or compromise Dudman's objectivity. Maybe Bissell silenced Dudman's dispatches from Dallas by telling him that, if the truth of Oswald's association with Russia was exposed, World War III would break out in the form of a nuclear war. It's funny how the Pentagon and the CIA enthusiastically urged Kennedy to commit to a nuclear first strike during the Cuban Missile Crisis, but somehow were hesitant to enter into a nuclear fight with the Russians after Kennedy died, even though the CIA had gone to great lengths to link the phony assassin with the Soviets and their assassination program.

In the end, Dudman was just one of thousands of reporters who surrendered their integrity to the wiles, pressures and inducements of the CIA. Dudman would have certainly denied being an active participant in Operation Mockingbird; however, the courtship was such a sly enterprise that he probably did not even know he was doing the agency's bidding. By early 1964 Dudman was no longer assigned to the Kennedy assassination, and the chances of getting at the truth of the matter were measurably diminished.

The Excellent Adventures of Lee in Mexico and Dallas

There is evidence that an impostor was using Oswald's name as far back as 1959, but the fake Oswald sightings spiked dramatically in the months before the JFK assassination. Sometime during the late summer and early fall of 1963 an Oswald lookalike or "double" began showing up in Dallas and, by his bizarre actions and words, endeavored to implicate the real Oswald in the crime of the century. Who was this fake Oswald? We do not know, because the CIA has withheld this information from us (as it has withheld thousands of documents relating to the Kennedy assassination). We can say with utter certainty, however, that this person did exist, he worked for American intelligence, and he bore a remarkable resemblance to the real Oswald.

The recurrent and contradictory sightings of Oswald prompted Warren Commissioner Richard Russell to conduct a secret inquiry. He had an Army intelligence officer look into Oswald's background and found that there were two birth certificates in the name of Lee Harvey Oswald and the certificates had been used by two different people.[89] Incredible as it sounds, the double identity of Oswald was a CIA scheme dating back to childhood. Author John Armstrong writes that two young boys, almost identical in appearance, were selected to be part of the CIA's MK-ULTRA program. The purpose was to merge their identities for clandestine espionage during the Cold War. Armstrong asserts that the use of "twins" allows intelligence agencies to use one twin as an alibi for the other who is involved in illegal activity.[90] Witness statements which verify that one twin was performing a routine or innocent activity can provide cover for the other twin who might be engaged in something illicit. This raises the possibility that one of the purposes of the two-Oswalds scenario was to discredit "unfriendly" witnesses and support "friendly" witnesses who might later come forward with information about Oswald's activities prior to and on November 22. Maybe the point was to give subsequent investigators of JFK's murder the option of choosing the Oswald sighting which best suited the lone-nut theory, and at the same time provide an excuse to dismiss other sightings as the faulty recollections of crackpots. To a large degree, this actually occurred. The Warren Commission and the HSCA accepted versions of Oswald sightings which fit their pre-formed theories and used other sightings to discredit "unacceptable" versions of Oswald sightings.

The problem with this tactic is that sophisticated observers (ones aware of spycraft techniques) would recognize that dual sightings of Oswald pointed to an intricate intelligence scheme. If Kennedy-assassination investigators had been savvy and honest enough to recognize this artifice for what it was, they might have seen right through it, and the ploy would have backfired.

A good example of the CIA possibly overplaying its hand in this regard is the case of Laura Kittrell, a Texas Employment Commission employee, who in October 1963 accepted the employment application of Lee Harvey Oswald. The problem was she already had a Lee Harvey Oswald on file. After noting several discrepancies between the second Oswald's application and that of the first Oswald's, Kittrell determined that the second Oswald was "pretending to be the [first Oswald]…and had been coached upon how to answer certain questions."[91] When challenged, the second Oswald got irate and made bizarre references to a man named Murray Chotiner.[92] Chotiner was a somewhat notorious lawyer involved in criminal enterprises, including serving as a counsel for the Committee To Re-Elect President Nixon. CREEP became infamous in the early 1970s for its connections to the Watergate scandal. Chotiner also represented racketeers like Bugsy Siegel and Meyer Lansky. Were CIA plotters trying to establish an assassination link to Nixon and organized crime, or did the second Oswald, having been caught in a lie, shoot off his big mouth when he should not have?

Another instance where the plotters misused the second Oswald occurred just two days before the assassination. A 27-year-old refrigeration mechanic named Ralph Leon Yates picked up a hitchhiker on his way into downtown Dallas. The hitchhiker was carrying a long, brown-paper package which he said contained curtain rods. The man, who bore a close resemblance to Oswald, then stunned Yates by talking of the possibility of shooting President Kennedy when he came to Dallas.[93] We know the hitchhiker Yates dropped off at the corner of Elm and Houston, across the street from the TSBD, was an impostor, because the real Oswald was working inside the TSBD at the time. Remarkably, though, the fake

Oswald's curtain rods story matches the real Oswald's story of carrying a curtain-rod package to the TSBD two days later. After the
assassination, when Yates identified his hitchhiker as Oswald he was
scoffed at by authorities who needed to dismiss his story in order to
maintain the fiction of there being just one Oswald. But Yates
insisted to the FBI that his story was true, and lending credibility
to it was the fact that Yates had told a co-worker about his strange
encounter with the hitchhiker *before* the assassination. The FBI's
reaction was predictable. Despite several interviews with Yates, the
Dallas field office could not break him. Finally, the FBI accused
Yates of being mentally disturbed and sent him off to an institution
for treatment. For the rest of his life, Yates was a psychiatric patient
at one hospital or another in Texas; he was fed debilitating drugs
and underwent shock treatments. Through it all, Yates never
wavered from his Oswald/hitchhiker story. He died at the age of 39,
a ward of the state; his only crime was telling the truth.[94]

Perhaps the most egregious example of the CIA's overexuberance
in regards to the Oswald "twins" ploy emerges when examining
Oswald's movements from September 27-October 3, 1963. While
the real or fake Lee took a mysterious trip to Mexico, the other Lee
showed up at the doorstep of Sylvia and Annie Odio in Dallas. The
Odio sisters were from a wealthy and prominent Cuban family;
their father had initially supported Castro's revolution, but Mr.
Odio fell out of favor with the new regime when he spoke out
against communism. He was incarcerated by Castro in the notorious Isle of Pines prison; meanwhile, Sylvia and Annie fled to the
U.S. In late September 1963 three men showed up at the Odio
sisters' residence at 1080 Magellan Circle, Apartment A, of the
Crestview Apartments, and scared the sisters with their menacing
message. The men spoke of killing President Kennedy and Fidel
Castro and asked the sisters for donations to accomplish the deeds.[95]
Two of the men were Latins and introduced themselves with their
"war" names—Leopoldo and Angelo. The other male was a white

man who was referred to as "Leon." The men were vociferously anti-Castro and made it clear to the sisters that they knew intimate details about their lives in Cuba and their father's suffering at the hands of Castro.[96] Months later when Oswald was arrested, Sylvia Odio recognized him as the Leon who had come to her door on that unforgettable night in September.

But the other Oswald was on his way to Mexico at this time. He entered the Mexican consulate in New Orleans on September 17 and applied for a tourist visa. He was promptly issued card number FM-82405.[97] Tourist card number FM-82404, the one granted just prior to Oswald's, was issued to a William Gaudet, a self-admitted CIA operative.[98] Gaudet claimed, unconvincingly, that it was a mere coincidence that he and Oswald were granted consecutive tourist cards and travelled to Mexico together. What is more likely is that Gaudet was shepherding Oswald to Mexico City.

Again the question of where Oswald got his money for the trip is at issue. He had quit his job in New Orleans and did not even have the money "to pay the $65 rent due on September 9."[99] Marina complained to Lee that he had money for Mexico but not for her. She chastised him for caring more for Cuba, Mexico and Castro than he did for her.[100] Ruth Paine saved Marina and her children by taking them into her Dallas home; meanwhile, Lee found the money for a bus ticket to Mexico City and almost a week's stay there. His meager unemployment check could not cover such an exorbitant trip.

On the bus ride south of the border, accompanied by Gaudet, Oswald, or an Oswald impostor, loudly bragged about the reason for his trip. According to author Priscilla McMillan, Oswald told "...an English couple...that he was secretary of the Fair Play for Cuba Committee...[he also] took out his old U.S. passport to show [two girls] his Soviet visa."[101] Oswald, as he often did in the weeks leading up to November 22, was demonstrative and unapologetic about his Marxist sympathies and made certain that witnesses would remember him. This leads one to believe that it was the Oswald impostor who made the trip to Mexico.

The consulates in Mexico City remembered him well for his fury at not being granted passage to Cuba. He arrived on September 27 and wasted no time going back and forth between the Russian and Cuban embassies. But despite the fact that the CIA bugged and photographed both embassies and the attached consulates, no photograph or recording of Oswald is known to have been taken. Several CIA sources claim to have seen photographs of Oswald entering and leaving the consulates, but no such photo has ever surfaced. Instead the CIA presented a photograph of an impostor—a man of stocky build with a crewcut, who weighed about a hundred pounds more than Oswald. This has baffled investigators for decades, but there is a simple explanation. The CIA, realizing after the fact that the "real" Oswald was seen in Dallas during the Mexico City escapades of the other Oswald, most likely destroyed any definitive photographic evidence of the Mexico City Oswald. Admission of two Oswalds would have been a dead giveaway of intelligence involvement in setting him up. The CIA also claimed to have no audio recordings of Oswald in Mexico City, though this is denied by Warren Commission counsel David Slawson who said that the CIA's Win Scott played for him tape recordings of Oswald at the Cuban embassy. If those tapes did indeed exist, they have since been destroyed or hidden away.

The Assassinations Record Review Board procured a transcript of a conversation between LBJ and J. Edgar Hoover in which they discuss Oswald's visit to the Soviet embassy, but even these two assassination "insiders" seem confused about the authenticity of Oswald's calls. LBJ asks Hoover if he has "established any more about the [Oswald] visit"; Hoover replies, "…that's very confusing…the tape and photograph of the man who was…using Oswald's name…do not correspond to this man's voice, nor to his appearance."[102] This was a case of the Dulles plotters bamboozling the Johnson plotters, and it indicates that, for plausible deniability purposes, the higher-ups did not dirty their hands with the day-to-day operational details of the plot. Hoover and Johnson are baffled because the surveillance of the Mexican embassies was a CIA task, and the CIA withheld many facets of its operational framing of Oswald.

All three KGB officers in the Mexico City consulate claimed they encountered the real Oswald.[103] One of these officers was Valery Kostikov. Kostikov was part of the KGB's secretive and deadly assassinations group—Department Thirteen. If the plotters' original plan was to use the assassination of President Kennedy as an excuse to start a war with the Soviets, linking Oswald with Kostikov would have served their purposes well. But in the end, the CIA decided that the ploy was too implausible even for a gullible public and a compromised Warren Commission. The agency had to admit that the real Oswald was never in Mexico City at all. The man who would have been in charge of such an operation, the CIA's Western Hemisphere chief, David Atlee Phillips, blurted out the truth in 1977. He said, "There is no evidence to show that Lee Harvey Oswald visited the Soviet Embassy … [and] no proof that he visited [Mexico City]"; this contradicted Phillips' testimony to the Warren Commission and the HSCA.[104] In the end, the CIA made the assessment that the negative repercussions of the public becoming aware of an Oswald doppelganger trying to frame the other Oswald prior to the assassination outweighed the propaganda benefits of linking Oswald to Castro or the Soviets.

The irony is that it was probably Phillips who concocted the Mexico City scenario in the first place. He met with Oswald in early September 1963, and it was likely at this meeting that he ordered Lee (or his double) to make the trip south of the border. The purpose of the CIA having one of the Oswalds visit Mexico City was to link him with Cuba and Russia before the assassination so that after 11/22/63 the communists could be blamed for Dallas.

The HSCA got close to uncovering the ruse fifteen years later only to have one of the CIA's best counterintelligence operatives, a man named George Joannides, step in to subvert the investigation. Dan Hardaway, a researcher for the HSCA has claimed that Joannides, as the CIA's liaison to the HSCA, lied to the committee, redirected its investigators to false leads, and withheld documents.[105] As a result, the totally false notion that the Russians and/or Castro participated in the assassination is still given credence in some quarters today.

What is no longer in question is that David Atlee Phillips wanted JFK dead. An anti-Castro Cuban named Antonio Veciana, who once worked for Phillips and the CIA, came forward to unequivocally state this in his 2017 book titled *Trained To Kill*.[106] (See the next chapter for more on Veciana's revelations.)

CHAPTER 4

Genesis of the Plot

"...we were ordered to say...that the Warren Commission found that [Oswald] acted alone. But was there more than one gunman? Yes, personally I believe so. And my personal opinion about Jack Ruby is that he was paid to kill Oswald."

—Secret Service agent
Jerry O'Rourke, who was
in Dallas on 11/22/63[1]

In his inaugural address JFK touched on themes that would have pleased Dulles, his CIA, and the military brass who eyed his election warily. Kennedy sounded like a typical Cold Warrior when he promised to "pay any price, bear any burden...and oppose any foe to assure...liberty." He pledged his commitment to the arms race: "We dare not tempt [our enemies] with weakness...our arms [should be] sufficient beyond doubt." He also implicitly stated that communist aggression against our allies anywhere in the world would not be tolerated, and the introduction of communism to the western hemisphere, Castro notwithstanding, would be met with rigorous opposition. The CIA must have interpreted this to mean that the new commander-in-chief would rubber-stamp covert anti-communist actions—legal or illegal, moral or immoral—around the globe. But buried in the subtext of Kennedy's speech were the seeds of confrontation with his own military and intelligence advisors. He did not directly threaten the Soviet Union, but instead he offered an olive branch: peace negotiations "...before the dark powers of [nuclear] destruction...engulf all humanity." It was this grave concern that finally defined Kennedy's presidency. He came to fully understand the danger of two superpowers pointing nuclear weapons at one another during the Cuban Missile Crisis; his steady hand, and his alone, saved the world from a nuclear war in 1962. It was then that he turned away, for good, from the strategy of winning the Cold War. Instead he endeavored to end the Cold War. And with that enormous paradigm shift, he permanently alienated himself from the U.S. military and intelligence establishment. In three short years JFK changed from a Cold Warrior to the Peace President. One has only to compare the two seminal speeches of his presidency—his inaugural address on January 20, 1961, and his American University "peace speech" on June 10, 1963—to comprehend his stunning transformation. After the stare down of Kruschev in October 1962, Kennedy was not at war with the communists but with a powerful cabal of Cold Warriors and business interests in his own country.

The deep chasm which developed between JFK and the CIA began with the Bay of Pigs. The CIA blamed Kennedy, and Kennedy publicly accepted the cross. Privately, however, Kennedy was furious, and, within a few months had cleaned house at Langley. Of this was born a mutual enmity between Kennedy and the agency that lasted until his death.

Where does the blame for the Bay of Pigs really lie? With the CIA itself, according to a long-suppressed CIA internal review. The review was not released until 37 years after the event for good reason. It called out the intelligence agency for "ignorance, incompetence, [and] arrogance...misinforming officials of Kennedy's administration, planning poorly...and conducting a military operation beyond [its authority]."[2]

In his disingenuous autobiography, the CIA's Bissell tries to have it both ways: diminish CIA culpability, yet disgrace Kennedy for not knowing that the agency was deceiving him, "…the president did not realize that the air strike was an integral part of the operational plan…we, the planners [did not make] it clear enough to him."[3] Or, in other words, JFK was intentionally duped. When the inevitable happened, the CIA had an easy out—the cancellation of air cover absolved it—and Kennedy took the brunt of public criticism. He also made some dangerous enemies in the intelligence community: people like the Cabell brothers; thousands of anti-Castro Cubans; and CIA snakes like E. Howard Hunt, Frank Sturgis and Gerry Hemming. Kennedy also roused the resentment of private businessmen—CIA friendlies who had provided funding and equipment for the operation. Among them was George H.W. Bush. His Zapata Petroleum Company provided cover for Cuban operatives who actually trained for the invasion on oil platforms provided by Bush's company in the Caribbean.[4]

A lot was riding on the Bay of Pigs' success—the CIA's overthrow of a communist nation 90 miles from our border, the profitability of American business interests and oil contracts in the Caribbean, and the Mafia's reclamation of its casinos in Cuba. When the mission failed, Kennedy's new enemies swore revenge against him. It is an oversimplification to assume that the Bay of Pigs was the impetus for plotting JFK's murder. The motives were far more extensive and involved many more people than a few pissed-off CIA chiefs, Mafioso and oilmen. What the Bay of Pigs, and later the Missile Crisis, told the generals and other right-wing hawks is that Kennedy was a free thinker unbeholden to their outdated modes of reactionary policies. He was his own man, who challenged the Joint Chiefs, particularly Curtis LeMay, whenever the matter of communist aggression and retaliation reared its ugly foreign policy head. During the Missile Crisis, JFK flat-out rejected nuclear first-strike advocates. He rebuked the CIA's false flag operations to whip up public sentiment (for instance, Operation Northwoods, an

Edward Lansdale project) for the ouster of Castro. He opposed CIA paramilitary operations in the Caribbean. And he threatened to scatter the CIA to the wind. In so doing Kennedy put himself in the crosshairs of the national security and defense establishment.

The seething resentment against Kennedy manifested itself in ongoing foreign policy conflicts. The generals and the CIA clamored for war against the communists; Kennedy resisted at every turn. James Douglass writes that the pressures on Kennedy became enormous—"…from the weapons-making corporations that thrived on the Cold War, and from the Pentagon and the CIA that were dedicated to 'winning' that war."[5] The Cold Warriors' enmity towards JFK knew no bounds; it was ruthless in nature, and it bordered on treason.

The aforementioned Operation Northwoods is a prime example. Northwoods, dreamed up by General Edward Lansdale, a CIA operative posing as an Army officer, was a plan to create fake attacks against Castro refugees in the U.S. and American military installations in the southeast and blame these attacks on pro-Castro Cubans. The purpose was to arouse American hatred for Castro and force Kennedy to authorize retaliation against Cuba. The plan was approved by the Pentagon and the CIA, before being angrily dismissed by Kennedy as a crackpot scheme. There were others even more dangerous.

At a July 20, 1961, meeting with Kennedy, the chairman of the Joint Chiefs of Staff, the director of the CIA, and others, presented plans for a surprise attack on the USSR.[6] Kennedy was stunned by the appalling brutality of such a plan. Knowing that its execution would have brought about a nuclear conflict that would have destroyed most of life on Earth, he left the meeting in disgust. Later he bitterly mused to Dean Rusk, "And we call ourselves the human race."[7] LeMay was so bent on nuclear confrontation with the Soviets that he openly discussed it at a Georgetown dinner party in 1961. In the midst of politicians and their wives, LeMay announced that a nuclear war was imminent and that major U.S. cities, such as New York, Washington, Philadelphia, Detroit and Los Angeles, would be incinerated. His advice to the party attendees was to seek safety in the high desert where they would not be poisoned by the radiation fallout.[8] Further right-wing hysteria was whipped up during the Cuban Missile Crisis by LeMay's deputy Tommy Power, whom even LeMay considered unstable. Power, without authorization from the President, took his Strategic Air Command to DEFCON-2, one step from nuclear war.[9]

It is understandable, then, that Kennedy came to view his military command as somewhat mad and willing to risk the survival of the planet to satisfy their bloodlust for all-out war with the Soviets. For their part, the Joint Chiefs came to view Kennedy as a communist appeaser, weak on defense and military action. It is also important to remember that Jack Kennedy was a lowly lieutenant in World War II and was outranked mightily by the men he now commanded; it was easy for the generals to think of the young President as their inferior, especially when compared to his predecessor Eisenhower, who had commanded them all in the great war. To compound the problem, the Vice President was taking sides with the Joint Chiefs behind Kennedy's back. Lyndon Johnson, though he was mostly silent in JFK's presence, privately joined in with the generals' grousing about the President's reluctance to take military action in Cuba, the Soviet Union and Vietnam. Johnson knew he would need these men as allies when it came time to execute the coup of 1963. The dead giveaway of a Johnson-LeMay partnership is the oral history that LeMay made for the LBJ Library. In it he calls the Kennedys "ruthless, vindictive cockroaches," whom Johnson should have stepped on.[10]

But there were many others who hated Kennedy too. In the gilded hallways of big business and big oil, Kennedy was a dirty name. When Kennedy proposed a cut in the oil depletion allowance, LBJ's friend and financier H.L. Hunt, the self-proclaimed richest oilman in the world, professed his desire to kill the President. According to author Craig Zirbel, Hunt "...announced that the President and his staff should be shot since there was no [other] way to get those traitors out of government."[11] While Hunt may have just been blowing off steam, he had the means and the temperament to murder a president. He was rich enough to get away with anything, as he proudly admitted to close associates. He also had a list of political enemies, much like Richard Nixon's, called his "kill list." According to John Curington, Hunt's lawyer, Hunt was fascinated with assassination as a means by which to eliminate his political enemies. And Hunt's actions before and after the JFK hit, should have put him at the top of the list of suspects. Jack Ruby was seen entering Hunt's office building in Dallas the day before the assassination, as was a paid killer named Eugene Hale Brading, alias Jim Braden. Braden was on parole at the time, and he was briefly detained by police in Dealey Plaza immediately after the shooting. Hunt was also busy after the assassination. He directed Curington to check out security surrounding Oswald at the Dallas jail, apparently with an eye towards the possibility of silencing the patsy. The same weekend Hunt flew to Washington, perhaps to visit his old pal Lyndon Johnson and congratulate him on their mutual success. Upon his return to Dallas, he entertained the FBI and Marina Oswald in his offices in the Dallas Mercantile building.[12]

Besides running his strip club, Ruby was known to be a small-time bookie on the side. Hunt, who loved to bet money on football games, may have just been settling gambling debts when Ruby visited his offices on November 21. But the other connections to assassination figures are more difficult to explain away. It's hard to construe an innocent explanation for a known killer like Jim Braden wandering into Hunt's offices and then showing up at the scene of the murder of the century the next day. Also, if Hunt had helped finance the JFK kill or provided a hit man and helped direct Ruby, he would certainly have a stake in what Marina Oswald had to say about her husband's guilt and possible associates. Hunt had the wherewithal and possibly the motive to control Marina. The fact that she was seen in Hunt's offices with an FBI man certainly raises the possibility of Hunt's guilt.

Hunt was not a Texas isolationist in the plot. He was well acquainted with the eastern establishment—intelligence, military and the FBI. He met with J. Edgar Hoover many times in the early 1960s.[13] Much of the information on Hunt's pre- and post-assassination activities comes from Curington, who so aroused Hunt's suspicions that Hunt went so far as to put a tap on Curington's phone; in fact, Hunt got so paranoid that he wiretapped many of his employees and associates who knew his secrets.[14]

Texas oilmen weren't the only business millionaires who despised JFK; he made enemies with U.S. Steel and its board members in a 1962 dispute that involved price hikes and wage increases. Kennedy intervened in the country's best interests to avoid an inflationary spiral; he correctly surmised that increases in steel prices would inflate the prices of many other commodities. He brokered a contract that minimized union workers' wage increases in exchange for the promise that Roger Blough, chairman of U.S. Steel would not increase prices. Four days after the contract was signed, Blough double-crossed Kennedy and announced a price increase anyway. Bethlehem Steel and others followed. An infuriated Kennedy retaliated by awarding defense contracts to smaller steel companies which had not raised their prices. Bobby Kennedy started a federal inquiry regarding price fixing. The President held a press conference in which he denounced steel executives as greedy profiteers whose "pursuit of private power…exceeds their sense of public responsibility."[15] Eventually the steel companies caved and rescinded their price increases, but the rancor they felt towards the Kennedys simmered beyond April of 1962. It was not just the steel companies that were embittered by Kennedy's intervention, it was the men—Wall Street titans, bankers and leaders of conservative foundations—who sat

on their boards of directors who denounced JFK. Henry Luce's
Fortune magazine expressed the antipathy in an editorial of the
period which called Kennedy's actions, "...a vitriolic and dema-
gogic assault."[16]

Kennedy's Cabinet Mistakes

It is now indisputable that JFK was surrounded by traitors—in the
intelligence community, in his Joint Chiefs staff and the Pentagon,
and even in his own cabinet. These were men who despised Kennedy
and his policies and would have been gleeful at his demise. Kennedy
knew this, yet when he took office he did not dismiss these men, as
it was his right to do. Why? There are many reasons. Kennedy won
the presidency by a very slim margin, and did not feel he had the
mandate to fire Langley sacred cows who did not share his world
view. Warmongering generals like LeMay and Lyman Lemnitzer
were also holdovers from previous administrations with whom Kennedy was stuck. But even the men he chose himself—cabinet
appointees like Secretary of Defense Robert McNamara and
McGeorge Bundy—were rock-ribbed Republicans, seemingly at
odds with the politics of the young Democratic president-elect.
Bundy, a Yale graduate, was a member of the super-secret Skull-and-
Bones club at Yale, and he turned out to be the CIA's covert spy
inside the Kennedy White House. Bundy's brother William, also a
Yale bonesman, was a CIA operative who counseled Pentagon generals and McNamara himself. According to Pentagon/CIA insider
Fletcher Prouty, William Bundy was well-known as a "CIA conduit"
whom the agency used to present its Vietnam scheming to McNamara and Rusk.[17]

As gatekeeper, McNamara is widely thought to have served JFK
well by countering and clarifying Pentagon and CIA misinformation. Despite his Republican background, he seemed to be a Kennedy loyalist and first presented JFK with the quarantine gambit
that gave the President a non-nuclear solution to the Cuban Missile

Crisis. JFK, in fact, credited McNamara's clear-headedness and strong stand against the war hawks in the administration for helping to keep America out of a nuclear confrontation.[18] McNamara also, at least under Kennedy, resisted escalation of American involvement in Vietnam. In October 1963 he presented a report to Kennedy, based on a fact-finding tour that he conducted with General Maxwell Taylor, which recommended withdrawal of all American military personnel.

But there is also some evidence that McNamara might have known what the traitors inside the Kennedy administration were up to and did nothing to stop it. For some reason he did not attend a high-level cabinet meeting in Honolulu on the day of the assassination; he and Mac Bundy were the only Kennedy cabinet members not flying over the Pacific at 12:30 pm, CST, on 11/22/63. Why was that? And what was so important about the Honolulu meeting just prior to the assassination?

For the answer, we have to back up momentarily to revisit the McNamara/Taylor report on American military involvement in southeast Asia. The report, while chastising the repressive tactics of the Diem regime, recommended that key adjustments in the South's military strategy could bring about the end of the conflict by 1964. It also stated that the Vietnamese could be trained to take over all U.S. military functions and that "it should be possible to withdraw the bulk of U.S. personnel by…the end of 1965."[19] Kennedy used this report as the basis for his National Security Action Memo 263 which called for a pullout of 1,000 American advisors by the end of 1963 and a complete withdrawal of all U.S. personnel from Vietnam by 1965.

For those historians who try to claim that Kennedy's Vietnam policies would have been no different than Johnson's, NSAM 263 is a problem; for the memo indicates, simply put, that there would have been no Vietnam War had Kennedy lived. Anyone who claims Kennedy would have escalated the war that wound up killing nearly

60,000 Americans and millions of Vietnamese, and costing billions of taxpayer dollars, as Johnson's war did, must overlook McNamara's insistence that Kennedy would have gotten us completely out of Vietnam. As recently as 1995 McNamara reiterated (ironically in a speech delivered at the LBJ Library) that Kennedy's NSAM 263 would have, without equivocation, put an end to American involvement in Vietnam by 1965.[20]

With NSAM 263, Kennedy once again had defied the wishes of his own military/intelligence advisors who wanted a war, any war, to confront communist aggression. Already considered a communist appeaser by the Pentagon and the CIA, Kennedy's Vietnam policy made him a marked man within his own administration. Those who wanted him out of office got their wish just six short weeks after the issuance of NSAM 263.

This leads back to the importance of the Honolulu meeting, as its findings formed the basis for the reversal of NSAM 263 and the implementation of Lyndon Johnson's NSAM 273. In other words, the purpose of the Honolulu meeting was to radically alter America's Vietnam policy *just hours before* Kennedy's death. As Prouty put it, "Who could have known beforehand, that this new…agenda would be needed in the White House because Kennedy would no longer be president?"[21] More to the point, JFK would not have ordered a meeting of his cabinet, diplomats and military advisors for the purpose of countermanding his own Vietnam policy. So who *would have* ordered such a meeting? Who had the power to do so? Whoever exercised this power committed a treasonous act.

There are those who believe that Bundy and McNamara were the traitors. Dr. Alen Salerian, former chief psychiatrist with the FBI's mobile psychiatry unit, is one. He examined the words and deeds of Kennedy's advisors in the weeks leading up to the assassination and found them suspicious. Behind Kennedy's back, Bundy sent a cable to the Vietnam ambassador, Henry Cabot Lodge—another bad JFK appointee—authorizing the overthrow of South Vietnamese President Ngo Dinh Diem. When Diem was killed in a coup engineered by the CIA's Lucein Conein, Kennedy was deeply shaken and probably understood then just how badly he had been betrayed. As author James Douglass put it, "[Kennedy's advisers] all thought …they knew better than their chief what had to be done to win the war."[21] Douglass also points the finger of guilt at McNamara, whom he said was duplicitous and two-faced. McNamara did not really want to withdraw from Vietnam; he only expressed this opinion behind closed doors with the President.[23]

At the very moment of the assassination, Bundy and McNamara were at the Pentagon. McNamara was in a routine budget meeting when the rest of the world became aware of the tragedy in Dallas; he continued the meeting for a full 90 minutes as if nothing had happened. He later said he was unaware of the assassination. This seems preposterous considering he was at ground zero for preparedness and military response to national emergencies. The question needs to be asked: Were Bundy and McNamara monitoring the situation in Dallas from the epicenter of national defense? Salerian believes that McNamara remotely chaired the Honolulu meeting from the Pentagon, though he has no definitive evidence of this.

While Salerian praises McNamara for the open apology he expressed in his book, Bundy does not get off so easily. Salerian writes that Bundy "…was a broken mind with an internally roaring fury at all the Kennedys…[and] his emotional, historical, political roots to [Allen] Dulles…coordinated demolition of the Kennedy White House."[24] And Salerian pulls no punches when he states that the Kennedy hit was an inside job, engineered by Bundy, McNamara, LBJ, Dulles, and Curtis LeMay in order to wage war in Vietnam.[25] But first the plotters needed NSAM 263 relegated to historical obsolescence, so that the path to Vietnam could be paved by the precedence of NSAM 273, the document that everyone but Kennedy endorsed.

If Salerian and others are correct, it seems only logical, in hindsight, that the point of the Hawaii meeting was to create a justification for the reversal of NSAM 263. The participants in the meeting returned to Washington late on the night of 11/22/63 with a report that was ready-made for the new president's wishes. Within days of Kennedy's assassination, Johnson reversed the policy initiatives of NSAM 263 with his own action memo, NSAM 273, which recommitted American military efforts to winning the Vietnam War. Subsequently, mere months after Johnson won a 1964 landslide election, an election in which he ran as the peace candidate, 50,000 ground troops were in southeast Asia and America was in a full-out shooting war that lasted for a decade. By December 1965, the month that Kennedy would have ended American involvement in Vietnam, Johnson had already sent thousands of Americans to their deaths and had steered America on an irrevocable course for the most useless, catastrophic and divisive war in the country's history.

The cataclysmic shift in America's Vietnam policy, occurring suddenly and dramatically over the course of just a couple weeks in the fall of 1963, begs the question: was Kennedy killed, at least in part, for his promise to withdraw from southeast Asia? If the answer is yes, then CIA and Johnson apologists would be desperate to prove that Kennedy would not have pulled out of Vietnam and would have prosecuted the war in the same way his successor did; lest, the CIA and Johnson could be ascribed a damn good motive for wanting Kennedy dead. Put another way, lone-nutters (people who ascribe Kennedy's death to a lone nut and, thus, relegate it to an act of political and historical randomness) must overlook the titanic shift in America's Vietnam positioning before and after the Kennedy assassination. To wit, before Kennedy died, America was on a course of entirely abandoning southeast Asia militarily; after his death, America's course was re-charted towards a path of a full-scale, ten-year war by the man who succeeded him and in whose state Kennedy died. That's one huge coincidence to overlook, but some of Dulles's best Mockingbird assets and some of the nation's most militant right-wing fanatics have tried their best to do it.

The most vociferous argument from lone-nutters, one which persists even today, is that most of Kennedy's advisors became Johnson's advisors, so one should assume that Kennedy would have done exactly what Johnson wound up doing—escalating the war. Not true. Kennedy had, under the crucible of fire, proved his steely resolve to resist his military and intelligence advisors time after time—at the Bay of Pigs, during the Cuban Missile Crisis, and in Vietnam. Kennedy was an independent thinker, and his overriding mandate was to keep America out of war. He wanted to end the Cold War, not win it. As he stated in his courageous peace speech of June 1963, his desire was to make the world safe for diversity not to destroy those who were different from us. To that end, he found very few allies in his own administration.

In the middle of all this calculus was McNamara. After Kennedy was killed McNamara seamlessly switched allegiances to Lyndon Johnson; some trick considering that Johnson immediately reversed Kennedy's Vietnam policy. McNamara seemingly turned from Vietnam dove to Vietnam war hawk overnight. Was McNamara's value system so flexible he was easily swayed by prevailing winds? Or was something more devious afoot? Some have suggested that McNamara, still close to Bobby Kennedy after Dallas, was trying to bring down LBJ's illegitimate presidency from the inside. The notion of McNamara deliberately sabotaging LBJ's presidency from the inside seems far-fetched though. It is unthinkable that he would sacrifice countless thousands of American lives in a savage, needless war just to get even with Johnson.

Nonetheless, McNamara himself admits in his memoirs that he saw the futility of Vietnam long before Johnson did; this despite the fact that in the beginning of the Johnson presidency McNamara was the one of the original proponents of military escalation in southeast Asia. As early as 1964 he advocated troop expansion; in the coming years he would design bombing strategies and micromanage targets. He warned of the domino effect the fall of Vietnam would set in motion.[26] He insisted, time and again, that victory in Vietnam was possible, and because of this he was Johnson's fair-haired boy.[27] But eventually, he saw the futility of it all. In 1966 he told an old Kennedy ally that, in essence, it would not matter at all in the world's scheme of things if South Vietnam fell to the communists. But it took something more dramatic for McNamara to come to his senses and fall out of Johnson's good graces: the emergence of Bobby Kennedy as a possible presidential candidate. Johnson despised Bobby, and the feeling was mutual. McNamara, even while serving in Johnson's cabinet, never really broke ties with the Kennedy family. According to author Jeff Shesol, Johnson became disinfatuated with McNamara because "he was on the wrong side of the war after his Kennedy friends turned against it."[28] Eventually McNamara's transformation from Vietnam dove to Vietnam hawk back to Vietnam dove was completed when he was fired by Johnson. In subsequent years, McNamara revealed some of his inner thoughts, but kept mum about key aspects of his Kennedy/Johnson years. He makes a tantalizing suggestion in *The Fog of War* that he knew something was amiss about the Honolulu conference which began the process of shredding Kennedy's NSAM 263 and paving the way for NSAM 273. But he never quite states it forthrightly.

The question that begs to be answered, then, is "Who was McNamara?" Whose side was he on, and how much did he know about Kennedy's assassination? I have assiduously researched his background and career, and I still do not know. The contradictions in his character were endless. He worked for Curtis LeMay during World War II, and blithely recounts how LeMay, as brutal and ruthless a military commander as ever there was, nearly firebombed Japan off the face of the earth. McNamara admitted that "LeMay and I should have been prosecuted as war criminals"; in the next breath, he claimed to have been a peace advocate.[29] He proposed complete withdrawal from Vietnam as Kennedy's advisor, but just days into the Johnson administration he had changed his mind. He seemingly had great affection for Kennedy; he was near tears in retelling the story of how he picked out JFK's gravesite in Arlington the day after the assassination. Still he shifted his allegiance to Johnson the same weekend. If McNamara had been genuinely conscience-stricken by his suspicions of Johnson's illegitimate rise to the presidency, it seems much more likely that he would have turned his back on LBJ after Dallas. Instead he stayed on and prosecuted the war as if he had never been in the Kennedy administration. As early as February 1964, Johnson told McNamara he had been foolish to recommend a pullout. Johnson bullied McNamara into submission by saying, "How the hell did [you] think that when [you're] losing the war [you] can pull men out of there?"[30]

Solving the McNamara conundrum may be as simple as this: he was just a dutiful soldier. All his so-called brilliance withered in the face of LBJ's orders. He was used by Johnson to lend the appearance of continuity from the Kennedy administration, in order to assuage any public suspicion that the murder of JFK had something to do with Vietnam.

But the possibility that McNamara willingly assented to the plotting of JFK's assassination still can't be dismissed. He once said of himself, "This man is duplicitous; he's held things close to his chest."[31]

McNamara's final words on the topic were as enigmatic as ever. When asked by documentary filmmaker Errol Morris why he didn't speak out against the war when he left the Johnson administration, he responded in the ambivalent, circular way that only McNamara could. He might as well have been responding to the question, "Who killed Kennedy and why?" "These are the kinds of questions that get me in trouble. You don't know what I know about how inflammatory my words can appear."[32]

You don't know what I know. McNamara, in the end, left us

hanging. Maybe more than anyone else in JFK's cabinet, he knew how and why we escalated the war in Vietnam, and in what way JFK's murder was related to that war. But he took the coward's way out, and, his weepy recollection of choosing JFK's gravesite notwithstanding, he, like so many others who owed JFK so much, betrayed him.

False Motives

While great effort has been put forth to hide the viable motives of some in Kennedy's inner sanctum, the effort to ascribe false motives to the patsy have been just as unrelenting. The dual tactics have always complemented one another: to wit, to deflect attention away from the real motives behind the killing of President Kennedy, the plotters have tried to smear the patsy with all manner of crazy and unsupportable motives. Some of the silliest came from Priscilla McMillan's disinformation book about Lee and Marina Oswald, titled *Marina and Lee*. One nonsensical passage reads, "Lee had tried to commit suicide…thus he may have been particularly spellbound by…Kennedy's close brushes with death…and the reason isn't that he hasn't been."[33] Huh? Somewhere in that tangled mess might be some reasoning, but I fail to grasp it. Oswald's suicide attempt was not genuine. The "official" story is that when the KGB rejected his request for political asylum, Oswald became despondent and tried to do himself in. The real story is that Oswald offered outdated, and possibly fake, radar codes to the Soviets who saw right through his phony defection and recognized him as a double agent working for U.S. intelligence. In a desperate attempt to avoid being deported, Oswald faked his suicide. The Russian doctors who treated him called his act "a show."[34] From McMillan's dime-store psychology evolves the preposterous narrative that Oswald had to kill Kennedy to fulfill his own death wish. People who are genuinely suicidal are fixated on their own deaths, not the deaths of others. Furthermore, if Oswald's intent was to make a name for himself by killing the most prominent figure in the world, why did he deny doing it? No lone-nutter has ever provided a satisfactory answer to that question.

Other crazy motives have been floated by the plotters and their media lackeys.

The Russians did it. Utterly laughable. Not a speck of legitimate evidence of Soviet involvement has ever surfaced. After Kennedy's "peace speech" in June of 1963, relations between the two Cold War giants had improved. A nuclear test ban treaty had been signed. Kruschev and Kennedy had open dialogue about ending the Cold War. Kennedy's declaration that "If we cannot end now our differences, at least we can help make the world safe for diversity," resonated in Moscow. Slyly, but without any proof whatsoever, LBJ raised the possibility of Russian involvement to convince his southern conservative friends to serve on the Warren Commission. He told Senator Richard Russell that "forty million Americans might lose their lives in a nuclear conflict if accusations about Castro and Kruschev weren't refuted."[35]

Castro did it as revenge for the Cuban Missile Crisis and CIA assassination attempts. Kennedy's peaceful resolution of the Cuban Missile Crisis saved Cuba from annihilation by American military forces, and Castro knew this. Kennedy was the only friend Castro had in the U.S. war room in October of 1962. The CIA did attempt to kill Castro, but these attempts were bungled and meant to embarrass Kennedy to renew strained relations with the communists. Castro was savvy enough to realize that Kennedy, at war with his own national security apparatus, was not behind the plots; enough so that he entertained Kennedy's backdoor emissary, Jean Daniel, in Cuba in November of 1963.

The Vietnamese did it. It is almost beyond laughable that "historian" Robert Dallek has the temerity to suggest this possibility. Without a scrap of evidence, and with no citation to back it up, Dallek writes that JFK might have been taken out by the "Vietnamese retaliating for Diem's death."[36] For over a half-century I have scoured the public records, perused photographs, interviewed witnesses, and read a mountain of books on the subject; nowhere have I found even a hint of Vietnamese conspirators planning and executing the murder of the century. Though I will make certain to again closely scan all Dealey Plaza photos for Asian faces and pro-Diem death squads. The only purpose Dallek's completely superfluous biography of Kennedy served, as far as a critical reader can fathom, is that it did not rankle the corporate media or the military-intelligence establishment.

Johnson and Dulles Prepare

If one views the Kennedy conspiracy as a business enterprise unto itself, then we can theorize that there must have been an organizational hierarchy with CEOs overseeing mid-level and lower-level participants. Something as challenging and world-changing as killing the U.S. president can't be accomplished without such a structure. There had to be bosses or high ministers who gave the orders. There had to be a mastermind, the creator of an elaborate scenario, who served at the pleasure of the chief executives. There had to be middle-level managers to implement the mastermind's plan. And there had to be ground-level operatives and "on-site soldiers," the assassins and their assistants, for instance, who carried out the managers' orders.

It is this book's contention that Lyndon Johnson and Allen Dulles were the "CEOs" of the plot. No other men had more power and cunning, despite the fact that, in their public lives, they had seemingly been consigned to insignificance. In 1963 it appeared that Dulles was an aging, irrelevant ex-spymaster, deposed by JFK after the Bay of Pigs; Johnson appeared to be an impotent political has-been, banished by the Kennedys and about to be indicted for a career of criminal behavior. But the private truth of these men's circumstances was much different. Dulles was still running a sort of

CIA in exile. He regularly communicated with Richard Helms, James Angleton, David Atlee Phillips, E. Howard Hunt and Edward Lansdale, his former CIA underlings. They were men who remained loyal to Dulles, even after his ouster, and despised Kennedy for what he had done to the "old man." Author David Talbot confirms this in *The Devil's Chessboard*, his book about Dulles. "Dulles did not relinquish his hold over…U.S. intelligence once he was 'retired' by JFK," writes Talbot, "…his Georgetown home [was] the center of an anti-Kennedy government."[37]

Extensive research has unearthed the direct involvement of "Dulles's men" in the assassination and its cover-up. Phillips himself was seen conferring with Oswald or Oswald's double just weeks before the assassination by a CIA operative named Antonio Veciana. Veciana, a Cuban accountant at the time of Castro's takeover of the island, helped form the violent anti-Castro group Alpha 66 with the aid of the CIA. As part of his involvement in the group he became acquainted with a high-ranking American CIA official he knew as Maurice Bishop (an alias used by Phillips). Veciana met with Bishop many times in the early 1960s, and at one such meeting he arrived to see Bishop conferring with Lee Harvey Oswald or an Oswald double. In the 1970s Veciana testified to this Oswald/Bishop (Phillips) meeting before the House Select Committee on Assassinations.[38] However, he did not definitively admit that Bishop was Phillips until he spoke publicly at a 2013 JFK assassination conference; he told the attendees that day at the Bethesda Hyatt Regency he was convinced the CIA organized the president's murder and that Oswald was a CIA operative whom the agency decided to blame for the killing.

Veciana, speaking through a translator, said he had once admired the CIA and Bishop for their anti-Castro activities. Now, however, he said he wanted to set the record straight because he had come to admire Kennedy, whom he and Phillips once regarded as a "traitor" for allowing Castro to remain in power. The turning point for

Veciana may have come in the late 1970s; after his HSCA testimony, someone tried to kill him. He was shot in the head but survived the assassination attempt.[39]

As for Phillips, he came close to admitting culpability for the assassination. After retirement from the CIA, he organized thousands of ex-intelligence assets to form the politically influential Association of Former Intelligence Officers. Phillips traveled the country promoting the organization and trying to rehabilitate the CIA's damaged reputation. On one of these occasions he made the mistake of debating CIA critic and assassination researcher Mark Lane. Lane shamed Phillips into admitting some of the CIA atrocities which had been committed under Phillips' watch. Phillips admitted to regretting many of the lies he had told about the events surrounding the assassination of President Kennedy; in essence, Phillips confessed that his intelligence agency was actively involved in framing Oswald.[40]

Johnson was wired into this anti-Kennedy government-in-exile. Despite his public reticence during his days as Vice-President, quietly he was maintaining alliances with CIA and military chiefs.[41] He commiserated with them when they vented their spleens over JFK's refusal to flex America's military might. From 1960-63 Johnson carefully nurtured the friendships he would need to ensure the success of 11/22/63. Like-minded men with vast resources at their disposal plotted together to wrest away control of the nation.

Johnson and Dulles were vicious men, accustomed to scheming and murdering their way into positions of power and surrounding themselves with a wall of secrecy to conceal their involvement in any wrongdoing. At the height of their reign, in the 1950s, they had nurtured and refined a network of men who arranged plots designed to topple their enemies—through disinformation, theft, corruption and murder. They were good at it, and they had learned how to get away with it. Dulles was quite adept at surrounding himself with a barrier of misinformation and stealth; plausible deniability of all its atrocities was the very essence of the CIA's business. No one in the CIA hierarchy, much less Dulles, has ever been held accountable in any real way for any crimes.

Johnson also relied on absolute secrecy; he refused to put anything in writing, so his unlawful activities were hard to trace. His dealings with his criminal partners—Billie Sol Estes, Cliff Carter and Mac Wallace especially—were usually in person, and on a cash-basis only.[42] Like a shrewd Mafia don, Johnson would insulate himself with several levels of intermediaries so as not to get his hands dirty. He was also protected by his close relationship with J. Edgar Hoover. His bond with Hoover was never as secure or vital as it was in the days following 11/22/63. It insulated Johnson from prosecution for the murder of John Kennedy.

Together, Johnson and Dulles were two untouchable powerbrokers completely beyond the reach of the law. Granted, before 1963 they had never been so bold and reckless as attempting the assassination of a sitting U.S. president. But they must have felt comfort and security in knowing a joint venture, combining their vast network of collaborators, had a good chance of succeeding.

Johnson and Dulles were acutely aware of the absolute power they would possess with Kennedy out of the way. After all, who was going to arrest them as suspects in the murder of President Kennedy? Certainly not Hoover. Johnson knew full well of Hoover's sexual proclivities, and Hoover had the goods on Johnson's criminal rise to power. Public disclosure of their scandals would have ended their careers. They were partners in self-survival.

Besides, Hoover despised the Kennedys, especially his young boss Bobby, the attorney general. With Jack out of the way, Bobby no longer had any control over Hoover, and both men knew it. Hoover made certain that the FBI implicated Oswald as the assassin and quashed evidence of a conspiracy. Bobby Kennedy could do nothing about it.

As for Dulles, his standing was restored after Dallas. His service on the "blue-ribbon" Warren Commission, at least at first, restored his name to public prominence. Privately, his command over a vast network of covert assets seemed, once again, omnipotent. No one in Washington had the wherewithal or nerve to challenge the grandmaster of CIA intrigue. He could have, and did, destroy many who dared to implicate him or the CIA in Kennedy's murder.

The Meeting

By the summer of 1963 the plot to kill Kennedy was in motion. The major players were making preparations. Assassins had been approached. The patsy was being moved around like a puppet. Dates and itinerary for the Texas ambush were being arranged. The CEOs held one final meeting in Austin to cement their alliance. Having a scheme that was so compartmentalized and far-reaching, LBJ and Allen Dulles each needed reassurance that the other was fully committed.

Wise in the ways of conspiracy, Johnson and Dulles were quite scrupulous in hiding their tracks. They left little or nothing in writing, and their public comments after the fact were mostly innocuous. Suspicious activity prior to November 22 was kept to a minimum. The two did, of course, meet with their "managers," but the public record of these events contain no smoking gun. However, Dulles and Johnson did make one slip-up. They met with one another in Texas sometime prior to the assassination, and the occasion was photographed by a Texas journalist. It likely took place sometime in the summer of 1963 at LBJ's ranch near Austin. The photo ran on page four in "The Opinions" section of the *Tribune* on August 15, 1963, under the caption—"IN TEXAS—The vice president shows off a horse to former C.I.A. director Allen Dulles as daughter Lynda and wife Lady Bird look on." David Talbot reports that the photo was published in the *Chicago Tribune*; however, this is probably erroneous. It is more likely that the photo ran in the *Texas Tribune* of August 15, 1963.[43] The photo depicts LBJ sitting on a horse as an amused Allen Dulles stands nearby and watches. Next to Dulles are Lynda and Lady Bird Johnson. Sitting on the horse, Lyndon raises his hat as a rodeo cowboy would. In the background is the Johnson home. The men are coatless, and the women are dressed in breezy summer outfits; it is reasonable to assume, then, that the photo was taken in the summer of 1963. Which leads to the crucial question: Why on earth would Dulles visit Johnson at that particular time? These two men were officially no longer relevant in public affairs, and they lacked any institutional power in the U.S. government. Dulles at the time had no official connection to any U.S. government agency, and Johnson's position was meaningless. The two would have had no cause to engage in policy discussions or intelligence briefings. They were persona non grata in the Kennedy administration; still they were not frivolous men, given to mundane activities or inane niceties. Dulles would not have traveled a thousand miles to spend a languorous summer day admiring Johnson's equestrian skills. It is highly unlikely they would have met in the summer of 1963 unless they had common business. So what did they discuss? We can't know for sure, but we do know that they shared a mutual disdain for the man who had taken away their power.

The Machiavellian Dulles and the manic, hyperkinetic Johnson were men of purpose who could not stand to be outside the center of action. Remember, they were just three years removed from the height of their powers in the Eisenhower era—Dulles as head of the CIA, and Johnson as king of the U.S. Senate. It is not a hyperbolic assertion to say that they had plummeted from their positions of immense influence and had become virtually insignificant in just 36 months. That's quite a fall for two men whose lust for power was unequaled by any other public servants in the 20th century.

Two more opposite personalities are hard to imagine. Though they were both outlaws, Dulles considered himself urbane and erudite. He liked to entertain his Georgetown friends with espionage tales at Eastern socialite cocktail parties. He would have considered Johnson vulgar and unmannered. For his part, Johnson would not have considered Dulles the kind of downhome "good old boy" he sought out as a drinking buddy. A real odd couple, Johnson and Dulles would have no shared interests save for one—the removal of their common antagonist, Jack Kennedy. It was Kennedy who had reduced them to insignificance. It was Kennedy's panache and power they envied. It was Kennedy who stood in the way of their return to status and prominence.

The LBJ/Dulles 1963 photo is often confused with another of Dulles and Johnson taken at the LBJ ranch on July 28, 1960, just after the Democrats nominated the Kennedy/Johnson ticket to run against Nixon. Dulles was ostensibly delivering the standard intelligence briefing accorded the vice-presidential candidate. The later photo, of LBJ on a horse, was clearly taken at a time after JFK had fired Dulles and before the assassination of JFK made LBJ president. The LBJ/horse photo, first published in August of 1963, was again published in the *Fort Worth Press* on November 14, 1963, under the headline "Kennedys To See Lots Of People." This referred to the President's upcoming Texas trip. Incredibly the LBJ/horse photo appeared again on the day of the assassination in a small Benton Harbor, Michigan, newspaper—the *News-Palladium*. Accompanying the photo was an article on the new role of Lady Bird Johnson as the first lady, under the shockingly tasteless headline "New First Lady: Dynamic, Charming, Wise." Below the headline was a photo of the brand-new first family in a smilingly playful pose. How is it possible that the editors and reporters of such a small paper, presumably with limited resources, gathered all this information in such a short time? Presumably, the paper did not even know of Kennedy's assassination until 1 p.m. central time, yet it managed to write six full columns, find three file photos, print, and distribute the November 22 issue in time for the afternoon/evening edition.

It is surprising that Dulles and Johnson allowed the LBJ horse/ photo to be taken at all; perhaps they thought it would appear in a small publication and then disappear from history. But they were mistaken. The photo offers tangible proof that the two most likely suspects in the plot to kill President Kennedy did actually meet just a few short months prior to the assassination. If nothing else, the meeting confirms that the two men who had the most to gain from Kennedy's death thought they had matters important enough to discuss in person, away from prying ears, in the days leading up to Dallas. Dulles and Johnson would have wanted assurances from one another that what they had set in motion was still a "go." They were nearing the point of no return, and they needed one another to pull off the coup. More importantly, they needed the network of operatives each had at his disposal to perform as expected.

All participants in the plot, in some manner or form, could be traced back to these two giants of the conspiracy. CIA assets answered to Dulles. Johnson had enormous influence over Hoover and the FBI, the Secret Service, Texas oilmen, politicians and police, and his own personal assassin, Mac Wallace. Some see the Mafia as a separate entity, but this was not so. The Mafia and the CIA had been partners in crime for years. Richard Bissell admitted to hiring gangsters to help in the failed attempts to kill Castro.[44] Ruby, a low-level hoodlum, was connected to Texas oilmen and organized crime.

Missing Tape

No recording of what Dulles and Johnson discussed at their summer 1963 meeting exists, but other recordings pertaining to their involvement in the plot do exist. The source for this information was a man named Colonel Trenton Parker, a CIA counterintelligence agent who ran a program called Pegasus. According to author Rodney Stich, "Pegasus was set up by...[President] Truman to spy on other CIA units...[to detect] any unlawful activities by the

CIA."[45] Truman always regretted forming the CIA on his watch; when the agency's power became uncontrollable, he fought back in the only way he could. He spied on the spies. As a result, Pegasus uncovered some stunning tape recordings. Parker, an expert in counter-espionage, bugged Hoover, Dulles and Johnson, among others. What he heard on those tapes were plans to kill JFK. "The individuals identified on the tapes were 'Rockefeller, Allen Dulles, Johnson of Texas, George Bush, and J. Edgar Hoover.'"[46] Dulles was linked to the Rockefellers through Sullivan & Cromwell, the Dulles brothers' Wall Street law firm which represented Rockefeller oil interests.[47] Writer Joseph de Burca describes the alliance between Dulles and David Rockefeller as a means by which Rockefeller transformed the CIA "into a truly diabolical organization dedicated to the overthrow of anyone who threatened Rockefeller global business interests...not to mention those of his fellow billionaires, many of who were friends and former clients of Allen Dulles...This accounts for [the CIA's] oft-quoted nickname: Capitalism's Invisible Army."[48]

Among the conversations on the Parker tapes was a cryptic message from Hoover to Rockefeller, "...we aren't going to have any problems. I checked with Dulles. If they do their job we'll do our job."[49]

The whereabouts of those tapes today is a mystery. Parker claimed to have turned them over to a Congressman from Georgia named Larry McDonald. The relationship between Parker and McDonald was unclear. Why Parker trusted McDonald with such explosive information is unknown. McDonald died in a plane crash in 1983. He boarded Korean Air flight 007 in New York City, headed for Alaska on September 1. The plane apparently crossed into Soviet air space and was shot down by Russian interceptors over the Sea of Japan. The Soviet news agency TASS reported that Richard Nixon was scheduled to be aboard the same flight, but the CIA warned Nixon not to board. He cancelled at the last minute.[50] This raises the obvious questions: How did the CIA have advance knowledge of the Soviet action, and why would an American intelligence agency warn Nixon but not McDonald or the other 51 Americans aboard the plane? One answer presents itself: If the CIA knew McDonald was a passenger on the flight and that he carried audio evidence of a high-level conspiracy, involving the CIA, to kill Kennedy, the agency could have used its KGB connections to notify the Russians of the illegal flyover. And the work of Pegasus and Parker might have ended up at the bottom of the ocean with the other 249 passengers.

CHAPTER 5

Execution of the Plot

"When they saw him from a distance and
before he came close to them,
they plotted against him to put him to death. They said to
one another, Here comes this dreamer! Now then, come
and let us kill him and throw
him into one of the pits; and we will say,
'A wild beast devoured him.'
Then let us see what will become of his dreams!"
—Genesis 37:18-20

Dallas and the Big Day

Nicknamed the city of hate, Dallas was the most frenzied hotbed of right-wing extremism in early 1960s America. The city was home to defense contractors, wealthy oil magnates, and a police force approved by the John Birch Society—a devil's brew of anti-Kennedy fervor. The leaders of the community gathered in private clubs—exclusive domains for a weird amalgam of business leaders, CIA agents, and conservative ideologues lurking on the fringes of lunacy—to share their hatred of the President and devise plans for his demise. Treason was in the air. Men like H.L. Hunt, without whose consent nothing ever got done in Dallas, pulled all the strings when it came to the commerce, politics and laws of the city. Hunt and oil millionaires like him made a fortune from the east Texas oil boom of previous decades, and they used the money to turn Dallas into their own pseudo-fascist playground. Hunt funded his own radio show (a forerunner of Rush Limbaugh's nationwide hatecasts) "Facts Forum" to lash out at the UN, immigration, gun control and fair taxation of the rich. Hunt later changed the show's title to "Life Line" when he incorporated evangelical Christianity into the broadcasts. He forced Dallas libraries to stock their shelves with his book *Alpaca*, Hunt's megalomaniacal fantasy world in which a small, super-wealthy class rules everything and everyone. The government, what there is of it, is controlled by this cabal; funding for essential services like public schools is slashed; the rich are not taxed; and like the Wild West, it is every man, woman and child for him- or herself. There are no civil rights or guaranteed equality. Only the wealthy survive. Congressmen and Senators are nothing more than wholly-owned subsidiaries of their rich overlords. At the time, the book seemed like the harmless ravings of a right-wing lunatic, but America since 1963 has gradually gravitated towards Alpaca. As more and more fanatical Republicans seize control of what's left of our democracy, Hunt's depraved vision is becoming reality. He would heartily approve of the neo-fascists, hatemongers and rabid nationalists populating the presidential administration elected under dubious circumstances in 2016. Dallas of 1963 was the prototype.

With Hunt's blessing and his funding, right-wing polemics infested all sectors of life—education, business, politics, law enforcement and religion. The John Birch and Patrick Henry societies were considered mainstream; the Christian Crusaders and the National Indignation Convention dominated evangelical dogma; the Minutemen thrived.[1]

That's the Dallas that Kennedy rode into on 11/22/63: seething with hatred, ready to end his life, and eager to move the country on a rightward trajectory. The killers were waiting for him; the assassins and the decoy were in place. For days, teams of killers rehearsed. They were timing their movements, assessing angles, looking for the perfect cover. But the plotters needed some luck with the weather. They got it. What started as a dreary, drizzly morning turned into bright sunshine by mid-day. Rain would have forced the President's limousine to have the bubble top on it, and assassination would have been nearly impossible. But with the sunlight came the open-air ride, easy access for killers and ready cover for their deed. The shadows on the knoll were deep and dark, hiding the riflemen lurking there. All they needed was the target to be driven into the kill zone.

The Strange Motorcade Formation

The Secret Service agents assigned to the Dallas motorcade exposed Kennedy to maximum danger. Besides being hungover (more on this later) and ill-prepared, the agents made certain that the Dallas police did not provide adequate protection either. Normally the presidential limo would have been flanked by motorcycle cops riding at the front and back bumpers. This was the accepted formation for most of Kennedy's motorcades. But at the last minute at Love Field, Dallas motorcycle cops were told to stay back of the limousine; specifically, no cop was to ride forward of the back bumper.[2] This opened up a field of fire for the assassins in Dealey Plaza.

For some perspective on historical presidential motorcade formations, one need only look at old newsreel videos of the parades involving Kennedy's three predecessors—FDR, Truman and Eisenhower. The National Geographic television channel recently broadcast clips of a Truman motorcade from March 1946, when he toured Fulton, Missouri, with Winston Churchill. Truman's car was surrounded by Secret Service agents, four in all, standing on the running boards, at the sides and the rear; in the front of the motorcade was an escort of motorcycle cops, ten deep.[3] There were also agents and police riding closely behind Truman's vehicle. Had Kennedy been flanked by such tight protection in Dallas it would have been nearly impossible to murder him. And the discrepancy of Secret Service protection in the two motorcades is even more telling when one considers some of the agents who served Truman, including James J. Rowley and Floyd Boring, also served Kennedy. Why such stringent protection for Truman but not JFK? Boring may have answered the question himself when he said, "Truman never came across as being superior"; other agents said he treated them like a son.[4] This is in stark contrast to the somewhat aloof, erudite, and Ivy League-educated Kennedy who was young enough to be a son to some of the SS agents. It is easy to see how the same agents who were so protective of the paternal Truman might resent Kennedy, the young and privileged patrician.

J.B. Marshall, one of those motorcycle cops in the unusual Dallas formation, provided verification that the route was changed by Secret Service agents. He and other officers were under the impression that the motorcade would travel straight down Main Street as it neared Dealey Plaza (this is the route which an FDR motorcade took in 1936), but at Love Field the cops were told by unidentified agents that the motorcade would make a right on Houston and left on Elm, passing right through the kill zone.[5] Without the zigzag turns, the limo would have been out of range of the assassins' bullets.

There were other motorcade irregularities. The press pool, which was usually positioned near the presidential limousine in order to have good photo opportunities, was placed well back in the procession. In other JFK motorcades, flatbed trucks of photojournalists were positioned directly in front of Kennedy's car. Also far removed from the presidential limo was the vice-presidential car carrying Lyndon and Lady Bird Johnson, as well as Texas Senator Ralph Yarborough. It was placed well back in the motorcade, ensuring that Johnson was safely out of the target area when the bullets flew.

Johnson's behavior was suspicious too. Motorcycle cops who escorted his car through Dealey Plaza claimed that Johnson ducked down a "good 30 or 40 seconds before the first shots were fired."[6] Support for this assertion can be found in the famous photo of the assassination taken by AP photographer James Altgens. Johnson cannot be seen in the vice-presidential car which has just made the turn from Houston onto Elm Street. Either he magically vanished from the car, or he was ducking down in his seat.

Johnson later tried to explain away his actions by claiming that his Secret Service agent Rufus Youngblood had vaulted into the back seat to cover Johnson during the shooting. But according to Yarborough this never happened; he told author Jim Marrs, "It was a small car. Johnson was a big man, tall. His knees were up against his chin as it was. There was no room for it to happen…Youngblood never left the front seat."[7] Yarborough also claimed that Youngblood had a small walkie-talkie radio and that Johnson hunched over to listen to it. The volume was too low for Yarborough to overhear what was being said.[8]

There were other men with walkie-talkies in Dealey Plaza. One was an unidentified dark-skinned man, who appeared to be Hispanic, standing on the sidewalk on the north side of Elm Street as the motorcade passed. Photos of the man showed what appeared to be a small radio in his back pocket. The man raised his hand in a defiant gesture as the first shots were fired. Next to him was "umbrella man"—a white male carrying a black umbrella on a cloudless day. He raised the umbrella and pointed it at the limousine just as Kennedy was struck in the throat. Some have suggested the man was a CIA agent firing a poisonous flechette to paralyze Kennedy and make him a defenseless target for rifle fire. Years later, it was revealed in Senate hearings that the CIA did possess such a weapon in 1963, but there was no evidence that it was used by the man in Dealey Plaza. In the 1970s Dallas resident Steven Louis Witt came forward to admit that he was "umbrella man" and that the umbrella he carried to Dealey Plaza was not a weapon but merely a device he used to heckle the President. He claimed to have never been in the CIA, and that he was merely in the wrong place at the wrong time. Furthermore, he neither knew nor ever saw again the man carrying the walkie-talkie, and insisted that the man was African-American rather than Latino. Witt appeared before the HSCA in the late 1970s and testified that he was sitting down on the grassy knoll when the motorcade approached. He then stood up and walked to a point near the death limo, but did not see the shooting because his umbrella was blocking his view.[9] The photographs taken in Dealey Plaza at the time of the shooting contradict every bit of Witt's testimony, but somehow the HSCA members failed to challenge him on this.

What Umbrella Man and Walkie-Talkie Man were really up to remains a mystery today.

Secret Service Involvement

In 1963 there existed a common misconception among Americans that the Secret Service was a professional, college-educated, buttoned-down, thoroughly dedicated group of elite and selfless individuals who were devoid of political preference and who were willing to give up their lives for the commander-in-chief. In reality, these agents were underpaid, overworked, undereducated and vulnerable to infiltration by those who wanted Kennedy dead. The older agents, especially, were right-wing partisans who despised Kennedy for his politics and his womanizing.

After the assassination, the Secret Service should have been held accountable for its outrageous protection lapses, if not for its active participation in the killing of JFK. Instead, the agents were cited for bravery, were provided excuses by the Warren Commission, and were given cushy jobs by the new President whom they had served well in Dallas. Emory Roberts, Secret Service shift supervisor in Dallas who told agents in the follow-up car to stand down during the shooting in Dealey Plaza, was appointed personal assistant to Lyndon Johnson. It was the only time in Secret Service history that an agent joined a presidential administration; Johnson once said that Roberts was "the man who greets me every morning and says good-bye to me every night."[10] Roberts' offspring also thrived in government service. His son Doug was active in Republican politics in the state of Michigan for many decades, and his grandson John worked in the George W. Bush White House.[11]

Other agents got rich from writing books about their abysmal performance in Dallas. Clint Hill created his own small cottage industry of assassination books. Nowhere in these books will one find admissions about Secret Service drunkenness in the early morning hours of 11/22/63 or the hatred many of the agents felt towards Kennedy. Thanks to one honest Secret Service agent from that period named Abraham Bolden, the first African-American member of the Secret Service to be assigned to the White House detail, we have proof of the agency's disdain for the man it was assigned to protect. Bolden's courageous book, *The Echo From Dealey Plaza*, contains these shocking passages: "I overheard [agents] making chilling racist remarks, referring to Kennedy as 'that nigger-lover'…[and] if shots were fired at the president, they'd take no action to protect him."[12] Bolden made the otherwise all-Caucasian White House detail so uncomfortable that he transferred to the Secret Service's Chicago office before the assassination. There he warned his superiors that "Kennedy's days were numbered" because of the lax security provided by SS agents.[13] Not only did the White House detail despise the President's politics and his privileged background, its members often caroused and drank to excess while on duty. When news came that JFK had been killed, one of Bolden's former colleagues on the White House detail shouted, "I told those playboys [SS agents] that someone was going to get the president killed if they kept acting like they did."[14]

Months before Dallas, Bolden himself had tried to warn Secret Service inspector Thomas J. Kelley and Secret Service Chief James Rowley of the inept and half-hearted protection the White House detail was providing the President. But Kelley and Rowley took no action. After the assassination, Bolden sensed that a cover-up was taking place. Orders came down the chain of command that "…

hinted at an effort to withhold, or at least to color, the truth...We were not to discuss Kennedy's protection, regardless of who asked us."[15]

Bolden, however, refused to remain silent. He tried to contact Warren Commission counsel J. Lee Rankin in May of 1964. His intent was to expose the Secret Service's protection of Kennedy as a "complete sham."[16] Rankin claimed that Bolden never contacted the commission and that, when given the chance, Bolden refused to testify.[17] Bolden was never called to testify, but his views on the assassination were well-known inside the agency. To shut him up, the government took the extraordinary step of framing him for a crime he did not commit. The FBI arrested him for supposedly selling a government file to a counterfeiter for $50,000. Bolden held a press conference to adamantly deny the charges. His first trial ended in a hung jury, but he was found guilty at his second trial in August of 1964. The purpose of the charade was summed up by Edward Hanrahan, prosecutor of the case, who made this public statement after the second trial: "The verdict completely rejects the outrageous charges made by the defendant and confirms the public's belief in the absolute integrity of the U.S. Secret Service."[18]

It was easy to railroad African-Americans in the racially charged year of 1964. America was largely a segregated country then, and bigotry was rampant. Blacks were considered second-class citizens without equal rights under the law. All-white juries regularly sat in unfair judgement of minority defendants. Bolden had no chance in the kangaroo court set up by federal authorities. Discredited by the sham verdict, his inside information about the assassination was ignored by the media.

After his conviction, Bolden was fired by the Secret Service. His appeal was denied, despite the fact that his accuser admitted to lying on the witness stand. He served 39 months in a federal prison. Meanwhile, no serious investigation of the Secret Service's involvement in the JFK assassination was ever conducted. Bolden's plight served as a warning to those who would dare question the official story.

Resentful of its client, derelict in its duties, and susceptible to treason, the Secret Service could have been, and likely was, co-opted by plot insiders. Those who contributed, in small or large ways, to the President's demise in Dallas were rewarded handsomely by Lyndon Johnson and treated with kid gloves by Dulles's Warren Commission. No SS agent lost his job after Dallas, and many went on to serve the new President in similar or better positions.

In subsequent years, some SS agents tried to blame the assassination on Kennedy himself. Gerald Behn and Winston Lawson are two agents who are cited as sources for the lie that Kennedy did not want agents riding on the back of his limo and that he wanted the motorcycle escort reduced and pushed back to offer bystanders a better view of himself and the first lady.[19] After-action reports filed by several agents, no doubt under pressure to cover their behinds, allege that President Kennedy had ordered agents off the rear of the limousine on November 18, 1963, in Tampa. When questioned by assassination researchers, SS agents later retracted their assertions that Kennedy stripped his own protection. Still the lie survived as recently as 2013. In a documentary which aired on the 50th anniversary of the assassination, Clint Hill asserted that JFK did not want the people to think he was inaccessible by having agents up on the back of the car in which he rode; in the same program, Westinghouse reporter Sid Davis claimed that Kennedy said, "He did not want the Secret Service running alongside the presidential limousine because he wanted the crowds to see Jackie."[20] These are utter falsehoods, as attested to by a multitude of others including Secret Service members themselves. SS agents Gerald Behn, Floyd Boring and Robert Lilly all affirmed the fact that at no time did JFK order agents off his limousine; moreover, the President never interfered with agents when they were protecting him and never dictated how they should perform their duties in any manner.[21]

On 11/22/63 it was Emory Roberts, the lead SS agent in the Dallas follow-up car, who can clearly be seen on local television newsreels ordering two agents—Don Lawton and Henry Rybka—off the rear bumper of the President's limousine as it departed Love Field. Roberts stands in the follow-up car and gestures to the agents to abandon their posts. One of the admonished agents (probably Don Lawton) raises his arms in confusion three times, as if to indicate his dismay at being waved off his post. This was an extraordinary lapse; films of previous JFK motorcades show agents routinely riding on the rear of the limousine. It indicates that something was amiss or out of the ordinary in Kennedy's protection detail that day. If Rybka and Lawton had been riding on the death car (there was a small platform and hand rail on either side of the limousine's rear bumper to accommodate agents) in Dealey Plaza, they would have cut off an assassin's view of the President, and would have been able to cover him quickly before the fatal head shot hit. Roberts' suspicious command made sure that Kennedy was not protected in this way. As the motorcade traversed downtown Dallas, the President was an open target for potential snipers. In the kill zone, another SS agent made an unthinkable blunder.

William Greer, the Secret Service agent who drove the presidential limousine in the Dallas motorcade, slowed the limo down, coming to a complete halt according to 21 witnesses, at the exact moment when the President was struck in the head.[22] The motionless car made Kennedy a stationary target for the assassins. At the same time, Greer took his left hand off the steering wheel and pointed it at the President as if he were aiming something at him. The Zapruder film shows no gun in Greer's hand, but witnesses in Dealey Plaza saw a gun in his hand. Standing near the limousine at the time of the shooting, Hugh Betzner said he "...observed what appeared to be a nickel-plated revolver in someone's hand in the President's car."[23] At this critical moment, Greer turned twice to look back at Kennedy, and did not speed up again until he saw that the man he was supposed to protect had his head blown apart. Greer lied about this to the Warren Commission, testifying that, "I didn't see anything of the President. *I didn't look* [emphasis added]. I wasn't far enough around to see the President."[24] A close examination of the Zapruder film also reveals some other oddities pertaining to Greer's movements. His body turned back and forth faster than humanly possible. It is my belief that only one explanation can account for this: Frames were removed from the Zapruder film to make it appear that the limo did not come to a complete stop (more on the alteration of the Zapruder film later in this chapter). The doctoring of the film, however, sped up movements of the people and objects in it. This was the price plotters had to pay for covering up Secret Service complicity in the assassination. In other words, Greer's inexplicable driving and the other agents' lack of proper response to the shooting would invite suspicions if the Zapruder film was seen in its pristine state.

Years later when Greer's son was asked how his dad felt about President Kennedy, he hesitated before admitting, "Well, we're Methodists and JFK was Catholic."[25] This raises the possibility that William Greer bore some animosity towards the President, perhaps having to do with the age-old Irish religious conflict between Catholics and Protestants. Greer also made dubious claims about being with Kennedy's body at all times "at Parkland or in transit."[26] He was certainly not in the cabin with the casket aboard Air Force One, nor did he accompany the body to Bethesda because it was already at Bethesda by the time Greer arrived there; however, he *was* with the body in Parkland's Trauma Room One during the time that confusion and chaos engulfed the hospital (the significance of this is explained later).

There is other evidence to support the possibility that Secret Service agents pulled out their firearms and shot at the President that day in Dealey Plaza. Several witnesses at ground level on Elm Street reported hearing, seeing or smelling gunfire either *inside* the

President's limo or nearby it. Jean Hill said that at least one shot came from the front seat of the car; Charles Brehm said that "shots came from in front of or beside the President"; Mary Moorman, standing just a few feet from the limo said that she heard shots "like a firecracker" right beside her; James Altgens suggested that a shot came from the left-hand side of the car; Austin Miller told the Warren Commission that shots came from "right there in the car"; Ralph Yarborough admitted to newsmen at Parkland that the "third shot may have been a Secret Service man returning fire"; and, most damning of all, George Davis, standing on the triple overpass above Elm, with a view directly into the limo, stated that he saw guns in the hands of the Secret Service agents inside the President's limousine.[27] There were only two agents—William Greer and Roy Kellerman—in that car.

Many more "nose" witnesses smelled smoke at ground level, including Yarborough, motorcycle escort officer Billy Martin, press photographer Tom Dillard, patrolman Earle Brown and bystander Virgie Rackley.[28] An early report was delivered on-air by Chet Huntley of NBC News just a short while after the shooting. He said, "Secret Service agents drew their weapons, but the damage had already been done." Also, one of the nurses who met the death car as it pulled into Parkland Hospital's emergency area reported that she could smell gunpowder in the limo itself.[29]

Regardless of whether or not a Secret Service agent fired at the President, there is an abundance of evidence to indicate that the agents on duty in Dallas were negligent, if not criminal, in their conduct. On November 21 ten members of Kennedy's SS detail stayed out partying all night and did not return to their Fort Worth hotel until just a few hours before JFK awoke. Excessive alcohol consumption and sleep deprivation certainly hindered their reflexes and alertness. Many of these agents had crucial assignments in the Dallas motorcade. The Cellar, the establishment which served drinks to the SS agents in Fort Worth, was owned by a man named

Pat Kirkwood who had loose ties to organized crime. Kirkwood "bragged…that [SS agents] were out having a few cocktails while the Fort Worth Fire Department [guarded] the presidential suite."[30] The Cellar's manager admitted that the SS agents "were bombed. They were drinking pure Everclear, grain alcohol sold at 151 and 190 proof."[31]

Emory Roberts further restrained his agents' effectiveness in Dealey Plaza by ordering them to stand down as shots were fired on Elm Street. Sam Kinney, the driver of "Queen Mary," the car carrying the agents, confirmed to author Vince Palamara that Roberts did indeed issue this command as the President was gunned down.[32] Clint Hill was the only agent who reacted, and his rush to the limo was delayed and futile. At Parkland, Roberts brusquely demanded that Mrs. Kennedy lift her arms off the President's head as she covered him up in the limo outside the emergency entrance; when Roberts saw that Kennedy's wound was fatal, he immediately abandoned the Kennedys for the Johnsons.

Phony Secret Service Agents

Though the Secret Service claimed that none of their agents were positioned on the ground in Dealey Plaza on 11/22/63, several law enforcement officers and civilians encountered SS agents near the grassy knoll and behind the picket fence immediately after the shots rang out.

Seymour Weitzman, a Dallas cop who witnessed the assassination, ran into the parking lot behind the picket fence on the grassy knoll because he'd heard shots coming from that direction. When he got to the parking lot Weitzman ran into a man who flashed Secret Service credentials and told him the situation was under control. The credentials looked genuine, so Weitzman moved on. Later, however, the Secret Service had to admit that none of its agents were on the ground in Dealey Plaza that day. It became apparent that the Secret Service agent was a phony, and Weitzman was pressured by the Warren Commission and FBI to change his story. Weitzman never did. What's more, he positively identified Bernard Barker as the man who was pretending to be a Secret Service agent.[33] Barker was a covert CIA operative who was convicted as one of the Watergate burglars in 1972.

The implications of this are enormous. Barker's presence at the scene of two apocalyptic covert operations, a decade apart, reveals that there was a CIA "putsch" team working behind the scenes to overthrow presidents and change history without the consent of the American people. This team was composed of undercover operatives who had been recruited into the CIA during Allen Dulles's tenure as head of the agency. When Dulles and his sponsors decided it was time to eliminate a head of state, either foreign or domestic, the team was activated. Dallas ended the presidency of JFK and ushered into office Lyndon Johnson—the man who established the Warren Commission; Watergate did in Richard Nixon and ushered into office Gerald Ford—one of the men who served on the Warren Commission. This is no coincidence.

When Weitzman refused to change his story, he was institutionalized after having a nervous breakdown. But when interviewed by authors Michael Canfield and A.J. Weberman for their book *Coup d'état in America*, Weitzman was quite lucid and definitive in his identification of Barker.[34] Barker was not the only Watergate burglar spotted in Dealey Plaza. E. Howard Hunt's presence in Dallas is detailed later in this chapter.

Dallas police officer J.M. Smith also ran to the parking lot after the shooting and encountered a phony Secret Service agent. Smith told the Warren Commission, "I pulled my pistol…and I put it back. Just as I did he showed me that he was a Secret Service agent."[35] Only later, when Smith realized he had been duped, did he admit to author Anthony Summers, "The man, this character… looked like an auto mechanic. He had on a sports shirt and sports pants. But he had dirty fingernails…it didn't ring true for the Secret

Service...[but] I have seen those credentials before, and they satisfied me."[36]

Defending his men, Dallas Police Chief Jesse Curry supported the notion that the Secret Service agent must have been bogus: "... certainly the suspicion would point to the man as being involved... in the shooting since he was in the area immediately adjacent to where the shots were—and the fact that he had a [Secret Service identification] would make it seem all the more suspicious."[37]

Police sergeant D.V. Harkness encountered two strangers at the back of the TSBD approximately six minutes after the assassination. The two men convinced Harkness they were Secret Service agents, and Harkness moved on.[38] But later he divulged that the men were "well-armed...[and] I assumed they were with the Presidential party."[39]

Another encounter with a fake SS man was reported by Gordon Arnold. A soldier on leave from his unit at the time, Arnold, camera in hand, was scouting Dealey Plaza in the moments before the assassination for the perfect place to take a home movie of the presidential motorcade. He was walking behind the picket fence atop the grassy knoll when he was stopped by a man who displayed Secret Service credentials; the man told Arnold, "I'm with the Secret Service. I don't want anybody up here."[40] Arnold was followed by the "SS" man until he went around the other side of the fence to film the motorcade from there. (More on Arnold's story later in this chapter and in chapter 7.)

People Will Talk

In addition to innocent witnesses who spoke out, there were many plot insiders who divulged what they knew despite the inherent risks to their well-being. The plotters were experienced in covert acts and knew the success of their mission required utmost secrecy. They belonged to organizations which not only valued secrecy, but which also punished in the harshest way those who violated oaths of silence.

Nonetheless, all involved knew there would be collateral risks of unwanted candor. A large enterprise, such as the one that took JFK's life, will inevitably spring leaks before and after the fact. Peripheral characters, who may or may not have understood the full impact of what they saw or heard, felt the need to reveal what they knew. Such a monstrous act as the killing of a president was too hard to keep to themselves.

Below are just a few of the insiders who couldn't keep what they knew to themselves. The statements of those with foreknowledge are just as powerfully (perhaps more so with their predictive weight) indicative of a conspiracy as those delivered after the deed.

Richard Case Nagell, reportedly a CIA operative in the 1950s and '60s, wrote two letters to the Warren Commission claiming that he had been aware of the plot to kill JFK months in advance of the actual murder in Dallas. In spite of this, the commission showed no interest in him or his astonishing story. Nagell claimed that he was part of the branch of the CIA which was trying to abort the murder, and he was tasked with stopping it, even if that meant "terminating" Oswald.[41] (It is much more likely that Oswald himself was part of the abort team than an actual assassin.) Author Dick Russell claims that Nagell was also a KGB double agent who was ordered to keep an eye on Oswald; both Oswald and Nagell were apparently monitoring the assassination schemes of disaffected anti-Castro Cubans in the months before Dallas. Nagell, sensing a trap, found a way out of the intelligence web which ensnared Oswald by getting himself thrown into jail before the assassination happened. In September 1963 Nagell walked into an El Paso bank, fired some shots, and then calmly waited for the police to arrive. He told author Russell that "right-wing extremists, including wealthy Texas oil interests and CIA renegades" were behind the assassination; however, the public never heard this because a "concerted effort to suppress [Nagell's] true motive for...his 'alleged bank robbery'" was presided over by Judge Homer Thornberry in Nagell's trial.[42]

Thornberry just happened to be LBJ's Texas crony. (Thornberry was in Dallas on 11/22/63 and was aboard Air Force One when Johnson was sworn in as president.) Nagell was convicted, and Thornberry handed down the maximum sentence. The conviction was later overturned; Nagell was released from prison in 1968 and spent much of the rest of his life in seclusion. He testified before the HSCA, but the records of his interview have, as of this writing not been released. He was found dead in Los Angeles the day after the ARRB mailed him a letter asking him to appear before the board in the early 1990s.

John Martino, an anti-Castro Cuban with CIA and Mafia ties, who was once imprisoned in Castro's Cuba, knew many of the characters involved in the plot to kill JFK. Before the President arrived in Dallas, he exclaimed to his wife, "They're going to kill him when he gets to Texas."[43] How would Martino have had access to such explosive information? Unless he was psychic, he would have obtained it from some of the principals in the plot—CIA operatives like Rip Robertson, Frank Sturgis, David Morales and E. Howard Hunt—with whom he was well-acquainted. Martino got to know his unsavory associates while working at the mob-owned Deauville Casino in Havana in the 1950s. He worked alongside a notorious Dallas hood and gambler, R.D. Matthews, and Jack Ruby's gun-running mentor Lewis McWillie.[44] Ruby traveled to Cuba several times in 1959, including visits to McWillie's boss, mob chief Santos Trafficante; Trafficante was in prison at the time, and Ruby, according to underworld sources, gained Trafficante's freedom by selling black-market jeeps to Castro.[45] This is just one of several incidents which expose the full extent of Ruby's intricate ties with organized crimes, ties which the Warren Commission ignored in order to divorce Oswald's murder, and by extension the murder of JFK, from Syndicate connections. Connections which could have unraveled the CIA/Mafia plots to kill Castro.

In any event, Martino knew Ruby and other Mob figures during the years he spent in Cuba. After he was released from jail and returned home to Miami, Martino renewed his ties with the CIA and its contacts in the anti-Castro Cuban community in south Florida.

Rose Cheramie (aka Melba Marcades) was another who predicted JFK's demise. On November 20, 1963, she was traveling to Dallas from Miami with two CIA-connected, anti-Castro Cubans named Sergio Arcacha Smith and Emilio Santana. Cheramie claimed she was thrown from a moving car by Smith and Santana somewhere in Louisiana. While being treated for her injuries in a hospital, Cheramie told a Louisiana state cop that JFK was going to be killed in Dallas on November 22 and that Smith and Santana were involved in the plot. The cop, Francis Fruge, did not believe Cheramie because of her shady background. She was a drug-addicted prostitute who seemed to be hysterical. But when Kennedy *was* killed in Dallas two days later, Fruge took her seriously and tried to inform the Dallas cops what Cheramie had told him. Dallas police ignored him. Two years later, Cheramie was found dead on Highway 155 near Big Sandy, Texas. The cause of her death is still disputed.[46]

The point here is that Cheramie and Martino and others were not making crazy, unfounded assertions when they predicted JFK's assassination. They were both acquainted with CIA/Mafia types who should have been considered suspects by the Warren Commission and the FBI. Sturgis, Robertson, Hemming and other intelligence assets were photographed in Dealey Plaza at the time of the assassination. These men were associated with Operation 40, a group of anti-Castro Cubans who were recruited and trained by the CIA prior to the Bay of Pigs invasion. Notorious Watergate burglar and CIA operative E. Howard Hunt, who was recruited by Allen Dulles himself, served as liaison and paymaster to Operation 40.[47] Several of these men show up in Kennedy assassination literature as having played a role in Dallas.

William Harvey, a CIA operative, also purportedly had advance knowledge of the events in Dallas. He was at one time in charge of the CIA's assassination program called ZR-RIFLE. Considered something of a loose cannon, even by CIA standards, Harvey was a reckless drunk whom many fellow spies found repugnant and dangerous. He despised President Kennedy and worked diligently to undermine the Administration's goals; during the Cuban Missile Crisis, Harvey engineered raids on Cuba. He was banished by Kennedy to an overseas post where he remained until 11/22/63. In Italy when he received word of the assassination, Harvey divulged to a fellow CIA officer named F. Mark Wyatt remarks that convinced Wyatt of Harvey's foreknowledge of the assassination in Dallas.[48]

Private First Class Eugene Dinkin, a U.S. Army cryptographer, also possessed foreknowledge of the assassination. Stationed in Metz, France, in 1963, Dinkin decoded military intelligence messages in the weeks preceding 11/22/63 which indicated that a right-wing plot to kill Kennedy would take place in Texas in November. He dutifully reported this information to authorities and media outlets (including CIA Mockingbird asset Henry Luce's Time-Life bureau in Geneva, Switzerland). Alerted to Dinkin's provocative predictions, the CIA, FBI and military intelligence tried to discredit him. In fear, Dinkin went AWOL from his unit and approached European embassies with his warnings, but could not get them to take him seriously. He returned to his unit and was arrested there by U.S. Army intelligence and confined to a psychiatric hospital ward just a week before Kennedy's murder. After the assassination occurred as he had predicted, Dinkin was transferred to Walter Reed Hospital in Washington, D.C., where he was threatened with electric shock therapy unless he recanted his story. He underwent intensive psychiatric treatment (a CIA euphemism for brainwashing per MK-ULTRA protocols). Eventually Dinkin declared that he deduced his Kennedy assassination prediction not from official intelligence cables but from newspaper stories leading up to

11/22/63. This gave the government a ready excuse for labeling Dinkin an eccentric kook, and it also permitted Dinkin a way to survive further persecution. He was released from Walter Reed in 1964, and he obtained a medical discharge from the Army.[49] But the CIA and Army intelligence could not expunge from history the story of Dinkin, whose prediction still reverberates today. He might have even discovered the identity of one of the assassins before 11/22/63. The information he derived came from monitoring cables from the French OAS; a French OAS assassin named Jean Souetre (or someone posing as Souetre) had been in Dallas at the time of the assassination, and was expelled from the United States shortly thereafter.[50]

A CIA memorandum dated April 1, 1964, confirms Souetre's presence in Dallas. In part, the memo reads, "[Souetre, aka Michel Roux, aka Michael Mertz] was in Fort Worth on morning of 22 November and in Dallas in the afternoon. The French believe he was expelled to either Mexico or Canada...Subject is believed to be identical with a Captain who is a deserter from the French Army... [the French] would like to know the reason for his expulsion from the U.S. and his destination."[51]

Jury Believed Hunt Was in Dallas

The story of E. Howard Hunt begins and ends with his complicity in CIA atrocities stretching over three decades. Largely ignored by the mainstream media, despite Hunt's deathbed confessions, Hunt's story is a revelatory tale of how the CIA directed the fate of America (and much of the rest of the world for that matter) and its public leaders through covert operations.

Hunt joined the CIA in the 1950s and "made his bones" in the Guatemalan operation which deposed President Arbenz in 1954. He reputedly was the CIA liaison to the White House during the Bay of Pigs planning under Eisenhower. (When Eisenhower left office, Kennedy inherited the operation.) There is evidence that

Hunt had direct contact with Oswald in the weeks leading up to 11/22/63. Oswald wrote a note to Hunt dated November 8, 1963, in which he asked Hunt for "information concerning my position...I am suggesting that we discuss the matter fully before any steps are taken by me or anyone else."[52]

Hunt's role in the Kennedy assassination appears to have been that of paymaster, Cuban ringleader, and disseminator of phony Secret Service IDs to plotters on the ground in Dealey Plaza. This is not baseless speculation. A Miami jury in 1985 found that Hunt was in Dallas the day Kennedy died and was involved in the assassination. A juror named Leslie Armstrong told reporters, "The evidence was clear...The CIA had killed President Kennedy [and] Hunt had been a part of it."[53] The jury's verdict came in a civil appellate trial in which Hunt forfeited the award he had won years previously from *Spotlight* magazine. *Spotlight* ran an article in 1978 claiming, in part, that Hunt was going to be made the CIA's scapegoat in the Kennedy assassination with the House Select Committee on Assassinations hearing looming. Hunt sued *Spotlight* and won a $650,000 award, but the judgement was reversed on appeal by the Miami jury.

The *Spotlight* article, written by CIA agent Victor Marchetti, asserted that a CIA memo from 1966 stated that the agency would someday "have to explain Hunt's presence in Dallas on November 22, 1963."[54] The nomination of Hunt as the CIA fall guy may or may not have been a genuine CIA "limited hangout," a maneuver employed by the agency when it needs to reveal a fragment of the truth rather than fully divulge an entire operation. Diversionary or inculpatory, the memo is one of the few public CIA disclosures of its involvement in the killing of Kennedy.

Why was Hunt chosen as the scapegoat? For an explanation we must return to his role as the burglars' supervisor in the Watergate break-in of 1972, a bungled CIA operation which may have been staged to bring down the presidency of Richard Nixon. Hunt may have become expendable during the Watergate affair when his CIA cover was blown, and his notoriety as a criminal became a matter of public record. To comprehend his role in Nixon's undoing, one must reexamine the real purpose of what appeared to be a second-rate burglary. The cover story is that Nixon White House "plumbers," Hunt and G. Gordon Liddy, were assigned to spy on the Democrats and dig up dirt on the opposition in advance of the 1972 presidential election. The reality is much more complex. The CIA and Hunt were fearful of another Kennedy presidency, even after Senator Ted Kennedy had been disgraced by the Chappaquiddick affair. Hunt, a Dulles acolyte who revered the old master and reportedly ghost-wrote the Dulles book *The Craft of Intelligence*, despised the Kennedys and was obsessed with destroying them. In his own book, *Give Us This Day*, Hunt in essence says that Kennedy deserved to die for his cowardice and treachery in the Bay of Pigs affair. He reasons that had Kennedy rained down the military might of the U.S. on Cuba in 1961, Castro would have been removed and Lee Harvey Oswald, a Castro sympathizer, would have had no need to kill Kennedy.[55] What Hunt is really saying in his book is that had the Bay of Pigs been a success, there would have been no need to create a patsy named Oswald to cover up the CIA's revenge murder of Jack Kennedy.

Hunt wanted so badly to discredit Kennedy that he went so far as to fabricate cables between the State Department and the U.S. embassy in Saigon in order to falsely implicate Kennedy in the Diem assassination.[56]

But spying on Ted Kennedy was hardly necessary; he was not a candidate for the presidency in 1972. The deeper motivation seems to have been to remove Richard Nixon from office in yet another CIA coup d'etat. One might wonder why the CIA wanted Nixon out. He had served the agency well as the action officer in the Guatemala invasion and the pre-Kennedy planning for the Bay of Pigs operation. But Nixon's good relations with the agency may have been severed when he began snooping around for information about the Kennedy assassination.

Ever the paranoid and distrustful sort, Nixon may have been worried about his own vulnerability to a coup attempt. There is evidence that he knew quite well who had been involved in Dallas and what their motives had been. In unguarded moments he described the U.S. intelligence/military monolith as a "wild beast" that even presidents could not control.[57] Shortly after taking office Nixon instructed CIA Director Richard Helms to hand over to the White House "thousands and thousands of documents" having to do with the final days of the Kennedy administration, but Helms refused; Helms subsequently admitted that Nixon wanted CIA files having to do with "violent removal of…heads of state."[58] There was concern among the spooks at Langley that the Nixon White House wanted to rein in the CIA; to counter this, the CIA purposely tried to sabotage Nixon, and, according to Nixon aide Bob Haldeman, all covert projects, up to and including Watergate, were failures intended to harm the Nixon administration.[59] This assertion naturally leads one to the obvious question: "Was Hunt acting as the CIA's clandestine agent in an attempted overthrow of the Nixon presidency?"

Nixon, no doubt, recognized CIA involvement in the Watergate affair and likely suspected the agency was coming after him for daring to challenge its authority. He was quite aware of Hunt's background and profile. Nixon, desperate to save his presidency, resorted to blackmailing the CIA. He sent messages to the CIA through his surrogates, John Ehrlichman and Bob Haldeman, that unless the agency intervened to thwart the FBI investigation into Watergate, Nixon would reveal what he knew about the Bay of Pigs. Nixon used the expression "Bay of Pigs" as a euphemism for the Kennedy assassination, and the CIA understood quite well what he meant; when CIA Director Richard Helms, another Dulles hire, was approached with the veiled threat, he erupted in anger which made

Haldeman wonder what was so explosive in the CIA/Kennedy assassination connection.[60] In the subsequent Watergate hearings, Helms had an uncharacteristic slip of the tongue which revealed his real feelings about the "Bay of Pigs/Kennedy Assassination" linkage. While twisting himself into a knot trying to come up with a coherent reason for erupting in anger at Nixon's subtle threat to expose the CIA's "Bay of Pigs involvement," he testified that "I don't know what he (Nixon) had in mind but I reacted to that question very firmly. Now the Bay of Pigs is the rubric for a very unhappy event in the life of the CIA...therefore, it is one to which I am likely to react and react rather quickly, for the simple reason that the Bay of Pigs was long since over, [and] the problems arising from it had been *liquidated*."[61] *Liquidated* is a common CIA term for assassination. Helms admitted that the man whom he thought was responsible for the Bay of Pigs had been liquidated.

Nixon, who had been in Dallas on November 22, 1963, knew plenty about Hunt's involvement in the assassination on behalf of the CIA. So when Hunt was arrested for Watergate, and then was linked to the White House, Nixon realized that the stakes were much higher than just a failed burglary attempt. He and Hunt became loose ends that the CIA needed to tie up.

After Nixon tried to use his information on Hunt to leverage the CIA into doing his bidding, Hunt returned the favor by trying to blackmail the Nixon White House. On Nixon's secret White House tape recordings he clearly acknowledges Hunt's threat, and responds with the stunning assertion that he can raise the money. The figure mentioned is $1 million. It's unclear how much money Hunt received, if any, but a suspicious plane crash in December 1972 points to a payoff. Hunt's wife Dorothy died in that crash while carrying $10,000 in $100 bills; Hunt's son blames the Nixon White House for the crash.[62] The following year Hunt entered a guilty plea in the Watergate matter and was sentenced to 33 months in prison. He felt his country was "punishing me for doing the very things it trained and directed me to do."[63]

Embittered by the CIA's betrayal of him, Hunt retired from the agency and went into semi-seclusion until the *Spotlight* article appeared in 1978. Defiantly, Hunt sued, refusing to again be the fall guy for his government's crimes. He won the suit, but on appeal he ran into Mark Lane, a lawyer and Kennedy assassination researcher who was keenly aware of the CIA's participation in what Hunt called the Big Event.

Rather than claim lack of malice in *Spotlight*'s defense, Lane ingeniously used the truth as his hammer. Hunt's prevarications were no match for Lane's expertise in the intricacies of the Kennedy assassination. On the witness stand, Hunt used his three children—aged 14, 13 and 10 in 1963—as alibis, claiming they were with him in his Washington-area home at the time of the assassination. The children were certainly of an age where they would have recalled with great accuracy what they were doing and where they were when news of the assassination came. Yet Hunt claimed he continually, over the course of many years, had to remind his children of being in their presence on the fatal day; thus, he admitted to the presumption that his children did not recall his being at home with them on 11/22/63. Lane used this against Hunt on cross-examination by asking him, "Why did you have to convince your children you were not in Dallas, Texas, on November 22, 1963."[64]

The jury was also swayed by the testimony of Marita Lorenz, who as a CIA operative had become Fidel Castro's lover and who was well acquainted with anti-Castro Cubans in the Miami area. Lorenz traveled from Miami to Dallas with Frank Sturgis and Cuban ex-pats, in a car loaded with weapons, just prior to the assassination. In Dallas she witnessed Hunt and Jack Ruby providing payoffs to Sturgis and the others at a motel on the night before the assassination.[65]

The verdict in Hunt's trial should have set off a firestorm of media publicity and been the impetus for renewed investigation of the death of the 35th President. Instead the news did not spread north of Miami. The national press and major media outlets, ever vigilant in guarding the CIA's secrets, refused to pick up the story, and soon the whole mess blew over. Hunt faded into obscurity until his deathbed confession over 20 years later. He told his son, St. John Hunt, in chilling detail, who was involved and why. He drew a simple graph, at the top of which appeared the name Lyndon Johnson, followed by lines connecting to CIA agents Cord Meyer, William Harvey, David Morales and a "French gunman on the grassy knoll (corroborating the CIA memo stating that Jean Souetre was in Dallas on 11/22/63)."[66] While stunning, this list is hardly a comprehensive roster of JFK assassination suspects. Hunt included tangential characters who, coincidentally, he was not fond of, and excluded the more likely and notable suspects—Allen Dulles, David Atlee Phillips and James Angleton—CIA contemporaries whom he admired and trusted. So while Hunt is one of many who believed LBJ was at the top of the conspiracy's hierarchy, he could not bring himself to implicate the plot's other CEO—Dulles, a man Hunt worshipped. Still Hunt corroborated what many researchers suspect—the involvement of the CIA and Lyndon Johnson in JFK's murder.

Zapruder Film Was Doctored

The plotters, steeped in intelligence methodologies of plausible deniability and disinformation, went to great lengths to cover up the truth of 11/22/63. In all three stages of the operation—the planning, the execution and the cover-up—there is evidence of diversion, deception and disguise. Fakery was extensively employed. Even the photographic images of the assassination can't be trusted.

The deeper one delves into the JFK case, the more evident it becomes that the depiction of the assassination portrayed on the Zapruder film cannot be taken at face value. There are just too many discrepancies between what witnesses saw and what the film purports to show. So much so that, all serious investigators evolve to a point in their analyses when they must seriously consider the possibility that the Z film is a false record of the way the assassination happened. The most glaring evidence of Z film manipulation can be seen in frames 290 to 369. Kennedy suffers the fatal head wound at frame 313, and his head and upper body are thrown violently backward and to the left, indicative of a shot from the right front, even though the blood spray and brain matter appear to eject to the right front indicating a shot from above and behind. No official investigation has ever attempted to explain this odd contradiction evident in the Z film.

Suspiciously, the area in the back of the head where Parkland personnel saw an exit wound is shaded and darkened. Also a large, mysterious blob of something appears to ooze from Kennedy's right temple. As the frames progress, the blob appears to grow larger, then smaller, then larger again as it revolves around the right side of the head. At one point the blob appears to emanate from his cheekbone and covers the area from his nose almost down to his chin. What is this blob? Lone-nutters try to argue that it is a portion of his scalp which has been separated from the skull by the force of the shot. But no loose scalp was reported by the Parkland doctors and nurses. They reported a fist-sized hole in the back of the head, parallel to the right ear; it did not extend into the front right portion of the head, and there was no "moving blob" oozing from the right front of the head. A sketch made by Dr. McClelland, one of the attending surgeons at Parkland, leaves no doubt that Kennedy was shot from the front and had no large exit hole in the top of his head. McClelland's sketch (recently put up for auction) shows an entry wound at the right top of JFK's forehead in the hairline. McClelland's notes that accompanied the sketch read, "Probable entrance wound at hairline altho [sic] I did not see this... on the right side of the head"; the sketch depicts a large exit wound at the back of the head near the bump parallel to the right ear with the notation "4x5 inch wound (exit)."[67] In addition, neither McClelland nor any other Parkland doctor reported a loose scalp flap, covering a large portion of the right side of JFK's head, as was depicted in some of the autopsy photos. The only reasonable assumption one can make is that the scalp flap was created by secret work done on Kennedy's head in between Dallas and Bethesda. And the only acceptable explanation for the incredible blob is that it was painted on by CIA special effects technicians who had access to the film after the fact. But where was this done? By whom was it done? And when was it done?

The logistics and time constraints of altering the home movie of the century seem prohibitive: the plotters needed quick access to the film, the wherewithal to develop the film and transport it from Dallas and back in a short period of time, and the facilities and expertise to doctor the film before frames of it could be released to the public. Yet, it is readily apparent that this was somehow accomplished. The dramatic contradictions in what the extant Zapruder film reveals and what we now know to be true leave no doubt that someone tampered with this critical piece of evidence. To reiterate: at the moment of the fatal shot, the film shows blood, skull pieces and brain matter from the President's head flying forward and to the right, while at the same time the President's head is propelled violently backward and to the left; limo driver William Greer, looks back towards Kennedy in frames 302-303, a movement which takes him just one-eighteenth of a second, faster than the blink of an eye; Greer then accomplishes another impossibly fast turn forward in frames 315-317; the limo does not come to a complete stop in the Zapruder film, but numerous eyewitnesses swore that the limo *did* stop right before the fatal shot was fired; the "blob" at the top-right of the President's head was a wound not seen at Parkland Hospital; and the wound which was seen by the Parkland doctors, an exit wound at the back of Kennedy's head, was covered in a suspicious shadow on the Zapruder film. These are just a few of the anomalies which cast doubt on the film's authenticity.

Covering up the limo stop in the Zapruder film would have been a simple matter of removing some frames from the film, thus making it appear that the limo had continuous movement. This would prevent undue suspicion being directed at the limo driver, William Greer, and the inexcusable inaction of his fellow agents. But it would have also created the comically obvious quicker-than-normal actions seen in the altered film. Besides Greer's lightning-fast head turns, Clint Hill, the only agent who sprang into action when the shots rang out, appears to run at super-human speeds to catch up to the death limo. Hill jumped off the Queen Mary (the Secret Service back-up car) at approximately Z310 (frame 310 of the Zapruder film) less than a second before the fatal head shot strikes; he reached the back bumper of the President's limo at precisely Z339 when he grabs the trunk handle. He slips momentarily and then regains his footing, and by Z378 both of his feet are off the Elm Street pavement as he mounts the footlift with both hands firmly around the trunk handle. By Z390 he has grabbed Jackie's arm as he scrambles to reach the back seat. This is a remarkable physical feat. We can time it calculating the elapsed frames per second. The extant Z film was exposed at approximately 18 frames per second. That means it took Hill just five seconds to disembark the back-up car, race to catch the limo, grab the trunk handles, climb aboard the trunk, and grab Jackie's arm. Even more amazingly, Hill made his "mad dash," from bumper to bumper, in less than two seconds (Z310 to Z339). If Hill could really run that fast, he missed his calling. He should have been training for the 1964 Olympics as a world-class sprinter instead of riding in the Dallas motorcade. Of course, his Jesse-Owens speed is just an illusion if frames were removed to hide the fact that the limo came to a complete stop on Elm Street.

The speed-distortion anomalies, spotted only years later by those who would dare challenge the film's veracity, were the simplest to accomplish. The other alterations—distorting the head wound, creating false blood spray, and removing a revolver from Greer's hand, for instance—would have required much more intricate alteration techniques. This process would have required the film—like the body—to be intercepted somewhere, and some grand hoax perpetrated at an unknown site. But tracing the film's movement can be a daunting endeavor. There exist several versions of the original film's disposition, how many copies were made, who obtained those copies, when those copies were obtained, and what was done with the copies. Determining which accounts are accurate can be a frustrating enterprise.

Most accounts agree that Zapruder's camera original was taken to the Eastman Kodak lab in Dallas for development and then three copies were made at Jamieson Film Company on the afternoon of 11/22/63. This is where the truth gets muddled. Richard Trask, author of *Pictures of the Pain*, asserts that two copies were turned over to the Secret Service in Dallas and the original and one copy were returned to Zapruder.[68] But author Dick Russell contends that one of the first-generation copies was sold to H.L. Hunt.[69] Hunt's possible involvement in the financing and planning of the assassination is documented elsewhere in this book; his purchase of the Zapruder film so soon after the assassination gives rise to many questions. How could he have known of the Zapruder film's existence and "availability" when only a select few people were even aware of it in the early afternoon of 11/22/63? Was Zapruder aware of the sale to Hunt, and, if so, why did he permit it? Trask's position is that Zapruder "obtained assurances from the [Jamieson] technicians that no additional copies had been bootlegged."[70] But the film identification numbers associated with the original and the copies show a mysterious gap in their sequence. The original is #0183 and the copies are #0185, #0186, and #0187. What happened to #0184? Was this the copy Hunt received? Kennedy assassination researcher James Fetzer speculates that #0184 could have been taken to the Kodak lab in Rochester as a "negative and turned into a positive which was then taken to the National Photographic Interpretation Center."[71] The NPIC, located in the Washington Navy Yard, was a CIA-run organization.

It is now known that a film of the assassination was hand-carried by a Secret Service agent named William Smith to Kodak headquarters in Rochester, New York, to be developed there. Since films are not developed twice, this assassination film could not have been the original Zapruder film developed in Dallas. It was Homer McMahon, an NPIC technician in charge of color photography, who revealed this stunning information in his testimony before the ARRB in 1997. McMahon was insistent that the film he saw in Washington was an original "because it was Kodachrome, and... it was a double 8 movie"; notably, McMahon consistently referred to the film as an amateur movie of the assassination, and at no time during his testimony did he refer to it as the Zapruder film.[72] This supposes the incredible possibility that a separate, secret movie of the assassination was made by persons unknown for the purposes of later alterations to fit the plotters' scheme of framing Oswald. But who would have made such a film, and where was his filming location?

To answer this question, it is informative to reexamine the photographs taken in Dealey Plaza on 11/22/63. There are several images of what appears to be a man leaning against a retaining wall situated at the front of the grassy knoll just steps from where Abraham Zapruder shot his home movie. This man is holding an object (possibly a camera) to his face and pointing it at the motorcade. (Some refer to him as "black dog" man as his prone posture resembles a sitting dog. See chapter 7 for further discussion.) The two angles (Zapruder's and black dog man's) would provide similar, if not identical, views of the assassination. If McMahon is correct, then it is possible that the man on the retaining wall might have been the source of the "amateur film" which was rushed to the

NPIC by Secret Service agent Smith. McMahon stated that Smith told him that he [Smith] "had personally picked up the film from the amateur who had exposed it" in Dallas, and that the film was to be analyzed at NPIC.[73] In this scenario, the film would have arrived at NPIC already altered to remove the limo stop, to distort the actions of the Secret Service agents in the motorcade, to change the appearance of Kennedy's head wound, and to remove evidence of shots from the front. Enlargements were then made and briefing boards were prepared for analysis. While McMahon surmised that "President Kennedy was shot…from at least three different directions…the opinion of agent Smith [was] there were three shots from behind from the Book Depository"; Smith's explanation for his divergent interpretation was "you can't fight city hall."[74] At the conclusion of the analysis process, all materials were turned over to Secret Service agent Smith who warned McMahon and his assistant Ben Hunter "don't discuss this with anyone."[75]

It is likely that William Smith was an impostor, as no Secret Service agent named William Smith has ever turned up on the SS roles circa 1963. Who was he then? Was he working for the plotters? It appears so, because the film he carried to the National Photographic Interpretation Center could not have been the Zapruder film. In his book, *Inside the Assassinations Record Review Board*, Douglas Horne writes, "…McMahon and Hunter were not working with the true [Zapruder] camera original developed in Dallas, but were instead working with a re-created, altered film masquerading as the original."[76] Horne is implying that there was not a second film made in Dealey Plaza, but rather the plotters made their own doctored film by optically forging one of the copies of the original Z film. He flatly states that the "extant film in the [National] Archives is…a simulated 'original' created with an optical printer at the CIA's secret film lab in Rochester."[77]

Reasonable objections to this theory have been made by those who point out that there was not enough time to alter the film in this manner, make copies of the altered film and return them to Dallas, get the camera-original or a re-creation of the camera-original to NPIC for analysis, and then submit the film to *Life* magazine to meet its publication deadline of Monday, November 25, 1963. (*Life* published only a few "safe" slides of the film in its 11/25/63 issue, not including the crucial head-shot frames.) But long-time Hollywood film editor David Healy asserts that time was not of the essence because very few people had seen the Zapruder film in the hours immediately following the assassination, and what they recalled of it could be easily swayed to a different point-of-view on subsequent showings of the altered film years later. In other words, if the plotters' scheme was to alter the original Zapruder film (or cobble together a new one from another unknown amateur film) there was no need to rush it. The camera-original and the first-generation copies were locked away by individuals who were either suspiciously allied with the plotters or, in some way, had ample reason to keep the film hidden away. *Life* publisher C.D. Jackson, a close friend and ally of Allen Dulles, released only a few select frames of the film after the assassination. The other film holders—the Secret Service, the FBI, H.L. Hunt and Zapruder himself—had every reason to keep the film from public view. So there was plenty of time for altered copies to be substituted for the camera-original and first-generation copies. Healy suggests that the plotters could "find a hiding place for a couple extra copies of the altered Zapruder film...exchange [the copies and camera-original]...then burn the actual camera-original."[78]

David Lifton, however, in his article "Pig on a Leash" published in *The Great Zapruder Film Hoax,* states his belief that the Zapruder film *was* altered over the weekend of 11/22-11/24. His argument is that the alteration process was not simple but that the technology did exist in 1963, and, since William McMahon did not receive it at NPIC until Saturday or Sunday night, there was enough time to do the job. Lifton writes that "a technical team [could have been] working on the film by Friday night" because Zapruder, according to his widow, had turned over his film to government agents on the day of the assassination shortly after it was developed at Kodak in Dallas. This is contrary to the official story which has Zapruder holding onto his film until it was sold to *Life* on Saturday morning. Erwin Swartz, Zapruder's business partner, backed up the story of government agents having early access to the film. Swartz delivered two film canisters to the Dallas Naval Air Station on Friday.[79]

If it's true, then, that the government had its hands on the Zapruder film before it was sold to *Life* and locked away in *Life*'s vault, could the film alterations have been made quickly enough so that a "new original" could have been cobbled together in time to be developed at the CIA's Hawkeyeworks plant in Rochester before it was delivered to the National Photographic Interpretation Center on Sunday? Simple frame removal was all that was necessary to eliminate the limo stop on Elm Street, but a more elaborate process was needed to alter Kennedy's head wound to eliminate evidence of a shot from the front. How was this done?

Dr. John Costella, an expert in theoretical physics who applied advance computer techniques to the Zapruder film and concluded that the extant film is a fraud, writes that "glass painting," a common and simple form of film editing, could have been used to create the forward blood spray which appears in frame 313 of the film showing the impact of the head shot. Glass painting consists of painting images onto a piece of glass and then superimposing these images over an existing film to create a new composite image by running it through an optical printer. The new image is simply substituted for the original image. Costella writes that "this [forward] spray could not possibly be a real spray of bloody matter…it disappears within a frame, which violates the laws of physics.[80] Glass painting could also account for the moving, translucent blob which appears on the President's head in Z313 (and subsequent frames) and the suspicious dark shadow which blocks evidence of a rear exit wound on the back of the head. This would account for the discrepancies between what the film images display and what the Dallas doctors saw in Trauma Room One.

If Zapruder turned over his camera-original to the Secret Service on Friday, and the film was then flown by military transport to the CIA's Hawkeyeworks Lab in Rochester for alteration, our understanding of what the Z film shows and what roles certain key characters played in it must be reevaluated. While Zapruder himself may have told us partial truths, he did not tell us the whole truth, or he was duped by the Secret Service and other government officials. He turned over the film to Secret Service agent Forest Sorrels, but Sorrels might not have returned the camera-original and one copy to Zapruder on Friday. Instead Sorrels, under orders relating to national security, may have shipped the Z original to Hawkeyeworks for alteration. But this would mean that the copies returned to Zapruder were not of his film, and what he sold to *Life* magazine on Saturday was not the film he took the day before. Eventually, his camera-original would be returned to him, but only after it had been altered. It sounds like a complicated subterfuge for the plotters to undertake, but if there were images on the Z film that could not be revealed to the public (images indicative of Secret Service involvement and multiple Dealey Plaza shooters), then it would have been a necessary undertaking. An altered film, one showing wounds not seen by the Dallas doctors, would have, and did, undercut the testimony of the Dallas doctors. One more vital element to all this is that the Z film had to remain unslit by the Kodak lab in Dallas to accommodate alteration. As Lifton explains, "To alter the film, it was probably necessary to [enlarge] it to 16mm and more likely 35mm."[81] Only an unslit film could be enlarged; it was Dallas SS agent Forrest Sorrels who ordered Kodak to leave the film unslit.[82]

Was a "shell game" played with the Z film in order to create a false version of the assassination? Were there two films, only one an authentic one? The theme of doubles recurs throughout the assassination planning, execution and cover-up. As we shall see, there were two caskets, two sets of doctors who viewed the wounds, two Oswalds, two rifles found in the TSBD, two ambulances at Bethesda, and two of just about everything else crucial to our perception and understanding of JFK's murder. By employing this tactic, the plotters constructed a duality of purposes: confusion and confirmation. Those who saw the officially acceptable version of events (the evidence which suggests Oswald did it alone) could be used to discredit those who saw the officially unacceptable version of events (evidence of a conspiracy). It also gave the plotters a sort of weird flexibility to pick and choose the version which best suited their aims; if one construction proved unviable, there was always another which could serve as a fallback. Mostly, though, the altered evidence was manufactured to simply hide the authentic evidence. But for those who look closely enough, these twin falsifications, in the end, are just another indication of conspiracy.

Other CIA Agents in Dealey Plaza

In addition to Bernard Barker, Frank Sturgis and E. Howard Hunt, there were other CIA operatives who were seen in Dallas on 11/22/63.

David Sanchez Morales was a fearsomely vicious CIA asset. Part Native American and part Mexican, he played a part in many agency adventures, from the killing of Kennedy to the capture of Che Guevara. During Vietnam he took part in Operation Phoenix, a ruthless CIA assassination program which targeted suspected Viet Cong sympathizers. A prodigious drinker with a bad temper, Morales's reputation as a murderer was legendary in intelligence circles. According to his close friend Ruben Carbajal, Morales admitted being in on the plot to kill JFK as revenge for the Bay of Pigs.[83] Gaeton Fonzi, who investigated Morales for the House Select Committee on Assassinations, was convinced Morales was a

CIA killer who once bragged about taking care of that "son-of-a-bitch" Kennedy.[84] A man bearing a striking resemblance to Morales was photographed standing near the intersection of Houston and Elm as Kennedy's motorcade passed. Morales also fit the description of a man driving a getaway car just minutes later. Sheriff's Deputy Roger Craig described the driver of the vehicle as a "husky looking Latin, with dark, wavy hair."[85] (More on this incident later in this chapter.)

Gerry Patrick Hemming was a CIA mercenary who trained assassination teams in Florida in the early 1960s. A tall, imposing figure who talked tough and had the credentials of a paid hit man, Hemming claimed he was twice offered a contract to kill Kennedy—in 1962 by Guy Banister, an ex-FBI man who conducted intelligence and right-wing paramilitary operations in New Orleans; and in 1963 by wealthy Texans, including the son of H.L. Hunt, at the Dallas Petroleum Club.[86] Hemming turned down the contracts, but some researchers believe that he was involved in the planning and execution of the assassination. There is a photograph of a man who appears to be Hemming, or his identical twin, standing on a sidewalk near the presidential motorcade as it enters Dealey Plaza. He knew Oswald and interacted with CIA chiefs like David Atlee Phillips and James Angleton. He confessed to being aware of international assassin Jean Souetre's presence in Dallas. He even provided details of where the assassination teams positioned themselves in Dealey Plaza. Despite all this, Hemming claimed not to have participated in the assassination and that he was not in Dallas on 11/22/63.

James Powell was a special agent with the 112th military intelligence unit based in San Antonio, who just happened to be in Dealey Plaza on 11/22/63. Powell claimed he was off-duty at the time, but his actions indicate otherwise. His job, according to his own words, was to provide photographic surveillance of suspected spies or enemies of the U.S. government. He traveled to Dallas with his camera and took several photos of the presidential party at Love Field and Dealey Plaza. Despite not getting good photo opportunities at Love Field, Powell knew he would have a second chance at Dealey Plaza, so he hurried there and beat the motorcade to Elm Street.[87] (Due to the underpublication of the Houston-Elm detour, all people with foreknowledge of this route, especially intelligence agents, should have had their stories closely scrutinized.) There he snapped several photos, but only one would be widely published—a photo of the Texas School Book Depository immediately after the assassination. This photo revealed no sign of a human face or form on the fifth or sixth floor, in direct contradiction of other amateur photos which *did* show human form and movement around the time of the assassination. Was Powell's photo manipulated by intelligence operatives? Was that Powell's mission on 11/22/63—to provide a photograph of the TSBD that could later be used to prove that there were no other shooters besides Oswald in the TSBD? Powell actually entered the TSBD after taking his photo and was questioned by police. He showed his official identification to the officers, who apparently thought nothing of the fact that someone from military intelligence was roaming the TSBD just minutes after the President had been shot. If, as Powell claimed, he was not on duty that day, he went to a great deal of trouble just to see and photograph JFK. Since Powell was based in San Antonio, nearly 300 miles south of Dallas, he could have just stayed home and seen the President because *the President had just visited San Antonio the previous day*. It seems much more plausible that Powell was on some sort of intelligence assignment in Dallas.

Edward Lansdale, CIA provocateur, Army general and one of Allen Dulles's hand-picked favorites, was photographed in Dealey Plaza on 11/22/63. He appears as a civilian who just happens to be walking past the three tramps who were under "police arrest" shortly after the assassination. Lansdale was identified by two military officers who knew him well—Fletcher Prouty and Victor Krulak. In a

March 1985 letter from Krulak to Prouty, Krulak confirmed what Prouty suspected: Lansdale was the man who was photographed with the tramps. This excerpt from that letter addresses the tramp photos and the legitimacy of the cops escorting them: "The pictures—The two policemen are carrying shotguns, not rifles. Their caps are different (one a white chinstrap, one black). One has a Dallas police shoulder patch, one does not and their caps differ from that of another police officer in photo 4. Reasonable conclusion—they are either reservists or phonys [sic]. And, as you know, city cops don't have anything to do with Sheriff's offices. As to photo no. 1, That is indeed a picture of Ed Lansdale. The haircut, the stoop, the twisted left hand, the large class ring. It's Lansdale. What in the world was he doing there? Has anyone ever asked him and who was the photographer? Why did he take the pictures? What did he do with them?"[88]

The tramps are suspected of having been CIA assets (discussed at length in chapter 7). St. John Hunt was convinced that one of the tramps was his father, E. Howard Hunt. He told *Rolling Stone* writer Erik Hedegaard that the facial features of the rear tramp match his father's. "I've got a gut feeling, that [it's him]."[89] Others who have closely studied the photos agree. JFK researchers Michael Canfield and Alan Weberman measured the height of the tramp who resembled Hunt against the wall he passed. They concluded he was five feet, eight inches tall, exactly the height of Hunt.[90] The Hunt tramp also has an open-mouthed expression which is typical of Hunt in other verified photos of him.

(Many others, however, including dedicated lone-nutters, insist that the older tramp is not Hunt and is, in fact, a man named Chauncey Holt. Holt was a counterfeiter who specialized in making fake government IDs; he worked on special assignments for the Mafia and the CIA. He admitted to researchers that he was in Dallas on 11/22/63 where he claimed to have provided his fellow "tramps"—known killers Charles Rogers and Charles Harrelson—

with Secret Service credentials and guns with silencers.[91] Rogers and Harrelson are discussed at length later in this chapter.)

As for Lansdale, his involvement in CIA covert operations dates back to the post-World War II era. In 1954, Dulles enlisted Colonel Lansdale as part of a liaison detachment of five American officers that had been accepted by the French as part of a diplomatic mission to Vietnam. This so-called Saigon Military Mission was a cover for Lansdale's real operation—to install Ngo Dinh Diem, a Catholic, who had lived in exile in the U.S. and Belgium, as puppet president. As Fletcher Prouty wrote: "After an election campaign carefully orchestrated by the CIA and Lansdale, Diem became Prime Minister of South Vietnam in October 1954."[92] The CIA, with Lansdale pulling the strings, controlled Diem and managed to enlarge the Vietnamese conflict into a full-on civil war. It was the Dulleses who were behind it all. They were maniacal in their desire to wipe out Ho Chi Minh. The communist movement in southeast Asia posed an existential threat to the American hierarchy of capitalists. Though there was little reason to believe that a communist-run Vietnam could somehow diminish America's wealth and influence, the Dulleses and their clients were ever paranoid about leftist regimes across the globe. According to David Talbot, Nelson Rockefeller, "had long fretted about losing our property to nationalist movements overseas."[93] When it became apparent that the French would be defeated in Vietnam, President Eisenhower, a savvy military mind, absorbed the lesson that the West could not win a land war in southeast Asia. He told his National Security Council that he was "bitterly opposed" to U.S. involvement in Vietnam. But the Dulleses publicly contradicted Eisenhower. John Foster intended to "raise hell" against the communists.[94] That's how much power he and Allen possessed. That's who really ran American foreign policy.

After Kennedy's election, Allen Dulles and the joint chiefs pushed the new President hard on escalating American involvement in Vietnam. Kennedy compromised by sending 16,000 military advisors. The CIA saw this as a weak response to the growing menace presented by Ho. Diem was also a problem. Lansdale was supposed to "coach Diem to popularity and ultimately to victory over Ho."[95] But Diem the puppet turned out to be an unpopular and ineffectual leader in dealing with the threat posed by the communist North. When Diem was no longer useful to the CIA, it was Lansdale and the CIA's Lucein Conein who were called on by Vietnam Ambassador Henry Cabot Lodge to overthrow Diem. Lodge wanted Lansdale's expertise in coup d'etats.[96] JFK denied Lodge's request, but Diem was assassinated by the CIA anyway just three weeks before JFK himself was killed. It was Conein who arranged the coup.

So what was Lansdale doing in Dealey Plaza on 11/22/63? Was he the operation's overseer? Or was he just another dupe in a more elaborate intelligence game? There is reason to believe Lansdale may have been set up to take the fall if any government investigation got too close to the truth of Dallas. According to David Talbot, "CIA officials loathed Lansdale" for his participation in a Kennedy-inspired charade called Operation Mongoose; supposedly the Kennedy administration's genuine effort to remove Castro from power, Mongoose was really just a "grab bag of raids, propaganda tricks, and psychological war stunts."[97] They were meant to appease the right-wing hard-liners of the Pentagon and the CIA who wanted Castro overthrown. The Kennedys had no intention of invading Cuba; Mongoose was just for show. It was never an assassination program, and CIA insiders knew it. Richard Helms and William Harvey viewed Lansdale as someone who was collaborating with the enemy.

However, for his service to the Kennedys, Lansdale did not receive the compensation he wanted: the Vietnam ambassadorship. That went to Cabot Lodge. Reportedly, Lansdale was incensed by this snub and held a grudge against JFK. Then, for whatever reason, he resigned from the CIA on November 1, 1963, the very day of the Diem coup in Vietnam. So it is hard to say what his true motivations for being in Dallas were. One way or another, though, his presence, along with other CIA agents, points to a complex clandestine operation.

Lucien Conein was something of a legend in CIA circles. One of the original recruits into the OSS in the 1940s, Conein was assigned to southeast Asia when the Vietnamese fought French colonialists. Prouty claimed that Conein became a genius at planning the details of operational scenarios and that the "JFK assassination had all the complex marks of being an operation planned by Conein. Records exist that Conein was in Fort Worth on 21 November...and Dealey Plaza the next day to see his plan in action."[98] There is a clear James Altgens photo of Conein, or someone who looked just like him, standing at the corner of Main and Houston as the limo makes a right turn onto Houston, headed for Elm Street.

Conein was a busy man in November 1963. According to the *New York Times*, he "was the CIA's liaison between the American Ambassador [Lodge]...and the man through whom the United States gave the [South Vietnamese] generals tacit approvals [for] the assassination...of Diem."[99] But Lodge and Conein were not carrying out the wishes of JFK. It was Lodge who, on his own initiative, resisted and countermanded Kennedy's orders regarding a possible coup in South Vietnam. Kennedy ordered Lodge to speak to Conein and Diem's generals about alternatives to killing Diem. But Lodge and Conein refused.

Lodge and Conein were not admirers of JFK. Lodge bore a political and religious animus against Kennedy dating back to the 1950s when Kennedy, the upstart Irish Catholic defeated Lodge, the Protestant Boston Brahmin, in the 1952 Massachusetts Senate race. The family rivalry dated back to 1916 when Lodge's grandfather had defeated JFK's grandfather, Boston mayor "Honey Fitz" Fitzgerald, for the same Senate seat. For generations after, the Lodges had controlled Massachusetts politics, but that changed for good with Kennedy's victory. Since then, no Lodge has held public office in Massachusetts, and one Kennedy or another held onto that Senate seat until Ted Kennedy's death in 2009.

In 1963 Bobby Kennedy warned his brother that Lodge would suborn the President's agenda. RFK's prediction came true almost immediately. Lodge, for his part, must have taken great glee in embarrassing his old political rival. Kennedy, as he did throughout his presidency, tried in vain to appease Republicans with his appointments. It almost never worked; Lodge, in fact, according to one of his assistants, intended to use his appointment as a stepping stone to the Republican nomination for the 1964 presidential election.[100]

As for Conein, he hated JFK in the same way that all Dulles acolytes did—they viewed Kennedy a presidential interloper who was soft on communism and an enemy of the CIA's invisible empire.

Together Conein and Lodge, perhaps knowing that JFK's days were numbered, defied the President and gave the go-ahead to kill Diem. The South Vietnamese generals, having been informed that Kennedy was going to pull out of Vietnam entirely by 1965, saw the regime change as their only chance to win the war against the North before America left.[101] On November 1, just hours before the coup, Lodge lied to Diem by telling him there was nothing to worry about.[102] Later that day Diem was assassinated. When JFK received the news he was, according to Arthur Schlesinger, "somber and shaken"; he knew the CIA, through their emissaries Lodge and Conein, had arranged the murder against his wishes. As he had done after the Bay of Pigs, Kennedy told intimates that he needed "to do something about those bastards; they should be stripped of their exorbitant power."[103]

In his own way, Kennedy was aware of the storm that was coming. He was, in all likelihood, the source for incendiary quotes about the CIA which appeared in major East Coast newspapers in the early fall of 1963; his intent was probably to alert an oblivious public to the dangers the CIA posed to American democracy. Scripps-Howard reporter Richard Starnes wrote an article for the *Washington Daily News* which ran on October 2 under the headline, "Arrogant CIA Disobeys Orders in Viet Nam." In it, Starnes quotes a high U.S. official saying that "if the United States ever experiences a *Seven Days in May* (a reference to a popular early 1960s fictional book detailing the overthrow of a U.S. president), it will come from the CIA and not the Pentagon."[104] The following day Arthur Krock wrote a sort of corollary piece which ran in the *New York Times* and was less harsh on the CIA. Still, Krock quoted "a very high American official [Kennedy]" who compared the CIA's growth to a "malignancy...[and] was not sure even the White House could control...any longer."[105]

Less than a month later, Conein pulled off the CIA-connected murder of Diem. Just three weeks after that, Conein was, quite possibly, in Dallas to witness the demise of the CIA's public enemy number one. On 11/22/63 he (or his identical twin) was photographed with a self-serving smirk on his face as JFK's limo passes. Kennedy is looking straight ahead and does not notice the Conein lookalike staring directly at him. Less than a minute after this photo was taken, the fatal shots rang out. If Conein played a part in the execution, it was the second time in less than a month that he helped topple a head of state. As Neil Sheehan wrote in *A Bright Shining Lie*, "[Conein] had accomplished the act that is one of the highest professional aspirations for a [secret agent]—setting up a successful coup d'etat."[106]

The Shooters

It is this book's contention that each of the groups or individuals who wanted Kennedy dead had to provide their own assassin, in order that there would be mutually assured involvement, culpability and deniability. In other words, no group or individual could rat out the other because each of them had the goods on the other. They were all equally guilty, and this ensured mutual silence. Thus, LBJ, rogue CIA, Texas oilmen, the Joint Chiefs, and the Mafia (all deadly JFK enemies) hired their own gunmen for Dallas. This is not just speculation; there is hard evidence of assassins linked to each of the Kennedy-hating groups in Dealey Plaza on November 22, 1963. Let's start with Malcolm "Mac" Wallace, LBJ's personal killer. Wallace's long history of doing Johnson's dirty work is documented in chapter one. Wallace's fingerprint was found on a box in the Texas School Book Depository on the day of the assassination. The print, according to A. Nathan Darby, a fingerprint expert with international credentials, was a positive match to known Wallace prints.[107] There is no innocent explanation for this. At the time of the Kennedy assassination, Wallace worked for Ling-Temco-Vought; LTV, whose principal shareholder was Texas School Book Depository building owner D.H. Byrd, was granted a large Vietnam-era military contract during the Johnson presidency. As stated previously, Byrd was a close friend and financial supporter of LBJ. They were photographed together at a University of Texas football game.

There are those who believe, however, that the Wallace fingerprint lift was fraudulent. Joan Mellen, author of *Faustian Bargains*, a book about the relationship between Wallace and Lyndon Johnson, denigrates Darby's credentials and his match of Wallace's fingerprint. She tracked down her own expert who declared that the TSBD print was not a match to Wallace. Whether or not it is Wallace's fingerprint, Mellen and others who deny his presence in Dealey Plaza must overlook a mountain of circumstantial evidence which suggests Wallace executed contract killings for Johnson and that Johnson wanted Kennedy out of the way. One imagines that Mellen would be shocked to learn that Allen Dulles travelled to LBJ's ranch in the summer of 1963, that LBJ delayed the takeoff of

Air Force One from Love Field, and that LBJ appointed a whitewash commission which suppressed the truth of the assassination.
Mellen herself admits that Bobby Baker, a crooked LBJ intimate,
reportedly said that "[Kennedy] would never live out his term and
will die a violent death."[108] Yet Mellen concludes that there is no
hard evidence to indict Johnson in the murder of his predecessor.
It is as if her extensive research into Johnson has paralyzed her
analysis. In the end, *Faustian Bargains* is just a contorted effort to
defend LBJ against charges of collusion in the assassination. Mellen
finds nothing suspicious about Wallace's LTV employment at a
California factory or his absence from same on 11/22/63.[109] Only a
coincidence theorist wearing blinders could ascribe innocent over-
tones to such sinister connections. One imagines that Mellen could
wake up soaked on a camping trip and diligently try to prove that
it had not rained the night before. (More on Wallace later in this
chapter.)

Another killer in Dallas on the day of the assassination was international hitman Jean Souetre (mentioned previously in this chapter), who was attached to the OAS, or Organization de l'Armée
Secrétée, a right-wing extremist group opposed to French President
Charles de Gaulle. The OAS engaged in acts of terrorism and assassination and opposed France's policy to grant the African nation of
Algeria independence from French rule. Souetre was feared by
democratic governments around the world; they considered him a
ruthless killer who would assassinate any head of nation for the
right price. According to intelligence sources, Souetre might have
been part of an executive action team sent to Mexico City to assassinate de Gaulle in 1964.[110] There is evidence to indicate that Souetre met with E. Howard Hunt in the spring of 1963 in Madrid.
Madrid, at the time under the rule of fascist dictator Franco, was a
hotbed of extreme right-wing activity. Ostensibly Hunt was recruiting Souetre for the hit on JFK. Later that spring Souetre came to
the U.S. to visit General Edwin Walker just before Walker was

supposedly shot at by Lee Harvey Oswald.[111]

Instead of being expelled from the United States after the Kennedy assassination, Souetre should have been picked up and turned over to the FBI. The CIA, naturally, never shared its awareness of Souetre's movements in November 1963 with the Warren Commission. Even if it had, Allen Dulles, the de facto head of the Commission, would have certainly suppressed this information.

A known member of organized crime, Eugene Hale Brading, also known as Jim Braden, was arrested in Dealey Plaza shortly after the shooting of the President. But he was released just hours later. The day before the assassination he visited (along with Jack Ruby) the offices of Dallas oilman Haroldson Lafayette Hunt. On 11/22/63 Brading/Braden admitted to being in the Dal-Tex building on the same floor where Hunt Oil kept an office. The office was vacant at the time, and its west window looked out over the parade route. It was perfect vantage point from which a killer could have shot at JFK as the motorcade turned down Elm Street.

Some witnesses to the assassination said they heard shots come from the Dal-Tex building which housed the offices of Dallas Uranium and Oil, believed to be a front for Hunt's oil company.

The dual identity of Brading/Braden seemed to fool the FBI and the Dallas police who interviewed him subsequent to his mysterious appearance at the site of the assassination. It took CBS producer Peter Noyes to uncover the fact that Brading/Braden was "headquartered at the notorious La Costa Country Club, in San Diego County. To intelligence officers in Southern California, La Costa [was] considered a monument to organized crime."[112]

Some curious facts about La Costa need mention here. It was located just 20 miles south of Richard Nixon's San Clemente home. During the Watergate cover-up, John Dean and his cohorts met at La Costa to discuss strategy. It was financed by Jimmy Hoffa's Teamsters pension fund. Brading/Braden regularly mingled there with "...far-right industrialists and political leaders of that area...

JFK and the End of America

and Mafia" consorts.[113] Noyes reported that "[Braden] was a man of mystery who acquired huge sums of money without visible means of support."[114]

Another man who was arrested by police, and then was mysteriously released on November 22, was an Air Force marksman named Jack Lawrence. Lawrence used phony job references to obtain a job at a car dealership in Dallas a short time before the assassination. He did not sell a single car, and the day before the assassination he borrowed a company car for personal reasons. The next morning, 11/22/63, he did not show up for work, and did not return the car he had borrowed. About thirty minutes after the assassination he finally hurried into the dealership looking disheveled and sweaty. Reportedly, he vomited in the men's room. In his book *Crossfire* Jim Marrs writes, "...[Lawrence's] actions caused suspicions among his co-workers."[115] Some claim that the car he borrowed was eventually located in the parking lot behind the picket fence in Dealey Plaza. But when interviewed years later, Lawrence said that he did not park the car behind the picket fence on the grassy knoll. He abandoned it near the downtown YMCA where he was staying, just a couple blocks from Dealey Plaza. After the assassination, it became impossible to drive the car back to the dealership due to heavy traffic, so Lawrence got out and walked to the dealership just two blocks west of the plaza. Lawrence's excuse for missing work that morning was his ferocious hangover. He claimed he had gone on a drinking binge with some friends the night before, and had simply overslept on 11/22/63. He awoke when he heard four shots come from the direction of the plaza about a mile away; he immediately tried to drive to the dealership, but because of the snarled traffic he had to leave the car at Ervay and Main and walk to the dealership. Lawrence said that the anxiety of being late and the vigorous walk he took might have made him flush, but he did not rush into the bathroom and throw up.[116]

Despite his protestations, many things about Lawrence's story do not ring true. The likelihood that he heard four shots in a closed room nearly a mile from Dealey Plaza is quite remote. Distance and walls between himself and Elm Street make it difficult to believe he heard the shots. But why would he lie, and why would he suggest four shots when the official story called for only three? His excuse for abandoning the car seems flimsy too. Photographs taken shortly after the assassination show traffic flowing through Dealey Plaza, both westbound on Elm and eastbound on Main. Traffic in and out of the area was not shut down by the police until much later. And even if he were trapped in traffic, there were alternate routes to the dealership which he ignored. Logic dictates that, rather than leaving a company car in a tow zone, he could have simply driven around Dealey Plaza. Lawrence also seemed to show a lack of inquisitiveness about the shots themselves. It's odd that he was not curious about who would be firing a rifle in the vicinity of downtown on the day that the President of the United States rode through it.

Lawrence's account of his actions the night before the assassination are contradicted by Beverly Oliver, a Dealey Plaza witness, who claimed that she danced with Lawrence at the Cabana Hotel. She knew him by another name, but she also stated that Lawrence frequented Jack Ruby's Carousel Club.[117]

For all this, Lawrence's participation as a shooter is still suspect. If he actually fired a shot from behind the knoll, and then ran back to the dealership, where did he store his rifle? No rifles were found abandoned behind the picket fence or along the two blocks leading to the Downtown Lincoln-Mercury showroom. And a car matching the description of the dealership demonstrator was never seen in or around the parking lot behind the knoll. Lawrence insisted he got a ride back to his borrowed car by an Air Force colonel who also worked at the dealership. This colonel could vouch for the location of the car being Ervay and Main, and not Dealey Plaza, if only he could recall the colonel's name. Interestingly enough, Phil Willis, who was a witness to the assassination, was a retired Air

Force colonel who worked at Downtown Lincoln-Mercury.

The one guy who shot no one was the fall guy Lee Harvey Oswald. At the time of the assassination he was seen calmly sipping a Coke in the Texas School Book Depository's second-floor lunchroom.

Eyewitnesses

The large majority of eyewitnesses to JFK's murder said shots came from locations other than the Texas School Book Depository. Witnesses at the epicenter of the target area were especially specific in providing accounts which differed from other witnesses who weren't as close to the death limousine. People who were close to or forward of the limousine described hearing more shots from more directions. Dallas motorcycle cop Bobby Hargis, who was riding just feet to the left and rear of Kennedy's limo, was splattered by the President's blood, brain and skull at the moment of the head-shot impact. The direction of the debris from Kennedy's head indicated that the shot had originated from the front right of the motorcade and not the rear. Hargis reacted accordingly. He dismounted his motorcycle and ran up the grassy knoll towards the picket fence looking for a killer there.[118]

A.J. Millican, who had been standing in front of the concrete pergola in between the picket fence and the TSBD, said he heard as many as five shots come from the area right behind "the arcade between the bookstore and the underpass."[119]

Ed Hoffman, a young man who happened to have an aching tooth on 11/22/63, stopped on his way to the dentist to watch the motorcade on that Friday. Hoffman was a deaf mute whose eyesight was sharper than most because he had developed it to compensate for his lack of hearing. His view of Dealey Plaza was also unique— he pulled over on the shoulder of Stemmons Freeway, just west of the plaza, where he had an unobstructed view of the area behind the picket fence. In the moments before the assassination, he saw two men acting suspiciously. One was dressed in a blue suit, and the other was dressed as a railroad worker. As the President's limo traveled down Elm Street, Hoffman watched as "suit man" crouched behind the fence, quickly lifted a rifle, and fired it at the motorcade. A puff of smoke wafted out over the fence as "suit man" tossed the rifle to "railroad man." "Railroad man" hurriedly broke down the rifle, put it in a bag, and ran off towards the railroad tracks; "suit man" composed himself and walked casually along the fence line towards the walkway that led to the inner part of the plaza. "Suit man" was confronted by a Dallas cop who asked for identification; he reached into his coat pocket, produced his credentials, and the cop let him go.[120]

Hoffman was eager to tell his story to the police, but when the news broke that the lone assassin was Oswald, Hoffman's family urged him to keep quiet. They were fearful that Ed would be misunderstood by authorities (sign language experts were not commonly employed by police forces in 1963), and that he would be placing himself in danger by coming forward to contradict the official government story. The most forceful warning to keep quiet came from Hoffman's uncle who was a detective lieutenant on the Dallas Police force. Thus Hoffman did not divulge what he had seen on 11/22/63 until 1967 when he contacted the Dallas FBI office. The agent who interviewed Hoffman offered him a bribe for his silence. Later, his own family members, in an attempt to protect Hoffman, convinced authorities that Ed was prone to exaggeration and his communication could easily be misinterpreted by those not versed in sign language interpretation.[121] Nonetheless, Hoffman stuck to his story for the rest of his life.

Other witnesses spoke of phony law enforcement and government agents in Dealey Plaza. Malcolm Summers ran up the grassy knoll after the shooting and was "…stopped by a man in a suit and he had an overcoat over his arm. I saw a gun under that overcoat."[122] The man with the gun warned Summers that he might get shot or killed if he proceeded any farther.

Jean Hill, standing on the grass just feet from the President's limo, saw a "…muzzle flash, a puff of smoke, and the shadowy figure of a man holding a rifle, barely visible above the wooden fence at the top of the knoll."[123] Hill was so certain that the shots came from in front of the motorcade that she searched behind the picket fence for a killer. What she saw there was a single uniformed policeman who "seemed to be guarding something"; the policeman was holding a rifle in his hand.[124] Just then, two men in plain clothes accosted Hill and identified themselves as Secret Service agents. One warned her to "be still if she knew what was good for her"; the other swiped Polaroid photos of the assassination from her pocket.[125] She was holding the photos for her friend Mary Moorman who had accompanied Hill to Dealey Plaza. Moorman had taken the pictures as the President had been shot, and she might have captured on film the shooter whose bullet hit JFK in the head.

One of Moorman's photos shows the image of what appears to be an assassin above the grassy knoll. The man's head and upper body are barely visible in the shadows behind the picket fence about five feet west of the corner of the fence. This assassin's position was verified by the House Select Committee on Assassinations using a sophisticated computerized analysis made of sound impulses in the late 1970s. Quite by accident, a Dallas police dictabelt recording of the assassination was made when a motorcycle cop left his microphone open during the Dealey Plaza shooting. The HSCA employed an acoustical scientist to convert the recording to digitized wave forms or impulses. The scientist filtered out unwanted noises and was able to identify six impulses which coincided with the gunfire in Dealey Plaza.[126] Professor Mark Weiss of Queens College in New York then used the impulses to locate the origins of the shots. He tracked one of the shots to an area behind the picket fence at a point precisely where Moorman's photo captured the shadowy figure.[127]

But photographic certainty of an assassin behind the fence might have vanished when Moorman's other photos were stolen by Jean Hill's "abductors." Hill was roughly escorted by the phony Secret Service agents across the street to the Dallas County Criminal Courts building. On the third floor of the building she was turned over to unidentified interrogators who had apparently watched the assassination from their window which faced Elm Street; they knew what actions Hill had taken during and immediately after the assassination. Hill's answers to questions about the number and origin of shots did not please her interrogators. She told them she heard more than three shots.[128]

In the years following the assassination, government agents followed Hill everywhere and conducted round-the-clock surveillance on her residence. Dallas FBI agent Gordon Shanklin insisted it was for her own protection, but protection from whom or what? The only people who were threatening and harassing her were the same government cabal of which Shanklin was a part. For a significant segment of her adult life, Hill was persecuted by federal agents who tried to break her down and get her to change her story.[129]

Hill's boyfriend, Dallas motorcycle cop J.B. Marshall, also witnessed the assassination. He was riding to the rear of the death limo, and he later told Hill that there were two assassins firing from in front of the motorcade. He heard what he thought were as many as six shots.[130] According to Marshall, for months after the assassination, Dallas motorcycle cops who were part of the President's motorcade were harassed by government agents who went through their personal stuff in police lockers. They dug up dirt on the cops to compromise their integrity. Marshall felt that the feds believed that someone in the Dallas police department was in on the assassination, or that they wanted the Dallas cops to keep their mouths shut about what they saw on 11/22/63. Marshall came to believe that the FBI or CIA wanted to eliminate Kennedy because he was too liberal.[131] Eyewitness Hugh Betzner said, "It looked like the

President's car was stopped...I saw what looked like a firecracker going off *in* the President's car...and a man in either the President's car or another car pulling out what looked like a rifle...[I] also observed what appeared to be a [gun] in someone's hand somewhere in the President's car."[132] J.C. Price, who had a panoramic view of the motorcade from his perch atop the Terminal Annex building on the south side of Dealey Plaza, said the shots came from behind the wooden fence on the grassy knoll where it joins the triple overpass. After the shots, he saw a man running toward the railroad tracks behind the fence. The man was holding something in his hand.[133]

James Simmons, a Union Terminal employee on 11/22/63, was standing on the railroad overpass when he witnessed the shooting. He heard shots from the area of the grassy knoll and a puff of smoke wafting through the trees; his fellow employees—Nolan Potter, Richard Dodd and Clemon Johnson—also saw smoke coming from behind the picket fence.[134] An NBC cameraman named Dave Weigman captured an image of this smoke in one clear frame of a film he shot in Dealey Plaza.[135] Billy Lovelady, who said he was seated on the front steps of the TSBD when the motorcade drove by, said, "The shots came from that concrete little deal on that knoll...I did not believe at any time that the shots came from the Texas School Book Depository."[136] Lovelady's presence at the site of the shooting is significant for another reason: he bore a strong resemblance to his fellow TSBD employee Lee Harvey Oswald. Both men had thinning hairlines, were of similar height and weight, and had similar facial features. Co-workers sometimes confused one for the other. And many researchers who have looked long and hard at the James Altgens photo of the assassination have raised doubts about the identification of Lovelady in the background of the photo. The man appears to be Oswald; he is standing on the west side of the TSBD's front steps. Naturally, if Oswald was standing on the front steps of the building at the time of the shooting, he could not have been an assassin. Of course, the Warren Commission claimed the man was, in fact, Lovelady. The problem with the Commission's claim is that Oswald was dressed like the man in the photo, and Lovelady was not. Oswald wore a solid, mottled, long-sleeved shirt with a white tee shirt underneath. What Lovelady wore that day has been in dispute for over half of a century. A documentary called "The Day Kennedy Died," which aired around the 50th anniversary of the assassination, has cleared up the matter once and for all. At about one hour into the documentary there is a brief shot of Lovelady seated in an office in the Dallas police headquarters as Oswald is escorted past him. Lovelady is wearing a checkered, plaid shirt which bears no resemblance to what the man on the TSBD steps wore as depicted in the Altgens photo.[137] Unless Lovelady changed clothes between 12:30 p.m., when he witnessed the assassination, and 2:15 p.m., when he was being questioned by police, the man in the Altgens photo is not Lovelady. If, instead, it is Oswald, then the theory that Oswald shot Kennedy can be entirely discarded.

Emmett Hudson, the Dealey Plaza groundskeeper, was standing on the steps leading from the Elm Street sidewalk up to the picket fence on the grassy knoll at the time of the shooting. Hudson told the Warren Commission that, "The shots I heard definitely came from behind and above me."[138] WC counsel Wesley Liebeler twisted Hudson's words and coerced him into saying that "above and behind" fit with the shots from the TSBD. But clearly, from where Hudson was standing, "above and behind" meant the picket fence on the grassy knoll. Victoria Adams, an employee of Scott-Foresman and Company, which had its office in the Texas School Book Depository, watched the motorcade from the fourth floor of the building, just two floors below Oswald's supposed sniper's nest. Adams told the FBI that the shots came from the area of the grassy knoll; Mrs. Alvin Hopson, standing on the same floor said, "It did not sound like the shots were coming from my building…[it sounded like firecrackers] had been set off on the street below."[139]

Conspiracy Ballistics

The best evidence for multiple shooters in Dealey Plaza has long been overlooked by investigators, perhaps because it is so obvious that it does not even register. It is simply this: The bullets which struck Kennedy had radically different impacts on his body. This is not what would be expected with multiple bullets fired from the same gun. In other words, the two confirmed hits to Kennedy (though it is quite possible there were more) indicate, from the damage each caused, that they were fired from separate weapons using unalike ammo; to wit, the throat wound was a neat, clean entry from the front caused by a bullet which did not exit the body, but the fatal head wound blew out the back of the President's head and left a jagged, blasted-out wound. Lone-nutters would object to this line of reasoning by claiming that the neck wound was a wound of exit, not entrance. But even in their unlikely scenario, the two bullets which struck Kennedy behaved very differently too.

Let us, for a moment, suspend reality and give credence to the magic-bullet theory of the case. This bullet, supposedly fired from Oswald's Mannlicher-Carcano, passed through flesh and soft tissue, exited at a high enough rate of speed to enter another body where it pierced soft tissues and broke bones, and then came to rest *nearly intact*. (Again, this preposterous conclusion reached by the Warren Commission is cited here only to be used against itself.) But the second bullet did not exit intact; it exploded the President's head and fragmented into small particles. "That isn't how it works," according to ballistics expert Howard Donahue, "…you don't get one shot that goes through and one shot that blows up from the same gun and the same ammo."[140] This is definitive proof that at least two weapons were fired in Dealey Plaza, and it is most unlikely that the Mannlicher-Carcano was used to kill President Kennedy; its ammunition is inconsistent with Kennedy's head wound.[141]

Remember, also, it is quite likely that a third bullet strike, separate and apart from the hits on Kennedy, wounded John Connally, who insisted this was true until the day he died. Combined with the shot that nicked bystander James Tague, it adds up to at least four shots in Dealey Plaza, too many for the Oswald-did-it-alone hypothesis.

Further proof that Oswald was not the assassin can be found in the lack of ammunition he possessed. There were no bullets found in the Beckley rooming house, at the Paine residence, or on his person.[142] The only bullets or cartridges that were ever linked with Oswald's rifle were the ones found at the "sniper's nest" in the TSBD: three spent cartridges on the sixth floor and one live round still in the rifle. Furthermore, no prints were found on those three cartridges and one live round. This evidence alone would provide a jury with ample reasonable doubt about Oswald's guilt. How could Oswald have no ammunition for his weapon except for the rounds found at the TSBD? He was either very frugal with his bullets and counted every last one so that he would have just enough to kill the President, or he had nothing to do with buying ammunition for the Mannlicher-Carcano. There were only two stores within miles of Dallas which sold that type of ammo, and those store owners were certain Oswald had not purchased bullets from them.[143]

Consider also that Oswald, or someone impersonating him, was seen shooting a rifle at firing ranges in Dallas before 11/22/63. If this had been the real Oswald, one would expect him to have made some purchases of Mannlicher-Carcano ammo for practice use. And bullets are not purchased individually; they come in bulk packages. If a shooter were going to practice his accuracy in preparation for the murder of the century, he surely would have bought plenty of ammo and would not have been down to his last three or four bullets on the critical day. But Oswald had no bullets stored at work, at home, or on his person. The only reasonable conclusion to draw is that the real Oswald did not buy or possess bullets for the Mannlicher-Carcano. Did the plotters forget to tell Oswald or his impersonator to drop into a Dallas gun shop so one or the other could be seen purchasing ammo?

In addition to the lack of prints on the spent cartridges and live round, Oswald's prints were not found on the Mannlicher-Carcano when the Dallas police tested it. All of this tells us that Oswald did not fire the weapon.

Piece of Junk

Besides having a defective scope, the Mannlicher-Carcano was considered inferior even by the Italian army which called it "the gun that could not shoot straight." Aussie cop and private investigator Colin McLaren called the Mannlicher-Carcano "…a piece of junk; it was Army surplus; it was prone to jamming; the sights weren't aligned properly."[144] One of the flaws in the plotters' scheme was the choice of such a poor weapon. Its only purpose was to frame Oswald as the killer; no professional assassin intent on using it as an instrument of death would have willingly chosen it. However, it is probable that someone using the Mannlicher-Carcano, and firing from above and behind, did hit Connally with a shot that *did not* pass through Kennedy first. The likely shooter was either Malcolm "Mac" Wallace, LBJ's personal killer, or an Oswald lookalike. Photographs and films of the TSBD just prior to the assassination show at least two men at the windows of the sixth floor. Eyewitness accounts describe one of the men bearing a remarkable resemblance to Wallace. Richard Randolph Carr, who witnessed the assassination, described a heavyset man wearing horn-rimmed glasses and a tan jacket standing at the sixth floor window one minute before the shooting.[145] This description matches Mac Wallace. Carr saw two men, one of them the Wallace lookalike, running from the behind the TSBD after the shooting. The men got into a Rambler station wagon and sped north on Houston Street.[146] Carr testified to this at the New Orleans trial of Clay Shaw, accused by District Attorney Jim Garrison of being involved in the killing of JFK. For his trouble,

Carr and his family were intimidated and threatened by the Dallas police who ransacked his home and accused him of possessing stolen property. After the Garrison trial, Carr was attacked and stabbed by unknown assailants.[147]

Wallace's connections to Johnson were deep and undeniable, despite the fact that LBJ biographers have overlooked them. Wallace was a prominent Texan in his own right. In the 1940s he was president of the student association at the University of Texas at Austin. He was active in politics and campus affairs, and became well known for being a bright and thoughtful guy. After leaving UT he drifted to the East Coast and took a series of academic jobs; in the late '40s, with the help of Lyndon Johnson he secured a job with the Department of Agriculture in D.C. This appointment might have been payback for some favors that Wallace did for Johnson when Johnson stole the 1948 Texas Senatorial election.[148] The two may not have been formally introduced then, but Johnson was aware of Wallace's Texas background.

As stated in the first chapter, Wallace's notoriety became widespread in 1951 when, upon returning to Austin, he became embroiled in a love quadrangle involving his wife Mary Andre; golf pro Douglas Kinser; and Josepha Johnson, LBJ's alcoholic sister. Kinser had affairs with both Wallace's wife and Johnson's sister. Embarrassed and enraged by his wife's infidelities, and perhaps prompted by sinister political motives, Wallace murdered Kinser in cold blood in October of 1951. Despite being found guilty of first-degree murder, Wallace served no jail time. He was represented by two very able attorneys, Pike Shelton and John Cofer, whose clients included Lyndon Johnson himself. Johnson was also a close acquaintance of the prosecutor, Bob Long. Gun residue tests, witnesses and a bloody shirt placed Wallace at the scene. Without his influential connections, it is likely he would have been sentenced to a long stretch in prison. It is therefore legitimate to wonder if Johnson used his power to help Wallace beat a murder rap. Was Wallace then in Johnson's debt for the rest of his life, and did he perform his role on 11/22/63 at LBJ's behest?

The FBI claimed to have investigated the Kennedy assassination thoroughly, but overlooking evidence of Wallace's involvement was a telltale sign that the fix was in. Hoover was not about to expose the association between his good friend Johnson and a convicted murderer whose presence in Dealey Plaza on 11/22/63 is now a certainty. And it's not as if Hoover was unaware of Wallace. Out on bail before his 1952 murder trial, Wallace had written Hoover seeking assistance in his criminal defense.[149]

Several others might have been with Wallace during the shooting. At least three accomplices were named by Glen Sample and Mark Collom in their book, *The Men on the Sixth Floor*. Wallace and his accomplices were able to operate in relative privacy because the TSBD's sixth floor was under renovations at the time. New plywood flooring was being installed, and, because of this, TSBD employees avoided the sixth floor unless they had to be on it.[150] According to Sample and Collom, Wallace, Oswald (this had to be the fake Oswald because the real one was on the second floor) and two others—a spotter and a back-up—were on the sixth floor of the TSBD at the time of the shooting. It's possible that Wallace thought he was shooting at Ralph Yarborough, a man who was despised by Lyndon Johnson. Yarborough would have been riding in the death car had Johnson gotten his way. Johnson would have liked nothing better than to knock out two of his political nemeses in one stroke. LBJ had lobbied Kennedy just hours before the assassination to replace Connally with Yarborough in the presidential limousine. Kennedy refused, but Wallace might not have known that the final seating arrangements would put Connally in his rifle sights as the limo passed by the TSBD. Wallace and the Oswald lookalike fired in unison on the spotter's signal.[151] These were the first shots fired at JFK, and, because they were simultaneous, witnesses heard what they thought was just one shot. One rifle used was the Mannlicher-Carcano, and the other was likely the German Mauser found by Officer Gene Boone on the sixth floor.[152] Several other Dallas authorities identified the sixth-floor rifle as a Mauser, among them Constable Seymour Weitzman, District Attorney Henry Wade and Captain Will Fritz.[153] The Mannlicher-Carcano, however, was found on a lower floor of the TSBD, according to Frank Ellsworth federal ATF (Alcohol, Tobacco and Firearms) agent who just happened to be near the TSBD at the time of the shooting; he claimed he was allowed into the building at the same time Dallas police captain Will Fritz arrived. Ellsworth, who was not called to testify by the Warren Commission, found the Mannlicher-Carcano on the fourth floor.[154] This supports the contention of those who believe that the TSBD shooters stashed their weapons on the upper floors of the TSBD and then delayed their escape from the building until they could dissolve into the ensuing chaos. The German Mauser discovery somehow disappeared in the official record, but the Mannlicher-Carcano was used to link the patsy, the real Oswald, to the crime. Once it was planted at the sniper's nest in the TSBD it was easily traced back to Oswald through the paper trail he used to order it by mail. The planted bullet at Parkland, and fragments found in the death car, likely planted by the Secret Service, were also used to frame the designated fall guy.

Lone-nutters dismiss reports of a German Mauser rifle being found in the TSBD as nonsense. They say it was simply mistaken for the Mannlicher-Carcano, the only rifle which was present in the TSBD. But the German Mauser was identified by men who were quite familiar with rifles and their dissimilarities. And if there were two men with two different rifles shooting from the TSBD, naturally two rifles would be found. The shooters could not very well have taken the rifles with them when they left the building; they would have been easily spotted. So they simply left the rifles in the TSBD. This was a problem the plotters had to deal with later, and, sure enough, the Mauser quickly disappeared because it contradicted the lone-gunman scenario. Sometime between the discovery of the weapon and the moment it was logged into evidence by Dallas police Lieutenant J.C. Day it became a Mannlicher-Carcano.[155] The Mauser had vanished.

At the heart of the mystery surrounding the rifles is this question: if Oswald was not part of the plot to kill JFK, why did he bring the rifle to the Book Depository, if, indeed, he did bring the rifle with him? If he did not bring it to the TSBD on 11/22/63, who did? The Mannlicher-Carcano, after all, was the rifle Oswald had purchased earlier in 1963. And Wesley Buell Frazier, who gave Oswald a ride to work on 11/22/63, said Oswald was carrying a long object wrapped in a paper package. Frazier has always insisted that Oswald told him the package contained curtain rods. Oswald, when asked, vehemently denied this. A CIA technical analyst named George O'Toole, who wrote a book about his use of the Psychological Stress Evaluator to research the assassination, offered an explanation for the discrepancy. Oswald, he theorized, thought he was merely selling the gun to someone at the Book Depository. The buyer was a fellow employee, either Frazier himself or another co-worker. O'Toole performed a PSE test (which works much like a lie detector but analyzes voice stress and not body stress) on recordings of Frazier, and it indicated deception when Frazier was asked about the "curtain rod" story. Frazier, according to O'Toole, might have concocted the "curtain rod" story to avoid having suspicion deflected towards himself.[156] But there is evidence that Frazier played a role in convincing Oswald to bring his Mannlicher-Carcano to the TSBD.

When arrested, Oswald had $13 on him, just about the price he would have gotten for selling the Mannlicher-Carcano. Was Oswald prompted to bring his rifle to work on 11/22/63 by Frazier's promise to buy it? Was Frazier lured into buying Oswald's rifle by one of the plotters? If true, this would have been a clever ruse by which to induce Oswald to bring his weapon to the murder scene so that he could be unwittingly framed for the crime. Frazier, just 19 years old at the time, would have been merely a dupe, unaware that he was assisting the plotters. Possibly fearing for his life, Frazier never divulged who approached him to buy Oswald's rifle, nor did he reveal how he came up with the "curtain rod" story.

At one point, it is quite probable that Dallas police captain Will Fritz bought into the theory that Frazier and Oswald were in cahoots. He had Frazier arrested late at night on November 22. Here, in Frazier's own words, is how that interrogation went: "[Fritz] thought I was guilty, so he had someone type up a statement. He said, 'Sign this.' It said I was involved in the assassination of President John F. Kennedy. I said, 'I'm not signing this. This is ridiculous.' He drew his hand back to hit me. I put my arm up to block...he got so mad that he grabbed the paper and pen and stomped out."[157]

When O'Toole put Oswald's words to the PSE test, he concluded that Oswald was telling the truth when he denied involvement in the assassination. When a reporter asked Oswald in Dallas police headquarters if he had shot the President, Oswald responded, "I didn't shoot anybody, no sir." His voice indicated "almost no stress at all," meaning that he was telling the truth according to O'Toole's PSE evaluation.[158] Verification of Oswald's veracity came from an Army intelligence officer named Rusty Hitchcock; highly trained in the methods and analysis of polygraphic sciences, Hitchcock also concluded that Oswald was telling the truth.[159]

Two Oswalds on the Move

The key to unraveling much of the mystery of the assassination lies in following the movements of the two Oswalds after the shots were fired in Dealey Plaza. To help alleviate confusion, it is necessary to distinguish between the two. For our purposes, the Oswald who worked as a stock clerk at the Texas School Book Depository will be referred to as the First Oswald. The Second Oswald will be the impostor. It is crucial to discern whether or not one of the Oswalds crossed paths with Dallas patrolman J.D. Tippit, and, if so, did one of them murder Tippit? For many, the killing of JFK and Tippit are intrinsically linked, but few understand how the two crimes are actually related. Clarity comes only from tracing the Oswalds' movements away from Dealey Plaza.

The First Oswald, the one we know as Lee Harvey, was not on the sixth floor of the TSBD at the time the shots were fired. It is simply not possible (see testimony of Victoria Adams below). The Second Oswald, however, *was* on the sixth floor, along with Malcolm Wallace. They did not rush to leave the building after the assassination; they lingered for a few minutes to assess the damage they had done.[160] The First Oswald was on the second floor lunchroom getting a Coke just a minute or two after the shots were fired. We know this because Officer Marion Baker and TSBD superintendent Roy Truly encountered the First Oswald there.

The First Oswald then left the building within minutes of the assassination. He walked east on Elm Street for several blocks before boarding a city bus that traveled west on Elm, *back towards the scene of the crime*. What sort of killer flees *towards* converging law enforcement instead of away from it? Just as odd, Oswald boarded a bus that he had never before taken; normally he rode home from work on the Beckley bus which dropped him near his residence, but on 11/22/63 he boarded the Marsalis bus.[161] The route of the Marsalis bus would not have taken Oswald nearer than a mile from his rooming house, but it would have passed right by the filling station where Officer J.D. Tippit was known to be sitting in his squad car at about 12:45 p.m. In fact, there was a bus stop right across the street from Tippit's patrol car, and Oswald needed to exit the bus there if he wanted to get within reasonable walking distance of his residence. Was the First Oswald attempting to meet up with Tippit? Or was it a trap to lure Oswald into being gunned down and silenced forever? The timing of this arranged Oswald-Tippit confrontation coincides with the first report of Oswald being wanted as a suspect in the killing of the President. At 12:45 p.m. the Dallas police dispatcher broadcast Oswald's description over police radio channels, even though there was no cause at that early hour to suspect Oswald's involvement. The First and Second Oswalds left the TSBD before 12:45 p.m., but no law enforcement personnel had called in their physical descriptions or officially filed reports of their suspicious activities until after 12:45 p.m. The TSBD would not be sealed off for another 15 minutes; an employee headcount had not yet been performed. So why was Oswald's description broadcast to all units? Apparently because Tippit needed an excuse to gun down the patsy as he confronted him near the Marsalis bus stop in Oak Cliff. If Tippit had not been notified to be on the lookout for a white male fitting the description of Oswald, he would have had no reason to apprehend Oswald much less kill him.

As fate would have it, the Marsalis bus got stuck in the snarled traffic that was a residue of the chaos in Dealey Plaza, and the First Oswald got off four blocks shy of the TSBD. He requested a transfer from bus driver Cecil McWatters, and then walked several blocks south to the Greyhound Bus Terminal at Lamar and Jackson. There he was easily within earshot of the blare of sirens just blocks away, yet the First Oswald did not attempt to flee the city by purchasing a ticket for a Greyhound bus which could have quickly and quietly removed him from the danger zone. If he were desperate to escape the crime scene, he was in the perfect spot to safely do so. He could have boarded any one of several buses leaving Dallas and been clear of the city, and beyond law enforcement's clutches, within minutes. Instead he chose to hail a cab driven by William Whaley and head back to his rooming house on Beckley Avenue. This is inexplicable behavior if the First Oswald had just killed the President. Not only did he choose to stay in the city, he returned to his residence and risked capture. It makes sense only if he did not, as he later insisted, shoot anyone, and had nothing to fear, or if he were carrying out some intelligence assignment and needed to meet his contact for further instructions. There is a third possibility. Perhaps the First Oswald was becoming aware that the plot he had infiltrated was turning on him, and that, in fact, he was its scapegoat. In this case, he would have sought out his handler and asked that he be brought in "from the cold," or, in other words, protected from those who would apprehend him for the crime. His subsequent actions support this supposition.

Some speculation as to the First Oswald's frame of mind or level of awareness might be useful here. What did he imagine his role was on 11/22/63? An acquaintance of Oswald named Tosh Plumlee, a CIA operative himself who was also in Dealey Plaza during the shooting, said Oswald was part of an "abort team," whose mission was to prevent the assassination.[162] Plumlee did not disclose how Oswald was supposed to do this, but if he's correct, it provides a plausible explanation for the First Oswald's movements after he left the assassination scene. It was dawning on Oswald that something had gone terribly wrong in Dealey Plaza, and that he might be the one fingered for the crime. He moved about deliberately and cautiously, trying to think on the fly of the best way to contact his handler without arousing police suspicion.

Logically then, the First Oswald requested that Whaley drop him a block away from his Beckley rooming house. He apparently was fearful that authorities were already waiting for him at his residence. Perhaps he now suspected that his scheduled meet-up with Tippit was a deadly ruse. When Oswald did not show at the filling station at the appointed time, Tippit took off for a local record shop where he used a public payphone. When he returned to his patrol car, Tippit had just enough time to drive to Oswald's rooming house on Beckley Avenue to try to lure out the patsy.

At 1 p.m. when Oswald saw no one in front of his residence, he entered quickly. He rushed past landlady Earlene Roberts without saying a word. He went to his room, got a jacket, and supposedly armed himself with a pistol, though Roberts, who regularly cleaned his small room, had never seen a pistol in any of his possessions. While Oswald was in his room, a Dallas cop car (presumably Tippit's) pulled alongside the residence and beeped the horn twice as if signaling Oswald. Exhaustive searches for the cop car have yielded little except that J.D. Tippit's was the only car known to have been in the area of Oswald's rooming house at the time.[163] Roberts stated the car's numbers contained a "1" and "0"; Tippit's patrol car was Number 10.[164] When Oswald exited the Beckley residence, the cop car had already left. Oswald walked to the corner bus stand, where soon would pass a bus headed in the *opposite direction of* the Tippit slaying. If the First Oswald had taken this bus, he could not have possibly murdered Tippit; the timeline would not have worked. But it is likely he did not board the bus, because an unused transfer, presumably the one McWatters gave him minutes earlier, was found in his pocket when he was arrested.

At this point, the timeline becomes critical in assessing whether or not the First Oswald shot Tippit. The First Oswald could not have been at the bus stop on Beckley earlier than 1:04 p.m., and Tippit could have been shot as early as 1:06 p.m. In fact, one witness to the crime, a Mrs. Donald Higgins, who said that the killer bore no resemblance to Oswald, placed the Tippit murder at *exactly* 1:06 p.m.[165] It is physically impossible to travel the distance, about one mile, from the Beckley rooming house to the Tippit murder scene on foot in just two minutes. Possible verification of Mrs. Higgins' story comes from T.F. Bowley who saw Tippit down and bleeding on East 10th street near Patton. Bowley looked at his watch and noted the time as 1:10 p.m.; since Tippit had already been shot, and several bystanders had already gathered, it can be presumed that Tippit's murder occurred several minutes earlier.[166]

The Warren Commission ignored this evidence and made up its own timeline to fit Oswald's presupposed guilt. Commissioners stretched the limits of logic and the clock to give Oswald more time to reach the Tippit murder scene. They claimed that Oswald walked from his rooming house at 1026 North Beckley to East 10th and Patton streets in time to shoot Tippit at approximately 1:16 p.m. Even if Oswald jogged part of the way he could not have made it in time. Moreover, the Warren Commission's assessment of Oswald's speed varied wildly in the journeys to and away from the Tippit murder site. The commission said Oswald covered the distance from Beckley to the Tippit murder in just 12 minutes. But it took him twice as long (24 minutes) to cover the distance (about a half-mile) from Tippit's murder to the Texas Theatre (where both Oswalds fled after Tippit had been shot). Why did it take twice as long for Oswald to travel half the distance, when presumably he would have been much more frantic to flee the scene of Tippit's murder than to arrive at it?

At the Tippit murder site, Oswald's wallet was found. But he was also carrying a wallet when he was arrested at the Texas Theater. Who carries two wallets around? And who leaves one at the scene of a murder he has just committed? The answer is, no one does. The wallet found at the Tippit murder was obviously a plant to incriminate the First Oswald. It was Dallas police Sergeant Kenneth Croy who allegedly turned over the wallet to Captain W.R. Westbrook, but no others—witnesses, policemen, emergency medical personnel or anyone else—at the scene actually saw a wallet lying in the street. Croy just happened to be the first officer at Tenth and Patton, arriving ten minutes before any other police arrived.[167]

Ballistics at the murder scene are another indication that the First Oswald was framed. He was arrested with a revolver in his possession, but the shells used to kill Tippit were from an automatic weapon. Sergeant Hill of the Dallas police verified that he saw the inscription of ".38 auto" on the spent cartridges; he also admitted getting on the police radio to report that his fellow officer had been killed by automatic weapon fire.[168] There is other evidence that indicates that two weapons were fired at Tippit. The killer or killers, whoever they were, tossed four cartridge cases—two made by Winchester-Western and two made by Remington-Peters—before fleeing the scene. But of the four bullets that struck Tippit, three were manufactured by Winchester-Western and the other by Remington-Peters. Moreover, Dallas police detective J.M. Poe, who insisted that he had marked the hulls with his initials, according to prescribed police regulations to maintain chain-of-evidence integrity, could not later positively identify his markings.[169] The dubious nature of this contradictory and confusing evidence should have, at the very least, cast doubt on the First Oswald's involvement in the Tippit killing; nonetheless, the Warren Commissioners, lone-nut troopers that they were, strained their necks looking beyond the messy details and "convicted" the First Oswald.

A more discerning look at the known movements of the two Oswalds makes it more likely that the Second Oswald was involved in Tippit's murder. The Second Oswald had the opportunity and means; the First Oswald did not. This is because the Second Oswald had a getaway car waiting to spirit him away from Dealey Plaza and into the Oak Cliff area where Tippit was waiting. While the First Oswald was cautiously wending his way back to his Beckley rooming house using various modes of transportation, the Second Oswald did not quickly flee the upper floors of the TSBD; as chaos unfolded in Dealey Plaza, he was perhaps waiting for the smoke to clear before making his very public escape. Knowing that he had confederates to help him avoid detection and that the First Oswald would soon be gunned down by Dallas police, the Second Oswald was not panicked. He did not run down the back steps immediately after the shooting. In fact, we know that neither of the two Oswalds ran down the steps from the sixth floor to the second floor immediately after the shooting, because of Victoria Adams' testimony. Adams witnessed the assassination from a window on the fourth floor of the TSBD with work colleagues. Immediately after the shots were fired they ran to the back steps and descended to the first floor. They would have collided with an escaping First Oswald if he had really shot the President and was hurrying to the TSBD lunchroom as the Warren Commission claimed. According to the Warren Commission timeline, Oswald had approximately 90 seconds to get from the sixth floor to the second floor for his encounter with Officer Marion Baker, the first Dallas cop inside the TSBD after the shooting. But Adams was on the steps in those same 90 seconds, and she did not see a frantic Oswald, or anyone else, running past her in a rush.[170]

We can surmise, then, that the men on the sixth floor, including the Second Oswald, lingered for a few minutes to plant the weapon and cartridges and make a sniper's nest after the assassination. They were seen by several witnesses including Lillian Mooneyham. In an FBI report dated 1/10/1964, Mooneyham, a court clerk who watched the motorcade and its aftermath from a judge's courtroom in an adjacent building, stated that she saw a man standing in the sixth floor window about five minutes after the shooting.[171] Several other witnesses reported seeing two men on the sixth floor. Arnold Rowland reported two men pacing back and forth about ten minutes after the assassination.[172] L. R. Terry, standing across the street from the TSBD, also saw two men in the southeast window.[173] A Dallas County jail inmate named John Powell, in his cell across the street from the TSBD, watched two men with guns on the sixth floor; one of them, probably Wallace, had dark skin.[174] Ruby Henderson, at street-level, noticed the same two men; one had a darker complexion than the other.[175] Neither of the men seen in the window could have been the First Oswald because he was in the second floor lunchroom at the time.

At about 12:40 p.m. the Second Oswald made his move. As stated previously, Roger Craig, a Dallas County Sheriff's Deputy, saw a man closely resembling Oswald fleeing the TSBD by hurrying down Elm Street and jumping into a waiting light-colored Nash

Rambler driven by a man who resembled CIA asset David Morales.[176] Craig was not alone; several other witnesses—including Helen Forrest, James Pennington, Marvin C. Robinson and Roy Cooper—saw the same thing.

Craig's keen observation tells us that at about the same time that the First Oswald was on the Marsalis bus stuck in downtown traffic, the Second Oswald was fleeing Dealey Plaza in a car driven by a getaway man. This uncomfortable fact caused great concern for the Warren Commission and the Dallas police, and it eventually ruined Craig's career. An honest and decorated cop, he stuck to his story until the day he died.

Craig also saw some suspicious goings-on before he saw the Second Oswald. He was on duty near Dealey Plaza when the shooting occurred. Upon hearing the shots, he ran towards the picket fence atop the grassy knoll and saw a woman trying to drive out of the parking lot behind the fence. He stopped the car, arrested the woman, and turned her over to another Dallas cop for questioning. Soon after, the woman vanished without a trace. The other cop offered no explanation for her disappearance, and there is no record of her arrest; Craig also noticed what appeared to be a sidewalk nick caused by a fresh-bullet strike on Elm Street—another indication that many more than three bullets were fired that day.[177]

Two other Dallas cops apparently noticed yet another bullet strike indicated by some turf uprooted on the south side of Elm near a sewer lid. Just minutes after the assassination, Officer J.W. Foster and Deputy Sheriff Buddy Walther were photographed bending over to inspect the ground near the alleged bullet strike. An unidentified man in a suit picked up an object from the grass and put it in his pocket. Walther and Foster showed deference to this man, indicating that he was probably a federal agent of some sort. The photographer who took the photo admitted that the lawmen were looking for "either bullets or…fragments of bullets." Decades later, researchers identified the man in the suit as FBI agent

Robert M. Barrett, but Barrett denied being the man in the photograph. Incredibly though, Barrett managed to be at the scene of every crucial event of 11/22/63. He was in Dealey Plaza around the time of the shooting; he was at the Tippit shooting scene; and he assisted in Oswald's apprehension at the Texas Theatre.[178] The day after the shooting, Barrett, according to a government memorandum, "made a crime scene search of the sixth floor" of the TSBD building. He was also involved in seizing or collecting various amateur films of the assassination. The FBI was contacted by the lawyer of at least one of these filmmakers, a man named Clyde Paschall, who claimed that the FBI did not return the original film to Paschall.

At about 2 p.m., when he heard that Oswald had been arrested, Craig hurried back to police headquarters to view the subject. He identified Oswald, the First Oswald, as the man he had seen running from the TSBD into the Rambler on Elm Street (though it was certainly the Second Oswald he actually saw). When the Dallas homicide chief, Captain Will Fritz, told Oswald that Craig saw him get into a car, Oswald responded, "That station wagon belongs to Mrs. Paine; don't try to drag her into this."[179] This response is telling in many ways:

One) The First Oswald who spoke these words was not the man who had jumped into the Rambler on Elm, so he could not have known whose car it was and that it was, in fact, a station wagon. He was not there.

Two) Why did he assume, then, that the car belonged to Ruth Paine? Did he suspect that Paine was somehow connected to the plot which had just ensnared him? Was he trying to protect Paine from law enforcement scrutiny because Paine was sheltering his wife Marina? As far as anyone knows, Paine's car was parked in her driveway in Irving that day, so Oswald's quick denial of her involvement in the getaway of his doppelganger was presumptuous.

Three) Why didn't Oswald immediately deny climbing into the

getaway car on Elm? He was several blocks away at the time. Surely he knew that the man Craig saw get into the Rambler was someone else who looked like him. Was he aware of the Second Oswald and trying to protect him? If so, why? Is it possible that the real Oswald assumed that the fake Oswald was his ticket out of trouble when push came to shove? In other words, maybe the real Oswald had been assured by his handlers that whatever trouble he got into on 11/22/63 would be blamed on his "twin" and that an "identity switch" would be made when the time was right. This ruse could have persuaded Oswald to keep quiet about the full extent of what he knew concerning the events surrounding the assassination. And despite moaning to cops that "Everyone will know who I am now," as if his twin cover had been blown,[180] he *did* keep silent about what he really knew until the very end. Even when dying after having been shot by Ruby, Oswald refused to confess to his role in the plot, whatever that might have been. Dallas cop James Leavelle told a mortally wounded Oswald, "Son, you're hurt real bad. If there's anything you want to tell me, now's the time"; Oswald hesitated for a few moments, and then slowly and firmly shook his head from side to side.[181] One would assume that if, as lone-nutters assert, Oswald killed Kennedy because he wanted to make a name for himself, he would have at least taken credit for the deed before he died.

Despite the fact that several witnesses in Dealey Plaza backed up Craig's story, his testimony to the Warren Commission on April 1, 1964, was not taken seriously by staffer David Belin. The idea of two Oswalds in the TSBD at the time of the shooting did not sit well with those who were trying to sell the lone-assassin story. When the report was published, Craig was appalled to learn that Belin had twisted his words and changed their impact. The Commission deemed him not credible, but Craig did not budge. For his integrity, he was hounded, threatened and attacked for the next 12 years. An honest, decorated cop before the assassination, Craig became a pariah after 11/22/63. He was fired from his job in 1967, survived several murder attempts in the 1970s, and finally died of a rifle shot in 1975, a death that was ruled a suicide.[182] Suicides by rifle fire are extremely rare because of the difficulty in manipulating such a weapon for shooting oneself. However, an alarming number of Kennedy assassination witnesses seem to have committed "suicide" with a rifle.

Craig's integrity cost him his life, but he advanced our knowledge of the elaborate deception involved in the conspiracy by chronicling with certainty that there were two Oswalds at the TSBD on 11/22/63; following their movements immediately after the assassination unmasks the deception. If we surmise that the real Oswald was supposed to meet his demise at the hands of J.D. Tippit when he got off the Marsalis bus, then we can assume that when the rendezvous was aborted the plotters had to improvise. When Oswald did not show up, Tippit rushed to a payphone in a nearby music store, Top Ten Records, presumably to contact his handler for instructions, but, according to the storeowners, after several unanswered rings on the other end, he put down the phone without saying a word.[183] Tippit's actions are suspicious for several reasons. His demeanor in the store was frantic and rushed, as if he had urgent business to conduct, yet he was patrolling an area of Dallas that was miles from the scene of the crime of the century. Every other available Dallas police car was converging on Dealey Plaza. Oak Cliff, furthermore, was a section of the city that Tippit did not normally patrol.

Perhaps the key to understanding Tippit's motivations lies in his precarious personal circumstances. He was a husband and father, and his wife was pregnant; concurrently, he was having an affair with a waitress who worked at a Dallas barbecue joint. There were rumors that Tippit wanted to divorce his wife and marry his girlfriend.[184] This could have been quite expensive for him. It's possible that Tippit's financial circumstances made him vulnerable to criminal corruption. For a tidy sum, he might have been persuaded to participate in the plot. As a bonus, he would become a national hero if he gunned down the man who presumably shot the President.

After his unsuccessful phone call at the Top Ten Record shop, Tippit proceeded to Oswald's Beckley residence and beeped his horn. Oswald did not immediately emerge, and Tippit must have assumed that he was not there so he drove away. Shortly past 1 p.m. Oswald emerged and walked to the bus stop across the street. Did Tippit circle back to Beckley, see Oswald waiting for the bus, and offer him a ride towards the Texas Theater? If so, why didn't Tippit kill Oswald then?

The more likely scenario is that Tippit was accompanied by the Second Oswald. Earlene Roberts saw two men in the cop car that honked twice outside Oswald's boarding house; she described both men as uniformed policemen.[185] But she may have just assumed that Tippit's companion was also a cop because he was inside a police car. And a man fitting Oswald's description was seen in Top Ten Records at about the time Tippit made his call.[186] (There is a possibility that the man who accompanied Tippit might have been Roscoe White who knew Oswald and bore a passing resemblance to him. Though not a real cop, White had access to a police uniform. See his story below.)

If the Second Oswald left Dealey Plaza in the Nash Rambler at about 12:40 p.m., he would have had plenty of time to catch up with Tippit at the filling station along the Marsalis route where Tippit was waiting to ambush the First Oswald. If this was so, then it is likely that the Second Oswald was used not just to frame the First Oswald, but also to lure him to his death. But what was the back-up plan of Tippit and the Second Oswald once the real Oswald escaped their net? When the First Oswald found a way to make it unharmed to the Texas Theatre, a secondary plan to kill him emerged on the fly.

After leaving Beckley, Tippit cruised around the Oak Cliff section of Dallas apparently looking for Oswald. Having missed his target twice within a span of less than thirty minutes, and having no further opportunities to kill the patsy, Tippit may have become more useful to the plotters as a sacrificial lamb. A murdered cop would make the rest of the Dallas police force more trigger-happy; Oswald the cop-killer would have been a marked man. If the First Oswald was indeed the fall guy, the plotters would have wanted him dead as soon as possible; if Tippit couldn't do it, someone else needed to before the patsy could be taken into custody. In addition, the plotters would have no more use for Tippit once he had missed his chance to eliminate the First Oswald; they would have wanted Tippit silenced, since he possessed knowledge that the First Oswald was the assassination scapegoat. This would have been motive enough for the Second Oswald to kill Tippit.

Sometime after 1 p.m., and before 1:16 p.m., Tippit encountered a man at East Tenth and Patton streets. The unknown man was seen leaning into the passenger window for a brief conversation. (The story of the pedestrian leaning into Tippit's passenger window is questionable because photos at the scene show that window was rolled up.) Tippit, apparently feeling safe enough to not draw his weapon, got out of the car and took two steps towards the front bumper when the killer opened fire. Was this man the Second Oswald? There is some evidence to indicate that he was. Several eyewitnesses described the shooter as a man who bore a resemblance to Oswald. The killer ran right by cab driver William Scoggins who identified the killer as Oswald.[187] But no one saw the man inside Tippit's car before the shooting (except for Earlene Roberts around 1 p.m. outside Oswald's rooming house). If we can believe the witness who saw the Second Oswald and Tippit at the Top Ten Records store just minutes before, it means that the Second Oswald must have gotten out of the car, and then for some reason Tippit drove up beside him to ask him a question. Reconnecting with a man who had just been a passenger in his patrol car would explain why Tippit was casual in his approach as he got out of his car. He did not have his gun drawn; thus, the Second Oswald easily got the drop on him and pumped several bullets into the unsuspecting Tippit.

But this theory of the Tippit shooting is contradicted by some witnesses who saw a second gunman, who did not fit the description of Oswald, fire at Tippit. Acquilla Clemons saw two men involved, one of whom was short and somewhat stocky.[188] Another Tippit witness was a man named Warren Reynolds; Reynolds swore that the killer was not Oswald.[189] Who this killer was and where he came from is hard to decipher. But the identity of one of Tippit's killers may have been revealed in a conversation overheard by a teenager who just happened to be in Dallas police headquarters after Oswald was arrested.

Mike Robinson, 14 years old on 11/22/63, witnessed the Kennedy motorcade with a friend of his whose father worked for the Dallas police. After the assassination, Robinson accompanied his friend to the police department right around the time that Oswald was arrested and brought in for interrogation. Robinson was in the basement locker room using a toilet stall when he overheard two cops in an intense conversation about the day's events. One cop chastised the other for shooting J.D. Tippit and for not shooting Oswald. Subsequently, Robinson identified one of the cops as Roscoe White.[190] There is other circumstantial evidence for pinning Tippit's murder on White. White, who bore a passing resemblance to Oswald, left a diary in which, according to his wife, he admitted murdering Tippit and claimed he was one of the gunmen who fired at JFK.[191] Since Tippit was seen in casual conversation with his killer right before the shots were fired and did not draw his police revolver when he got out of his patrol car, it is quite likely that Tippit knew his killer. Tippit and White were well acquainted, as they lived across the street from one another in Dallas.

Who was Roscoe White and what role did he play on 11/22/63? First of all, White was not a real cop, but he was a paid city employee in training to be a cop. So he had access to a police uniform, but he was not officially on assignment that day. In other words, he was free to roam the city pretending to be a Dallas policeman. (A policeman's uniform was reportedly found in the back seat of Tippit's car.) That would have been quite useful for cover purposes if he were carrying out some assignment for plotters. He had an intelligence background; incredibly, he served with Oswald at the Atsugi Air Base in Japan in the 1950s. In fact, he and Oswald arrived at Atsugi on the same Marine troopship in September of 1957. As clarified in a previous chapter, Atsugi was a CIA base where U.S. soldiers were trained in intelligence operations.

There is compelling evidence that places White in Dealey Plaza on 11/22/63. A Dealey Plaza witness, Beverly Oliver, ran up the grassy knoll after the shooting and saw Roscoe White near the picket fence area. He was dressed in the uniform of a Dallas cop.[192] This is not an identification to be sneered at. Oliver knew White well; she worked in Jack Ruby's nightclub, a place that also employed Geneva White, Roscoe's wife. Ruby's Carousel Club was often frequented by Roscoe White and other "real" Dallas officers. White's son Ricky also believed his dad played a role in the plot to kill JFK. On August 6, 1990, Ricky White held a press conference at which he presented evidence that his father Roscoe was the "grassy knoll" assassin. Supposedly, White fired the fatal shot at JFK and then hopped the fence to accost soldier Gordon Arnold, who, on leave from his unit, took a home movie of the assassination (see previous mention in this chapter).[193] This verifies Arnold's story of filming the assassination from in front of the picket fence and having his film stolen by a Dallas police officer after the shooting. But no photograph or film taken on 11/22/63 shows White or any other Dallas cop confronting Arnold (see chapter 7 for further discussion of Arnold's story). This does not mean the incident did not happen; we know that many photos and films were turned over to the authorities and then were either doctored, destroyed or never returned to the rightful owners (Oliver included). Still, Ricky White's account of his father's actions has come under attack by many researchers who now believe it was a publicity-seeking hoax meant to procure a lucrative book deal for White.

Regardless of Ricky White's intentions, no one disputes that Roscoe White and Lee Harvey Oswald were stationed at the same CIA base in the 1950s; in the early 1960s they both worked at Jaggers-Chiles-Stovall Company, a defense contractor in Dallas that performed classified mapping and photographic work (requiring security clearances) for the U.S. government; and they were both identified as being in Dealey Plaza on 11/22/63. This is either a coincidence of enormous, unfathomable proportions, or it is an indication that White and Oswald were both involved, at some level, in clandestine intelligence operations for the CIA and their activities were connected to the assassination of the President.

White died in a mysterious fire in 1971 (the same year that Mac Wallace died) that some believe was set by John Liggett.[194] Liggett, who served in the same Louisiana Civil Air Patrol unit as David Ferrie and Oswald, was a murderous mortician whose involvement in the Kennedy assassination is discussed at length in the next chapter.

Two Arrests at the Texas Theatre

If we presume that the Second Oswald was with Tippit and did, indeed, play a part in Tippit's murder, where was the First Oswald when all this was going on? Recall the timeline supplied by landlady Earlene Roberts—she last saw the First Oswald across the street from her boarding house at approximately 1:04 p.m. He was standing at a bus stop, but it is unlikely that he took the bus to the Texas Theatre. We know this for two reasons: 1) according to the Texas Theatre concession stand attendant Butch Burroughs, the First Oswald arrived at the theatre as early as 1:07 p.m., not enough time for Oswald to travel from his rooming house to the theatre on a bus; 2) the First Oswald had an unused bus transfer on his person when he was arrested. This means that the First Oswald must have been driven by car to the theatre, and, thus, it was impossible for him to have been Tippit's killer. Burroughs was certain that he sold popcorn to Oswald at 1:15 p.m., and then observed Oswald sit next to a pregnant lady despite the fact that there were over 800 empty seats in the theatre. Oswald moved from seat to seat, apparently looking for his intelligence contact. He waited a minute or two at each seat, and moved on when he it became clear to him that the person next to him was not his contact person.[195]

Meanwhile, the Second Oswald did not arrive at the Texas Theatre until approximately thirty minutes after the First Oswald was seen there. A shoe salesman named Johnny Brewer saw the Second Oswald sneak into the theatre at about 1:45 p.m.[196] Shortly thereafter, as if on cue, the Dallas police arrived and cautiously entered the theatre looking for a cop-killer and possibly a presidential assassin. The Second Oswald probably climbed the steps into the balcony, while the suspicious-acting First Oswald was below him on the main floor. The cops approached the First Oswald with guns drawn, but, miraculously, after a brief struggle, the First Oswald was not gunned down. The plotters must have cursed their bad luck to discover that the real Oswald had again escaped death. He was dragged into a Dallas police car and driven off just before 2 p.m. But this presented a problem. How should the Second Oswald leave the theatre? Witnesses saw the First Oswald being arrested and taken away at the front of the Texas Theatre, so the plotters were again forced to improvise. A second arrest was quickly arranged. The Second Oswald was apprehended at the back of the theatre a few minutes after the First Oswald had been taken away. A shopkeeper named Bernard Haire who worked just a few doors from the Texas Theatre witnessed the Second Oswald being put into a cop car in the alley behind the theatre. Who did this, and how was it staged so quickly? There are hints in the official record. Dallas police homicide reports indicate that Oswald was arrested in the *balcony* of the Texas Theatre. Detective L.D. Stringfellow reported the same thing to his superior.[197] This is a reliable sign that someone inside the Dallas police department was working with U.S. intelligence agencies to stage manage the assassination and its aftermath. If there were two Oswalds, there had to be two arrests to account for both of them being whisked away from the theatre. Immediately after the arrests, though, it was time for the Second Oswald to vanish. With the First Oswald in custody, it was unnecessary and dangerous to have the Second Oswald being sighted in Dallas. The First Oswald would have to be disposed of while in jail; the Second Oswald was no longer of any use. While the real Oswald was being driven to police headquarters, the fake Oswald was released by police a short distance from the Texas Theatre. However, the Second Oswald's evacuation from Dallas, like all other things in the complex but flawed plot, did not go smoothly.

Escape of the Second Oswald

The challenge that presented itself to the plotters was how to remove the Second Oswald from Dallas quickly and at minimum risk of exposure. Buses, trains and commercial airplanes were too public. An escape by automobile was slow and roadblocks were a potential hazard. A CIA plane was the best option, but where to find one in Oak Cliff? There was no obvious landing and take-off facilities. Love Field was, of course, not an option. Red Bird Airport, site of suspicious activity anyway, was miles away. The plotters needed a private airstrip, far from prying eyes, that was not an airstrip at all. What they came up with was a floodplain near the Trinity River. The Second Oswald was seen boarding a CIA plane there at approximately 3:30 p.m. on 11/22/63. Aboard that plane was an Air Force sergeant named Robert Vinson, who had quite innocently and accidentally hitched a ride aboard the C-54 transport at Andrews Air Force base in Washington. Vinson was trying to return to his place of employment at Ent Air Force base in Colorado where he worked for NORAD as a communications and electronics clerk. He had no idea that he had hopped onto a plane that was headed for Dallas and the secret evacuation of the Second Oswald.[198]

At 12:30 p.m. as the C-54 was somewhere over Nebraska, Vinson, who was alone on the plane except for the pilots, heard one of the pilots on a loudspeaker say, in a monotone, "The President was shot at 12:29"; immediately thereafter the plane made a dramatic turn south and headed for Dallas.[199] How was it possible for the two crew members on the plane to know that the President had been shot at the very instant that it happened? Ostensibly, no one outside of Dealey Plaza knew this fact until minutes later when Kennedy was carried into Parkland Hospital. The rest of America had no inkling of the shooting until it was broadcast over television a half-hour later. Because of phone overloads and downed circuits, some government officials had trouble getting the word. Only plot insiders who were in radio contact with CIA personnel could have transmitted the information instantaneously. The CIA plane on which Vinson was a passenger certainly had state-of-the art communication equipment and would have been in touch with whomever was running the plot. But who was running the plot and from where? A possibility is suggested by author David Talbot in his book *The Devil's Chessboard.*

Talbot tells us that Allen Dulles spent the entire weekend of November 22-24, 1963, at the CIA's secret facility at Camp Peary near Williamsburg, Virginia. Known colloquially as "The Farm" among agency insiders, Camp Peary "was a bustling clandestine center that Dulles himself had inaugurated soon after taking over as CIA chief."[200] What was Dulles doing there? If he were indeed monitoring and directing the plot in Dallas, The Farm would have been the perfect place to conduct his business. Its sophisticated operation and communication facilities would have allowed him to be in touch with his agents on the ground, and in the air, surrounding Dallas, Washington, D.C., and anywhere else the plot was unfolding in real time. Dan Hardaway, an investigator for the HSCA, said The Farm was just an alternative headquarters for Dulles from where he directed covert operations.[201]

The presence of Dulles at the Farm, commanding the covert operation which took President Kennedy's life, provides an explanation for how the plotters might have been able to improvise and coordinate so quickly. Having a high-level manager, or more likely a management team, at the controls, and in contact with military, intelligence and police officials on the ground could account for the alternate plans which developed immediately when original plans went awry. Thus, there were covert operatives in Dealey Plaza coercing, threatening and influencing eyewitnesses in Dealey Plaza within minutes after the assassination. Photos and films were confiscated. When five or six opportunities to kill the real Oswald were missed, new stage directions were promptly applied. The body switch, the autopsy controversy, the choice of a post-mortem hospital made on Air Force One, and the ambulance/casket mix-up at Bethesda all could have been byproducts of instantaneous shifts in plans directed by someone at The Farm.

Collins Radio

One of the companies that supplied the CIA with its advanced communications wizardry was accidentally exposed by the men who were picked up by the C-54 when it landed on the Trinity River floodplain late in the afternoon of 11/22/63. According to Vinson, two men boarded the plane as the engines were still running. One looked like a dead ringer for Oswald (Vinson would not make the connection to the President's assassin until he watched TV a day or two later), and the other was a tall, husky Latin man, perhaps David Morales. Without saying a word or even acknowledging Vinson, the two men took their seats, and the plane took off. It landed at Roswell Air Force Base (technically Walker AFB, but more commonly referred to as Roswell) in New Mexico that evening where, hurriedly, the pilots, the Second Oswald and the Latino exited without saying a word. Vinson was stranded, and had to make his way back home to Colorado on his own. There he saw the TV image of Oswald and swore to his wife it was the same man he had seen on the C-54 flight from Dallas.[202]

Why did it not bother the CIA operatives on the plane that Vinson, a man they didn't know and who was not associated with the plot in any way, was riding with them? In large CIA operations, compartmentalization of assignments is essential in providing plausible deniability. Agents operate on a need-to-know basis for their own protection and the protection of others. Thus, Vinson was protected from probing questions and suspicious looks. The others simply assumed he was part of the conspiracy; accordingly, he was left alone. Only later did the CIA realize that Vinson was a "security" risk.

After landing at Roswell, the Second Oswald vanished into the mists of history. But how did he get from the streets of Oak Cliff to the C-54 getaway plane on the Trinity River floodplain? This much we know—he was spotted in a 1961 red Falcon, license plate PP4537, at a Mexican restaurant's parking lot at about 2 p.m. while the other Oswald was on his way to jail. The license was registered to a Carl Amos Mather, an employee of Collins Radio. Founded by Arthur Collins, a man who had a close connection to famed polar explorer Commander Richard Byrd (who just happened to be the cousin of CAP founder and TSBD owner D.H. Byrd), Collins Radio was a CIA contractor that installed high-tech communications systems for the agency. Some research on Collins Radio reveals that it was employed by the Strategic Air Command, under the auspices of virulent Kennedy hater General Curtis LeMay; by the CIA for its foreign ventures in Guatemala and Cuba; and by NASA for its space flights. When Oswald returned to America from the Soviet Union, George DeMohrenschildt introduced Oswald to Collins executives with the idea of getting Oswald a job with the company. On 11/22/63 Collins headquarters was the relay station for all classified communications between the Pentagon, the White House, Air Force 1 and 2, and Andrews AFB. It is not a stretch to say that Collins was the hub of all classified and secret messages to and from plotters before, during and after the assassination.

If this is not stunning enough, consider this: Mather and his wife were close friends of Mr. and Mrs. J.D. Tippit; on the afternoon of the assassination Carl and Barbara Mather drove to the Tippit home to console Marie Tippit after her husband had been murdered.[203] The conspiratorial entanglements make the mind reel. To put it another way, how can lone-nutters offer an innocent explanation for these connections: to wit, J.D. Tippit, who was seen in the company of an Oswald lookalike (and in fact may have been murdered by same), was good friends with a CIA-connected communications expert in whose car the Second Oswald was seen less than an hour after Tippit's murder? Was it possible that Carl Mather was the CIA's emissary sent to console the widow Tippit because her husband was not supposed to die on 11/22/63? (Tippit's widow was not the only widow who received consolation from a Collins employee. Marina Oswald, Lee's widow, married Kenneth Porter, an ex-Collins employee, in 1965. That same year Marina accused Porter of slapping her and had him arrested by the Dallas police.)

The original plan appeared to call for Oswald dying at the hands of Tippit, not the other way around. When things went awry, perhaps Carl Mather felt the sting of regret because he had been the one who recruited Tippit into the plot. We do not know for certain, however, because when interviewed by the HSCA, Mather admitted to no wrongdoing and stated he was merely friends with Tippit; he denied ever owning a red Falcon.

What we do know for certain is that the Dallas police and

Collins Radio maintained a working partnership. The intelligence division of the Dallas PD planted an informant at Collins who spied on potential subversives and reported on security risks within the company. Left-leaning employees were ferreted out by the undercover cop and exposed to management. This cozy relationship between Collins and the Dallas PD could have evolved into personal and "business" relationships for other government projects like the one Mather and Tippit participated in on 11/22/63.

Mather spoke to the House Select Committee on March 28, 1978, only on condition of immunity from prosecution. Significantly, he did admit to personally wiring LBJ's Air Force 2 at Andrews AFB.[204] Apparently, though, it did not bother the HSCA that the man who benefited most from the assassination had a communication system installed in his plane by the best friend of the man who was supposedly shot by JFK's assassin. That's a lot of smoke, and it took considerable apathy to look past the fire. In the end, it was just another in a string of endless coincidences that would have made honest investigators froth at the mouth.

It was Dallas TV reporter, and eventual Dallas mayor, Wes Wise who brought the story of PP4537 to the attention of federal authorities. Wise was approached by Mack Pate, who owned a service garage in Oak Cliff. It was an employee of his named T.F. White who had made the identification of Oswald in the red Falcon; Pate verified White's identification of the car, parked in the lot of El Chico's restaurant, and the Oswald lookalike inside of it. White, an auto mechanic, had heard the sirens blaring up and down the street next to Pate's garage on 11/22/63, and with an alert eye he noticed the red Falcon parked at a strange angle across the street and went to investigate. He got within a few feet when he stared the Second Oswald straight in the eye, and later had no doubt he had seen the man who had been arrested for the President's murder. He wrote down the license plate number and told his boss about the incident. Pate decided to tell Wise, and Wise never forgot White and Pate and their collision with history. Later when elected mayor of Dallas, Wise preserved the TSBD and Dealey Plaza for future investigators.[205] As a TV newsman, Wise also did a little digging on his own. He met the Mathers for dinner one evening, and found Carl to be quite nervous and unable to eat his food. Mrs. Mather, on the contrary, was "very, very cool."[206]

For the plotters, the "civilian" encounters of the Second Oswald by Robert Vinson and T.F. White were serious kinks in the plan; nevertheless, with a sleeping media and compliant "investigations" on their side, the plotters had little to fear. The men who killed Kennedy must have anticipated that things would go wrong when so many moving parts were involved, but surely they were buoyed by the certainty that no matter how many witnesses saw things they were never meant to see, no matter how much the planting and handling of ballistic evidence got bungled, no matter how terribly the autopsy and body alteration got botched, no matter how many doctors, politicians, Secret Service, law enforcement and media personnel had to be co-opted, Lyndon Johnson, Allen Dulles, J. Edgar Hoover, Curtis LeMay, and the other co-conspirators knew they would come out on the winning side. With JFK dead, they held all the power. They controlled the government and all information disseminating therefrom. No real investigation would be conducted. No indictments would be brought against them. No one, not even Bobby Kennedy, had the power to prosecute the traitors as long as President Kennedy did not escape Dealey Plaza alive. The plotters were invincible; no higher authority existed after 11/22/63.

The Vinson/White incidents did not gain traction in the press and were buried among the clutter of a hundred thousand government documents on the JFK case. The plotters, in advance, expected slip-ups. The elasticity and, at times, sloppiness of the plot were not a deterrent. Witnesses could be wiped out, institutionalized or discredited. Disinformation could be spread through CIA-friendly media assets. Johnson headed off Texas and congressional investigations with his own hand-picked, rigged commission. The coup d'etat was complete when the phony report was issued, records were sealed, and participants were rewarded. More than fifty years on, we are still trying to unravel the mystery—the contradictions, inconsistencies and coincidences. This is what the plotters wanted: to create confusion; to weave such a tangled web that future investigators who discovered coffin switches and body doubles and Oswald lookalikes would come off looking like wild-eyed kooks.

Ruby Does the Job
Once the Oswald impersonator had been removed from public view, the plotters focused their attention on eliminating the real Oswald. Time was of the essence; the longer Oswald lived, the greater the chances he would reveal too much. Having missed several opportunities to kill Oswald in the immediate aftermath of the assassination, the plotters' choices were limited once Oswald was taken into custody. Few criminals die while in police protection. Killing Oswald in his jail cell deep in the bowels of the Dallas police headquarters would have been too suspicious. The cops would have been blamed, and talk of their complicity would have been rampant. It would have been one thing to kill an armed and dangerous Oswald fleeing from the Tippit murder or hiding in the Texas Theatre. Those incidents could have been explained away as self-defense; the cops would have been hailed as heroes. But it would have been quite another thing to murder a jailed and unarmed Oswald. The cops would have had a lot of explaining to do. No, an outsider, ostensibly unconnected to Oswald, needed to do the job. And it needed to be done in a very public way so that Americans could see for themselves who was responsible. The solution was a sleazy strip-joint owner who acted on his own.

Ruby was able to gain access to the city jail because he was well-known to the cops. For years he had plied them with free food and booze, and he had treated them as VIPs when they visited his strip club. Cops knew if they wanted to get laid, make a bet, or sip a free beer, Ruby was their guy. Many of Ruby's strippers ended up as wives or girlfriends of Dallas policemen. So Ruby's face was a familiar one at the city jail, and no one batted an eye when he showed up for Oswald viewings over the long weekend.

Still, Ruby was not the perfect choice; his Mafia connections were conspicuous, and it would take little effort to connect him to Santos Trafficante in Cuba in 1959 and H.L. Hunt in Dallas just the day before the assassination. But who else could they find on short notice? And who would be willing to do it? Perhaps Ruby was the back-up plan all along, and when Oswald made it to the jailhouse alive, Ruby started building his cover story. He told several people he didn't want poor Jackie Kennedy to have to make the trip to Dallas for a trial.

The slightest peek into Ruby's past indicates he was beholden to gangsters most of his life. In the year prior to the assassination he made phone calls to at least seven organized crime members who had been prosecuted by Bobby Kennedy and the Justice Department. A Ruby stripper with a stage name of Gail Raven told Jefferson Morley in August 2016 that "Ruby had no choice but to kill Oswald," implying that he was ordered to do so by his superiors in organized crime. Oh, and that "saving Jackie a trip to Dallas" story? An absolute lie, said Raven.[207]

Ruby's phone records also reveal that he made several calls to his friend Breck Wall on November 23. Wall, at the time, was in Galveston, Texas, with David Ferrie, CIA recruiter and puppet master in the Louisiana Civil Air Patrol.[208] Ferrie also worked as the private pilot of New Orleans mob king, Carlos Marcello. Dallas was part of Marcello's territory, and all organized crime activity conducted by Ruby or anyone other hood in Dallas came under Marcello's control. Ruby's calls on November 23 might have been an attempt to receive instructions from Marcello, relayed through

Ferrie and Wall, on how and where to eliminate Oswald.

Marcello, one of the most powerful gangsters in the country, had a special hatred for the Kennedys. In April 1961 he was apprehended by agents of Robert Kennedy's Justice Department, flown to Guatemala, and unceremoniously dumped there. He had been deported without warning and without having the chance to pack or notify his family. He was not a man to suffer these indignities meekly. For the next two years he groused angrily about getting revenge. He likened the Kennedys to a "stone in his shoe," and, referring to JFK's assassination, he remarked that if you cut off a dog's head (Jack's), the tail (Bobby) stops wagging.

Regardless of who gave the order to kill Oswald, Ruby could not have accomplished his task without inside help from the Dallas police. Ruby said as much himself—"...who else could have timed it so perfectly by seconds?...someone in the police department is guilty of giving the information as to when Lee Harvey Oswald was coming down."[209] Testifying to the Warren Commission, Ruby admitted that it was "...a million and one shot, that I should happen to be down there at that particular second when this man comes out of whatever it was—an elevator or whatever it was—all these things—plus the fact...that they saw us [Ruby and Oswald] together at the club..."[210]

Ruby's rambling, and sometimes incoherent, statements offered stark contradictions and a hodgepodge of tangential names and dates. Mixed in were conspiracy innuendos, alternating with his insistence that he was not part of any conspiracy. Taken as a whole, Ruby's words seem a desperate plea to Earl Warren, implying that his family was in danger and that he could only tell the truth in Washington under the protection of the federal government. When he was denied that protection, he reverted to his ludicrous cover story—he acted out of pity for Mrs. Kennedy, and killed Oswald without any forethought or malice. Ruby, perhaps tricked into believing that a plea of extreme emotional distress would get him

off, laid the groundwork for his defense by telling many acquaintances of being overly distraught before he shot Oswald. He even
went so far as to approach local broadcaster Wes Wise to pre-estab-
lish his phony rationale; Ruby lamented that it would be "terrible
for that little lady [Jackie]" to have to come to Dallas for a trial.
Sure enough, Wise was called as a defense witness at Ruby's trial to
testify about the accused's extreme emotional state before he gunned
down Oswald.[211]

Still in all, Ruby was doomed as soon as he pulled the trigger in
the city jail on Sunday morning. He couldn't refuse the plotters'
orders, and once he had done it he knew he was in a terrible spot.
If he divulged his real reason for killing Oswald, he knew he and
his family could be harmed by the plotters. He was trying to save
his own neck, but didn't know quite how to do it. He must have
been wondering how high in the government the plot went, and
was testing the waters with Warren. "I have been used for a purpose...you have a lost cause, Earl Warren. You don't stand a
chance," he told the head of the commission.[212]

Ruby's other lame attempt at proving that his shooting of Oswald
was impulsive, emotional and unconnected to a larger plot was the
money wire he sent to one of his strippers just minutes before the
assassination. Ruby shot Oswald at precisely 11:21 a.m.; just four
minutes prior to that, he stopped at the Western Union office about
a block from the Dallas jail, to wire $25 to Karen "Little Lynn"
Carlin, one of his nightclub performers. Supposedly Carlin called
Ruby earlier that morning and said she needed a quick loan for rent
and food. This was meant to provide Ruby a reason to be in the area
of the Oswald transfer. But according to Dallas reporter Bob Huffaker, Ruby told Carlin that he was headed downtown anyway.[213]
Why was Ruby headed downtown anyway? The only plausible
answer, given his penchant for being everywhere the action was that
weekend, is to be in the city jail basement for the Oswald transfer.

By informing Carlin that he was going to be downtown that

Sunday morning anyway, Ruby proved that his entrance into the jail at the exact moment Oswald appeared was not simply a weird coincidence. His admission of pre-planning destroys the lone-nutters' argument that if Ruby had pre-planned the killing of Oswald, he would not have risked stopping at a Western Union office for a transaction that could have held him up for several minutes, thus missing Oswald's transfer and the opportunity to kill him. In fact, Ruby's admission compels us to look at the timing of the Ruby-Oswald confrontation in quite a different way, one which is much more in line with the weekend's other events: namely, there were just too many coincidences to explain away. If the circumstances of Oswald's transfer from the city jail to the county jail were a set-up, arranged so that Ruby could silence Oswald once and for all, then it didn't really matter if Ruby arrived at 11:20 a.m. or 11:30 a.m. or midnight. Oswald's transfer was detained until Ruby was in place to shoot the prisoner in the Dallas police basement. In other words, it is much more logical and likely that the exquisite timing of the Ruby-Oswald confrontation was a product of planning than it was coincidence; because if it wasn't, then all we are left with are fortuitous happenstances to account for the timing, and that is one more overstuffed coincidence that is just too big to swallow. One Dallas officer, Elmer "Sonny" Boyd, later conceded that Ruby could not possibly have planned the murder by himself. [214]

The Warren Commission would have us believe that Ruby just happened to show up at the Western Union office on Main street, a short distance from the Dallas jail, just minutes before Oswald was moved; that Ruby just happened to be carrying his revolver in his jacket pocket, something he normally did not do; that Ruby, after sending his wire, a transaction which luckily did not last too long, just happened to wander down the street to the Dallas jail and easily find a way into the supposedly heavily guarded basement; that Ruby just happened to walk right into the perfect position to murder Oswald, whose transfer had fortunately been delayed just long enough for Ruby to appear on the scene; and that Oswald's bodyguards just happened to be inept and distracted. It is a ludicrous narrative, full of flukes and accidents. It makes sense only as the product of scrupulous pre-planning. Ruby's actions were purposeful, and Oswald was being held until his killer arrived.

This leads to the question, which Dallas officers aided Ruby? Researchers have zeroed in on several suspicious circumstances. Sergeant Patrick Dean was a close acquaintance of Ruby, and he was in charge of security for Oswald's transfer.[215] Dean could have quietly let Ruby in via an alley entrance in order to avoid Officer Roy Vaughn who was stationed at the main ramp. To his dying day, Vaughn swore that Ruby did not pass by him that day. If Vaughn told the truth, it is almost certain that Ruby was ushered into a side entrance by someone in the Dallas police department. Dean vehemently denied doing this; however, no less than Warren Commission counsel Burt Griffin doubted Dean's story. Griffin accused Dean of lying when Dean testified that Ruby had walked down the Main street ramp past Vaughn.[216]

If it's true that the Oswald transfer was delayed until Ruby's arrival, who was responsible for this and how was it justified? Chief Jesse Curry's actions may provide some clues. The timeline of the transfer was given flexibility by Curry; he told reporters that it would not happen before 10 a.m., but gave no specifics beyond that. Curry also rejected Sheriff Bill Decker's suggestion that they "abort the public transfer" and move Oswald early in the morning when no press would be there.[217] Ultimately the transfer of the prisoner was delayed when Curry received a phone call from Dallas mayor Earle Cabell.[218] If Curry had taken Decker's suggestions, or refused to linger on the phone with Cabell, the Ruby-Oswald confrontation would not have occurred as it did. A 2017 release of long-suppressed ARRB documents verifies that Earle Cabell, like his brother Charles (fired by JFK in 1962), was a CIA agent. He had a 201 personality file, and he signed his CIA secrecy agreement in October of 1956; for unknown reasons, these documents were considered irrelevant by ARRB overseer John Tunheim. Having now been outed, Cabell's activities on the weekend of the assassination warrant closer scrutiny. He oversaw some of the motorcade arrangements; he greeted the President at Love Field, and Cabell's wife presented Jackie with red flowers, not the customary Texas yellow roses which would have been garishly smeared by the bloody massacre Cabell knew was coming; and he distracted Chief Curry just long enough to allow Ruby time to plug the patsy in the basement of the Dallas jail. Were these his duties as a CIA operative on the weekend of 11/22/63? He certainly had motive, means and opportunity to aid and abet the plotters. And he was intricately intertwined with the other suspicious characters in Dallas.

But Ruby needed even more inside help to accomplish his mission. Even the HSCA stated that it was unlikely Ruby entered the basement without police help. In the minutes before Ruby's arrival, security guards were removed from the area where it is suspected Ruby entered the garage. There were also unlocked doors along that side of the building. The Dallas police withheld this information from the Warren Commission.

Getting Ruby to the kill zone at the exact right moment was only half the challenge. He needed an opening, and he got it from the casual formation arranged around the accused presidential assassin. Dallas police officers did not surround their prisoner as they should have. Officers James Leavelle and L.C. Graves, who escorted the prisoner, made no attempt to stop Ruby. Leavelle, in particular, gazing in another direction and positioning himself away from the crowd of people to Oswald's left, seemed to be unconcerned with his prisoner's safety until it was too late. Prior to escorting Oswald, Leavelle joked with his prisoner that he hoped any assassin would be a good shot. Minutes later, Oswald *was* shot. Was this just a spooky premonition? Leavelle used the copious TV cameras and photographers' flashes as his excuse; he was temporarily blinded by the light. Fair enough, but why were news reporters and cameramen allowed in the basement in the first place? Dallas police should have restricted the area to law enforcement only; as it was, the people who were permitted in were not required to show identification.

Leavelle's post-assassination activities raise alarms about his integrity. He intimidated witnesses and made up strange stories for his own purposes. He showed up one night at the home of assassination witness Victoria Adams and frightened her with his presence. Adams, recall, descended the stairs of the TSBD right after the shots were fired and insisted to the Warren Commission that she heard and saw no one on the steps of the TSBD at the very time Oswald, if he had fired shots from the sixth floor and then run down to the second floor, should have passed her on those steps. Leavelle told Adams that she needed to be re-interviewed because all the original witness statements had been lost in a fire. No report of any such fire exists.[219]

Later in life, Leavelle, exploiting his dubious role as the man who failed to protect the most important prisoner of the 20th century, became a mini-celebrity and toured the country spreading lies about the assassination. Even in his 90s Leavelle was earning speaker's fees and signing autographs for the gullible who attended his lectures. Capitalizing on the 50th anniversary of the assassination, Leavelle spoke to an uncritical crowd at Washburn University in 2013 and made these outrageous, unsubstantiated claims that were swallowed whole by the audience: 1) JFK's body showed no evidence of shots from the front; 2) Only three shots were fired and all three were fired by Oswald from behind; 3) No shots missed their mark.

My first thoughts were: 1) Does anyone teach history at the universities where Leavelle makes his speeches? 2) Who would pay 92-year-old Jim Leavelle, who failed at the most important task he ever had in his life, to spread his preposterous falsehoods? 3) What sort of real college students/journalists would let him get away with it? Leavelle said, "...the first shot struck Kennedy, the second shot struck Texas Governor John Connally, sitting in front of Kennedy, and the third hit Kennedy."[220] In other words, no shots missed their targets. This would certainly be news to bystander James Tague who was struck in the face by a piece of pavement dislodged by a shot that completely missed the limousine. And his fellow Dallas detective Roger Craig would have certainly refuted Leavelle's bullet count. Craig saw fresh metal marks on the Elm Street curb, indicative of a second missed shot. And Leavelle must have overlooked the widespread reports of bullets found by his fellow officers in the grass in Dealey Plaza. Apparently Jim considered himself an expert in medical evidence too. His assertion that there was no entrance wound is refuted by Parkland doctors. Leavelle also claimed that three tramps arrested a few blocks from the Kennedy shooting were just tramps travelling through Dallas. No mention of the fact that two of the tramps were identified as CIA killers Charles Rogers and Charles V. Harrelson. And he ignored the fact that the "policemen" who made the "arrest" let an interloper come between them and their "prisoners." The interloper was positively identified as Edward Lansdale, Air Force general and CIA officer who many believe was the operational manager on the ground in Dealey Plaza.

The bitter irony is that if Leavelle had done his job on November 24, 1963, we might have gotten much closer to the truth much sooner, possibly soon enough to actually round up the culprits. Through his own bungling, Leavelle ensured a long, secure life for himself, albeit one based on lies. When he let Ruby just walk right up and murder Oswald, he furthered the cause of the plotters, and rather than being chastised or punished for his incompetence, he went on to profit from it at the expense of the dead President.

Jack Ruby, the murderer Leavelle failed to see right in front of him, eventually came to understand that, like other dupes in the plot, he was doomed. His sponsors couldn't prevent his conviction, and Ruby, probably feeling abandoned by them, bitterly spurted the real truth before he died: "Everything pertaining to what's happening has never come to the surface. The world will never know the true facts, of what occurred, my motives. The people that had so much to gain and had such an ulterior motive for putting me in the position I'm in, will never let the true facts come above board to the world."[221]

Asked if these men were in very high positions, Ruby replied, "Yes."

Ruby appeared to be in good health until late 1966 when he suddenly came down with what was, at first, diagnosed as a common cold and then pneumonia. It turned out to be cancer, and within weeks Ruby was dead. Before he died, Ruby told others that he had been injected with cancer cells.[222] JFK researchers have focused their suspicions on Dr. Louis Jolyon West, a CIA psychiatrist who "examined" Ruby while Ruby was incarcerated. West studied the effects of sleep deprivation on brainwashing.[223] His work in MK-ULTRA, the super-secret CIA program that dealt with mind control on human subjects, is now a known fact. MK-ULTRA was responsible for the deaths of many innocent subjects. West's mere presence in Ruby's cell suggests that the CIA was invested in either brainwashing Ruby or silencing him permanently. Ruby died on January 3, 1967, but not before telling the world that a whole new kind of government was going to take over America. He was referring to a kind of fascist state where our leaders, having learned the lesson of Dallas, would be controlled by the military-intelligence state and a small group of the wealthiest businessmen in oil, finance and the war industry.

Oswald Reaches Out

Alone in the Dallas city jail, fully comprehending that he was the patsy in an elaborate scheme, Lee Harvey Oswald took a desperate measure. He tried to call a CIA intermediary whom he apparently hoped would rescue him by contacting his case officer. Two phone

numbers were handed to Dallas city hall switchboard operator Lou-
ise Swinney, both connected to men named John Hurt of Raleigh,
North Carolina. One of the Hurts, John David, had a military
intelligence background.[224] Swinney, probably under orders from
her superiors, pulled the plug on the call before it went through,
and then discarded the phone number into a waste basket. Her co-
worker, Alveeta Treon, fished the number out of the trash and made
a copy of it. The number was traced to John David Hurt, a special
agent with U.S. Army Counterintelligence. When tracked down,
Hurt denied knowing Oswald; he also claimed he had never been
contacted by Oswald and did not have any idea why Oswald would
have tried to contact him.[225] Some in intelligence believe Oswald
was calling his predesignated "cut-out," standard procedure for a
CIA agent who is in deep trouble. But why someone in North Carolina? One possible explanation is that The Office of Naval Intelligence ran a training center for double agents in Nag's Head, on
North Carolina's outer banks. This is where, in 1959, fake American
defectors were trained before being sent to the Soviet Union. And
we know Oswald received this type of training before his own journey to Russia. The CIA's Tosh Plumlee, confirmed that he had
received instruction in intelligence operations with Oswald at Nag's
Head.[226]

In the end, Oswald was something of a sympathetic character.
Caught up in the lethal machinations of the CIA, and not fully
comprehending his part in it until it was too late, Oswald should
be pitied for being duped the way he was. Intelligence work, no
matter how low-level it was, lifted him from an otherwise dreary
and unrewarding life. He seemingly took his work seriously and
believed he was acting as a patriot in the service of an agency that
turned out to be run by traitors. When he suspected that the plot
to kill the President was real, Oswald tried to warn his superiors.
They didn't listen. Less than twelve hours after trying, in vain, to
save his own neck by calling his cut-out, Oswald, framed for a

crime he didn't commit and abandoned by the CIA, was dead.

A Tale of Four Presidents in Dallas

Of all the circumstantial oddities of Dallas, the most interesting one might be the presence of four presidents, a sitting one and three future presidents, in or near Dealey Plaza on 11/22/63. Their confluence was not accidental. They each played a role, directly or indirectly in the tragic events. Another future president, Gerald Ford, though he was not in Dallas, served on the commission that covered up the truth. The lesson for the cynic who does not believe the synchronicity of Dallas was unintentional is that the powers who really run this country were picking their own presidents, manipulating them for their own purposes, and teaching them a lesson they should never forget. If it is hard to imagine that the United States was controlled by a small, quasi-fascist cabal in 1963 and beyond, consider this: In the half-century after Dallas, roughly half those years saw the White House occupied by a man, or his offspring, who had some insidious connection to the events of 11/22/63.

Lyndon Johnson's role as one of the chief plotters has been discussed at length. But what is not widely known beyond a small band of JFK researchers is that future Republican presidents Richard Nixon and George H.W. Bush (and quite possibly his son George W.) took part in activities that should be closely scrutinized.

Bush

Bush 41's connection to Dallas was revealed publicly for the first time when he was asked an innocent question around the time he ran for and won the presidency in 1988. A reporter asked him where he was on 11/22/63; Bush could not recall. For members of his WWII generation and Baby Boomers, it is a shared experience and common point of reference that they *all* remember where they were when they heard the news of Kennedy's assassination. In fact, George H.W. "Poppy" Bush is the first person I have ever heard of who could not recall where he was on 11/22/63. It later became apparent that there was good reason for his faulty memory.

Bush's extensive CIA contacts, including close ties to Allen Dulles, and his active role in covert CIA operations, have been detailed in chapter one. What has been assiduously hidden from public view is what he did on 11/22/63. At the time of the Kennedy assassination he was in Tyler, Texas, not far from Dallas, about to address a Kiwanis club meeting. Bush and his wife Barbara were traveling around Texas with friends Al and Doris Ulmer. According to author Russ Baker, Al Ulmer was a close confidant of Allen Dulles, and "embodied the attitude that nobody could tell the CIA what to do."[227] After hearing of the assassination, the Bushes, according to Barbara's own words, "flew back to Dallas."[228] If Barbara can remember where she was, why couldn't her husband?

The issue came up in a *San Francisco Examiner* article during the Bush campaign for the presidency. The article claimed that Bush called the FBI office a short time after the assassination to try and lay the blame on a man named James Parrott who supposedly had been talking of killing the President. Bush knew of Parrott because Parrott, a low-level Republican functionary, had worked on the Bush campaign when Poppy (the insider nickname for Bush 41) ran for office in Texas. Bush, at first, denied making the call, and then days later a Bush aide said that Bush did not remember making the call.[229] The problem for H.W. was that there was an FBI hard-copy record of the call. It read in part: "At 1:45 p.m. [on Nov. 22, 1963] Mr. George H.W. Bush, President of Zapata Off-shore Drilling Company, Houston, Texas...telephonically [stated] that he wanted to be kept confidential but wanted to furnish hearsay that...one JAMES PARROTT has been talking of killing the president when he comes to Houston." The FBI memo concludes with "Bush [stating] that he was proceeding to Dallas, Texas," but does not include the fact that Bush had actually been in Dallas the night before the assassination. This created the illusion, possibly intentionally, that he was outside Dallas both before and during the assassination. As for Parrott, he was nowhere near Dallas at the time of the assassination, and it is quite probable that Bush knew this. So why did he make the call? In spycraft it's called creating plausible deniability.

By calling the FBI an hour and fifteen minutes after Kennedy was shot, to point the finger at a former campaign worker of his, Bush was creating the appearance that he was genuinely trying to help track down JFK's killer, and, by making the phone call from Tyler, Texas, he placed himself miles away from the assassination scene; this call would forever contradict any witnesses who saw him in Dallas before or at the time of the assassination. (There is a photograph of a man who bears a remarkable resemblance to Bush in Dealey Plaza just hours after the assassination. The man, of same height, hairline and facial features as H.W., is standing near the front steps of the TSBD conferring with officials in plain clothes. Another photograph appears to show him standing next to Edward Lansdale near the sidewalk at the bottom of the grassy knoll.) The call established that not only was he outside of Dallas at the time of the crime but that he cared enough about rounding up JFK killers to point the finger at a suspect. In reality, he despised JFK. All the Bushes did. Prescott Bush, H.W.'s father, once wrote that he would never forgive JFK for firing his good friend Allen Dulles after the Bay of Pigs.[230]

Subsequent to the Parrott memo, Bush's carefully constructed deniability crumbled with the disclosure of another FBI memo, this one from J. Edgar Hoover to the State Department. The memo confirmed that an informant named George Bush of the CIA had inside knowledge of the attitudes of anti-Castro Cubans in Miami after the assassination of President Kennedy. When the memo was discovered in the late 1980s, Bush's staff tried to claim that the George Bush named in the memo was another George Bush entirely. There *was* another George Bush who worked at the CIA, but he was a paper shuffler and would have had no access to knowledge of the anti-Castro community in south Florida in 1963. Hoover may have been trying to cover himself and his beloved FBI with this disclosure. As an intimate of Lyndon Johnson, Hoover was aware of a conspiracy to kill Kennedy and might have wanted to deflect attention to the non-LBJ culprits in the assassination—George H.W. Bush and his CIA cronies.

The Kennedy assassination was just one of the many catastrophic attacks on the stability of American democracy that Bush and his family have been right in the thick of. Prescott and his partners, including the Dulles brothers and their clients, made a fortune from funding the rise of the Third Reich. George H.W. helped organize and finance the Bay of Pigs. He was instrumental in convincing Nixon to resign just days before he did. And in 1980, in an attempt to get himself and Ronald Reagan elected, Bush made a deal with the Iranians to delay the release of the American hostages until after the 1980 U.S. elections. Heinrich Rupp, another Nazi war criminal who went to work for the CIA after World War II, accompanied Bush, Vice Presidential candidate at the time, to Paris to meet with Iranian officials in the fall of 1980. The "October surprise" sank the Carter reelection bid and secured the election for the Reagan-Bush ticket; just months later, Bush almost gained the throne when Reagan was shot. The hostages were released on January 20, 1981, only minutes after Reagan and Bush were sworn into office. In return, Rupp promised release of Iran's frozen assets, laying the groundwork for the Iran-Contra deal. So Rupp, the Paperclip Nazi, helped steal an election, control U.S. foreign policy, and precipitate one of the worst scandals of the 1980s.

As Vice President, Bush played a prominent role in the looting of Savings and Loans in the 1980s—covering up for the bad guys and making a tidy sum for all his crooked cronies. (Hyman Roth's line from Godfather II comes to mind, "I always make money for my partners.") And, of course, George W., Bush's son, was president when the 9/11 attacks occurred. W. himself may have been in

Dealey Plaza on 11/22/63. One of the photos of the aftermath of the assassination depicts a young man bearing a stunning resemblance to W., 17 years old at the time, crossing Elm Street towards Houston sometime that afternoon. (W. was a prep student at the time, but might have been home on break.) There is no definitive proof that the Bushes were there, beyond the photographic speculation; however, H.W. Bush's subsequent attitude and remarks about 11/22/63 cast doubt on his innocence.

Does the Bushes' mere proximity to these events make them guilty? Maybe not, but whenever something horrible has happened to America in the last century, the Bushes should be one of the first families investigated. Their labyrinthine connections to a subterranean world of oilmen, defense contractors, intelligence chiefs, ex-Nazis, drug dealers and international financiers create the appearance that they are at the heart of a secret empire that operates without oversight to manipulate and control the destiny of America for their own gain and the gain of their partners in the clandestine enterprise. Their shrewd employment of tradecraft and deception and their close association with immense power brokers have kept them immune from prosecution of any sort; still, their dirty dealings are more than obvious to the critical eye.

The Bush family-George DeMohrenschildt relationship alone screams JFK assassination connection. The two Georges knew one another from their days in the Texas oil business, but after 11/22/63, H.W. appears to have cut ties with DeMohrenschildt. When Bush was appointed head of the CIA by Gerald Ford in 1976, DeMohrenschildt made an unwelcome return to Bush's life. As the HSCA was gearing up to re-investigate the Kennedy assassination, DeMohrenschildt's name resurfaced. The CIA under Bush, naturally, would want to suppress the Bush-DeMohrenschildt-Oswald link, but DeMohrenschildt got nervous and went public when he got spooked by mysterious government agents who began pressuring him. He got so fed up with it that he took the extraordinary measure of writing a letter to his old pal Bush. The letter, dated September 5, 1976, is written in intelligence-coded language that both Georges would have understood quite well. It contains the tone of a desperate man, begging the one person he knows can save him from his coming demise. It reads, in part, "Maybe you will be able to bring a solution to the hopeless situation I find myself in. My wife and I find ourselves surrounded by some vigilantes; our phone bugged; and we are being followed everywhere…[possibly by] FBI." What exactly prompted DeMohrenschildt's hopeless situation? He tells Bush that, "I tried to write, stupidly and unsuccessfully, about Lee H. Oswald and must have angered a lot of people," and then implores Bush to "remove the net from around us."[231]

When DeMohrenschildt sent the letter, he signed his own death warrant. No information could have been more dangerous to the CIA and Bush than their direct connection to the Kennedy assassination through Oswald's best friend in Dallas before the assassination. The fact that DeMohrenschildt had attempted to reveal the truth of the assassination in his own book almost ensured that he would be called as a witness before the HSCA. Bush and the CIA could not allow this to happen.

Bush's response to DeMohrenschildt was cordial, but sent a diabolically subtle and unmistakable message to his friend. It read, in part, "…my staff has been unable to find any indication of interest in your activities on the part of Federal authorities in recent years… I believe I can appreciate your state of mind in view of your daughter's death a few years ago and the current poor state of your wife's health."[232] Translation: *The CIA has checked into your matter, and has found nothing to support your allegations that government agents are targeting you or that your life is in danger. It must all be a figment of your imagination due to your deteriorating mental condition, caused by your daughter's death and your wife's poor health. Contacting me was a huge mistake.*

After reading Bush's response, DeMohrenschildt must have deduced two things for certain: 1) He could expect no help from Bush and the CIA. He was out in the cold, and they were not going to bring him back in; and 2) His days were numbered.

DeMohrenschildt fled for Europe and stayed there until the spring of 1977. Upon returning to the U.S., he was scheduled to appear before the HSCA which sent an investigator to DeMohrenschildt's Florida residence. That very day, DeMohrenschildt was found shot to death in his home; a shotgun was found nearby. It was ruled a suicide by police, but his wife Jeanne, the former Jeanne LeGon who worked with Abraham Zapruder at Nardi's in Dallas, vehemently disputed this. A year later she had the courage to speak freely to the *Fort Worth Star-Telegram*. She stated that her husband George had not committed suicide and that Oswald was a government agent who had not killed the President. She also implied that the CIA had killed Kennedy.[233]

Found in DeMohrenschildt's belongings was the address of "Bush, George H.W., 1412 W. Ohio also Zapata Petroleum, Midland, Texas."[234] This was not the only JFK suspect who was found dead with Bush's information on his person. CIA pilot and drug runner Barry Seal, who may have flown a getaway plane out of Dallas on 11/22/63, had George Bush's private phone number in his pocket when found shot to death.

Richard Nixon

Like many other happenstances associated with the assassination, Richard Nixon's presence in Dallas on the fateful day is somewhat mysterious and murky. At the time, Nixon was practicing private law for a firm in New York. One of the firm's clients was Pepsi-Cola, and Dallas was the site for the national bottlers convention during the week of Kennedy's visit to Texas. This provided a good excuse for getting Nixon to Dallas, if this was the plotters' intent, but what was his role, if any, in the plot? It may have been just a coincidence that the man who narrowly defeated him for the presidency in 1960 was murdered just blocks from the site of Nixon's business dealings in Dallas. But stacked against a thousand other coincidences we must explain away, and given Nixon's deserved reputation for being a furtively malevolent schemer, the skeptical mind wonders what he was really up to.

Well, for one thing, he reminded Lyndon Johnson what was at stake if Kennedy lived to run for a second term. Nixon granted an interview to a Dallas news reporter the day before the assassination in which he asserted that Johnson might be a liability to Kennedy in the 1964 election. The article, which ran the next day in the *Dallas Morning News* under the headline "Nixon Predicts JFK May Drop Johnson," was picked up by wire services and was published in newspapers nationwide, including the Allen Dulles-friendly *New York Times*. The article quotes Nixon as saying that Johnson had become an embarrassment to the Kennedy administration, in part because of Johnson's entanglement in the Bobby Baker corruption scandal being investigated by the Senate that very week.[235]

This begs the question: How did Nixon know what few people in Washington did, namely that JFK was dropping Johnson? JFK never publicly admitted it, and only let on his intentions to a very small group of intimates. He certainly would have not told Nixon or anyone even remotely associated with Nixon. Was there a traitor in JFK's inner circle? Did that someone pass along this crucial information to the plotters who then prompted Nixon, wittingly or wittingly, to play his part?

There is another possibility. Johnson and Nixon might have discussed the matter privately between themselves the night before the assassination, when (as previously mentioned in this text), according to Johnson's mistress Madeleine Brown, they were together at Clint Murchison's "kill Kennedy" party. Also present were John McCloy (future Warren Commission member) George Brown of Brown and Root, J. Edgar Hoover and H.L. Hunt.[236]

Many question the credibility of Brown's account, because Nixon and Johnson each had an alibi which placed them elsewhere on the eve of the assassination. Nixon was seen in the company of movie star and Pepsi executive Joan Crawford at the comedic performance of television actor Robert Clary. Johnson had witnesses which placed him at his hotel in Fort Worth. But it is possible that the gathering at Murchison's mansion outside Dallas took place well after midnight, a time after which both Johnson and Nixon were free to attend.

Regardless of whether Nixon attended Murchison's party, it is a matter of indisputable fact that his presence in Dallas helped PepsiCo and other soft-drink bottlers keep their convention location, the Statler Hilton, from being taken over by the Kennedy advance team during the planning of the Texas trip. The Hilton was one of just a few sites which could have accommodated the JFK luncheon in Dallas. Because it was unavailable, however, the Trade Mart was chosen, and the motorcade route was forced to pass through Dealey Plaza where assassins lay in wait. A motorcade toward the Hilton would have taken JFK away from the kill zone.

By happenstance, Jack Ruby was also linked to PepsiCo and, by extension, to Nixon. Ruby was a friend of a man named Lawrence Meyers whose brother Ed owned a PepsiCo bottling plant in New York in 1963. Ed Meyers was in Dallas at the bottlers convention with Nixon, and their paths likely crossed there just a day or two before the assassination. According to JFK authors Canfield and Weberman, the Meyers brothers met with Ruby on the evening of 11/21/63 at the Cabana Motel.[237] Ruby's presence at the Cabana was confirmed by a CIA operative named Marita Lorenz, who had traveled to Dallas in the company of one Frank Sturgis (aka Frank Fiorini). Sturgis had transported weapons to Dallas from Miami in the days leading up to 11/22/63. At the Cabana, Lorenz saw E. Howard Hunt distributing cash payments to Sturgis.[238] This was also the motel where known killer Eugene Hale Brading stayed the night before the assassination. As previously stated, Brading (aka Jim Braden) was picked up by police in Dealey Plaza just moments after JFK was killed.

Nixon's association with Meyers and Ruby indicated he had something to hide, and his statements after the assassination only underscore this. He offered three different stories about his actions and whereabouts on 11/22/63. In one version he claimed to fly out of Dallas before the Kennedy entourage arrived. Nixon said he landed in New York at 12:56 p.m., and then took a cab into the city. As the cabbie was waiting for the light to change, a man rushed up to the vehicle and said Kennedy had been shot. (The time alone is suspicious because at 12:56 p.m. eastern time on 11/22/63, Kennedy's plane was just about to land in Dallas. He was not murdered until 1:30 p.m. eastern time.) In another version the cabbie got lost and a hysterical woman hailed it down to tell Nixon of the tragedy in Dallas. In a third version, reporters who greeted Nixon's plane at Idlewild Airport told him of the assassination. Nixon's memory, like George Bush's, was either muddled, or he was trying to cover up the true nature of his trip to, and return from, Dallas. In the 1970s, an executive from the Pepsi Company who had been with Nixon in Dallas claimed that Nixon was still in Dallas at the time of the assassination.[239]

Regardless of which version of the story is the truth, Nixon knew more about Dallas than he ever let on publicly. He knew enough to secretly threaten the CIA with exposing his knowledge of its involvement in the assassination, but he paid a steep price for that threat: the loss of his presidency. He learned, as all presidents have, that there are more powerful forces at work just beneath the surface of American politics. All presidents after 1963 were at the mercy of these forces. What Nixon called the "wild beast." Presidents didn't publicly acknowledge the beast; they had to maintain the pretense of being in control for the sake of appearance. But they knew that the real power over America lay elsewhere and could destroy presidents who didn't play ball. Wars, coups, looting of the national treasury, deep corruption, intelligence catastrophes, stolen elections and collusion with the enemy have drastically diminished the office's prestige and potency.

The president is no longer the president, but the creature least resistant to the malevolent impulses of American culture and power. And today even foreign oligarchs pull the strings. In the age of Trump the presidency is a laughingstock. Compare Kennedy's soaring, inspirational speeches to that of Trump's barely literate, third-grade-level rhetoric. Where once JFK made politics a noble profession, today it is a haven for schemers, scammers and scoundrels of all manner. People enter public service for their own selfish ends, and that is fine with the moneyed interests who have their hands on the levers of America.

Gerald Ford and the Warren Commission

Of all the things the mainstream media overlooked in the wake of the assassination, one of the most blatant indicators of Lyndon Johnson trying to cover his tracks was his cunningly shrewd selection of Warren Commission members. Republicans were in the majority, and nary a liberal was to be found, unless we count Earl Warren. As its titular head, Warren imbued the panel with an integrity it did not deserve; he had a reputation for progressive values and was despised by the extreme right-wing. Johnson saw his appointment as a way to appease liberals and Kennedy loyalists. But Warren was a reluctant appointee, and he rarely showed up for any of the hearings. The meat of the commission work was performed by Kennedy haters.

Johnson appointed just two Democrats—Richard Russell and Hale Boggs—both southerners who had opposed JFK's domestic agenda especially in the area of civil rights. This is a polite way of saying that even the Democrats on the Commission were not Kennedy admirers. It is easy to forget that the Democratic party in the early 1960s was evenly split between conservatives and liberals. Southern Democrats were nearly unanimously right-wing ideologues; much the same way that Republicans are today. Many of them, like John Connally and Strom Thurmond, switched their party affiliation from Democrat to Republican when the domestic strife of the '60s caused politicians to choose sides that more closely identified with their policies. Today southern Democrats are as rare as southern Republicans were in 1963. The point is, Johnson could rely on his Dixiecrat friends to avoid digging too deeply into the ugly truths of who really planned and executed the murder of a President for whom they bore no love. Still in all, despite their political opposition to JFK, Russell, Sherman Cooper (Republican) and Boggs had misgivings about the commission's findings that a single bullet struck both Kennedy and Connally. Not until John McCloy came up with compromise language did the three dissenters acquiesce to the others' magic-bullet charade. But Russell, according to author Gerald McKnight, never understood the full ramifications of conceding to McCloy. McKnight writes that, "Because of Russell's chronic absenteeism he never fully comprehended that the final report's no-conspiracy conclusion was inextricably tied to...the single-bullet theory.[240] Cooper may have been similarly oblivious—he attended barely half the meetings. Boggs' attendance was also sporadic, but his dissent appeared to disturb the commission's hierarchy more than others. He was bugged and followed by the FBI for years, and he vehemently objected to J. Edgar Hoover's Gestapo tactics. (Boggs' post-Warren Commission troubles and his mysterious disappearance are addressed in a later chapter.)

Over the life of the commission, it was three of the Republicans who exerted the most influence on the eventual whitewash: Allen Dulles, Arlen Specter (Dulles's intrepid and ambitious lawyer) and Congressman Gerald Ford. Specter expertly badgered and discredited hostile witnesses (read, witnesses who had knowledge of conspiratorial activity) and concocted the magic-bullet scenario which allowed the commission to frame the dead patsy for the crime. Because of the time constraints inherent in a frame count of the Zapruder film, Oswald had only six seconds to fire three shots, and two of them—the complete miss and the head shot—were already accounted for. That left just one bullet to do the rest of the damage. Specter's strained contrivance took care of that problem for the plotters. One bullet, he said, despite all evidence to the contrary, entered the President's back, exited his throat, entered Connally's back, broke his wrist, tore through his ribs, landed in his leg, and came out on a Dallas stretcher in pristine condition. No one but Specter saw this as an even remotely logical occurrence; still it exists in the official record today, despite the fact that no bullet fired in the history of the world has ever duplicated this feat, and despite the fact that no Parkland medical personnel saw a rear entry wound on the President's body. The Bethesda doctors *did* see a rear entry wound, but the wound was too low on the President's back to have exited his throat. The only way that wound could have been made was by body alterationists in transit from Parkland to Bethesda. The body alterationists created a wound that couldn't be easily accounted for. Specter tried, but he needed a big assist from Gerald Ford to complete the sham.

The problem for the plotters began when a medical illustrator named Ida Dox made an exact-replica drawing from autopsy photos of the rear entry wound on the President's back.[241] She placed it to the right of the midline in the President's back and parallel to the top of his right shoulder. Such a wound, if Oswald had made it by firing a bullet on a downward angle from the TSBD's sixth floor, would have had a corresponding exit in the middle of the President's chest. But somehow, Specter found a way to have the bullet travel upward and leftward from the President's shoulder to exit at his throat. That is some trick. The commission so feared that Specter's fraud would be widely ridiculed that Gerald Ford stepped in to falsify the final autopsy report. Thirty-three years after the fact he finally admitted that he moved the back wound up a few inches to accommodate Specter's hoax. He claimed that the change, in defiance of the autopsy's photographic record, "had nothing to do with a conspiracy."²⁴² *Then what did it have to do with?* Certainly not a search for the truth. Ford tried to make his evidence-tampering seem benign and unimportant. In fact, his manipulation of the wounds is just as criminal, and as essential to the perpetration of a false version of the assassination, as the Zapruder film alteration. The irony is that it was the plotters who necessitated the Specter/Ford fraud by altering the Z film that created an artificially speeded-up version of events in Dealey Plaza.

Ford's service to the plotters continued when he stumbled into the presidency after the Watergate debacle forced Nixon from office. In 1975 Ford appointed Malcolm Liggett to his cabinet. Malcolm, the brother of murderous Dallas mortician John Liggett, who played a critical role in the postmortem cover-up of JFK's wounds, was given a position in the Office for Wage and Price Stability and reported directly to the President.

Both Malcolm and John served in the Air Force in the 1950s. Then their paths diverged. After a stint in the Louisiana Civil Air Patrol, John became a mortician, renowned for his skills as a reconstructionist, and he "moonlighted" as a contract killer for covert intelligence and organized crime interests. Malcolm became an academic and a legal mediator, and won prestigious positions at universities across the land. Despite this, he reputedly associated with seamy characters in the Dallas area. According to family relatives, he was photographed in the company of Jack Ruby at Ruby's Carousel Club sometime before the assassination. Until he died in 2008, Malcolm always denied being the man in the photograph with Ruby. When the picture was broadcast as part of a documentary series presented by the History Channel in 2003, Malcolm filed suit against the TV channel. Also objecting vociferously to the documentary ("The Men Who Killed Kennedy"), which accused

Lyndon Johnson of planning JFK's murder, were Johnson apologists Jack Valenti, Bill Moyers, Jimmy Carter and Gerald Ford. Establishment historians were enlisted to aid the cause, and, in the face of such overwhelming criticism, The History Channel caved. It issued an apology, and the documentary has since disappeared from the airways.[243]

But John Liggett's family members did not keep silent. They insisted that Malcolm was working behind the scenes with powerful forces. When John was arrested for murder in Dallas in 1974, Malcolm, despite the risks to his reputation, came to John's assistance. He warned Lois Liggett, John's ex-wife, to stay away from John while he was in jail, implying that John was under close watch by the plotters and Lois should not get involved. The fate of John Liggett, and a full rendition of his suspicious activities on the weekend of 11/22/63, is presented in detail in the next chapter.

CHAPTER 6

From Washington to Dallas and Back Again

> "It seems fitting that…we should have
> two histories…a 'Disney'version…and
> a second one that remains secret, buried,
> and unnamed."
> —from *Spooks: The Haunting of
> America*, by Jim Hougan

When considering the plotters' plans and obstacles, it is reasonable to assume that there were three main challenges: 1) how to get JFK to Dallas; 2) how to get his motorcade to pass in front of the designated patsy's place of work; 3) and how to conceal the true nature of the shooting.

The first and second assignments were taken care of by Lyndon Johnson and his political protégé John Connally. Nicknamed LBJ (Lyndon's Boy John), Jr., by snarky insiders, Connally served as Johnson's political muscle in Texas for years. He was Johnson's campaign manager at the time Lyndon stole the 1948 Texas Senate Democratic election. Connally conveniently was away from Ballot Box 13 when the theft occurred, and he claimed to know nothing about it. Regardless, he ran interference for Johnson, whether the work was dirty or clean, corrupt or legal. Through Johnson, Connally was introduced to the real moneymen and kingmakers in

241

Texas politics—oil millionaires. The same people who financed and endorsed LBJ, and who despised Kennedy's politics, were the same people who backed John Connally. D.H. Byrd wanted Connally in the White House in the 1970s.[1] Sid Richardson was once a client of Connally's when he practiced law.[2]

At LBJ's urging, Connally was appointed Secretary of the Navy by JFK in 1961, but he resigned to run for governor of Texas in 1962. With Johnson's help Connally won in a landslide. It turned out to be a convenient circumstance for Johnson that Connally was governor when the time came to plan JFK's Texas trip. With some intense arm-twisting, the two Texans convinced Kennedy it was imperative for him to show up in their state for some political fence-mending. Connally headed up the conservative wing of the Democratic party. On the liberal side was Senator Ralph Yarborough. The two sides were bickering, and Connally and Johnson, in the spring of 1963, made a plea to the President to come to Texas as a show of party unity before the 1964 elections. Kennedy had to walk a political tightrope that made it appear that he stood with both sides and could appeal to a wide spectrum of voters, a nearly impossible trick. That's the official story anyway. The truth is that Kennedy was suckered into coming to Texas by cunning political enemies who were, literally, gunning for him.

For his part, Yarborough was an honest Kennedy supporter, and he tried to warn the President's aides what kind of treachery was waiting for him in Texas. Jerry Bruno, JFK's advance man, went to Texas in October to go over the itinerary for the President's whirl-wind two-day tour in November. Yarborough told him, "[Connally and Johnson would] be after John Kennedy in a minute if they thought they could get away with it."[3] Bruno was cowed and intimidated by Connally who forcefully told Bruno where the President would go and when he would go there. This was quite unusual for a Kennedy trip. As Tip O'Neill put it, "Kennedy…advance men had the power to make their own decisions…and quickly bypass all of…[the] local factions and conflicts."⁴ But not in Texas. A Connally spokesperson told Bruno, "You're coming into Texas…and Connally is the governor."⁵

In spite of the political bickering, the only major conflict was over the luncheon site for the Dallas leg of the trip. There were three possibilities being considered by Bruno—the Hilton Hotel, the Women's Building auditorium at the state fairgrounds, and the Dallas Trade Mart. As stated previously, the Hilton was booked by a bottlers convention, including Pepsi-Cola people for whom Richard Nixon was an attorney. The bottlers refused to give up the booking, so the Hilton was out.

Of the remaining two sites, the Women's building was preferred by Bruno and the Kennedy people. It could accommodate a large crowd and would have been open to a cross-section of Dallasites. According to Bruno, "We could have organized labor committees, Chicano committees, women and blacks to turn people out."⁶

But Connally and Johnson pushed hard for the Trade Mart site. It was a closed venue, accessible only to the Dallas elite and under the control of the Dallas Citizens Council, whose members included D.H. Byrd, H.L. Hunt and other Kennedy haters. Connally was so determined to get his way that he threatened to call off the whole trip if Kennedy did not have lunch at the Trade Mart. Finally Kenny O'Donnell, JFK's political advisor and chief protector, relented and told Bruno, "We're going to let Connally have the Trade Mart site."⁷

The important thing to note here is that the Trade Mart luncheon site forced the motorcade to pass near the Texas School Book Depository building and the ambush that lay waiting for JFK. If the luncheon had been scheduled for the Women's Building or the Hilton, Kennedy's motorcade would not have been in range of the snipers in Dealey Plaza. Once the motorcade was forced to travel to the Trade Mart, Kennedy's fate was in the hands of the Texas power brokers, and he would soon be a sitting duck in a shooting gallery.

Still, there was no need to make the jagged turns off Main Street onto Houston and then Elm. The motorcade could have reached Stemmons Freeway by continuing straight on Main Street and avoiding the kill zone on Elm. The Warren Commission, while avoiding the luncheon site conflict altogether, tried to convince the public that taking Main Street would have been inappropriate because it required the motorcade to make an illegal turn. But making illegal turns to protect a president seems a logical thing to do, and official parades routes are often designed to go where normal traffic does not. The commission also made reference to a concrete riser on the road between Main Street and the expressway as another factor in the motorcade taking its implausible detour through Dealey Plaza. Author Craig Zirbel destroyed this lame reasoning in his book *The Texas Connection*: "The riser was not an impediment…[it] was similar to a speed bump [and] was illegally traversed every day by Dallas motorists to get onto the expressway from Main Street."[8]

On October 4, 1963, Connally traveled to Washington and finalized the plans for the Texas trip with White House officials; he also met privately with Johnson. After his meeting with Connally, Johnson left for Texas and remained there for most of the seven weeks leading up to the assassination.[9] It was in this time period that the patsy secured a job in the building overlooking the parade route. Oswald, with the help of Ruth Paine, began working in the Texas School Book Depository just twelve days after Connally's bullying tactics made sure that the President's car would pass right below the Depository and into the midst of a crossfire from which Kennedy would not escape alive.

This would have never happened, of course, if Kennedy had just declined to go to Texas. Perhaps the possibility of losing Texas in 1964, and its huge electoral numbers, had an impact on JFK's decision. To enact his peace initiatives, his ambitious governmental restructuring (including the dismantling of the CIA), and his civil rights legislation, he knew he had to win reelection by a good margin. And that meant carrying Texas. He knew that Dallas was "nut country," but Kennedy was fearless and had stared down death many times in his short life. Kennedy's friends and advisors urged him not to go to Texas. "I told him so," wrote Tip O'Neill years later. "I didn't see the point of the [Dallas] trip…It just didn't make sense."[10]

Kennedy could not have been happy about embroiling himself in local squabbles in an area of the country that overwhelmingly did not share his views. But in the years following Dallas, Connally tried to convince the world that it was JFK's idea to visit Texas, and that he and Lyndon tried to talk him out of it. It is a despicable lie; one that the mainstream media never called him on. JFK aide Ralph Dungan settled the matter years later when he insisted that Kennedy made the Texas trip only at Johnson's insistence and as a political favor to his Texas vice-president.[11]

After Johnson's death, Connally tried to shift the blame away from himself and solely onto his co-conspirator. Under the influence of a few stiff drinks, Connally let slip this whopper, "You know I was one of the ones who advised Kennedy to stay away from Texas. [But] Lyndon was being a real asshole about the whole thing and insisted."[12] Pressed on the matter of a conspiracy, Connally insisted to *Capitol Hill Blue* reporter Doug Thompson, "I do not, for one second, believe the conclusions of the Warren Commission…[and] I will never speak out publicly about what I believe."[13] In an undated video (circa 1988) Connally even made the preposterous assertion that Kennedy insisted on attending five different banquets. Connally's wife Nellie, in the same interview, giggles and makes a tasteless joke about Kennedy's appetite. "Gobble, gobble, gobble," she says.[14]

If Connally's machinations concerning the Texas trip were nothing more than the typical gamesmanship employed by ambitious politicians, he could have ascribed his intense desire for a Trade

Mart luncheon to the need for raising campaign money from Texas fatcats. (Even after the date and place of the luncheon were confirmed, he and Johnson made little effort to drum up attendance. They knew that JFK would never arrive.) But Connally never used this excuse to explain away his suspicious tactics in luring the President's motorcade through Dealey Plaza; this leads one to believe that there is no innocent explanation for what he did. And there can be little doubt that his actions were prompted by his mentor, Lyndon Johnson, who benefitted immensely from the assassination.

After John Connally's death, Nellie Connally became indignant at suggestions that her husband was in on some conspiracy to murder the President. Her defense is one that, on the surface at least, has a solid rationale: Why would her husband concoct a scheme which would put him in the death car and at the mercy of a hail of bullets? The simple answer is: Connally assumed that he would *not* be riding in the President's car. His partner in crime, LBJ, tried to get him out of the death car before its fateful journey. JFK and LBJ had a bitter argument on this very topic the night before the assassination in the President's hotel suite. With words loud enough to be heard by Jackie and the hotel staff, the two men fought about the seating arrangements in the Dallas motorcade. Johnson demanded that Yarborough replace Connally in the President's limousine, but Kennedy would not hear of it.[15] The next day, Connally, instead of safely riding with LBJ several cars behind Kennedy, was positioned in the firing line amid a flurry of bullets.

This leads one to speculate about Johnson's true motives. Even though he knew that his long-time friend and ally was going to be in harm's way, Johnson did not call off the assassination attempt. It speaks to Johnson's ruthlessness that he was willing to sacrifice Connally to get to the White House. To hypothesize even further, perhaps Connally's death would have been seen by LBJ as good political cover and the closing of a loose end. There weren't many (outside of his lawyers, his personal assassin and Allen Dulles) who knew of Johnson's complicity in the crime, but Connally was likely one who did. It would have served Johnson's interests to have Connally silenced. Moreover, whoever shot Connally missed JFK by a good deal, as if the assassins who fired from behind the motorcade were aiming at Connally and not Kennedy. (Remember, Connally always told the truth about one thing: he was shot by a separate bullet; his testimony alone destroyed the Warren Commission's theory that he and JFK were hit by one magic bullet.)

Then again, the wounding of Connally might have been unintentional. At least two other bullets shot from the rear missed the motorcade altogether, which indicates perhaps that those who fired from behind the President were firing only to distract witnesses from the real killers to the front. Under this scenario, Connally could have been shot accidentally.

There is a third possibility for the shooting of Connally: mistaken identity. Johnson fought hard to get his hated political rival Ralph Yarborough into the death car. This may have been the plot all along: to kill Johnson's two hated rivals at once. Since it wasn't determined until just hours before the Dallas motorcade who was going to be riding in which car, the assassins might have thought they were actually taking aim at Yarborough—the other limo occupant Johnson wanted dead—and not Connally.

However his shooting occurred, Connally must have been petrified when he found out that his old pal Lyndon could not get him out of the death car. Connally's foreknowledge of events is written on his face in the photographs of him that day. In nearly all pictures taken, from Love Field to Dealey Plaza, Connally is seen as worried, pensive and tense. Though the day is beautiful and the crowds are enthusiastic, Connally is not happy. His brow is furrowed, and no smile crosses his lips.

When the fatal shots rang out, Connally made a "dying declaration"—"My god, they're going to kill us all."[16] "They," not "he." In a moment when he was struck by a bullet and feared that he might be losing his life, Connally uttered the truth. He knew shots were being fired from different directions and various guns.[17]

How Body Alteration Changed the Evidence

The third, and most crucial, element of the plotters' strategy was the most diabolical and macabre. Their plan, as bizarre as it sounds, was to snatch JFK's corpse and alter his wounds before an official autopsy could reveal the true nature of the wounds.

In any murder, the cause and manner of death are critical in determining who killed the victim. In cases of gunshot fatalities, doctors can readily discern the direction, number and origin of the shots by examining the wounds on the victim's body. The first examination of JFK's wounds by the Parkland Hospital doctors indicated that he had been shot at least once from the front and possibly twice.

Dr. Malcolm Perry and the others who attended to Kennedy at Parkland Hospital were highly trained and experienced physicians who saw gunshot wounds on a daily basis. Dallas in 1963 was, perhaps, the most right-wing and violent city in the country. They were Second Amendment lovers, and they were armed to the teeth. If you were a Dallasite and you weren't packing, you just weren't trying hard enough. Gunplay was a common occurrence, and Parkland was where most gunshot victims were taken. As Dr. Charles Crenshaw put it, "Parkland [was] a M.A.S.H. unit for Dallas County's war zone...we doctors there referred to the trauma team as those who treated the 'knife and gun club.'"[18] The doctors could easily distinguish exit wounds from entry wounds. Dr. Perry immediately recognized JFK's throat wound as a clean, neat and small wound of entry, and he had no problem saying so to news reporters. Imagine Perry's surprise when the autopsy revealed a much larger throat wound than the one he had seen in Trauma Room One. The Dallas doctors must have suspected that somehow, someone somewhere had altered the President's wounds before the body arrived at

Bethesda. And this fact was used against them when they testified before the Warren Commission. The Dallas doctors were chastised by Commission attorney Arlen Specter for being inaccurate and negligent in the assessment of Kennedy's wounds at Parkland.

The plotters' body alteration effectively compromised the integrity of the Dallas doctors whose descriptions of JFK's wounds were undercut by the autopsy findings which were based on a medical forgery—a corpse which had been manipulated to erase shots from the front. But even before the autopsy was released, the intimidation of the Dallas doctors began. According to Parkland nurse Audrey Bell, Dr. Perry looked haggard and worn when he reported for work on the day after the assassination. He told Bell that he had not gotten much sleep because unspecified Bethesda personnel had been harassing him by phone all night in an attempt to get him to change his opinion about the throat wound being one of entry.[19] In a hastily arranged press conference shortly after the murder, Perry had insisted three times that JFK's throat wound was one of entry; in other words, the President had been shot from the front. Later, when the Bethesda autopsy doctors saw a gaping throat wound and declared it was one of exit, the Warren Commission was able to discount Perry's testimony. Allen Dulles even encouraged him to make a public apology for his erroneous observations of the throat wound.

Less than a month after the assassination, Secret Service agents showed up in Dallas to present the autopsy findings to a few of the doctors who worked on Kennedy. The intimidation tactics worked. Dr. McClelland quickly reversed his opinion as to the direction of the shots which killed the President.[20] Secret Service agent Elmer Moore told researcher James Gochenaur that he pressured Dr. Perry into changing his testimony about the frontal-entrance throat wound.[21] Moore, who called JFK a traitor and said "maybe it was a good thing" that he died, admitted that "from Washington, [I] got [my] marching orders...I did everything I was told...or we'd get our heads cut off."[22]

The same tactics were used on McClelland. Federal agents showed him the autopsy report; he was shocked to discover that he and the other Parkland doctors had apparently missed two wounds entirely—an entry wound in the back of the head and an entry wound in the upper back. In the face of the seemingly authentic autopsy findings, McClelland, Perry and the others were shamed into admitting they had been wrong in stating that JFK had been shot from the front. But, as previously discussed, McClelland's true impressions of the wounds he saw were expressed in the sketch he made after the assassination which depicted frontal wounds to the President's head and throat. That sketch also contained a rear entry wound in the back.

But were the rear entry wounds seen at autopsy genuine wounds? That is to say, were they incurred at the time of the shooting in Dealey Plaza? The actions and observations of Parkland personnel immediately after the shooting suggest these wounds were made after the assassination as part of the alteration process that disguised the true nature of the shooting. No Parkland doctor or nurse saw any *rear* entry wounds on the President's body on 11/22/63. Warren Commission defenders argue this is because the President's body was not turned over while he was in Trauma Room One; the doctors were focused on saving his life and simply missed the rear-entry wounds. However, close scrutiny of the statements of Parkland personnel reveals some, indeed, could have and should have spotted the rear wounds if those wounds were actually present. Dr. Robert Carrico made a manual examination of the President's back and detected no bullet entry wound. Likewise, the Parkland nurses, Diana Bowron and Margaret Henchliffe, who removed the President's clothing as soon as he was wheeled into the emergency room, saw no bullet entry wounds at the rear of his body. Presumably the nurses would have needed to lift the President up to remove his shirt, and in so doing would have had a clear view of his back and neck. Subsequently Bowron and Henchliffe, assisted by two other nurses and an orderly, "...washed the blood from the President's face and body."[23] During this process, they had another chance to detect entry wounds on the back of the body. Again, four Parkland nurses and one orderly noticed nothing.

How, then, did the wounds to the back of the President's body get there? If they were not seen in Dallas, but they were seen at Bethesda, then only one conclusion can be drawn—the person(s) who altered the President's wounds had the ability to not only erase inconvenient wounds that pointed away from Oswald but also to add convenient wounds that pointed to Oswald's guilt. A man who had the prerequisite skills and the necessary connections to do such things was one John Liggett, and his actions on that fateful weekend in November will be discussed at length below. His work, and the work of others, forever distorted the assassination medical records, and have made the task of finding the true killers a confounding one. This, I assume, was the goal all along.

The Dallas doctors, faced with documented evidence from an official government autopsy, grew reticent to speak publicly and challenge the official story of Oswald as the lone gunman. After the Warren Commission filed its fraudulent report, Parkland personnel were wary of government agencies and media perusal. The man who pronounced JFK dead at Parkland, Dr. Kemp Clark, voiced his disgust in a succinct way, "Well, I guess the only person who got anything out of this deal was [Warren Commission counsel Arlen] Specter."[24]

All this does not change the fact that, before they were pressured into revising their professional observations, the Dallas doctors spoke the unvarnished truth in the first minutes, hours and days after the assassination. Perry, in a press conference on the afternoon of 11/22/63, told reporters three times that Kennedy's neck wound was one of entrance.[25] Dr. Kemp Clark said the bullet which caused the neck wound "was a small entrance wound below the Adam's apple."[26] [The bullet] ranged downward in [Kennedy's] chest and did not exit...the second [was] a tangential wound...that struck the right back of his head."[27] Dr. Robert McClelland said, "I think [the President] was shot from the front."[28] Dr. Charles Crenshaw described the wounds to Kennedy's head and throat as "...caused by bullets that struck him from the front, not the back."[29] Dr. Paul Peters stated that "...we saw a wound of entry in the throat and noted the large occipital wound...of exit."[30] To a man, the Dallas doctors were convinced the President had been shot from the front.

As the years went by, however, the men who worked on Kennedy at Parkland got the message that it was safer for them to publicly change their stories or just keep their mouths shut about what they really saw. Crenshaw revealed that "Parkland Hospital and the United States government have never been overtly subtle about their desire for us doctors to keep quiet and not divulge what we heard, saw and felt...a gag order was issued warning [us] not to confer with Oliver Stone [during the filming of *JFK*, the movie]."[31] The intense efforts to suppress the truth began just moments after Kennedy died, when the Parkland Emergency Room director, Dr. Charles Baxter, mandated an edict of secrecy to his fellow doctors.[32]

Another source of controversy has been Perry's tracheotomy incision performed on Kennedy during life-saving measures in Trauma Room One. It just so happened that the President was shot in the throat at precisely the point where a tracheotomy incision is best placed to provide an airway for a patient who is having difficulty breathing. When he cut into the President's neck, Perry forever distorted the small entry wound below the Adam's apple. But the incision as performed in Dallas was much smaller than the incision seen by the Bethesda doctors. Perry recollected an incision that was no more than two to three centimeters (about an inch in length); the Bethesda doctors reported an incision that was seven to eight centimeters long (approximately three inches).[33] No competent or reputable surgeon would make such a large tracheotomy incision.

It is another indication of the body being intercepted and altered by unknown parties prior to arrival at Bethesda; apparently, the plotters had to enlarge the throat wound in order to remove the bullet because it was not fired from Oswald's gun. The bullet was fired from in front of the President and it did not exit the body.

Shots From the Front

Scores of witnesses on the ground in Dealey Plaza contradicted the official story of three shots fired from above and behind. Jean Hill, standing just feet from the Presidential limousine, heard "...four to six shots...They were different guns being fired."[34] She also "...saw a man fire from behind the wooden fence...[and] a puff of smoke and some sort of movement on the Grassy Knoll."[35] Union Terminal Railroad employee Sam M. Holland said at least one of the shots came from behind the picket fence; he also saw a puff of smoke lingering under the trees.[36] Beverly Oliver, standing on the south side of Elm, saw a figure "behind the picket fence and smoke there."[37] Another witness, Maurice Orr, thought there "could have been as many as five shots."[38] JFK's close political advisors, Dave Powers and Kenny O'Donnell, riding just a few cars behind the President, were certain that two shots came from behind the fence atop the knoll.[39]

J.C. Price, Ed Hoffman, Gayle Newman, Charles Brehm, Lee Bowers, Phil Willis, Hugh Betzner, Mary Moorman, Officer Bobby Hargis and Secret Service agent Paul Landis were among over a hundred other eyewitnesses whose accounts discredited the official government story of the murder. In all, there were many more witnesses who disagreed with the Warren Commission version of events than agreed with it. The account of Willis, a retired Air Force officer, was extremely compelling. He groused that neither he nor other photographers were called to testify by the Warren Commission, and he was convinced that the head shot came from "the right front, from the knoll area."[40]

The plotters knew ahead of time that they would have to counter all these eyewitness statements and the Dallas doctors' frontal-entry observations. They knew that the emergency room doctors and witnesses in Dealey Plaza could and would provide an abundance of testimony indicating that Kennedy had been shot from the front. And shots from the front would point away from the designated patsy, and this fact would put the plotters at risk. If it could have been definitively proven that Oswald did not do it, then the search would have begun for who did. Dogged and honest investigators might have gone down trails that led them to the real culprits. The real culprits could not let that happen, and so they devised a scheme so daring and improbable that, even now, it is difficult to fathom— the President's wounds were altered by someone who had access to the corpse between Parkland and Bethesda hospitals. Sometime between 12:30 p.m. central time and approximately 8 p.m. eastern time on November 22, 1963, the chain of evidence was broken, and the President's body was illegally intercepted for purposes of medical alteration. There is an abundance of evidence to indicate that this happened. Most critically, the Parkland doctors saw a different set of wounds than did the Bethesda doctors. Moreover, autopsy x-rays and photos do not match the Parkland doctors' descriptions of the wounds. The House Select Committee on Assassinations put it rather succinctly. Its report, issued in the late 1970s, reads, "…if the Dallas doctors are correct, particularly with respect to the gaping hole in the back of the President's head, then it would mean: 1) the autopsy photographs and x-rays had been doctored to conceal this hole; 2) the body itself had been altered, either before its arrival at Bethesda or during the autopsy…; or 3) the photographs and x-rays were not President Kennedy."[41] Official records and eyewitness accounts support the fact that some form of all three of these deceptions might have occurred.

The fist-sized, blasted-out wound at the lower back of the President's head, about which the Dallas doctors were unanimous in their description, was not depicted in the Bethesda photographs. In fact, the autopsy photos indicate no damage to that area of Kennedy's head. Likewise, the Dallas doctors saw no damage to the top of the President's head, but six hours later at Bethesda the autopsy doctors described a large hole in the top of the President's head. The damage seen at Bethesda was so extensive that, at first, the autopsists did not think it was entirely caused by a bullet. Dr. James J. Humes noted "surgery of the head area, namely in the top of the skull."[42] Surgery? What surgery? No surgery had been performed on the President's head in Dallas; if any doctor had done so, it would have been akin to medieval butchery. And the autopsy doctors certainly did not perform postmortem surgery. So where did this surgery take place and when? And by whom was it performed? The statement's source is indisputable. It was found by researcher and author David Lifton in a Supplemental FBI report submitted by agents James W. Sibert and Francis X. O'Neill who were present at Bethesda on the night of Kennedy's autopsy. They reported the words spoken by the autopsy doctors.

Proof that bullet fragments were removed from the President's head prior to autopsy was provided by none other than Dr. Humes. His description of the condition of JFK's brain as seen on the evening of November 22 is delivered in medico-technical language that is indecipherable to the layman, but when translated into plain English it is stunning to contemplate. Author David Lifton asked a neurosurgeon friend of his to do just that—interpret Humes' autopsy report. The neurosurgeon told Lifton that the "brain had been sectioned."[43] Sectioning a brain which has been injured by a gunshot is normally done *at* autopsy, not *before* autopsy. It is a process by which a series of deep parallel cuts are made for inspection of the damage, trajectory determination and possible bullet removal. All of which aid in evidentiary discoveries for possible prosecution in a criminal proceeding. The neurosurgeon assured Lifton that such cuts could not have been made by a bullet's entry into and exit from the brain, and that "the damage sounded like it had been made with a knife."[44] Again, Humes saw this damage to the brain just as the autopsy began and *before* he or his colleagues actually did any sectioning of the brain.

The implications of this are incredible. It means that someone sectioned Kennedy's brain sometime after it left Dallas and before it arrived on the autopsy table in Bethesda. Naturally it leaves one wondering how this could have been done. And why did the plotters take such extraordinary and risky measures to cover up their crime? The answer to the second question is: the fervor of JFK's enemies to remove him from office was urgent, time-sensitive and maniacal. The plotters wanted and needed him dead; therefore, the attempt on his life was an all-or-nothing proposition. The mission had to succeed; there would be no second chances. If the attempt had failed (had Kennedy escaped Dallas alive), an honest, transparent and scrupulous investigation would have followed. Kennedy and his loyalists—particularly his brother, the Attorney General of the United States—would have undoubtedly rooted out the real traitors: Lyndon Johnson, the Allen Dulles/CIA-in-exile group, the Secret Service conspirators, the FBI, the Texas oil cartel, the Joint Chiefs and organized crime elements. Bobby Kennedy would have zealously prosecuted all involved, no matter where the trail led, no matter how many "respectable" government and military figures were involved, no matter how shocked the public would be. Even J. Edgar Hoover would not have been immune from indictment.

Once the public became aware of the conspiracy, no government agency no matter how esteemed; no oil billionaire, no matter how powerful; and no Mafia figure, no matter how dangerous, would have been safe. The plotters knew this from the start, so their attitude surely must have been, "We have but one chance, and we'd better get him. If we don't, we are doomed." (The aborted Chicago attempt on JFK's life three weeks before Dallas had merely been a ruse, one that gave the Secret Service some cover when its agents failed miserably in Dallas.) The gunmen in Dallas had to succeed, no matter how many shooters it took, no matter from where JFK was shot, no matter the number and placement of his wounds. Medical evidence could be distorted and covered up later; doctors could be compromised after the fact; witnesses who said the wrong thing could be killed; photos and films could be seized, manipulated and/or destroyed to suit the official story; evidence could be planted, lost or faked as needed. As long as Kennedy was killed, all other problems could be fixed on the fly during the cover-up phase.

The plotters prepared for any contingency that might develop, and must have had confidence in their power to create and support a false narrative of the assassination, as long as JFK did not leave Dallas alive. A non-fatally wounded JFK, with his mental faculties intact, would have jeopardized the fortunes, status and freedom of the plotters. That's why there were many teams of shooters, firing many different weapons from many directions in Dealey Plaza: to ensure success.

But this wild, turkey-shoot mentality, with shooters in front of, behind, aside, above, at street-level and *in* the motorcade itself presented many challenges for the plotters in the cover-up phase. Angles, directions and trajectories of gun shots are readily discernible by competent emergency and autopsy doctors in their examination of the wounds on the body. That risk, however, did not dissuade JFK's plotters from their assassination attempt. They were willing to accept the danger of being exposed by the clear evidence of multiple shooters in Dealey Plaza. They also had an ace-in-the-hole to mitigate against their risk: a world-class body reconstructionist to alter the President's wounds after the assassination and before the autopsy. Diabolically clever, the plan was as simple as it was ingenious. Hard to accomplish, yes, because intercepting the President's corpse after the fact was going to be difficult (but not impossible if the President's bodyguards were compromised, and they were). Body alteration accomplished two critical tasks: 1) It implicated Oswald as the lone assassin firing from above and behind; and 2) It made the Dallas doctors look foolish and subjected their expert medical opinions to ridicule.

Since the two sets of doctors saw two different sets of wounds at two different places and times, they could not compare notes and discuss what the incredible discrepancies meant, at least not on 11/22/63. Later, the images of the President's body, as photographed and x-rayed at Bethesda (which amounted to medical forgery), were used to discredit the observations of the Parkland doctors. There was one doctor, however, who saw Kennedy's wounds at *both* Parkland and Bethesda—Admiral George Burkley, JFK's personal physician, who was in the motorcade in Dallas and who flew back to Washington on Air Force One. Burkley should have been the one qualified medical person who could have attested to the disparate wounds and their meaning as relates to a possible conspiracy.

In 1976 Burkley was contacted by an investigator for the HSCA named Richard Sprague. Through his lawyer, Burkley made a statement to Sprague that "others besides Oswald must have been involved," indicating that Burkley had correctly surmised what the wound discrepancies meant. But when Sprague, an honest and scrupulous man, threatened to expose CIA involvement in the assassination, the agency used covert media manipulation to assail him and remove him from his position.[45] Subsequently, Burkley backed off his original statement and instead issued an affidavit to the HSCA which stated, among other things, that: "I was at Parkland Hospital and later at Bethesda Naval Hospital on the evening of November 22, 1963. There was no difference in the nature of the wounds I saw at Parkland Hospital and those I observed at the autopsy at Bethesda Naval Hospital."[46]

The above statement is noteworthy for many things, the most remarkable of which is this: Dr. Burkley, possibly the only medical person who saw the body in both places (Parkland *and* Bethesda), stated that the wounds he saw were unchanged from Parkland to

Bethesda. All other medical personnel testimony contradicts his affidavit—the Dallas doctors saw one set of wounds; the Bethesda doctors saw another set of wounds. Therefore, Burkley's statement is at odds with all other known medical testimony concerning JFK's wounds. One then must choose to believe Burkley or all the other doctors (and there were dozens). I tend to discredit Burkley's affidavit, because it is refuted by all other medical descriptions of the two wound patterns.

The Grand Deception

The plotters' initial medical challenge was how to prevent an autopsy from being performed in Dallas as prescribed by Texas law. An honest autopsy performed before body alteration took place would have exposed the true nature of JFK's wounds. This problem was solved by sheer physical force and threat of violence. When the Dallas coroner, Dr. Earl Rose, tried to step in at Parkland and perform his legally sworn duties, Secret Service agent Roy Kellerman drew his weapon and promised to shoot Rose if he interfered with the Secret Service getaway. Researchers have always pointed to this brazen "highjacking" of the President's body as proof that the conspirators did not want a credible autopsy performed in Dallas. But what if the real reason the Secret Service illegally rushed the President's casket out of Parkland is that the casket was empty or that there was a substitute corpse in the casket? As far-fetched as it might seem, there is evidence which points to the possibility that JFK's corpse had already been "switched out" at Parkland by the time the Secret Service rolled out the expensive, ornamental casket provided by Oneal funeral home. The plotters needed access to Kennedy's body to alter the wounds, so why not steal the body at the source, amid the chaos and confusion at Parkland Hospital? In all the bedlam, no one noticed that there were two funeral home ambulances present. While Oneal was the official funeral home summoned to bring a casket to Parkland, there was another "unofficial" funeral home represented at Parkland that day. Despite not getting the job of providing a casket and hearse for the dead President, Restland Funeral Home mortician John Melvin Liggett drove his hearse, possibly containing a casket with a pre-wrapped corpse inside of it, to Parkland shortly after hearing of the assassination.

We know this because a source with inside information has come forward to verify this and tell an incredible story of deception and medical forgery that is at the heart of the plan to cover up the truth of JFK's murder. She has requested anonymity, for the sake of herself and her family. I'll refer to her by the pseudonym Gwen DiBoard. Gwen knew John Liggett very well and divulged his secrets over the course of a year in a series of revealing interviews with this author. She claims that Liggett somehow got access to the President's body and altered his wounds between the time it entered Parkland and the time it arrived at Bethesda Medical Center near Washington, DC. How did the plotters know of Liggett's skill, and how did he come to be recruited into the plot? One needs to examine Liggett's background for the answers. His story begins, as do many others in this sordid tale, in the Civil Air Patrol.

Born in 1933 to Francis and Neva Liggett, John had six siblings, one of whom, named Malcolm, was tangentially associated with Jack Ruby and Lyndon Johnson, and came to serve the U.S. government in extraordinary ways (see the previous chapter). For his own part, John also worked with government operatives in more secretive settings. He was first recruited into intelligence work in the same way that Lee Harvey Oswald, David Ferrie, Barry Seal, Charles Rogers and James Bath were—in D.H. Byrd's LCAP. The cover story for the creation of LCAP was that the U.S. Air Force needed an auxiliary unit to patrol our borders during war time and serve as a training ground for future military pilots. The reality of LCAP was much different. Close scrutiny of its personnel and operations reveals its obvious connections to the CIA.

Cadets, Creeps and Killers

Running the country and the world required the CIA to raise its own money in order that its operations be kept secret. Using more than its rationed share of public funds would have risked exposure. Even though oil and banking millionaires chipped in for big events, like the murder of a sitting U.S. president, the CIA had to be mostly self-sufficient. It did this by, among other things, selling narcotics and running guns. And in order to sell drugs it needed pilots who could fly all over the world to make pick-ups and drop-offs. So the CIA came up with a novel idea—it would recruit young, impressionable, adventure-seeking cadets from the Civil Air Patrol who aspired to a life of daring and stealth. The ideal recruit would also lack morals or a social conscience, or, in the alternative, would be a loner, willing to commit abnormal or questionable acts without resistance.

Subsequently, an unusually high number of these CAP cadets became psychopathic killers, CIA pilots, or gullible, low-level fall guys. In order to facilitate its recruitment of CAP cadets, the CIA needed mesmeric leaders who had sway over young men. It found one such leader in David Ferrie, a defrocked priest, a skilled pilot, a hypnotist and a pedophile. Ferrie, we now know, was well acquainted with numerous players in the JFK assassination drama, including Oswald, Liggett, Seal and Rogers. Oswald did not become a drug-running pilot, but there were plenty of other CAP members who did, like Barry Seal and Charles Rogers.

Seal was entrusted by the CIA to fly drugs out of southeast Asia, Central America and South America; guns in and out of troubled nations across the globe; and operatives to secret CIA missions whenever it needed a democratic or socialist leader overthrown. As previously stated, when Seal was murdered in the mid-1980s, he was found to have on his person the private phone number of George H. W. "Poppy" Bush.

Another CAP alumnus who became notorious was Texas native

Charles Rogers, CIA pilot and murdering psychopath. Rogers was as brilliant as he was disturbed. A graduate of the University of Houston, Rogers worked as a seismologist for Shell Oil in the 1950s before joining the CIA. It is a seismologist's job to determine if the underlying rock or substrata of any particular area is fertile ground to drill for oil or natural gas. This was and is vital information to oil companies; thus, seismologists and geologists are in great demand. But that kind of life was apparently not adventurous enough for Charles. So in 1956, he applied with the CIA and was interviewed in the offices of Shell Oil's law firm, Fulbright-Jaworski (yes, the Leon Jaworski of Watergate fame); DeMohrenschildt conducted the interview.[47] The CIA always had a cozy relationship with big American oil companies. Much of the business required international knowledge and enterprise, for which CIA operatives were well-prepared. Also, uncooperative or socialist foreign governments sometimes were resistant to American oil companies taking over their natural resources; the CIA often used its "influence" to convince them otherwise. In return, the CIA got much of its funding from big oil.

On DeMohrenschildt's recommendation, and with a good word from David Ferrie, Rogers was hired by the "Company." He was assigned to Latin America, where his piloting experience came in handy. As an avowed anti-communist, Rogers enthusiastically flew men and weapons into and out of Guatemala and points south in preparation for the Bay of Pigs invasion. Rogers and his CIA cohorts blamed the president for the abysmal failure of the operation. But an internal investigation released in 1978 blamed the CIA's "ignorance, incompetence and arrogance" for the disaster.[48] The report absolved President Kennedy, saying that he was misinformed and misled.

In any event, Rogers next showed up around the time of the assassination. What his exact role was is unclear, but Rogers was photographed in Dealey Plaza on November 22, 1963. He was one of the three "tramps" being led away from the scene of the crime by men dressed as Dallas police officers; he was identified as such by a Houston police department forensic artist named Lois Gibson.[49]

Just weeks before the Kennedy assassination, Rogers met up with Oswald (or, quite possibly, the Oswald impostor) and a contract killer named Charles Harrelson in Houston. A neighbor of Rogers, a minister named Elmer Gerhart, allowed Oswald and Harrelson into his home for a meal and some rest while they waited for Rogers. Gerhart, a virtuous and conscientious man who had no reason to lie, claimed that Harrelson and Oswald had travelled together on a bus from New Orleans and that they were meeting up with Rogers for the next leg of their journey: Mexico. After JFK was killed, Gerhart recognized newspaper photos of Oswald as the man he had let into his home two months prior.[50] On November 22, 1963, one of the hobos seen with Rogers in the custody of Dallas police in Dealey Plaza bears a remarkable resemblance to Harrelson. In 1980 Harrelson was convicted of killing a federal judge in Texas; upon his arrest, he implied that the CIA was involved in the assassination of Kennedy.[51] (See chapter 7 for more discussion of the three tramps.)

After 1963, Rogers led a secretive, mysterious existence. His parents became so concerned about his covert activities that they contacted the Veterans Administration (Charles had served in the U.S. Navy) in seeking help for their strange son. The threat of exposure prompted Charles to murder his parents by beating them to death with a hammer on Father's Day 1965.[52] Afterwards he cut them up into small pieces and stuffed their mutilated corpses into a freezer; then he simply disappeared off the face of the earth. It is known only that he worked as a CIA pilot, and sightings of him were sketchy and rare.

James R. Bath turned out to be another "illustrious" grad of Byrd's Civil Air Patrol. Bath served in the CAP in the mid-1950s, about the time Oswald, Ferrie, Seal, Liggett and the other CIA recruits were active members. But it's what he accomplished after his CAP training that makes him notorious.

After leaving active duty with the Air Force, Bath joined the Texas Air National Guard in 1965 where he met his great pal, George W. Bush, just as the Vietnam War was escalating. The Air National Guard was considered a hideout for those pilots who wanted to avoid combat, and W. and Bath were given special privileges not accorded to other pilots. While officers without political connections fought and died in Vietnam, the sons of a powerful few skated through without flying a single war-time mission. These "special cases," like Bush, shirked their training duties without suffering the consequences. The 147th Fighter Group in Houston was a "champagne" outfit; its roster included John Connally's son, Senator Lloyd Bentsen's son, the grandson of H.L. Hunt, and two sons of Bush-connected oilman Sid Adger. Bush himself apparently went AWOL from the unit in 1972.[53]

Bath began a lucrative CIA career when he was recruited into the agency by "George [H.W.] Bush himself."[54] According to author Pete Brewton, Bath was used by Bush in several notorious CIA operations, including the Savings and Loans/Iran-Contra scandals of the 1980s; he also worked for Edward du Pont's Atlantic Aviation, a CIA subsidiary; he became a trustee "for two of the richest families in Saudi Arabia...that provided financing to Adnan Khashoggi around the time of the Khashoggi-Ghorbanifar arms-for-hostages transactions"; formed a Cayman islands laundering operation for Oliver North; obtained a "sweetheart" contract for his gas company as repayment for his loyalty; and profited from the S&L collapse.[55] There is also evidence that Bath was the link between the bin Laden family and the Bushes. A Texas businessman named Bill White, who had inside knowledge of the arrangement, claimed that the bin Ladens were investors in Arbusto, W. Bush's oil company, and it was Bath who brokered the deal.[56] The dirty and secretive connection between the bin Ladens and the Bushes was evident on 9/11 when the bin Ladens were quickly and safely spirited out of the country by forces at the highest echelons of the American government.

So anxious were the Bushes to disassociate themselves from Bath and the Saudis, they redacted his name from White House documents turned over in the investigation of 9/11; according to author Craig Unger, Bath was a witness to "…how the richest family in the world, the House of Saud, and its surrogates courted the Bush family."[57] Bath went far with his Bush connections, and he is not the only one. The Bush family's bizarre and suspicious connections to the characters involved in the JFK assassination are explored in another chapter.

Liggett's Role

Of the odd-lot of treacherous and inscrutable Louisiana Civil Air Patrol/CIA recruits who were peripherally or directly involved in the plot to kill President Kennedy and cover up his death, no one played a more diabolical role than John Liggett. Liggett served in the unit in the 1950s at about the time Oswald and Ferrie first met. Since LCAP records have been destroyed, there is no way to know if these men served together. What we do know is that Liggett went on to serve in the Air Force where he worked as an attache, often a euphemism for intelligence work. After being discharged sometime in the late 1950s he learned the mortuary trade. He studied at Gupton Jones, which later became the Dallas Institute of Funeral Services. Around 1960 he got a job as a mortician at Restland Funeral Home in Dallas. Restland had a shady reputation in the 1950s and '60s. It was known as the place where Mafia figures and covert intelligence types had bodies buried. An adjacent graveyard was known derisively as the "field of honor," for being the final resting place of hoodlums and various others whose deaths needed to be covered up.

Liggett became so good at his craft that he was known as one of the best "body reconstructionists" in his industry. If someone died a violent death and the family or other interested parties needed the victim to look presentable in the casket, Liggett was the man to call. One of his colleagues, Charles Smith, said, "If [Liggett] had to build a lip or nose or…an eye orbit or ear he may work all night long doing the reconstructive work on someone that had been shot in the face or [injured in an] automobile accident. He was the best."[58]

Liggett's "side work" often took him away from his normal duties at Restland. Co-workers often wondered what he was up to, and why he was such a privileged character; however, they learned not to question his whereabouts. They knew Liggett was protected by powerful interests, and that he was allowed to come and go as he pleased. Still, he lay low in his personal life until 1962 when he met and married a widow named Lois Godwin whose husband had been killed in a plane crash.

Gwen DiBoard, who was close to the Godwin family, now thinks the plane crash that killed Lois Godwin's first husband, Charles Godwin, Sr., was no accident and was in fact arranged by interests who wanted to give Liggett an air of legitimacy and normalcy as the "Big Event" of 1963 approached. Godwin was a pilot with his own small aircraft, an asset always coveted by the CIA, and he knew many of the movers and shakers of Dallas. He and his wife Lois were musicians who would often play gigs at the homes of wealthy and connected Dallasites, including D.H. Byrd. Coincidentally, the Godwins' hosts would often find their residences robbed of jewelry; DiBoard has reason to think that Charles Godwin might have been the notorious King of Diamonds cat burglar who was looting Dallas homes in the early '60s. Or he, in some way, played a part in helping the King of Diamonds by "casing" victims' homes.

My interviews of DiBoard are presented below in transcript form.

GD: "Charles Godwin knew everyone important in Dallas,

and had access to all the richest homes and hotel parties in town. He and his wife were the hot musician duos for these private gigs. If, say, they were playing an event at the Baker Hotel and knew in advance who would be attending the party, they might have alerted the thief of whose house to break in. I also think these thefts were inside scams for the insurance money. So the owners might have been in on it. Remember, Billie Sol Estes (LBJ's swindling partner) was a big insurance scammer, and he travelled in these circles. And Iris Campbell (LBJ's events coordinator), a friend of Lois Godwin's, participated in criminal schemes with a group of jewelers who staged robberies of themselves for the insurance payout. I also saw cigar boxes full of jewelry at the Godwin residence in Grapevine (a Dallas suburb). Charles would take them apart and get the stones out. There was also this curious incident at the Byrd mansion when the Godwins played a private party there shortly before Charles was killed. Lois Godwin found an expensive diamond watch on the ground which belonged to Mrs. Byrd, with an inscription from D.H. Byrd. Lois returned the watch the next day, and did not accept a reward." Was it possible that this personally inscribed item was of no use to the burglars because it would have been easily identifiable?

All this points to the Dallas underworld and moneyed elites, in particular D.H. Byrd, being quite aware of Charles Godwin and his activities. It is not a stretch then to imagine that he might have been approached by them. DiBoard speculates that Mafia/intelligence operatives, always in need of pilots who were at ease with covert and criminal operations, may have offered Godwin a job working for them. When he refused their offer, Godwin met his end. The cause of the 1962 crash remains a mystery. Regardless, when he died, Liggett took his place. Godwin left behind a widow and four children, but soon Liggett married Lois Godwin, and became stepfather to three young girls and one boy. "It was as if he walked into a ready-made family for himself. The perfect cover for whatever secretive stuff he was up to," said DiBoard.

As friends of the Godwin children, DiBoard often visited their home and got to know Liggett very well. She describes him as a smooth operator, one who was brilliant and yet seemed to be hiding something just beneath the surface.

> GD: "I never saw him lose his temper; he never harshly disciplined those kids. He loved James Bond movies and jazz. He smoked a lot. He liked his cocktails, but I never saw him drunk. There was no change in his demeanor when he was drinking. He was tall and lean, about six feet, two inches. He had incredible blue eyes. Always neat, clean and well-dressed. He was a chess master and professional poker player. He was always well-groomed, and he never had facial hair. He couldn't grow it. I liked him, but the kids told me it was like living in a hurricane. John was calm in the middle, but strong, uneasy forces were nearby at all times."

On November 22, 1963, Liggett was officiating the funeral of his wife's aunt at Restland Funeral Home, when he was suddenly called away from the graveside shortly after 12:30 p.m. He returned to the grieving relatives a few minutes later to tell his wife that Kennedy had been shot and he had to go to Parkland Hospital. When Lois asked him if Restland was going to get the job, John replied that he did not know but that she should not try to contact him. This was quite unusual. Normally when Liggett was on a job or on call, his wife and kids visited him at the funeral home. Never before had he instructed them to stay away. Equally as strange, Liggett did not return home until the next day. When he arrived he seemed worn and disheveled, quite unlike his customarily cool comportment and dapper dress.

What had Liggett been up to for those missing 24 hours? His stepchildren had some very provocative thoughts on that and shared them with DiBoard over the years.

> GD: "Given his unique skills, his dark connections, and his secretive ways, the family believed he had something to do with altering JFK's body postmortem to disguise the truth of who really killed him."
>
> TF: "What makes them believe that?"
>
> GD: "John told them he went to Parkland that day, and he was in a rush to get there. A Restland employee named Wes Allen saw Liggett leave in a hearse with another co-worker; it is believed they brought a coffin with them."
>
> TF: "What time would they have arrived at Parkland Hospital?"
>
> GD: "They could have been there as early as 1:10 p.m."
>
> TF: "Shortly after the President had been pronounced dead."
>
> GD: "Correct. They would have known this by the time they arrived there."
>
> TF: "Does the Godwin family think Liggett and his co-worker were trying to solicit the mortuary work for Restland?"
>
> GD: "No. They did not want to be part of the official record of events that day. Their purpose was secretive. They were most likely appearing as if they were supposed to be there. It was not at all unusual for Restland employees to be hanging around Parkland. John

actually called Lois from the hospital, and she could hear the noise and chaos of all the commotion in the background."

TF: "What was Liggett doing there, then?"

GD: "The family thinks he was there to remove JFK's corpse and substitute it with another corpse, one Liggett brought with him from Restland already wrapped in sheets and pre-soaked with blood around the head area. Liggett somehow got access to the Emergency Room and made the switch there."

As astounding as this story is, there is corroboration for it which comes from LBJ's corrupt sidekick, Billie Sol Estes. In his book, *Billie Sol Estes—A Texas Legend,* Estes claims that sometime prior to the assassination Liggett used his unique body alteration skills on an unknown corpse, similar in height and weight to JFK, to create a medical forgery. Liggett "constructed" a rear head-wound entrance on the corpse to make it appear the man had been shot from behind. Pictures and x-rays of the false wound were taken and then introduced into the official record of JFK's assassination. The impostor's brain was even used as a substitute for JFK's. As sensational as these allegations are, they do provide an explanation for the many discrepancies in JFK's autopsy x-rays and photographs, as well as the mysterious disposition of his brain (matters that will be discussed later). Liggett stored the "fake" corpse at the Restland morgue until the day of the assassination.[59] Estes does not reveal his source, but such sensitive information which was at the heart of the plotters' deception could only have come from a powerful insider. And Lyndon Johnson was the only powerful insider that Estes knew.

At least one of Estes's claims is suspect. According to him, the fake corpse was flown to Washington on a private plane. If this were true, there would have been no reason for Liggett to rush off to

Parkland Hospital on November 22; he could have simply escorted the fake body to Washington without switching it for JFK's corpse at Parkland. Why would Liggett undertake the trouble of a dangerous and difficult body switch at Parkland if his job were merely to fly his "pre-altered corpse" to Bethesda?

> TF: "But there are no reports in the literature of another coffin or dead body at Parkland about that time." (I later learned there *were* reports of another critically wounded patient entirely separate from Kennedy and Connally.)
>
> GD: "No one knows for a fact exactly how it occurred, but the family thinks Liggett finessed his way through the corridors of Parkland. There were many entrances and exits to the hospital and he knew them all. He was there before the Oneal coffin arrived. Perhaps he wheeled in the fake corpse in a linen basket, and with the Secret Service's help made it into the Trauma Room. There were reports of clean-up being done by orderlies or nurses. How did the towels and sheets get in there? There was a period when no one was in the room except for the Secret Service. When the Oneal coffin arrived and the body was loaded into it, it was already wrapped in sheets. The Godwins believe this was the substitute corpse John had brought with him. Once this corpse was inside the Oneal casket, the Secret Service was not about to let anyone near it. It was sealed and would not be opened until it got to Bethesda. Aubrey Rike, Oneal's guy, did what the Secret Service told him to."

Much of what DiBoard says above is corroborated by other sources. At one point, according to an FBI report, Secret Service agent William Greer was the only agent stationed inside the Parkland emergency room with JFK.[60] The same William Greer who drove the death car into Dealey Plaza and kept his foot on the brake until JFK's head had been blown off. The same William Greer who looked back twice at the President as he was being hit by gunfire and still did not speed away or take evasive action until he saw that the President had been hit in the head. The same William Greer who once worked for Henry Cabot Lodge, Kennedy's political rival. The same William Greer whom Clint Hill claimed pulled out a handgun during the motorcade and pointed it right at Hill as he jumped onto the trunk of the death car during the shooting.[61] The same William Greer who was photographed smiling and laughing with his Secret Service side-kicks Kellerman and Hill after their Warren Commission testimony on March 8, 1964. The same William Greer who, at Bethesda, first posed the theory of the magic bullet to confused autopsy doctors who found no bullets in JFK's body.[62]

Rike told David Lifton that Secret Service agents wouldn't let him out of the room once he put the body in the casket.[63] Rike also explained how he and his co-worker 'Peanuts' McGuire "…lifted the President, wrapped in sheets, into the coffin. The casket had been lined with a piece of plastic."[64] Several Parkland nurses reported washing the President's body and covering him with a sheet, but they did not claim that they *wrapped* him in a sheet. Dr. Phillip Williams, Nurse Pat Hutton and Nurse Doris Nelson said they thought the body was laid in a mattress cover.[65] This was probably the piece of plastic to which Rike referred. The important point here is that none of these personnel did the wrapping of the body, which begs the question: who did?

There were also reports of other undocumented bodies being wheeled around Parkland early that afternoon. Nurse Beth Lozano reported that "…a technician came to the desk and asked me to expect a private patient who was bleeding…blood technicians came to ask me who 'Mr. X' was who did not have an ER number.

Hematology also came with the same problem and was told the same thing."[66]

The Parkland elevator operator, an Otis Elevator employee named Nathan Pool, saw a body being rolled out of the Trauma Room by Secret Service agents. The body was not in a coffin, but rather on a stretcher, and was hidden by a purple cover. Other Secret Service agents remained behind in the Emergency Room. Pool assumed the corpse under the purple cover was JFK, but how could this be if JFK's body had been loaded into the Oneal casket inside Trauma Room One. If the supposed Secret Service agent Pool had seen was actually John Liggett, then Pool might have unwittingly witnessed the "body switch" deception.

Parkland administrator Jack Price also encountered a possible phony agent; a man, supposedly a Secret Service agent "who had been bruised or had a minor injury," approached Price to ask him about alternative ways out of the hospital, and Price showed him a secret "tunnel" passageway.[67] This secret exit was obviously not used to remove the Oneal casket (ostensibly with JFK's body inside) from Parkland. So what was it used for? Why did a Secret Service agent (assuming he was an agent) go to so much trouble to explore possible secret exits from Parkland? Was this the exit used by Liggett and an accomplice to remove JFK's corpse? No record exists of an agent receiving treatment for a minor wound at Parkland. The question, then, of the legitimacy of the agents inside Parkland needs to be raised. Posing as Secret Service agents was a subterfuge used by several of the plotters, including the shooters in Dealey Plaza, on November 22, 1963. This might have been the ruse that helped Liggett to accomplish his task inside Parkland.

Pool was someone to be taken seriously, as the House Select Committee on Assassinations did when it interviewed him in 1977. It was Pool, and not Darrell Tomlinson (as reported in the Warren Commission), who actually discovered the pristine bullet (soon to be known as the magic bullet or CE 399) on a stretcher inside

Parkland Hospital. Pool found it near some bloody sheets on an abandoned stretcher that could not have been either JFK's or Connally's stretcher. An internal HSCA memo describes Pool as a credible witness, and it admits that a Secret Service agent was "close enough to the elevator to plant a bullet."[68] The planted bullet, supposedly fired from Oswald's rifle, was supposed to be matched to the back wound seen on JFK's body at the Bethesda autopsy, in order to incriminate Oswald; instead, it became a major kink in the plotter's scheme. Once the plotters realized that the bullet had to account for many more wounds than just the one on Kennedy's back, the unscathed nature of CE 399 opened the Warren Commission up to ridicule. How could a pristine bullet rip through Kennedy's back and throat, strike Connally in the back, tear through his chest, break his wrist, and leave fragments in his thigh? Only a super-bullet, one with magical qualities, could do that. But that's the only explanation Arlen Specter's crazy magic-bullet theory left for the plotters. No matter that the original autopsy findings did not allow for a transiting bullet (Dr. James Humes probed the back wound and found that it did not extend beyond his fingertip.). No matter that the back wound was placed much lower than JFK's throat wound, suggesting an impossible upward trajectory. And no matter that no one in Dallas, including John Connally himself, described CE 399 as passing through both Kennedy and Connally.

Liggett and the Corpse

One of the many enduring mysteries in the Kennedy case is why Liggett went to Parkland at all. Why intercept Kennedy's corpse there? Presumably, there was no realistic opportunity to alter JFK's wounds at Parkland with so many witnesses there. Logic dictates that Liggett, and ostensibly an autopsist who knew how to section a brain, needed to work in a private place away from prying eyes to do their dirty work. I asked DiBoard about this.

TF: "If we look at the plotters' alteration scheme, it is basically this: steal the body at Point A, alter the body at Point B, and reintroduce the body to the Oneal coffin at Point C. We know from the public record that Point C was Bethesda Naval Hospital. But where were Points A and B?"

GD: "I really think that Point A was Parkland Hospital. Why else would Liggett go to Parkland shortly after the President was rushed there? The plan was to switch the bodies and then perform the alterations somewhere else. It went according to plan until the coroner stepped in."

TF: "Dr. Rose got in the way."

Dallas coroner Dr. Earl Rose insisted that an autopsy be performed on Kennedy, per Texas law, before the body left the state. It led to an ugly confrontation between Secret Service agents and Rose. With guns drawn, and bodily harm threatened to anyone who dared to get in their way, the agents illegally commandeered the body out of Parkland.

GD: "Right. This almost threw a major monkey wrench into the plot. Can you imagine if Rose had opened the coffin to find an impostor inside?"

TF: "How did the impostor corpse get there?"

GD: "Remember, Wes Allen (a Restland Funeral Home employee) saw Liggett drive away from Restland in a hearse that had a casket loaded inside of it. Caskets like that were easily accessible to morticians. In fact, on Halloween the Godwin children and I would play with the shipping caskets that Liggett brought home for a prop...you know, to scare kids on Halloween. I believe Liggett, not necessarily alone at this, transported a 'pre-wrapped' body of a male of similar weight and size to that of the President in that Restland casket. Easy enough for a funeral home like Restland, and a mortician like John, to have a corpse obtained in advance and ready for the call that came on November 22."

TF: "This corpse must have been someone who did not have any family or who had died under questionable circumstances…circumstances unknown to the public?"

GD: "Exactly. I'm the one who told you about the 'field of honor,' remember? Restland did that sort of thing. There was a shady element to the business, and Liggett was at the center of it."

TF: "So, let's get back to the timing of this. The Oneal coffin did not arrive at Parkland until 1:40 p.m.; if Liggett got there just after 1 p.m., he would have had a little over half an hour to do his work. At some point, TR1 is cleared out, not even Jackie was inside… only SS agents."

GD: "Yes. The pre-wrapped body replaces JFK's body on the table in TR1, and John somehow wheels JFK out on a stretcher or in a linen cart beneath some sheets and towels. He would have then loaded the body into the Restland coffin, probably a cheap shipping casket, and driven off to the airport. Though likely not Love Field. More likely Red Bird where a CIA pilot was revving his engines and waiting for him."

TF: "It would have taken a lot of, what, fearlessness or audacity to wheel the President's body out of Parkland. Did Liggett have the moxie for something like that?

GD: "Only people who knew John Liggett personally, could totally understand how he could pull this scenario off...cool as a cucumber and totally in control. You have to know his charisma and genius."

It is hard to recreate in words the utter bedlam that prevailed at Parkland in the minutes and hours that the mortally wounded President was there. William Manchester, author of *The Death Of A President* writes, "...the emergency area had been overwhelmed... There were too many people...an almost total collapse of discipline."[69] Dr. Crenshaw put it more succinctly: "It was a goddamn madhouse in the Emergency Room...people running, yelling."[70] The Secret Service agents, out of guilt or paranoia or culpability, were wildly unruly. They challenged everyone in sight; no one knew whom to trust, and everyone was on guard. Clint Hill waved a handgun at doctors.[71] Someone who knew the score and had the temperament and credentials to keep his composure—someone like John Liggett—could have worked calmly and purposefully with Secret Service agent plotters to abscond with the most important evidence in the murder, the President's body.

TF: "However, I have read no account, seen no pictures, heard no witnesses' claims as to another coffin (Restland's coffin) leaving Parkland at about the same time as the Oneal coffin did."

GD: "That's because Liggett probably did not bring the fake corpse into Parkland inside a casket. He likely left the casket he brought with him in the Restland hearse parked outside Parkland. If he did wheel the coffin into Parkland, though, it would not have seemed unusual. This was his business; Restland personnel were known to do this. And the Restland coffin would have left before the Oneal coffin did. They didn't leave at the same time or at the same exit. Restland left earlier, after being 'dismissed' from duty if you will. As for witnesses or pictures...to my knowledge there were never any pictures even of the arrival of the Oneal coffin, so who knows if there was one, two or 50 coffins around the place? If those are never in the same room at the same time, who would really pay that kind of attention under the circumstances? Only the Secret Service. And we know whose side they were on. There are a lot of ways in and out of Parkland. And the Oneal coffin was only photographed when it was loaded and leaving from the dock, supposedly with the body in it. Why? Because people only wanted to photograph the coffin they were told contained the President's body. The one they had been waiting for. Unlike today, when everyone is photographing literally everything with cell phone cameras, etc., that was not the case back then."

TF: "So amid the confusion, Liggett moves quickly to the exit claiming to all within earshot that Oneal has gotten the job and Restland is certainly sorry for being so presumptuous."

GD: "Well, something like that would be likely. But John would NOT have moved quickly to the exit! He would have rolled out smoothly. I can imagine him mentioning, *if necessary*, to anyone who looked too curious or asked questions, that Restland's services simply weren't needed...an actual statement of fact. It could have been assumed they were there for someone else who died that day, for example. To mention specifically to anyone, at that time, that Oneal 'got the job' doesn't even sound like John's style. If I take liberties at times, describing what I imagine a conversation or scene was like, it is because I lived in those historic times and, more importantly, I did know

John Liggett...the smooth operator that he was."

TF: "Somewhere in here John calls his wife to tell her he has to leave and not to contact him."

GD: "Yes, he did place a brief call to her from there. But, he had *already* told her not to attempt to contact him, that he had to leave (meaning the funeral of a relative) and he would be 'on call.' He did that when he was standing beside her at Restland, directing his wife's aunt's funeral and had just gotten the 'news' of the assassination. He left her immediately. I guess he just called her later to briefly say good-bye. He knew he was undertaking his most dangerous assignment and wanted to hear the voice of his wife before he left."

TF: "Lifton, of course, believes that the body theft occurred elsewhere, mainly because the body showed up in a government-issued body bag and cheap shipping coffin at Bethesda. I doubt that Restland would have put the body in a body bag and shipping coffin inside Parkland."

GD: "No. No way. Like I said before, I think Liggett wheeled JFK's body out of Parkland on a stretcher or a cart of some sort. And then it was loaded into the hearse out of eyesight of nosy witnesses whose attention was focused elsewhere. But if it *was* placed in a coffin inside Parkland, it was certainly not a cheap shipping casket. It would have been put (switched) into Restland's nice coffin at Parkland and then transferred to the cheap shipping casket at some later time...maybe where the alteration took place. But to show up at Parkland hospital with a nice 'regular' coffin, suitable for a president is what Restland would have done...supposedly to offer their services to provide a coffin and take it to the airport...which is all

Oneal ultimately did. To have a regular coffin, or two, rolling around in Parkland would not have looked that odd, whereas a cheap shipping coffin would have. Once Restland [Liggett] left the hospital, who would have known or paid any attention to where they went?"

TF: "If the theft of the body did happen at Parkland, it answers a lot of questions I have about the timing of the body alteration. Once he had control of the President's body, Liggett presumably drove to Red Bird Airport where the coffin could have been loaded into a CIA plane and flown to Washington in plenty of time for the plotters to alter the body. Lifton's scenario, that JFK's body left Parkland in the Oneal coffin and was transported via Air Force One to Andrews Air Force base near Washington, leaves precious little time for body alteration prior to the commencement of the autopsy."

GD: "Right. Liggett and company would have needed more time to alter the wounds and remove the bullets than Lifton allows under his theory."

TF: "Lifton suggests that the body was stowed in a closet on Air Force One and put aboard a helicopter after landing at Andrews AFB."

GD: "Whatever! He has to sell books...I don't."

TF: "Others believe that the body was flown back to Washington on Air Force 2. They have circumstantial support for this: Roy Kellerman's shirt and suit were soaked in blood, presumably from moving the body from AF1 to AF2 during LBJ's swearing in; the bloody shirt was confirmed by the AF2 pilot. Aboard Air Force 2 were the Secret Service culprits: Kellerman, Greer and Roberts (and possibly John?). So they could have secured the environment for alteration there."

GD: "There were so many people watching AF1 during the swearing in time; it seems highly unlikely that Liggett and the Secret Service took JFK's body to Love Field. Someone would have noticed a second casket being loaded onto AF2. Kellerman could have gotten bloody from moving the body while in Parkland when he helped Liggett lift it off the emergency room table and onto a stretcher or into a cart."

I agreed with DiBoard about that. A Love Field theft and transfer of the body to AF2 was unlikely, but there were plenty of other odd activities aboard AF1. Most notably, LBJ employed some highly suspicious delay tactics, and made some strange requests before departure for Andrews AFB. Johnson insisted that his swearing-in ceremony (neither sanctioned nor required by the Constitution) be conducted aboard AF1. While the plane was sitting on the tarmac at Love Field, and, supposedly, the body of the dead President was lying in a rear compartment, Johnson sent for Sarah Hughes, a Dallas judge and his personal friend, to officiate the ceremony. If JFK's corpse actually was aboard AF1 during this time period, why would the plotters want to waste valuable time just idling at Love Field when the time could have been put to better use? It makes more sense that JFK's corpse was elsewhere, and that LBJ's stall tactics were meant to give the plotters more time to transport and alter the corpse before reuniting it with the Oneal casket in Washington.

Author David Lifton has advanced the theory that JFK's body was removed from the Oneal coffin aboard AF1 and stowed in a luggage compartment while everyone else on AF1 was witnessing LBJ's swearing-in; thus, the contention is that the swearing-in was a diversionary tactic meant to give the conspirators the time and privacy they needed to remove JFK's corpse. But the coffin was being watched by Kennedy aides who refused to attend the swearing-in ceremony. Surely this would have dissuaded any conspirator from removing the corpse from the coffin. However, for argument's sake, let's assume that the conspirators did manage to steal the corpse aboard AF1 and stow it elsewhere on the plane. Once the plane landed at Andrews AFB at approximately 6 p.m. eastern time, the corpse, according to Lifton, was secretly removed from the "back side" of AF1 and loaded onto a helicopter for a quick flight to the alteration site. This would have put the body at this site by approximately 6:10-6:15 p.m., where parties unknown altered the corpse and removed bullets from it and then delivered it to Bethesda. Common sense tells us that this is simply not enough time to perform all these tasks.

How do we know there was not sufficient time to do all this? Because Bethesda Navy hospital corpsman Dennis David, Chief of the Day on November 22, testified under oath that Kennedy's body arrived at Bethesda in a cheap shipping casket (*not the Oneal casket it supposedly left Dallas in*) at 6:30 p.m.[72] If David is right, and there is no reason to disbelieve him, it seems that Lifton's scenario is untenable. And it is preposterous to suggest alteration and bullet removal was done on AF1 or in the helicopter between Andrews and Bethesda.

David's account *is* proof that JFK's corpse was separated from the Oneal coffin at some point because the corpse arrived at Bethesda *before* the Oneal coffin did (the Oneal coffin arrived at about 7 p.m. in a Navy ambulance). Kennedy's body had either been removed from the Oneal casket somewhere between Dallas and Washington, or it had never been placed in the Oneal coffin in the first place. It is the contention of this book that it was never placed in the Oneal casket; however, regardless of which scenario is true, what is known for certain is that Kennedy's corpse arrived at Bethesda in a cheap shipping casket and was enclosed in a body bag, which means some serious postmortem deception and chicanery was going on with the

President's body. The casket subterfuge is a direct result of the plotters needing more time to perform the medical forgery and a private place to do it.

Let's review. 1) The Parkland doctors described wounds that were radically different from the wounds the Bethesda doctors saw. 2) It stands to reason, then, that President Kennedy's wounds were altered somewhere between Parkland and Bethesda. 3) Kennedy's corpse arrived at Bethesda before the Dallas casket did. 4) This means that the corpse was either removed from the Dallas casket or it was never placed in the Dallas casket; either way, the purpose of body/casket switch must have been to alter the wounds and remove the bullets. 5) Removing the corpse from the Dallas casket while it was aboard AF1 would have left the plotters with insufficient time to perform alterations. 6) If the corpse was never placed in the Dallas casket, and was, instead, "intercepted" at Parkland, the plotters would have had enough time for alterations necessary to frame Oswald for the assassination. 7) This leaves Parkland as the likely place where the body theft took place; once the plotters had the corpse in their possession, they were free to fly it anywhere for alteration and bullet removal and then reunite it with the Oneal coffin at Bethesda.

As implausible as it might seem, this scheme is easier to accept when we consider that John Liggett—a CIA- and Mafia-connected mortician who kept company with David Ferrie, who served in Lee Harvey Oswald's LCAP unit, and who was a master of deceit and body reconstruction—was at Parkland during the 68 minutes between the time Kennedy was declared dead and the departure of the Oneal coffin. DiBoard's scenario is frighteningly tenable. Even Lifton concedes this was a real possibility: "If [Dennis] David's account was correct, plotters had obtained access to the body *before Air Force One left Dallas* (emphasis added)."[73] Either the Oneal casket was empty when it was lifted onto AF1, or Liggett had accomplished his body switch at Parkland and a phony corpse had been substituted into the Oneal casket. Interestingly, there is no testimony in the official record of anyone who handled the Oneal casket commenting on its surprisingly light weight.

Parkland Diversions

A common tactic employed by intelligence operatives in covert situations is a diversion. If Liggett did indeed steal JFK's body at Parkland, he might have benefited from two bizarre and clamorous diversions. One involved the obstinate intervention of the Dallas County Medical Examiner, Dr. Earl Rose; the other involved a priest of all people.

The protracted and ugly confrontation involving Dr. Rose, who insisted the body be kept in Dallas for an autopsy, and Secret Service agents who demanded that Rose release the body, began shortly after the Oneal coffin arrived at Parkland. Rose stubbornly stood his ground in the face of threats of violence. Author William Manchester called it, "…the loudest and largest uproar of the afternoon…"[74] Oneal employee Aubrey Rike who witnessed the argument said, "I was scared to death…we'd start pushing and someone would grab us and…pull the casket back."[75] It lasted for more than 30 minutes, and it got so heated that the Parkland hallways became jammed with irate combatants and spectators whose emotions ranged from disbelief to fear for their own safety. Kennedy aides—Powers, O'Donnell and Larry O'Brien—joined in the fracas, but for reasons other than the SS agents did. The Kennedy men did not fear an autopsy which would reveal the absolute truth about the nature of the President's wounds and how he was shot; they wanted to spare Jackie, and themselves, four more hours in Dallas, a place they considered a violent, un-American hellhole after what had happened minutes before in Dealey Plaza. They were mortified at the thought of an autopsy being performed by the same Texas hicks who had just murdered their President. But the motives of Kellerman, Greer and the other agents were quite different. Having done nothing to protect the Chief Executive they were sworn to protect, and, in fact, having contributed directly or indirectly to his murder, evading an honest autopsy was in their best interests. And if Rose had opened an empty coffin, or one containing a corpse other than Kennedy's, the plotters' ruse would have been exposed.

It is quite likely that as the altercation raged on, confusion and chaos reigned. Attention was diverted away from the President's corpse. People came and went; Trauma Room One was left unguarded. Even Vernon Oneal vacated his post to see what all the shouting was about.[76] This would have been the most opportune time for Liggett to pull off the body switch. With everyone's attention focused on the pitched battle for control of the corpse, the corpse itself might have vanished.

This brings into question the real motives behind the Rose incident. Was he genuinely concerned with Texas legalities, or was he just another pawn in a larger game being played out in Dallas that day? Rose's intractability surprised Oneal who knew him well and always found him "100%" cooperative with funeral directors.[77] Even Kennedy loyalists wondered about Rose's motives; they thought "perhaps he had been sent to delay them."[78] At one point a Dallas cop backed up Rose by pulling out his gun; this only escalated the confrontation, and made the Kennedy people more determined to resist Rose and the Dallas authorities.[79]

The other odd distraction was a Catholic priest named Father Cain. He first approached Jackie outside of the trauma room and offered his sympathy and indulgence. Then he began behaving abnormally. He flitted about erratically, babbling nonsense in the guise of prayers. He offered to lay a relic of the True Cross beside the dead President, and with Jackie's permission entered Trauma Room One. But when he returned to the hallway with the relic still in hand, Jackie and the others got disgusted and dismissed him.[80] However, Father Cain was there for the duration. He lingered at Parkland and made a spectacle of himself until the Oneal casket was loaded into the hearse at 2:08 p.m. Cain tried to follow the casket as it was loaded into the ambulance, but he was pushed aside by the Kennedy people.

Jangled nerves and rampant terror accompanied the ambulance to Love Field, where Larry O'Brien feared that the Dallas cops would board AF1 to take back the Oneal casket. He, General Godfrey McHugh (JFK's military aide) and Ken O'Donnell demanded that the plane take off immediately. When Johnson demurred, O'Brien asked himself a question that goes to the heart of Johnson's secret agenda, "What would he have done if we hadn't come?"[81] Exactly. How did Johnson know there would be no autopsy performed at Parkland? Certainly, he would not have waited on Air Force 1 while it idled at Love Field for four hours. At the least, we can assume that he had some awareness that someone at Parkland was managing things to turn out as the plotters intended. He knew the coffin would follow shortly after he left Parkland. He stated that he would not leave Dallas without the President's widow, and Jackie was not going to leave Parkland without the casket. This presumes then, that Johnson knew no autopsy would be performed in Dallas.

Bethesda Corroboration

The validity of Dennis David's account is verified by several Bethesda employees. One is x-ray technician Jerrol Custer, who, on the evening of the assassination, took several sets of x-rays of the dead President. In order to process the x-rays, Custer had to pass through the lobby of Bethesda on his way from the morgue, where the autopsy took place, to one of the upper floors of the hospital. On his second or third trip, his hands full of undeveloped film, he saw Jackie Kennedy enter the lobby having just arrived in the Navy hearse from Andrews AFB.[82] The hearse, of course, contained the Oneal coffin, and did not arrive at Bethesda until 7 p.m. This supports David's contention that JFK's corpse was at Bethesda long before Jackie and the Dallas coffin were.

Additional confirmation of David's story comes from a report submitted by a Marine Corps sergeant named Roger Boyajian who supervised a security detail of ten men at Bethesda on the evening of 11/22/63. The detail was ordered to report to Admiral Galloway at Bethesda at approximately 6 p.m. eastern time. This detail witnessed a cheap shipping casket (not the Oneal coffin), containing the dead President's body, arrive at the morgue entrance at approximately 6:35 p.m. According to Boyajian's report, "…the casket was received at the morgue entrance and taken inside"; the report also adds that "For the remainder of the evening, members of the detail were posted at various places throughout the corridors and morgue entrances…Their primary duty was to prevent anyone from taking photographs of any activity that took place therein."[83] So not only did the security detail of Marines bear witness to the casket shell game, they prevented any media personnel from recording the strange goings-on at Bethesda that night. Since Bethesda employees were military personnel they were easily dissuaded from divulging what they knew at the time, but many years later they came forward to contradict the official government lies. In all, eight Navy and Marine enlisted personnel swore that JFK's body was delivered to Bethesda at 6:35 p.m., or thereabouts, wrapped in a body bag and enclosed in a cheap metal coffin; it was not wrapped in sheets and not enclosed in the large ornamental coffin provided by Oneal Funeral Home in Dallas.[84] The cheap coffin was transported to the Bethesda morgue's loading dock in a black Cadillac hearse, from which several men in suits and two men in mortician smocks emerged.[85] Could one of the men wearing a smock have been John Liggett? It stands to reason that whoever was involved in the body alteration scheme would have helped deliver the stolen corpse to Bethesda for the official autopsy.

If we assume that the men in suits accompanying the shipping casket to Bethesda were Secret Service agents or plotters with Secret Service credentials, then at some point their actions needed a cover story in case suspicions were aroused. They would have met the corpse at a Washington-area airport around 5 p.m., offloaded it into a hearse, transported it to the alteration site (see the Walter Reed scenario below), and then driven to Bethesda by 6:35 p.m. The cover story for an extra coffin and body might have been that there was an agent killed in Dallas that day, and the corpse needed to be escorted to Washington for an autopsy. There *was* such a report of a dead agent which surfaced on November 22. NBC broadcast it as part of its assassination coverage that afternoon. As a result, Secret Service agent James K. Fox was ordered to "…put together a group of senior agents to meet a plane that day to receive the body of a dead agent."[86]

The Puzzle

To revisit the body/coffin-switch puzzle, we must return to Dallas. Assuming the Oneal casket had a phony corpse in it as it was loaded onto AF1 at 2:14 p.m. Dallas time, where was Kennedy's body? Presumably in flight back to the Washington, D.C., area, but aboard what plane? There was another jet parked at Love Field—Air Force 2—the Vice-President's plane. Was it possible that the conspirators secretly flew Kennedy's corpse back aboard Air Force 2 ahead of Air Force 1's landing at Andrews AFB? This is not likely, because records indicate that, even though Air Force 2 passed Air Force 1 in flight on the way back to Andrews, Air Force 2 did not land in Washington until 5:30 p.m., which allowed the plotters about a half-hour more to do the dirty work; this might have accommodated body altera-tion, but there is a problem with the AF2 theory. The plane's pilot and flight engineer both swore that no coffin or body was surrepti-tiously loaded onto AF2 in Dallas.[87] This brings us back to DiBoard's contention that Kennedy's body was probably flown out of Dallas aboard a CIA plane departing from Red Bird Airport. Liggett and his cohort(s) could have driven the body to Red Bird from Parkland as early as 2 p.m. central time. If this is so, the body, Liggett, and whomever else the plotters had hired to help alter the corpse and remove incriminating bullets could have arrived in Washington as early as 5 p.m. eastern time. This scenario allows a much more reasonable amount of time in which to perform alterations. But where did the alteration take place, aboard the CIA plane or at a location near Washington? More than half a century after the fact, this remains an open question because body alteration was never a consideration in any formal government investigation of the Kennedy assassination; therefore, one can only speculate based on the known testimony of relevant witnesses and the circumstances evident in the public record. A reconsideration of the timeline from Parkland to Bethesda is revelatory.

A proper investigation would have more closely examined the activities in and around Parkland on November 22. Much of what happened is lost to history, but we do have many indisputable things with which to work. We know that the Oneal casket left Parkland at or near 2 p.m. (Dave Powers noted the time as 2:08), and it arrived at Love Field approximately fifteen minutes later.[88] But was it empty or did it contain a corpse? And was the corpse JFK's or a "body double?" The casket was loaded onto AF1 with some great effort (the handles had to be removed so the casket could fit through the plane's door). Then the plane needlessly sat on the tarmac for about an hour. Kennedy loyalists were irate. Kenny O'Donnell ordered General McHugh to get the plane off the ground.[89] But Johnson refused, and one must ask why he did, for this is at the heart of the plotters' casket/body alteration timeline.

Johnson's delay tactics began at Parkland when he refused to leave the hospital in spite of the desperate pleas by Secret Service agents Roberts and Youngblood to get back to Love Field and take off for Washington as quickly as possible. The agents tried to explain to Johnson that he would be safer in the air than on the ground in Dallas. They provided all the excuse he needed to flee Parkland. Still he stalled. What were Johnson's motives for staying at Parkland?

Always aware of the political ramifications of his actions, Johnson might have been fearful of being seen as a power-hungry usurper who wanted to snatch the White House away from Kennedy before Kennedy's body was cold. Johnson told the men around him that he would not budge until Kenny O'Donnell gave him the go-ahead. But it's just as likely that Johnson had other motives, such as giving fellow conspirators time to fly Kennedy's body back to Washington ahead of AF1. Johnson even proposed the idea of moving AF1 to nearby Carswell Air Force Base because the plane would be more secure there. It was a preposterous idea, and it was quickly rejected.[90] Besides the added time and unnecessary bother of flying AF1 from Love Field to Carswell, the Johnson entourage (and later the Kennedy entourage) would have been forced to take ground transportation to Carswell from Parkland, about an hour's drive, much longer than the short distance from Parkland to Love Field.

If Johnson were an innocent man and had no knowledge of the plot that took his predecessor's life, why would he look for every excuse to stay near the scene of the crime of the century? If, as he intimated many times afterwards, there was a widespread conspiracy which presented a danger to his life, why not hurry back to the safety of Washington? An innocent Johnson, unaware of who really killed Kennedy and concerned only with the one thing which guided his entire life—his own well-being and survival—would have fled Parkland, without hesitation, for AF1 and the safety of flying high above the country. Only when seen through the prism of his culpability for the assassination do his actions make sense. Johnson knew there was no threat to his safety; the plot began and ended with the death of JFK. He knew that there were no hidden gunmen stalking his every move from Parkland to Love Field or anywhere else. If he had been genuinely afraid of being shot and killed while traveling in a car, a fate which had just befallen his predecessor, he would not have been willing to risk a long car ride from Parkland to Carswell Air Force Base. Johnson's words and deeds make sense only if he knew that Kennedy was the only one to be killed that day.

Johnson and Lady Bird finally left Parkland at about 1:20 p.m. They were driven back to Love Field under the protection of Secret Service agents and Dallas Police Chief Jesse Curry. By 1:30 p.m. they boarded AF1, not AF2. In a galling display of callousness and a complete disregard for the martyred President and his widow, the Johnsons commandeered the President's plane as if it were their own. They headed for the Kennedys' bedroom in the first minute onboard AF1.[91] Johnson had finally attained the position to which he had long aspired; he was going to avail himself of all of its privileges. He even had the audacity to transfer Lady Bird's luggage from AF2 to AF1, a completely superfluous activity since AF1 and AF2 were headed to the same destination in Washington. One might expect a normal Vice-President to be paralyzed with shock and grief over the sudden slaying of his President, but not Johnson. There was no mourning period for him, and he showed only token concern for the grieving widow and the people in the Kennedy entourage. Lady Bird herself was so insensitive to Jackie's feelings that she had the temerity to tell the widowed First Lady, "What wounds me most of all is that this should happen in my beloved state of Texas."[92]

O'Donnell, who did not get to Love Field from Parkland until much later than Johnson, was shocked to find Johnson aboard AF1 instead of in-flight headed back to Washington on AF2. Johnson later claimed that O'Donnell had suggested, at Parkland, that the new President should take AF1 back to Washington. However, O'Donnell emphatically denied this.[93] He insisted that if Johnson had broached the idea to him he would have rejected it. "Anything that would delay Johnson's departure from Texas was a bad move... he never discussed [using] Air Force One."[94] For the rest of his life, O'Donnell never wavered from his assertion that he and Johnson had agreed at Parkland that Johnson would take AF2 back to Washington.[95]

Johnson also lied to General McHugh. He told McHugh that he needed to fly back to Washington aboard AF1 because it had more sophisticated communications systems. The truth was that the planes were identical in that regard. Plane 26000 (AF1) was no more advanced electronically than plane 86970 (AF2), and Johnson knew it. According to McHugh, Johnson "just wanted to be on Air Force 1."[96]

There were more surprises awaiting O'Donnell on AF1. He was flabbergasted to learn that Johnson wanted to take the oath of office on the plane; Johnson told O'Donnell that he had received approval from Bobby Kennedy to do it. But Bobby Kennedy later denied this. He had never given Johnson the go-ahead to take the oath.[97]

When Jackie Kennedy boarded AF1 at 2:15 p.m., she was stunned to find Johnson and Secret Service agent Youngblood in her bedroom. According to some reports, Johnson was actually lying on the bed; a stunned Jackie retreated to the aft cabin beside her husband's casket.[98] For decorum's sake, the Johnsons realized they had to resort to some respectful posture and at least accord Jackie the appearance of consoling her. Lady Bird sat her down and promptly uttered an outrageous lie: "You know we never wanted to be vice-president, and now, dear God, it's comes to this."[99] The operative word is "we"; Lady Bird let slip that she intimately shared her husband's relentless political ambition. And the truth is, Lyndon Johnson lusted after the vice-presidency because, once JFK had sewn up the 1960 nomination, he knew it was his only path to the presidency. According to author Philip Nelson, "Johnson, Speaker of the House Sam Rayburn, and FBI Director J. Edgar Hoover threatened to blackmail Kennedy if he didn't give [the VP slot] to Johnson."[100] When asked by Clare Boothe Luce why he accepted such a worthless position, Johnson told her, "One out of every four presidents die in office. I'm a gambling man."[101]

The rancor between the Kennedy and Johnson camps grew as the liquor flowed and the temperature soared inside AF1. The Captain of the plane, James Swindal, disconnected the air conditioning from the mobile power unit, and the atmosphere became suffocating. Still, Johnson stalled. He put out a call for his crony judge, Sarah Hughes, knowing full well it would take 30-45 minutes for her to arrive at Love Field. Johnson's choice of Hughes was not random. It was a calculated swipe at Bobby Kennedy. In 1961 Johnson had asked Bobby to appoint Hughes to a federal judgeship. Bobby turned him down, saying that Hughes, at age 65, was too old.[102] Though Hughes was later appointed to the bench, Johnson never forgot the slight.

As the sun beat down on the hot metal of the plane, the Kennedy people became increasingly incensed that AF1 was not airborne. O'Donnell told McHugh to order the pilot to take off. The pilot, in deference to the new President, refused. McHugh stormed through the entire length of the plane looking for Johnson. He finally found him cowering in a bathroom and crying like a baby. He reportedly told McHugh that an international plot was afoot and that they "were going to get us all."[103] Johnson, the consummate manipulator, was probably putting on an act to disarm McHugh. A Kennedy loyalist who could come off as intimidating even to the most powerful of men, McHugh was not one to be dissuaded easily. Even Johnson, an imposing figure himself, could have been frightened by McHugh's demeanor. To most others Johnson seemed unusually calm and collected after the assassination; he switched gears quickly to appease McHugh and keep the plane on the ground.

While waiting for Hughes to arrive, Johnson couldn't resist planning for his new administration. In an unseemly twist, he turned on the charm and began schmoozing the Kennedy people in an effort to win them over and allay their suspicions. He needed as many Kennedy people as he could persuade to stay on in the new administration, in order to convince the world that he did not play a role in killing his predecessor. Some of Kennedy's people enlisted with Johnson; others did not. On AF1 O'Donnell ignored Johnson's overtures.

Hughes finally arrived, and Johnson told O'Donnell another lie about Jackie insisting on coming forward for the swearing-in ceremony.[104] It was Johnson who sweet-talked Jackie into attending the ceremony. She refused to change her clothes, though, and was photographed wearing her bloody dress and stockings. Small flecks of her husband's brains were stuck in her hair.

The ceremony was as macabre as the rest of the day. Photographer Cecil Stoughton's now famous roll of photos shows Lady Bird smiling and LBJ barely able to contain a smirk. LBJ aides eagerly crowd around the new king; a supporter, Congressman Albert Thomas, gives LBJ a celebratory wink. Jackie, her dress still dripping with her husband's blood, stands forlornly at Johnson's side. After the swearing-in, Lady Bird happily chatted up Jackie. The other plotters, especially Dulles and his minions, must have been shocked at the Johnsons' barely contained joy. One can imagine them telling Lyndon and Lady Bird, "Tone it down." The Johnsons were much more subdued at Andrews.

At 2:47 p.m. the plane finally took off from Love Field, and Johnson went right to work. While others were in a state of shock, Johnson took over as if he had been preparing for the moment for years. He talked to his military aides. He arranged to meet with Bundy and McNamara upon his return to Washington. He cobbled together a speech with his aides Bill Moyers and Jack Valenti.[105] Always frenetic anyway, Johnson, having achieved his life-long goal, must have been in a state of euphoria. Armed with a foreknowledge of November 22's events, he was already prepared for the first days of his administration. Meanwhile, his predecessor's body, in the hands of conspirators, was about to be mutilated to bury the truth of Johnson's crime.

Back in Washington the Kennedy loyalists who had been on the Dallas trip were eager to tell Bobby Kennedy of Johnson's loutish and insensitive behavior aboard AF1; McHugh described it as "obscene."[106] O'Donnell and O'Brien provided a vivid picture of two enemy camps tensely occupying the same place.[107] There were even cruder indignities in Johnson's takeover of the White House. The morning after the assassination, Johnson encountered a weeping Evelyn Lincoln, Kennedy's secretary, sobbing inconsolably in the Oval Office. Without offering condolences, Johnson ordered her off the premises, saying he needed his own girls to take over. Lincoln had her stuff packed and gone within hours.

Johnson was now the supreme ruler, and would let nothing stand in his ruthless way. He took over the country in much the same way as he had taken over Air Force 1 for the flight back to Washington, a flight that was more of a getaway than anything else.

The Walter Reed Scenario

On the flight back from Dallas, communication channels were engaged, and the radio chatter of military and government personnel indicates that many officials suggested or implied that Walter Reed Hospital was the Oneal coffin's destination. This might have been due to genuine confusion as to where the autopsy would be performed, but it could also be the unintentional residue of the plotters' surreptitious plans to alter the body at Walter Reed prior to the official autopsy at Bethesda. The two-hospital scenario is in keeping with the conspirators' dual storylines running through important aspects of the plot; to wit, there were two corpses, two Oswalds, two coffins, two funeral home representatives at Parkland, shots from two directions or more in Dealey Plaza, two sets of wounds, two Oswald wallets (one found at the Tippit murder scenes, the other on Oswald at his arrest at the Texas Theater), and two rifles found on the sixth floor of the Texas School Book Depository.[108] The duality of evidence and circumstances was the plotters' attempt at deception and disguise. It also served to provide the plotters with the means by which to undercut witness accounts which were "unfriendly" to the official version of events.

Walter Reed was the Army's equivalent of Bethesda Naval, and the two hospitals were only a short distance from one another in Washington. There seems to have been a disagreement between military officers and Secret Service agents aboard AF1 about which hospital would serve as the autopsy site. On AF1 radio transmissions, General Chester Clifton, the senior military officer on November 22, can be heard requesting of General Heaton, commander of Walter Reed, "...an ambulance and a ground return from Andrews to Walter Reed, and we want the regular...ah, postmortem that has to be done by law, under guard, performed at Walter Reed. Is that clear, over?"

Heaton acknowledges the transmission, but then later in the tape these arrangements are countermanded by Secret Service officials. Jerry Behn (code named Duplex), the White House Secret Agent in Charge, tells Clifton, "...there's been arranged to helicopter, helicopter the body to Bethesda...and everybody else aboard [AF1], arrangements have been made to helicopter into the South Grounds [presumably the White House South Grounds]." Behn, wittingly or unwittingly, reveals some of the plotters furtive plans here. His words betray some advance planning regarding details in two areas: President Kennedy's body was not going to be transported from Andrews AFB to Bethesda in the Dallas coffin, and members of his traveling party were not going to make the trip to Bethesda. The former turned out to be true; the latter did not. Is it possible that the plotters did not want the Kennedy family members (namely Jackie and Bobby) at Bethesda? If so, for what reason? What was Behn's level of awareness of the plot's machinations? Did he know that the Dallas coffin contained a "corpse double"? Was he trying to convince Clifton that Walter Reed was not going to be used, when secretly it was?

It seems feasible now that Walter Reed was the site of the first alteration of JFK's corpse; the body might have been flown into the

Washington area from Red Bird airport in Dallas, and then Liggett and company went to work. The site had numerous advantages: 1) it offered a secure environment for the secretive work; 2) it was a military installation (just like Bethesda), so that any personnel who may have stumbled onto the body alteration scheme could be sworn to secrecy by threat of court-martial; 3) it was a short distance from Bethesda, the official autopsy venue, and the body, once altered, could be easily and quickly be transported there with a short helicopter or ambulance ride. Recall that Dennis David saw a black ambulance roll up to the Bethesda morgue at 6:35 p.m. Out of the ambulance hopped several men, some in suits and some in smocks, who carried a cheap shipping casket bearing the body of the dead President. Obviously, the ambulance came from a location that was nearby Bethesda; Walter Reed is a logical possibility.

The mention of Walter Reed in AF1 transmissions might have also been a cover for the plotters in case their scheme blew up on them. They had to know that someday investigators would uncover their corpse/casket skullduggery; if Walter Reed were revealed as the initial destination of Kennedy's body, the plotters could claim that it was their intention to go there all along, but for security reasons they made a public show of transporting the Oneal casket to Bethesda. They could then claim that nothing sinister happened at Walter Reed, just some preliminary observations and photos before the body was transported to Bethesda.

This seems like a flimsy cover; nonetheless, there is corroboration for it. There were some post-mortem photos of JFK taken somewhere other than at Bethesda. Upon viewing some of the JFK autopsy photos, Earl McDonald, a Bethesda autopsy photographer, saw these discrepancies: 1) JFK's head rests on a Y-shaped stirrup; McDonald never saw this head support in his time at Bethesda. 2) Wooden furniture appears in the background of some photos; McDonald did not recall wooden furniture in Bethesda's autopsy room. 3) The telephone is in the wrong location. 4) McDonald did not recall the bare tile walls depicted in the photos; rather he recalled a room cluttered with lockers, cabinets and a chalkboard which obscured the tile walls.[109] These discrepancies suggest some preliminary photography was taken at Walter Reed after the first attempt at body alteration. McDonald also enumerated many flaws in the photographs which make them appear to be taken in a hurried manner by someone who was not a professional in the field.[110] The plotters were against the clock in trying to do their work and still meet the Oneal casket when it arrived at Bethesda.

The AF1 transcripts contain many more suspicious references to Walter Reed. While transcribing her boss's words aboard the plane, LBJ's secretary made a note which read, "Body...to Walter Reed."[111] Dennis David said the black ambulance (containing the cheap shipping casket with JFK's altered body inside a body bag) he saw at the back gate of Bethesda had come down Fourteenth Street.[112] This is the route the ambulance would have taken if it had come from Walter Reed, a distance of merely five miles. And Admiral Burkley, JFK's military physician, wrote in his report that "Arrangements were made...for departure to Walter Reed...or Bethesda...as the case may be."[113]

Other radio transmissions between Behn and his Dallas agent, Roy Kellerman, are more revealing. Kellerman, recall, had been riding shotgun in the death car in Dealey Plaza, and had pulled a gun and threatened violence in order to commandeer the Oneal casket out of Parkland. If anyone had inside knowledge of the plot in Dallas it was Kellerman. In the following transcript, Kellerman's code name is "Digest"; Behn is "Duplex." "Volunteer" is LBJ, and "Crown" refers to the White House:

Digest: "...Suggest we have a 2 hour 15 minute flight into
        Andrews. We have a full plane of at least 40."
Duplex: "OK, go ahead."
Digest: "I'll have to call you again after the, ah body...However,

I'm sure the, ah, Volunteer boys will go ov.r his car and
so forth. We will need [garbled] and several others."

Duplex: "All right, let me know what Volunteer wants to do
when they, ah, land if they want to come into Crown
by, ah, helicopter."

Digest: "That's a roger. I'll call you again."

Duplex: "OK."

When Kellerman referred to the "body," he certainly meant JFK's
body. But what did he mean by "after the, ah, body…" and "Volunteer boys will go over his car and so forth?" A suspicious mind,
given all the other evidence of Secret Service involvement in a plot,
might calculate that Kellerman knew that something which needed
to be done to the body had not yet taken place. Could he have been
referring to alteration? And was Kellerman notifying Behn that he
would let him know when it had been done?

The reference to the Volunteer boys and the car can mean only
one thing: LBJ's agents were going to destroy evidence of shots
from the front by cleansing and deconstructing the death limousine. Some of the process had already taken place at Parkland. A
photograph of the exterior of Parkland shows a Secret Service agent
using a bucket of soap and water to wipe the blood, skull, and brain
matter from the car's interior. Another photo shows a through-and-
through bullet hole in the car's windshield. Later that weekend the
limousine's windshield was replaced. The plotters could not afford
to have evidence of too many bullets being fired in Dealey Plaza.
The staged crime scene on the Book Depository's sixth floor contained only three spent cartridges—one each for: the "magic bullet"
that passed through both Kennedy and Connally; the head shot;
and the stray bullet which nicked a bystander, James Tague. No
more bullet strikes were allowed, or else the case for a second
shooter could have been made.

Secret Service agents took other measures at Parkland to frame the patsy. Bullet fragments from Oswald's rifle were planted in the limousine, and inside Parkland an unidentified agent placed the magic bullet on a hospital stretcher.

The Coffin Shell Game

While he has written a voluminous book (*Inside The Assassinations Record Review Board*) full of stunning revelations, Douglas Horne's core assumption that wound alteration was performed by the Bethesda autopsy pathologists is suspect. Horne makes the assertion that James Humes and Thornton Boswell, pressured by their superiors, entered into an impromptu conspiracy to conceal the true nature of President Kennedy's death. But there are several obvious problems with this hypothesis: 1) How did the plotters convince Humes and Boswell on-the-spot to do this postmortem surgery to cover up such a momentous crime? 2) Why was it necessary to intercept the President's body en route from Parkland to Bethesda, in order to play an elaborate and risky shell game with the corpse and two caskets? 3) Why did Lyndon Johnson go to such extraordinary lengths to delay the post-assassination departure from Love Field? In other words, if the plan all along was for the Bethesda pathologists to alter the dead President's wounds, why didn't the plotters simply leave the body in its original Dallas/Oneal casket and transport it directly to Bethesda for pre-autopsy alteration? This far-less-complicated scheme would have saved the plotters the trouble of stealing the President's body, loading it into a second coffin, secretly altering it at an unknown location, reloading it back into the second coffin, and then transporting the second coffin to Bethesda where it was received in the morgue just after 6:30 p.m. and reunited with the Dallas coffin before making its "official" appearance in the autopsy room.

JFK's body made its second [or possibly third] entrance into Bethesda at 8 p.m., after it had been "re-introduced" to the Dallas coffin, and was lifted onto the autopsy table. Dr. Humes said the head fell apart in his hand.[114] Then he uttered the statement about head surgery. If he was the one who altered the head wound, per Horne's theory, why would he draw attention to it by claiming he noticed surgery of the head area? If he had altered the head wound earlier in the evening at Bethesda it is unlikely he would let the others in attendance know this. Witnesses saw him with a small saw, but that is a tool normally involved in any autopsy where parts of the skull need to be removed. And if the skull was in pieces when he got it, the saw's use would have been limited anyway.

Still, the plotters needed the early entry at Bethesda for some reason. Bethesda lab assistant Paul O'Connor testified that the skull was empty when he first saw it; there was no brain inside the cranium. That must have been what the plotters were up to at Bethesda between 6:35 and 8 p.m.—manipulating the brain to make it appear as if Kennedy had been shot from above and behind. This indicates that the first body forgery done at Walter Reed (or some other location) was imperfect, done in a rush because the body had to be at Bethesda by the time the Oneal casket arrived at Bethesda from Andrews AFB. The motorcade from Andrews, with Jackie and Bobby Kennedy and the Dallas coffin inside the gray Navy ambulance which had departed Andrews at approximately 6 p.m., pulled up in front of Bethesda at precisely 6:55 p.m. JFK's body had already been at Bethesda for at least 20 minutes, but the plotters needed more time still to complete the body forgery. What they did to buy more time was conjure up a scene straight out of a Keystone Kops movie. Another ambulance, referred to as a decoy by many who were there that night, showed up at the entrance of the hospital. As high-ranking military officers stood around Bethesda's main entrance and discussed their next move, Admiral Calvin Galloway, Humes' commanding officer at Bethesda, got behind the wheel of the "decoy" ambulance (which did not contain the Dallas casket) and led the casket team on an ambulance chase around the entire perimeter of the hospital grounds.[115] Meanwhile the gray Navy, non-decoy ambulance went around to the back of the hospital where the Dallas casket was off-loaded and made its first entry into the morgue at about 7:15 p.m. The casket team, a military honor guard provided by the joint services, led by Lieutenant Sam Bird, dutifully followed Admiral Galloway's decoy ambulance to a destination that led nowhere. In this interim, Kennedy's body was put into the Dallas coffin which was then loaded into the non-decoy ambulance. After nearly 45 minutes of a wild goose chase, the casket team finally followed the correct ambulance and wound up at the morgue's entrance where they carried the Dallas casket into the hospital and left it in an anteroom. Secret Service agents, probably Roy Kellerman and William Greer, who seemed to be the omnipresent directors of every part of the November 22 sham, sealed off the area.

What happened to the fake corpse (if there was one) and the cheap casket, no one knows. But we do know what happened to the Oneal casket. It was dumped into the ocean years after the assassination when investigators like David Lifton first started becoming aware of the casket shell game. It is commonly believed that Robert Kennedy ordered this destruction of evidence, but the facts point to someone else. It was Johnson, through his Attorney General Nicholas Katzenbach, and Earle Cabell, covert CIA operative and the mayor of Dallas on 11/22/63, who instigated the casket disposal scheme. The cover story was that JFK's coffin should not become a ghoulish museum piece somewhere. This excuse does not seem plausible, for there are many ghoulish exhibits of the assassination accessible to the public—from the head shot in the Zapruder film to photos of JFK's autopsy and pictures of his bloody clothing. All of which are much bloodier and gruesome than an empty coffin. There must have been another reason for disposing of the coffin, and I believe it was to destroy evidence of blood, which did not match JFK's blood type, being found in that coffin. Some blood did leak through the wrappings and the sheets which lined the coffin.

Once researchers began to dig into the coffin/body switch, it was only a matter of time until someone demanded that the blood found in the Oneal coffin be forensically examined. The plotters certainly could not have hard evidence of their chicanery being discovered. Not even the stoutest Warren Commission defenders could have explained that away, and it might have blown the lid off the conspiracy. As a result, in 1966 the Oneal casket was loaded onto an Air Force C-130 transport and secretly dumped into the Atlantic Ocean. The American public was not informed of this outrage until many years later.

The Riddle of Early Entry

While a counterargument to Douglas Horne's theory of pathologists' altering the body at Bethesda is presented above, there is a problem with the theory of alteration being finished by the time the body arrived at Bethesda. It is clear why the plotters needed to highjack the body and remove the bullets before the autopsy: they needed to conceal the truth of how the assassination had really occurred. But why was it necessary to bring the body (arriving in the shipping casket at approximately 6:35) into the Bethesda morgue and place it on the autopsy table before it was transferred to the Dallas/Oneal coffin? Why not just wait for the Dallas coffin to arrive from Andrews and make the body/coffin switch *before* introducing the body into the Bethesda autopsy room? Why not avoid the introduction of the cheap shipping casket into the equation? Why risk having so many witnesses like lab assistants Paul O'Connor and James Jenkins, and the pathologists themselves, see Kennedy's body encased in a body bag and arriving in the shipping casket, when the body transfer could have been made (and later was) out of eyesight of non-plotters? (There were several other witnesses to the body arriving at Bethesda in a cheap shipping casket, including Joe Hagan of Gawler's funeral home which was contracted for its embalming and funereal services. Hagan wrote on his First Call Sheet [a standard industry report] that the "body was removed from metal shipping casket at USNH Bethesda."[116]) Why use the wrong casket to unload the President's body, and why allow witnesses to see two casket openings? A satisfactory answer to these questions is not readily available, except to conjecture that there was not enough time to make a perfect forgery at the location where bullets were removed. But if further "corrections" to the body were required before it was transferred into the Dallas/Oneal coffin, then Humes and his fellow pathologists were the only ones who could have done it. And these changes could only have been done in the approximate hour between the time the shipping casket arrived at the morgue and the "official" opening of the Dallas/Oneal coffin at 8 p.m. If this conjecture is accurate, Humes' statement about "surgery of the head area" must be reevaluated. If Humes did perform some reconstruction work himself before the body was placed into the Dallas/Oneal coffin, then his statement regarding surgery may have been his feeble attempt at covering up his role in alteration by blaming the massive head wound on the Dallas doctors. It didn't work, of course, because it was later revealed that the Dallas doctors performed no such surgery.

If Humes was involved in the cover-up, then so were his assistants, Drs. Thornton Boswell and Pierre Finck. It is hard to imagine that they would willingly participate in such a monstrous deed, but there seems to be no other logical explanation for why the shipping casket made its early entry into the Bethesda autopsy room. The rushed attempt to make the President's wounds "look right" at Walter Reed (or elsewhere) was insufficient, and "repairs" needed to be done before photos and x-rays were taken. Indications of shots from the front could not be allowed into the official photographic record. But in a frantic hurry to cover up the truth of the murder, the plotters made several problems for themselves.

As part of the original alteration process, the bullet fragments which did not match Oswald's ammunition needed to be removed from the brain; this meant the brain needed to be removed from the skull. This procedure would have required making a huge hole in the head, beyond the size that any of the medical personnel at Parkland saw. It is possible that Humes and associates tried to "fix this" at a pre-autopsy autopsy. It would have required trying to piece together fragments of skull and bone, but it was shoddy work and it created an anomaly that was not fixable—namely that there is no photographic record of the brain inside the head.[117] To clarify, since the plotters had to extract the brain for bullet removal purposes, they created a hacked-up brain that had been "sectioned" and would have obviously looked that way to any qualified pathologist. To photograph this brain in the President's head would have been an obvious indication of forgery. (See discussion of "Two Brains" later in this chapter.) So what we are left with is the paradox of a hole in the top of the head too small to have blasted out the President's entire brain; the only deductive conclusion is that the President's brain was removed before the official autopsy by persons unknown, and then an attempt was made to reconstruct the skull to match the government's emerging story of how the assassination occurred.

So what, exactly, did Humes do? An eyewitness named Tom Robinson, a Washington mortician, sat in the autopsy room gallery and witnessed Humes using a saw to open the head. This process is part of a normal autopsy, but usually does not occur at the beginning of an autopsy. The beginning of the autopsy of a body which has died by gunshot wound should be devoted to discovering the number and direction of bullets and their paths through the body, not distorting the wounds. According to Robinson, Humes distorted the genuine wounds as inflicted in Dallas. Robinson claimed that one of the original wounds appeared to be small and round, located high on the President's right forehead in the hairline, as if it had been made by a bullet's entry from the front.[118] Why would Humes cover up this wound? Horne writes that "...the postmortem surgery was a damage control exercise, performed by pathologists who had already been told that…evidence of frontal shots had to be suppressed for reasons of national security."[119] Another question arises from this presumption: How did Humes and his fellow autopsists keep this secret for over three decades which included testimony in front of three panels—the Warren Commission, the HSCA, and the ARRB? Humes may have provided the answer when he declared, after his HSCA interview, "They had their chance, and they blew it. They didn't ask the right questions."[120] Maybe they never wanted to ask the right questions.

So Horne may be correct after all. There may have been a two-part pre-autopsy alteration process which constituted a desperate attempt to get the body to "look right" for the second, and "official," casket opening at Bethesda.

Medical Evidence

If there is a smoking gun in the Kennedy assassination it is the medical evidence; more specifically, it is the unreliability of the medical evidence in the official version accepted by the government and the mainstream media. In fact, if Oswald had lived to get his day in court, the medical evidence which the plotters jimmied up to frame him would have been thrown out by any honest judge because the chain-of-evidence on the body had been broken. As President Kennedy's body was being transported from Dallas to Bethesda on November 22, 1963, it was highjacked for the purposes of covert alteration of his wounds; thus, if there had been a trial of Lee Harvey Oswald for the crime of the century, the prosecution could not have presented evidence of the President's wounds as a means of convicting Oswald. And without this evidence it is highly unlikely Oswald could have been found guilty. Jack Ruby took care of the Oswald problem for the plotters, but the chain-of-evidence break still exists and has been laid bare by researchers for all the public to see. The handiwork of the plotters is ugly and brutal, but there can now be no doubt that President Kennedy's body was desecrated by plotters for the purposes of deceiving the American people.

In keeping with the duality element mentioned previously, there were at least two different sets of autopsy photographs, filmed by two different teams at two different times at Bethesda. The photographs show conflicting wounds on the President's body, so one set of photographs needed to be destroyed. There were two entirely separate descriptions of Kennedy's wounds at Bethesda, described by two different sets of equally qualified witnesses. There were even x-rays taken of two different brains.

To reiterate, these twin storylines were intentionally created by the plotters in order to provide seemingly reasonable alternatives if and when the official story of the assassination was ever challenged. In other words, if accounts of two casket openings at Bethesda surfaced in the record then one, whichever suited the plotters' purposes, could be completely dismissed as inaccurate because of the existence of the other believable casket opening. Just as the testimony of the Bethesda autopsy doctors served to help negate the Parkland doctors' testimony, the arrival at Bethesda of the Dallas/Oneal casket which contained a phony corpse wrapped in Parkland/Restland sheets served to negate the earlier Bethesda arrival of the cheap shipping casket which contained the real corpse enclosed in a body bag. If this seems confusing, let's back up for clarification.

Remember, no bullets were in the body at Bethesda. At least none were reported by the autopsy doctors. Humes called Parkland to find out if any bullets had been found there; magically, Commission Exhibit 399 had been found at Parkland, and suddenly Humes was provided the bullet he needed to explain the shallow back wound he saw on the President's corpse. The problem was, this wound was not seen in Dallas; none of the Parkland doctors, nurses or orderlies noticed any bullet holes or wounds of any kind on Kennedy's back. So how, when and where did the wounds get there, and, more importantly, who put them there? If the Parkland medical personnel were correct, the back wounds had to be added by alterationists before the body arrived at Bethesda. Humes himself considered the outrageous possibility that the Dallas doctors had inflicted the wounds themselves; incredibly, he telephoned Parkland's Dr. Perry, to ask if the Dallas doctors had *made any wounds* on the President's back.[121] If Liggett or one of the other plotters made these wounds on the body after the President's death, then, of course, they would have also made corresponding holes in the President's clothing to account for a bullet's passage through the clothing from the rear. Proof that the clothing holes were made after the assassination is provided by the size of the holes; the bullet holes in the clothing (the coat and the shirt Kennedy wore when he was killed) were about three times the size of a Mannlicher-Carcano bullet.[122]

But who removed the bullets and added the back wounds? Certainly not Humes. As noted previously, this does not mean that Humes was above reproach. He burned the original autopsy notes, and his subsequent testimony to the Warren Commission was full of inconsistencies. One of the most ponderous statements he made was that the bullet which struck the President in the head *entered and exited from the rear*, a physical impossibility unless a bullet made a U-turn in the President's head.[123] Also Humes did not address, for obvious reasons, the possibility of pre-autopsy surgery in his testimony.

Those who defend Humes point out that he did not have the credentials to perform the work he was asked to do, and he was at the mercy of his military superiors who barked orders at him during the autopsy. Being the obsequious sort, Humes did as he was told. Many at Bethesda considered him a butt-kissing toadie who always kowtowed to his superiors; by contrast, he treated the enlisted personnel with disdain and disrespect. Dennis David despised Humes so much that he called him a "little Adolf Hitler."[124] David Lifton was kinder to Humes. He believed Humes tried to relay the truth to the Warren Commission in coded medical language that the Commission simply did not understand or refused to investigate further.[125] And in fairness to all the Bethesda doctors, they were trying to perform their work in a "three-ring circus."[126] Just like the Dallas doctors, Humes and his colleagues were surrounded by chaos and hysteria. Bethesda x-ray technician Jerrol Custer testified that inside the autopsy room "the commotion level was astronomical. The decibel level was extremely high. You had to scream at people at times."[127] Tom Robinson described the atmosphere as similar to a "cocktail party" and a "circus."[128] Generals and admirals were shouting commands that hampered the doctors' progress. Humes, Boswell and Finck were just military men whose function was not to get at the truth but to obey orders.

The medical evidence is further complicated by the deep discrepancy between what the official autopsy photos and x-rays show and what medical personnel at Bethesda actually saw. In his Warren Commission testimony Humes stated that he saw 30-40 tiny bullet fragments in JFK's head.[129] These minute particles would be consistent with damage caused by a frangible bullet, quite unlike the ammunition used in a Mannlicher-Carcano rifle. The logical conclusion is that the bullet which struck Kennedy in the head did not come from Oswald's rifle. However, there was an attempt made by the authorities to alter the x-rays to make it appear that Oswald's rifle had been used to inflict the head wound. A few days after the autopsy Doctor John Ebersole, assistant chief of Radiology at Bethesda, was ordered to the White House to meet with the Secret Service. At this meeting, Ebersole was handed bullet fragments which he was told came from ammunition that was linked to Oswald's Mannlicher-Carcano. Ebersole took the fragments back to Bethesda and ordered Custer to *tape the fragments to images of JFK's skull*.[130] In other words, Custer was forced by his Bethesda superior to falsify evidence in order to frame Oswald. Threatened with imprisonment if he did not keep his mouth shut, Custer refused to disclose the fake x-rays until he was deposed by the Assassinations Records Review Board in 1997.

Five skull x-rays were taken at Bethesda on 11/22/63; two of those x-rays are now missing.[131] The three remaining skull x-rays have been exposed as forgeries by Dr. David Mantik. Mantik, a scientist with impeccable credentials who has been understandably ignored by the medical quacks who support the lone-gunman nonsense, made quantitative analyses of the extant skull x-rays at the National Archives in the 1990s. His findings back up Custer's claim of x-ray fraud; to wit, "the largest metal-like object (6.5 mm across and nearly round) on the extant skull x-rays was not present on the original x-rays."[132] The plotters used Ebersole and Custer to superimpose the image of a Mannlicher-Carcano bullet fragment on an x-ray of JFK's skull. But the bullet on the forged x-ray is larger than any existing bullet fragment in the National Archives. In other words, *no bullet of the size indicated on the fraudulent skull x-ray was ever extracted from the President's head during the Bethesda autopsy.* Mantik's research unearthed other deceptions, including altered autopsy photos and brain substitution.[133]

This explosive evidence was not available for almost thirty years, because of a secrecy order invoked at Bethesda in 1963. All personnel who were in any way involved with the autopsy were under orders not to speak about what they had seen and done. This included Custer and Ebersole, and anyone else who had taken or processed x-rays and photos. Photographer Floyd Reibe, who turned over at least 100 photos to the Secret Service and never saw them again, was constrained by the gag order.[134] The photos he took did not match the ones he later saw published. Another Bethesda photographer named John Stringer took photos that showed not just Kennedy's body, but also the personnel in the background, including military officers, Secret Service personnel and other unidentified federal agents. These photos were destroyed.[135] It is noteworthy that the man to whom the photographers turned over their rolls was none other than SS agent Roy Kellerman.

Stringer and Reibe were not the only autopsy photographers. One of the official White House photographers, Robert Knudsen, was also at Bethesda taking photos of the dead President. He was also forced to turn over his film to the Secret Service and, in subsequent years, claimed that some of the images he took disappeared or were altered. Knudsen showed confidantes two versions of Kennedy's rear head area—one with a large bullet wound, the other with no wound at all. Knudsen told family members that the exit wound in the back of the head had been concealed by hair being drawn over the blasted-out bullet hole.[136] That was not the only strange thing about Knudsen's recollections. Despite the undeniable presence of Stringer and Reibe, *Knudsen believed he was the only photographer to record the autopsy*; in fact, he met Air Force 1 at Andrews AFB and rode with some Secret Service agents in the last car of the motorcade to Bethesda.[137] The only explanation for Knudsen's recollection is that Knudsen's pictures were taken at a different stage of the autopsy (a process that took up to eight hours and was not finished until well after midnight according to some) than were Stringer's and Reibe's photos. The idea that separate autopsy photo sessions were conducted is supported by Stringer and Reibe who said that no other personnel were taking photos while they were. Apparently the plotters felt compelled to take many photos, at various stages of the autopsy/wound reconstruction process, to cover a myriad of eventualities, so that they would have a set of photos to match whatever version of the crime emerged as the most convenient or workable. Why else would it be necessary to have separate photographers, completely unaware of one another, and multiple photographs revealing contradictory images? And why would most of the images subsequently vanish? An honest autopsy procedure, one that did not involve body manipulation and evidence destruction, would have ardently preserved any and all photographs taken.

Knudsen stated that 1) he was at the autopsy from the very beginning; 2) probes had been inserted into the corpse to determine bullet trajectories; and 3) the top of the President's head was almost completely gone and very little brain was left. Knudsen's recollection of Kennedy's head wound conforms to the testimony of many others at Bethesda who saw most of the top of the head missing and most of the brain gone, confirming that someone had tampered with the body between Parkland and Bethesda. However, some at Bethesda saw no body probes and swore that the head wound was localized to the back of the head, more consistent with the Parkland doctors' testimony. These variances were likely a byproduct of the ongoing "work" on the body. The imperfect forgery created before the autopsy had to be reconfigured as the night wore on to try to match the evolving ballistic and trajectory evidence coming from Dallas. Wounds appeared and vanished; trajectories were probed and reconsidered; the doctors were following orders rather than conducting a real autopsy; many rolls of photographs were taken, most of which were destroyed because they would have revealed an inconvenient truth. Oswald was being framed on the fly, and the conspirators were frantic to create a false record of how the assassination occurred.

As they tried to do their jobs, the Bethesda autopsy doctors—Humes, Boswell and Finck—were "managed" by mysterious government agents and high-ranking military officers. These men were gathered in the gallery of the autopsy room, and, according to Douglas Horne, were an "impatient and demanding" group; they provided "suggestions and directions as to what to look for next and even what [the] findings should be."[138] Who were these men? There is evidence that one of them was Air Force Chief of Staff, and Kennedy hater, Curtis LeMay.

Jerrol Custer testified that a "four-star general" general kept issuing orders from the bleachers during the autopsy; Custer identified the general's shirt as light-blue in color, the same color of shirt worn by Air Force personnel.[139] Bethesda Corpsman Paul O'Connor, who was also present during the autopsy, corroborated Custer. O'Connor said that at one point Humes complained about the cigar smoke in the autopsy room, and he instructed O'Connor to find the culprit and tell him to stub it out. O'Connor followed the smoke right to General LeMay who, rather than putting the cigar out, smugly blew the smoke in O'Connor's face. Humes, realizing his mistake, did not challenge LeMay again.[140]

With LeMay in charge of the autopsy, the Naval pathologists and technicians who participated in it were under his command. It was a military operation, and LeMay outranked everyone there. Finck testified that the doctors were ordered not to dissect the organs of the dead President's neck; this unusual command, one that flies in the face of normal autopsy protocol, prevented the doctors from recognizing the hole in the President's neck as a bullet wound. They thought, at first, it was merely a tracheotomy that was performed as part of the life-saving measures at Parkland. Only later, with the aid of the "producers of the charade" who magically found a bullet for them, did it "dawn" on the doctors that the hole in the neck was a bullet wound of exit (or so they were told). But where, then, was the wound of entrance? The doctors were "guided" to the conclusion that the entrance wound seen on the President's back was the entrance of the bullet which passed through his neck and continued on to strike John Connally. This provided a convenient solution to the autopsy doctors' quandary of why they found no bullets in the body. It also explained how the holes in the body were connected.

Even then, the doctors could not keep their stories straight. Humes insisted to the Warren Commission that he did not "connect the dots" of the back and throat wounds until the morning *after* the autopsy (this is the excuse provided by Humes for *burning his original autopsy notes*, an act that violated standard autopsy protocol in a criminal case); Boswell, however, testified to the

Assassination Records Review Board in 1996 that he connected the wounds *during* the autopsy.[141] Over thirty years after the fact, Boswell's memory may have faded; Humes insisted that during the autopsy, in Boswell's presence, he tried to probe the back wound with his little finger and could only go as deep as the tip of the finger. There was no bullet pathway through to the President's neck. And without a pathway completely through the President's body, the Warren Commission's magic-bullet theory would have been exposed as a hoax. The FBI's own autopsy report stated that the bullet did not transit. This presented a difficult hurdle for the Commission to overcome.

But the commission's Arlen Specter came to the rescue with the most laughable conclusion of the entire 26 volumes—the magic bullet. Specter, out of thin air and a desperate need to protect the plotters, proposed that one bullet caused the President's back wound and neck wound, and then continued on into Connally's back, chest, wrist and thigh. An impossible feat for an intact bullet, but it was all the plotters could come up with given the limited number of shots that the patsy was able to get off in the time allotted (six seconds).

The doctors were also coerced into making their various conclusions about the head wound. They were astounded that such a massive head injury could have been caused by a gunshot. Humes, at first, ascribed the wound to surgery, as would be done in the postmortem dissection of a brain. Areas of entry and exit were hard to discern. But as the evening wore on, solutions were provided by the mystery men. Boswell testified that bone fragments displaying evidence of damage caused by bullets suddenly appeared halfway through the autopsy, having made their way from Dallas.[142] It is probable that these fragments were the remnants of the pre-autopsy wound alteration, and they were presented to the doctors when it became necessary to provide the "appropriate solution" to the crime.

One must keep in mind that the plotters were devising the scenario of the assassination by making it up as they went along on 11/22/63 and into the next day. Naturally, inconsistencies, contradictions and improbable happenstances would be part of the fiction.

Two Corpses and Two Brains?

If it is true that Liggett had a fake corpse in waiting at Restland for the day it was needed, was the brain of this fake corpse photographed and x-rayed to create a false record of the assassination? There is startling evidence that this happened. Varying descriptions, some wildly divergent, of the damage to Kennedy's brain exist in the accounts of those who saw the wounds at Bethesda. Some like Paul O'Connor saw no brain at all in Kennedy's cranium.[143] Others saw minimal damage. This leads to the inevitable, question: were two brains from two different cadavers examined, photographed and x-rayed at Bethesda? The weight of a normal brain in a 46-year-old (JFK's age at the time of his death) is approximately 1350 grams; however, Kennedy's brain was weighed at 1500 grams, despite having parts of it splattered all over Dealey Plaza and the Trauma Room floor at Parkland Hospital on 11/22/63.[144]

Called to testify at the Assassination Records Review Board hearings in the late 1990s, Francis O'Neill, one of the FBI agents present during the autopsy at Bethesda, added his support to the two-brain ruse. He told the ARRB that the brain he saw removed from the President's cranium was not as large as the brain depicted in the extant photos of the autopsy, implying that the photographed brain was substituted in the official records for the President's brain.[145] This makes sense only if the plotters knew that the President's brain had undergone so much damage, during pre-autopsy sectioning and probing, that it would not match the government's story of how the assassination took place. They needed a brain that appeared to be injured by a single bullet passing from back to front, causing its most critical damage as it exited the front and right of the President's head. O'Neill told the ARRB that he was present when the President's brain was removed from his cranium, and that "there was not too much of the brain left"; on the contrary, the brain depicted in the autopsy photos, while damaged, retained most of its matter.[146] O'Neill's FBI partner, James Sibert, also testified before the ARRB and also cast doubt on the official autopsy photos. He said the head wound he observed at Bethesda was larger than the wound depicted in the photos.[147]

Further proof of different brains can be deduced by comparing Dr. Humes' Warren Commission testimony of the condition of the brain as he saw it at autopsy with the brain which was turned over to the Secret Service after the autopsy. Humes noticed "parasagittal lacerations that extended from the tip of the occipital lobe to the tip of the frontal lobe."[148] Translated into layman's language, this means that there were deep exploratory cuts, probably performed by someone with medical expertise, inside the President's brain. These cuts are typically performed at autopsy when the victim has been wounded by a bullet to the brain. But no such cuts were made by the Bethesda doctors; the cuts had already been made by the time the body arrived at Bethesda. And these cuts, uniformly parallel and running the entire length of the brain, could not have been made by a bullet. Bullets don't behave that way when fired into a brain. Remarkably though, the brain turned over to the National Archives by the Secret Service in April 1965 contained no such cuts, or coronal sections, as seen by Humes and his colleagues.[149]

The two-brain scenario was probably necessitated by the extensive pre-autopsy wound alteration. In expanding the head wound to three times its normal size in order to extract the non-Oswald bullets and to disguise the authentic direction of the shots, the plotters caused more skull and brain damage than was caused by the actual shooting. The brain, then, as seen by the Bethesda medical personnel had more damage than such experts would expect to find in an examination of a death-by-gunshot corpse. The plotters needed a second brain, which could be substituted for the real brain and made to look like a typical gun-shot-damaged brain, so that it could be photographed for posterity.

O'Connor and his Bethesda cohort James Jenkins may have inadvertently seen the ploy by which the second brain entered Bethesda. They recalled the story of a stillborn baby being wheeled into a hospital corridor around the time of the autopsy. The "baby" was just a small object covered by a sheet. A check of the Bethesda records for 11/22/63 revealed no stillborn births on that date. Was it possible that this was the second brain? There must have been two, because O'Connor saw no brain in the skull cavity when JFK's corpse was lifted onto the autopsy table, yet Jenkins was adamant that he injected a brain (which he believed was JFK's) with formaldehyde as part of a normal autopsy procedure.[150]

Another person who testified to the existence of two brains was Saundra Spencer. Spencer, a First-Class Petty Officer who in November 1963 worked as a photographer's mate in charge of the White House Lab at the Naval Photographic Center in Anacostia, developed autopsy photographs on the day after the assassination. In testimony before the ARRB in the 1990s, Spencer recalled a photograph of the dead President lying next to a "*brain that was laid beside the body*" (emphasis added); incredibly, though, the President's skull showed no indication that it had been cut into as would be necessary to remove the brain. Spencer then made the unforgettable remark, "As to whose brain it was, I cannot say."[151]

An even more macabre fact is that today there is no brain to examine. The brain which was turned over to the Secret Service after the autopsy may or may not have been JFK's brain; regardless, it is now missing. After being in the possession of the Secret Service for an undetermined time, it was transferred to the National Archives in a stainless steel container. That container was removed sometime in 1966 and has not been seen since. The mystery is confounded by the fact that, supposedly, the only two people who had access to the container were Robert Kennedy and Evelyn Lincoln. How, why, and under what circumstances the brain was taken remain a mystery.

In addition to her shocking statement about JFK's brain, Spencer made other statements that corroborated the Dallas doctors' observations of shots from the front. She recalled a hole of two inches in diameter at the back of the skull behind the right ear, and she said the forward right side of the President's head was intact.[152] The photos Spencer described were likely pre-alteration photos, taken at the site of the alteration. But why would the plotters permit should photos to be taken and developed? At such an early stage in the cover-up, the plotters might not yet have known if the Oswald-as-lone-gunman scenario was going to be the official story. Perhaps there was still a possibility of trying to frame a lone-gunman who had shot the President from the front. At the time the pre-autopsy photos were taken, Oswald had not yet been charged with the murder of Kennedy. Still, the inclusion of an extra brain makes the photos seem counterproductive to the believability of any false version of the crime. Letting an enlisted Naval lab worker see the pre-autopsy photos empowered a witness who could testify that the post-autopsy photos were fraudulent. Indeed, Spencer did just that. When showed post-autopsy photos of the heavy damage to Kennedy's head, Spencer denied seeing it in the photos she developed. She also insisted that the paper on which her photos were developed did not match the paper on which the extant photos were made.[153]

The matter of the placement of the head wounds, and the description of their size, has evolved into a Litmus test for which side of the controversy one falls—the truth or the scam. Those who place a massive exit wound at the top and the right side of the President's head are confused, deceived, or in on the plot. Those who place a smaller exit wound, about the size of a fist, at the rear of the President's head are telling the truth. Within these categories are some discrepancies. Even the government's own experts have contradicted one another many times. One egregious example is the HSCA's own medical "star," Dr. Michael Baden, the man who made a career out of being a paid trial expert for whomever ponied up enough dough, placed a wound on Kennedy's head where the Clark Panel, appointed by Johnson's attorney general, said one did not exist.[154] But, in general, the witnesses can be divided into pre-alteration and post-alteration groups. The pre-alteration group is, naturally, limited because wound alteration took place just hours after the assassination; however, the post-alteration group is quite large because the forged extant photos have been viewed for over half of a century. This absurd disproportion in groups is what, at least in part, accounts for the endurance of the cover-up.

Liggett Returns Home

Whether one believes that post-mortem body alteration was at the heart of the JFK cover-up or not, there is no getting around two undeniable facts: 1) the body arrived at Bethesda before the Dallas coffin did; and 2) the body wounds had been radically altered somewhere between Parkland and Bethesda. The children of John Liggett, and the family friend with inside knowledge of Liggett's movements on November 22, are convinced that Liggett played a role in both of these deceptions.

Liggett did not return to Dallas until November 23, approximately 24 hours after he had abruptly departed Restland Funeral Home for Parkland Hospital. He showed up at the doorstep of his Dallas residence on Saturday appearing haggard and worn. He was pale, and looked as if he had not slept the previous night. His normally well-groomed hair was out of place, and his clothes were wrinkled. He quickly ordered his wife and kids to pack their things; they were going on a road trip. They headed south out of Dallas, and along the way Liggett stopped for clandestine meetings with unknown men out of the earshot of his family. Confused by the mysteriousness of it all, Lois Liggett felt that her husband John was

---

keeping some dark secret from her that had something to do with the momentous events of that weekend. "Throughout this journey," she said, "there were conversations that went on between John [and others]…they knew something I didn't know."[155]

The Liggetts finally settled into a motel room in south Texas for the evening, and on the morning of November 24 they awoke to watch the live telecast of Jack Ruby murdering Lee Harvey Oswald. When Oswald was pronounced dead, John Liggett breathed a deep sigh of relief and told his wife and kids that it was okay to return home. Though he did not tell his family why, it was apparent to them that Oswald's death meant that whatever role Liggett had played in the Kennedy assassination would be hidden from public view. Liggett must have assumed that the story the patsy had to tell died with him. It stands to reason that if Oswald had lived to testify at his trial the entire plot would have unraveled and everyone involved would have been at risk. Oswald may have been duped into participating in what he thought was a fake attempt on the life of the President, but once he realized that the attempt was real and successful, and that he had been betrayed by his handlers and "shepherds," he would have been motivated to reveal all that he knew about the plot. That included the LCAP background he shared with John Liggett and the common ties they had to David Harold Byrd; this would have opened up a sordid can of worms for Liggett. And once alternate shooters were exposed, there would have been closer scrutiny of Kennedy's wounds and the integrity of the chain of evidence as the body moved from Parkland to Bethesda. Eventually Liggett would have been exposed as an accessory after the fact.

With Oswald dead though, Liggett was free to pursue a protected and privileged existence. After the assassination, he came into a good deal of money which he used to purchase a home for his family in an upscale Dallas neighborhood. With the change in lifestyle came a more reckless and less guarded Liggett. He hosted all-night poker parties attended by Dallas lowlifes, including Russell

Matthews, a local burglar and hitman who was associated with Jack Ruby. Liggett was also visited by David Ferrie, Oswald's captain in the LCAP, who apparently carried CIA/Mafia assignments. The Liggett stepchildren vividly remember Ferrie because of his bizarre appearance. They made fun of his orange wigs and fake eyebrows. (They once infuriated Ferrie by taking his car for a joy ride.)

Concurrent with Ferrie's visits to Dallas, Liggett embarked on a side occupation of hired killer. He was suspected in several murders, some at least tangentially related to the cover-up of the Kennedy assassination. He may have been involved in the strange death of assassination eyewitness Lee Bowers. Bowers was a Union Terminal railroad employee in Dallas who watched the assassination from his tower overlooking Dealey Plaza on November 22, 1963. Bowers told the Warren Commission that he saw three cars circle the area behind the picket fence just prior to the assassination. These cars were interlopers because the police had supposedly closed off the area to traffic that day. At the time of the shooting, Bowers saw a "commotion" behind the picket fence and two or more strange men who were partially obscured by the trees.[156] There is a feeling among some in the conspiracy community that Bowers, out of fear, neglected to tell all he knew. The hazy recollections he gave the Warren Commission were intentionally vague. But Bowers did, reportedly, admit to Canadian researcher Al Navis that the shooters he saw behind the picket fence were two men dressed as Dallas policemen; Navis claimed to have a letter from Bowers divulging this information, but was unable to produce it when asked.[157]

In August 1966 Bowers met an untimely and mysterious end. He was killed in a one-car accident near Midlothian, Texas, on a clear day. Those who found him said he appeared to be in some sort of shock or a drug-induced state. His widow sensed foul play. "They told him not to talk," she said.[158] It is only conjecture that Liggett was somehow involved, but it is a fact that Bowers was cremated, just two days after his death, at Restland, Liggett's place of employment, without an autopsy being performed.[159]

Liggett's involvement in other attacks in the Dallas area after the assassination is without dispute. He was arrested and charged in March 1974 for the attempted murder of Dorothy Peck, widow of LBJ cousin (and doppelganger) Jay Bert Peck. Liggett met Peck at a bar and talked his way into coming home with her and then assaulted her. According to the *Dallas Times-Herald*, "Mrs. Peck... was beaten with a hammer and left on the bed while [Liggett] stuffed clothing beneath the bed and set it on fire...the attacker's method was similar to the one used in the Feb. 10 slaying of Susan Payne Thompson, a 41-year-old Dallas legal secretary."[160] Thompson's death was seemingly unrelated to the JFK case, but the assault on Peck had conspiratorial implications. Peck, as the wife of Lyndon Johnson's relative, may have been privy to information that made the plotters nervous.

This prompts the question: In addition to his role in the JFK cover-up, was Liggett also a serial killer with a murderous appetite for middle-aged women? If he was, his children did not suspect it, because he was normally cool and composed with them, never losing his temper or disciplining them harshly. Liggett might have had multiple personalities then—skilled mortician and family man by day, contract killer by night, and random serial killer in his spare time. DiBoard acknowledges that Liggett's stepchildren believe that Liggett killed random non-JFK assassination-related victims as a cover for those victims who *were* JFK assassination-related; however, this seems an extreme measure for a hired assassin to take—why risk exposure by committing extraneous murders that have no purpose other than to convince authorities who may later arrest him that he was not involved solely in killing JFK witnesses? The more likely explanation for Liggett's killing rampage is that he was a psychopath with a dual personality, able to contain his murderous impulses around his family and co-workers. These traits would have been very useful to the CIA.

Liggett's modus operandi was to burn his victims after he had killed them in order to destroy as much evidence as he could. Curiously, the New Orleans murder of Mary Sherman, an associate of Oswald's lover, Judyth Vary, fits this pattern. She was shot in bed and then set on fire.[161]

By the time of Liggett's attack on Peck, Liggett and Lois had been divorced for many years, but during his incarceration Lois was contacted by John's brother Malcolm Liggett and warned not to have anything more to do with John. Behind bars for a year without being tried, Liggett tried to escape jail in 1975 and was apparently shot dead by a Dallas policeman. The word "apparently" is applied here because his widows have reason to dispute his demise. Leona Liggett, who was married to John at the time of his "death," said she did not recognize him as he lay in his casket. The corpse had a moustache, and John Liggett was unable to grow facial hair. So what really happened to the authentic Liggett?

Newspaper accounts from 1975 report that he was shot and killed as he tried to escape the custody of Dallas County Sheriff's deputies. He was being transported back to jail with several other inmates after a court appearance when he "somehow freed himself from his handcuffs. When the paddy wagon doors were opened, according to officers, Liggett bolted."[162] While running north on Houston street, ironically just a block from Dealey Plaza, Liggett or someone who was identified as Liggett, was gunned down by Deputy Joe Crawford. Liggett, or his substitute, was still alive when carted off to the emergency room, but he was pronounced dead at (fittingly) Parkland Hospital that same day. Was this really Liggett, or was it an elaborate trick to free Liggett so that he could go underground and start a new life. The men who employed Liggett's services for years may have been testing his ability to keep silent when he was incarcerated for 11 months after the Peck attack. Apparently he passed the test and was granted a reprieve from conviction. Faking his death would have been little more than a minor challenge for the men who arranged the murder and cover-up of a U.S. President. Perhaps Crawford had shot and missed Liggett, and instead of Liggett being transported to Parkland he was simply set free. It would have been easy enough to substitute the corpse of another who could have been identified as Liggett at Parkland. Somebody goofed, however, when Leona Liggett was allowed to see the fake corpse in the casket.

Further proof that Liggett was not killed in February 1975 in Dallas comes from his first wife Lois. She was vacationing in Las Vegas years after John had supposedly died when she saw him working as a pit boss in one of the casinos owned by Dallas gambler and gangster Benny Binion. Binion was a mob-connected bigshot in Dallas in the 1940s and 1950s when the city still had the reputation of being a cowboy outpost. Nonetheless, he owed fealty to Carlos Marcello, Mafia kingpin of New Orleans whose territory included Dallas. David Ferrie, the captain of Liggett's CAP unit and the "freak" who visited Liggett's residence in the mid-1960s, was once Marcello's private pilot. Perhaps it was Marcello who gave the order to free Liggett from jail and provide a new life and new identity in Vegas. That's where Liggett's trail ends. The where and when of his real death are unknown.

To this day, Liggett's precise purpose for being at Parkland remains undetermined. And despite a considerable number of circumstantial clues, the Parkland body-heist supposition is speculation rather than definitive fact. Since the time that DiBoard first introduced me to the possibility, I have searched tirelessly for more evidence to support her hypothesis. In that quest, I came across an interview of Aubrey Rike by JFK researcher Joel Wagoner in early 1992. In it, Rike laughs at the suggestion that JFK's body was stolen or switched out at Parkland. He assured Wagoner that once he helped load the body into the coffin, the body was not removed by anyone; Rike was there the whole time. But then he added a curious caveat: "Of course, I can't say what might have happened before I put the body in it."[163]

I circled back to DiBoard for her reaction to Rike's statement. She responded with a mixture of amusement and exasperation: "He doesn't get it. The switch was accomplished before he loaded the fake corpse into the casket he brought from Oneal. Did anyone ask him if he was sure that the body he put into the casket was really the body of JFK?" To my knowledge, no one ever did. Rike's presumption must have been that it had to be JFK's body. He did admit to Wagoner that even when he was in Trauma Room One with the body, *he could not see it* [emphasis added].[164] Rike is dead now, so the question lingers. DiBoard added, "Besides, he was a smoker. Tell me, under all that stress, he didn't sneak out to have a cigarette?" Sure enough, Rike told Wagoner that he left Trauma Room One to buy a pack of cigarettes.[165]

One last puzzle involving Rike at Parkland is this—according to Warren Commission Document 1245 dated May 28, 1964 (as part of an FBI report), "[Aubrey] Rike stated that he was advised by a Secret Service Agent at Parkland Hospital that his ambulance was not to be moved because they might need to move the President to another location."[166] Where was this other location? Was the original intent of the plotters to alter the body in Dallas at an undisclosed location after removing the body from Parkland? Rike's hearse was eventually used to transport the Oneal casket to Love Field, but the President's body might not have been in it.

CHAPTER 7

The Cover-Up, Then and Now

"[JFK] was struck in the right temple [by]
…a German Mauser"
—NBC broadcast on 11/22/63

Unraveling the truth of the Kennedy assassination has been like peeling back layers of an onion that seems to have endless layers. As we get closer to the center, more obstacles present themselves, and there are more layers to strip away. That was the mastermind's plan all along—to make it a multi-layered puzzle. On the surface it appears that Oswald did it alone; the planted evidence indicates that. But dig a little deeper and you'll find other layers of partial truths: 1) the anti-Castro Cubans planned it and Oswald was supposed to stop it; 2) Carlos Marcello and the mob planned it, with the help of some lower-level CIA factions; 3) Texas oilmen executed the plot; 4) Rogue CIA and FBI agents pulled it off with the help of disaffected Secret Service agents; 5) Kennedy's military chiefs were to blame. At each of these levels one can find evidence to indict someone. But the full truth lies deeper. One must slice into the core—at the rawest, most dangerous place—to find Lyndon Johnson, Allen Dulles and their sponsors. And it was their sponsors who ultimately gave the go-ahead. These were men who really ruled America. They owned most of the riches and resources and still do. They financed the careers of front men like Johnson and Dulles, men who were the gatekeepers of government. They amassed vast fortunes in oil, communications, weapons manufacturing, finance, transportation and engineering. They profited immensely from war and saw no future in a peace economy. That's why Kennedy had to go.

Unraveling what they did requires persistence. It becomes a ceaseless project. New mysteries and contradictions present themselves, and we are left to our own devices to discern the truth. In this process, it is easy to get caught up in what I call "vacuum discussions," discussions of limited scope over some very specific matter that can get lost in a vacuum. Often it becomes a debate between two people who are at different "layers of the onion." Those who are stuck at the peel usually insist the Oswald-did-it evidence is the best evidence and will doggedly defend their flawed views with vacuum discussions. They lose perspective and ignore the fact that there are thousands of other pieces to consider, the preponderance of which point dramatically to conspiracy.

For instance, lone-nutters like to use the spent Mannlicher-Carcano shells on the sixth floor of the TSBD as absolute proof that Oswald shot the President from behind. But this easy presumption ignores a wider universe of evidence that Oswald could not have fired the shots. For one thing, neither the FBI nor Dallas police could definitively find Oswald's prints on the rifle, until mysterious federal agents lifted them from Oswald's corpse at the funeral home where he was embalmed. Paul Groody of Miller Funeral Home in Fort Worth claimed that he witnessed postmortem fingerprinting of Oswald's corpse two days after the assassination—"I was there... that's exactly what [FBI agents] did."[1] For another, no witness saw or heard Oswald run down the steps from the sixth floor to the second floor in the ninety seconds before he was seen there by Marion Baker and Roy Truly. For another, Parkland doctors and nurses saw frontal-entry and rear-exit wound patterns on the President. Given the wider universe of evidence, it is more likely, then, that Oswald did not fire the Mannlicher-Carcano that left the spent cartridges on the sixth floor. This means that either the spent shells were planted, or someone else fired from behind and missed the President. And this would, by definition, indicate conspiracy, a place where lone-nutters are loath to go.

To grasp the full scope of the conspiracy that took JFK's life one must avoid vacuum traps, though they are easy to fall into. Many so-called experts limit their knowledge by failing to step back and assess the larger field of evidence. Illustrative of this problem was the August 10, 2017, NPR broadcast ("Fresh Air") which featured JFK assassination writer Philip Shenon. Shenon, author of a *Cruel and Shocking Act*, got bogged down in a discussion of Oswald in Mexico City. He claimed that documents have been uncovered which reveal that Oswald was at a "twist" party there with a woman named Silvia Duran, a Cuban consulate employee, in late September of 1963. According to Duran, this Oswald stated very clearly that JFK needed to be killed. Meanwhile, apparently unbeknownst to Shenon, another Oswald, at the very same time, showed up at Silvia Odio's residence in Dallas (see chapter 3). Shenon is either oblivious to the fact there was an Oswald impersonator framing the real Oswald in the weeks leading up to the assassination, or he has dismissed Odio's eyewitness testimony. (As a reminder, Odio's account of seeing Oswald is quite credible. She recognized him as the same man she saw on TV after the assassination.) Either way, Shenon, operating in a vacuum, discredits his own research by failing to understand there were two Oswalds. He is also seemingly unaware that the communist consulates in Mexico City were constantly monitored and bugged by the CIA. Yet the CIA could produce no recording or photo of an Oswald visiting either the Soviet or Cuban embassies. How is that possible? Why didn't the CIA make public its proof of Oswald's presence in Mexico City? Shenon, lobbed gratuitous softballs by the hosts of "Fresh Air" who seemed even less informed than he, provided no hint that he was aware of, or understood, the meaning of the two Oswalds' encounters with the two Si[y]lvias 1,100 miles apart on the same day.

But there are other lone-nutters who know better, yet refuse to admit their near-sightedness. One of the most prominent is author Vincent Bugliosi, who is fond of blaming conspiracists for taking what should have been a simple murder and turning it into the most complicated case in history. I beg to differ. It is the plotters who made it the most complicated murder case in history. Purposefully so. False leads, planted evidence, misinformation, photography and film manipulation, body alteration, official corruption and criminal complicity are what have made the Kennedy assassination the hall of mirrors that it is. I am convinced this was the conspirators' intent: lay a trail so winding, steep and treacherous, that it would be nearly impossible for investigators to scale the summit to the truth. This hypothesis is supported by the words of a man who had inside knowledge of the plot. CIA operative Gerry Hemming explained to British author Noel Twyman that one of the prime methods of obscuring the truth of a covert event like the assassination of a head of state is to employ intentional deception. "There will be confusion as to who the assassins and sponsors [are]…leads are given that are decoys and strays…[or someone] could be proven to be a principal, an aider and abettor."[2] The purpose is to confound outsiders looking in, by making it hard to separate the decoys from the real perpetrators.

The seeds of covert deception were planted in all compartments of this complex scheme. Relatively speaking, accomplishing the deed was straightforward; the more insidious part of the plot was blocking all avenues by which the truth of it could be unearthed. The tricks of illusion, red herrings and fakery began before 11/22/63 and kicked into high gear the moment Kennedy was hit.

In Dealey Plaza, the smell of gunpowder was still in the air when conspirators on the ground began their work. They sabotaged evidence, intimidated witnesses, created false leads and facilitated assassins' escape. They did this by employing men with false government identification badges at ground zero, Dealey Plaza. We have seen from a previous chapter that there were literally dozens of intelligence-linked assets in the immediate area of the assassination, many of them posing as Secret Service agents. Some were dressed in Dallas police uniforms. Others were disguised as tramps or railroad workers. All had a specific role to play; all had rehearsed their assignments and, thus, were well-prepared.

In the chaotic aftermath of the killing, these undercover operatives were able to carry out their nefarious tasks without much resistance. Civilian witnesses and honest Dallas cops were looking in many directions for killers, but they did not recognize them in their very midst because they were well-disguised. The killers, and the accessories to the crime, were hiding in plain sight. Only those aware of the plot and its mechanics would have had any inkling of who was involved and who wasn't. Witnesses were shocked, panicked and frenzied; they would have been susceptible to misdirection and manipulation.

The Photographic Clean-Up Crew

There were many photographers and filmmakers in Dealey Plaza on 11/22/63, but a considerable number of the films and photos they took that day have not survived in their original, unaltered state. As stated previously, the only publicly known film of the assassination to be taken from the north side of Elm Street was Abraham Zapruder's. But there were many who took pictures from the south side of Elm. Photographers Phil Willis, Hugh Betzner and Jim Towner stood near the corner of Elm and Houston; Beverly Oliver, Mary Moorman and James Bothun stood in the grassy triangle south of Elm. Professional James Altgens was at the west end of Elm near the underpass. Amateur filmmakers near Houston and Main, and south of Elm, included Robert Hughes, Marie Muchmore, Orville Nix and Charles Bronson. With so much coverage of the event, there should have been a complete photographic record by which many of the mysteries could have been solved. However, most of the photographers reported that the images they recorded were stolen, altered, deleted or simply ignored.

We now know that one of the tasks of the covert agents was to "clean up" the photographic evidence. These agents made off with films or photographs of the assassination, or secured information about the photographers and home-movie makers so as to procure their films at a later date. The FBI also contacted film processors in the Dallas area to flag assassination pictures and turn over these images to the local FBI office. On the surface of it, these measures could be construed as legitimate investigative procedure; however, in more cases than not, the films were suppressed or manipulated to prevent the secrets they held from being exposed.

Nix turned over his film to government agents, and years afterwards he told his granddaughter, Gayle Nix Jackson, that he believed the footage he shot had been altered. Jackson publicly asserted that the government had kept her grandfather's original film and returned a doctored copy to the family, because there was something in the original frames that the plotters did not want American citizens to see. She claimed that the HSCA was supposed to turn the original over to the National Archives, but the National Archives has not returned it to her. Jackson brought a $10 million complaint in 2015 after the National Archives and Records Administration told her that her grandfather's original footage had gone missing, along with the chain-of-custody index.[3]

In 1991, extreme blow-ups of the Nix film revealed human movement behind a concrete retaining wall near the steps on the grassy knoll.[4] In the same area, a Willis photo reveals what researchers have dubbed the "black dog man." An image of someone in a classic shooting position, holding an object that is pointed towards the motorcade, can be seen. The object is indiscernible, but some have speculated that it is not a weapon but rather a camera that the man is pointing at the motorcade. (See the discussion of a possible alternate home movie of the assassination in chapter 5.) The image is black and resembles a dog in a sitting position, but moments later it has disappeared. The Nix film also captured what appeared to be a rifleman, in a classic shooting pose, leaning against a car in the parking lot behind the picket fence as he takes aim at the motorcade. The film passed through various hands in an attempt to examine it more closely. Eventually it wound up at Itek, a Massachusetts firm with expertise in photographic analysis. Itek concluded that the "rifleman image" was nothing more than shadows and highlights. But it later turned out that Itek executives were ex-CIA agents, and more than half the company's business was provided by the intelligence agency.[5] In short, the CIA's analysis of the Nix film was that the CIA was not involved in the assassination.

The black dog controversy was partially resolved in 1978 when the HSCA authorized a study of it. Photographic experts from the University of Southern California and the Aerospace Corporation concluded that the black dog image was of "an adult person standing behind the wall." That person was holding an object in his hands which could not be identified, but which appeared to be pointed at the presidential limousine.[6]

A Canadian journalist named Norman Similas claimed that his photo of the TSBD's sixth floor at the time of the shooting was not returned to him after he submitted the photo for publication to the *Toronto Telegram*. The newspaper told Similas the photo had been lost; as compensation, Similas was sent a check.[7]

Beverly Oliver (Babushka Lady), another amateur filming from the south side of Elm, said that she was approached by FBI agent Regis Kennedy just days after the assassination. Kennedy said the FBI was aware of her film and wanted to develop it for evidence. The agent confiscated the film she made with her new Super-8 Yashica camera, and Oliver never saw it again.[8] Oliver's film, had it not been stolen, could have settled once and for all the controversy of who, if anyone, was firing from behind the picket fence atop the grassy knoll. Her camera was aimed directly at that area at the time of the shooting, and of all the home-movie makers in Dealey Plaza on 11/22/63, Oliver might have been closest to the President.

Oliver's story does not end with stolen film. She ran up the grassy knoll after the shots had been fired, and recognized a man named Roscoe White (husband of an acquaintance who worked for Jack Ruby) dressed as a Dallas cop. On November 22, White was not officially a member of the Dallas Police Department, but did have access to a police uniform because he was in training to become a cop.[9] He is suspected of being one of the Dealey Plaza shooters by some researchers; there is also evidence that he played a role in the killing of Officer J.D. Tippit the same day (see chapter 5).

Oliver knew other organized-crime characters who were associated with events surrounding the assassination. She worked for Jack Ruby in one of his Dallas nightclubs. One night she was introduced, by Ruby, to a man named Lee Oswald of the CIA. Shortly after the assassination she married a Dallas underworld figure named George McGann. McGann's best man was Russell Matthews, a known criminal associated with the Mafia in Dallas. Matthews was a mentor to assassin Charles Harrelson, and he played poker with the murderous undertaker John Liggett. Oliver claimed that she and McGann met with Richard Nixon in his hotel room in Miami during the 1968 presidential campaign.[10]

But there are parts of Oliver's story which need closer scrutiny. How did a young woman like Oliver, 19 years old on 11/22/63, who was involved with so many organized crime figures in Dallas, end up being in perfect position to film the crime of the century with a brand new home-movie camera? In 1963 strippers who worked for Ruby were barely able to pay their rent, much less afford expensive cameras. We can surmise that, since federal agents confiscated her film shortly after the assassination, they had probably been alerted to Oliver's presence in Dealey Plaza by Ruby, Matthews, McGann or some other shady figure. Perhaps Oliver was yet another amateur filmmaker who was supposed to be where she was, because some of the plotters encouraged her to be there. They even provided a new camera for her. It was just as important for the plotters to know how the assassination happened, as it was for law enforcement, so they would know what needed to be covered up.

Phil Willis, standing on the south side of Elm Street with his family, swears he took a picture of Jack Ruby walking in front of the Texas Book Depository right after the shooting. Ruby said he was not in the plaza at the time of the shooting, and proof of his presence there would have sent conspiratorial shockwaves through the investigation. When Willis got his photo back, he saw that it had been cropped right through the image he claimed was Jack Ruby.

Mary Moorman took one of the most famous photos of the assassination. It was a picture of JFK just as the bullet which killed him struck his head. Moorman's photo has obviously been cropped. How do I know? Look closely sometime. *There is no one driving the car.* Limo driver William Greer, who some say pulled a gun and pointed it at JFK, has been cut out of the picture.

It is quite possible that we will never know how many images were confiscated and destroyed on 11/22/63. Some photographers remain anonymous. Illustrative of this is an incident which occurred at Parkland Hospital shortly after the President's limo arrived there. A boy with a "small, cheap-looking box camera" snapped a shot of the limo's interior which was splattered with blood and brains. A Secret Service agent brusquely confiscated the camera and destroyed the film; as he did this, he chastised the boy.

Other photographers' work simply disappeared. Congressman Henry Gonzalez snapped photos inside Parkland, but his camera was stolen before he could develop the shots.[11]

As mentioned previously, Gordon Arnold took a home movie of the assassination while standing almost directly in the line of fire by the picket fence on the grassy knoll. A 22-year-old soldier on leave, Arnold at first intended to film the motorcade from behind the fence line, but he was forcefully told to move by someone who flashed Secret Service credentials. Arnold dutifully shifted to the other side of the fence but stayed near the top of the grassy knoll. He began filming as the motorcade approached when "...a shot went off over my left shoulder. I felt the bullet rather than heard it, and it went right past my left ear...and [I] heard several other shots."[12] He hit the deck and covered up as he had been taught to do in basic training. Quickly two "cops" emerged from behind the fence and demanded, at gunpoint, that Arnold turn over his camera. One of the cops was carrying a rifle and the other was sobbing uncontrollably. The cop with the rifle yanked the film out and threw the camera back at Arnold. Terrified by what happened, Arnold quickly left Dealey Plaza without reporting the incident to anyone.[13]

Some have called Arnold a "kook" and dismissed his story, but corroboration of it comes from a very credible source—Senator Ralph Yarborough, who was riding in the same car as Lyndon Johnson, just a few cars behind the President's. Yarborough said, "My eye was attracted to my right...I saw a man jump about ten feet... I thought to myself there's an infantryman who has either been shot at in combat, or he's been trained thoroughly. When you hear firing, get under cover."[14]

Arnold's story also informs us that it is quite likely that assassins were disguised as Dallas police officers in Dealey Plaza. This diabolically shrewd deception is one that the CIA could have concocted. How better to hide the killers in plain sight than by dressing them up in policemen's uniforms? There were also plain-clothed men posing as Secret Service agents. How did these men get their authentic-looking credentials? It is likely only those inside the government with high-level access to the changing codes and symbols of Secret Service identification could accomplish such a forgery. (It is significant to note here that just weeks after the assassination, all Secret Service agents were required to turn in their IDs—or commission books—and were issued new ones in January of 1964.) The

fake IDs deceived an authentic Dallas cop from perhaps apprehend-
ing one of the assassins just moments after the gunfire. Convinced
by witnesses that shots had been fired from the front right of the
motorcade, Officer Joe M. Smith scurried into the parking lot
behind the picket fence before the smoke cleared. There he encountered a man dressed in a sports shirt who flashed Secret Service
credentials. The ID looked authentic to Smith, and he did not
detain the man. But later he regretted it because the man "...looked
like an auto mechanic...he had dirty fingernails...and it didn't ring
true for the Secret Service."[15] Secret Service agents in 1963 wore
dark suits, white shirts, and narrow ties. They did not dress in sports
shirts while on duty. Smith made another critical observation: he
detected the lingering smell of gunpowder "around the hedges lin-
ing the parking lot."[16] He was one of scores of witnesses who
smelled gunpowder at or near street level (see previous discussion
in chapter 5), strong evidence that shots were fired from locations
other than the Book Depository building.

Other films, like the one taken by Charles Bronson, were initially
considered of such little consequence that they were ignored as evidence. Bronson filmed the motorcade with his eight-millimeter
camera from atop the concrete pillar at the corner of Main and
Houston. His movie offered a good view of the TSBD as the President's car approached Elm Street. When examined closely years
later, Bronson's film revealed two human figures moving about the
sixth floor just seconds before the assassination.[17] Thus, it verifies
that if Oswald (or his doppelganger) was there, he was not alone.
The HSCA found the film significant enough to recommend further official scrutiny of it. However, after years of legal wrangling
and government obfuscation, the Justice Department dismissed the
film's evidentiary value. In the final year of Ronald Reagan's presidency, as George H.W. Bush was actively campaigning for the same
office, Assistant Attorney General John Bolton claimed that the
National Academy of Sciences had already disproved the HSCA's

basis for considering the Bronson film proof of a conspiracy.[18] This, in effect, forever killed any possibility that the government would acknowledge the film as a crucial piece of evidence. Bolton's career subsequently skyrocketed when he was hired by two Bush administrations—H.W.'s and W.'s—to serve in various State and Justice Department positions. He was involved in the Iran-Contra affair; as an archconservative and war hawk, he promoted aggressive American military action around the globe. He was the most bombastic and reviled Ambassador to the U.N. America has ever appointed. He also worked in the Agency for International Development which has long been associated with CIA covert activities.

Other photographs which went unnoticed for years include several taken by Dallas-Fort Worth professionals which show three tramps being arrested in Dealey Plaza on 11/22/63. *Fort Worth Star-Telegram* staff photographer George Smith captured the tramps as they were led away from a railroad box car towards Dealey Plaza. The tramps' procession to the city jail was also photographed by William Allen of the *Dallas Times-Herald* and Jack Beers of the *Dallas Morning News*. These photos were not published until many years after they were taken, and it is unlikely that the tramps' arrests would have become public knowledge had the photos not surfaced. This perhaps explains why the photos were unaltered, unsuppressed and intact. It is probable that not even the plotters knew of their existence before they were "discovered" in the late 1960s.

In a prior chapter, I explored the possibility that the tramps were CIA-connected operatives Charles Rogers, Charles Harrelson and E. Howard Hunt. But by no means have the three tramps been identified with absolute certainty to the satisfaction of all researchers. Some lone-nutters cling to the innocent explanation that the arrest of the tramps was entirely incidental to the assassination and involved nothing more than hobos innocently hopping a freight mere yards from the murder of the century. Researchers Ray and Mary LaFontaine, in the early 1990s, even attached names to the bums—John Forrester Gedney, Gus W. Abrams and Harold Doyle.[19] In subsequent years two of the three were tracked down (Abrams died in 1987 before he could be located by investigators). Gedney and Doyle gave similar versions of why they were in Dallas; they were just traveling the rails, aimlessly roaming the country. In a recorded interview in 1992, Doyle claimed he and the other tramps were told about the assassination before they hopped onto the railroad car near the assassination site; almost immediately thereafter, they were surrounded by police and dragged off the box-car.[20] However, the timing does not correlate to the known facts. The tramp photos were not taken until almost two hours after the assassination. If, as Doyle claims, he and his companions were arrested right after the assassination which occurred at 12:30, how is it possible that it took them two hours to walk about 200 yards to the city jail?

The circumstances under which the names of Doyle, Abrams and Gedney were released are also suspicious. For nearly 30 years there existed no arrest record, no files and no paperwork at all on the three tramps in the Dallas police department. But in 1992 (shortly after Oliver Stone's movie *JFK* caused renewed interest in the tramps), suddenly out of nowhere, the tramps' arrest record was miraculously found buried in the Dallas police department's old files. Looking past the fact that it is highly unusual that a police department would even retain a 30-year-old record on three hobos who were charged with no crime, there are strange notations on the arrest record. The arresting officer is listed as W.E. Chambers, but photographs of Chambers in 1963 do not match the photographs of the arresting officers in Dealey Plaza. In fact, it is still unclear who the arresting officers were. Some believe they were Patrolmen Billy Bass and Marvin Wise; others claim they were Officer D.V. Harkness and an unknown cop.[21] Many researchers say the cops were phony, and their arrest of the tramps was part of a CIA ruse to safely escort CIA operatives Rogers, Harrelson and Hunt from the scene of the crime. The cops' uniforms had minor variances from standard Dallas police uniforms of that time, and one of the officers had an earpiece in his right ear. Interestingly, the oldest tramp seemed to also have an earpiece in his right ear, suggesting covert coordination between the arrestors and the arrestees.

Throw into this mix the presence of CIA operative Edward Lansdale, who, at one point, walks through the "cops/tramps procession" without any resistance or interference from the arresting officers (see chapter 5). It violates routine police procedure to let a civilian come between the arresting officers and those they have apprehended. Reading body language as this trespass occurs reveals something else that is suspicious. The tramps lower their heads in an apparent attempt to avoid the gaze of Lansdale. At the same time, the taller tramp betrays recognition with a self-satisfied smirk, as if he is acknowledging the approval of his case officer, Lansdale.

The arrest record also contains another timing inconsistency. It reads, "These men were getting on a boxcar right after President Kennedy was shot"; however, the time of the arrest reads "4 p.m." The assassination occurred at 12:30 p.m. What were the tramps and their arrestors doing for over three hours? It doesn't take that long to walk from the railyards to the city jail. As stated above, the photos were taken between 2:15 and 2:30 by Smith, Allen and Beers. The cops and tramps were either the slowest walkers in the world, or the arrest record and Doyle's story are fabricated.

Serious researchers who have studied the three tramps and their relationship to the assassination, have cast further doubt on the assertion that the hobos were incidental victims caught up in circumstances in which they played no part. In their book, *Coup D'Etat in America*, authors Michael Canfield and Alan Weberman insist that the photographed tramps were not Abrams, Gedney and Doyle, and that Doyle, especially, bore no resemblance to any of the tramps in Dealey Plaza.[22] But this, like many other matters surrounding the assassination, may be beyond any definitive resolution because of conflicting accounts and the plotters' insertion into the official record of dubious or doctored evidence.

The CIA Began Linking Oswald to Castro Just One Day After JFK's Murder

An obscure memo uncovered among the documents in Boston's JFK Library directly links the Central Intelligence Agency to a Miami publication which, just one day after JFK's assassination, accused Lee Harvey Oswald of being an agent of Fidel Castro. In one stroke the CIA was trying to plausibly deny its own involvement in Kennedy's murder *and* provide the U.S. with the pretense for overthrowing a communist government 90 miles from our shore. JFK researcher Jefferson Morley recently brought these facts to light; as of this writing, he is suing the CIA for release of over 1,000 files related to the JFK assassination. (All government records pertaining to the assassination were supposed to be released in October 2017, but most of them were held back by Donald Trump at the insistence of the FBI and the CIA.)

The magazine the CIA used to make its false allegations on November 23, 1963, was *Trinchera*, Spanish for "Trenches." According to Joseph Lazzaro, writing for the *International Business Times*, *Trinchera* was published by a group which called itself the Cuban Student Directorate or DRE (Directorio Revolucionario Estudantil). The JFK Library memo states that the DRE received $51,000 per month from the CIA; that's the equivalent of $389,000 in 2013 money, or over $4 million per year. Records declassified under the Freedom of Information Act indicate that the CIA liaison who paid the DRE its money was George Joannides. Stationed in Miami, Joannides formed and advised the DRE in covert operations designed to sabotage Castro and promote right-wing propaganda in the U.S. Joannides, who has other sinister links to the Kennedy assassination, was head of PsyOps at the CIA's Miami station. He was also the CIA's liaison to the House Select Committee on Assassinations (1976-78) which reopened the JFK investigation.[23] As the CIA's point man, Joannides destroyed documents, intimated witnesses, misled committee members, and obstructed justice at every turn. He was vigilant in guarding the CIA's secrets and preventing the committee from connecting the CIA to the assassination.

Without Joannides' interference, the HSCA investigation might not have been derailed. Its original Deputy Chief Counsel, Robert Tanenbaum, once told researcher Robert Groden that, "This conspiracy goes to the highest levels of government, and we're going to blow them out of the water."[24] But when it became apparent that the committee was headed in the wrong direction, Tanenbaum quit. He refused to be part of an investigation meant to deceive the American people.

The HSCA's Chief Counsel Robert Blakey later claimed that if he had known of Joannides' background and mission he would have put him under oath and been suspicious of all CIA source material provided by Joannides.[25] Of course, by the time Blakey figured out that Joannides was nothing more than an obstructionist and a propagandist it was much too late. Joannides died in 1990.

Blakey's admissions are shocking. In essence, he is telling the American people that the HSCA investigation he chaired was a complete sham and cannot be trusted. He told PBS's Frontline that "I no longer believe we were able to conduct an appropriate investigation of [the CIA] and its relationship to Oswald....[because] Oswald had direct dealings with [the DRE] during the time that Joannides was linked to the DRE...and I was not told of this."[26] The big conclusion reached by Blakey and his committee, namely that Oswald killed Kennedy, is flawed because they failed to seriously consider CIA involvement. The HSCA was stumbling around in the minor leagues while the CIA was playing big-league baseball. The CIA, with Joannides as its project leader, established the DRE, also known as AMSPELL, in September 1960 and disbanded it in

December 1966.[27] The timing is significant, as the DRE's origins
and termination correlate to the presidential campaign of 1960 and
the post-Warren Commission era when serious doubts about the
report were first being expressed in America. It raises the possibility
that whomever was elected in 1960 would be subject to intense
pressure brought by the CIA to remove Castro by hook or crook.
When Kennedy failed, he was dealt with accordingly. In preparation for the assassination, DRE conducted covert operations which
implicated Oswald as a pro-Castroite in New Orleans in August of
1963. It was the DRE that organized the Fair Play for Cuba organization; its imprint was affixed to the leaflets Oswald handed out
to create the false impression that he was a Cuban agent. After the
assassination, the DRE needed to be terminated for fear it would
be seen as a CIA tool for redirecting suspicions away from itself.

Legal maneuvers to obtain the classified files on Joannides under
the Freedom of Information Act have failed. According to Lazzaro,
the CIA has also refused to release the files of other JFK murder
suspects—David Atlee Phillips, E. Howard Hunt and William Harvey. The "if only we had known" attitude towards Joannides continued with the Assassination Records Review Board (ARRB). Jack
Tunheim, ARRB chairman, said that had the board known about
Joannides' activities in 1963, it would have been a no-brainer to
investigate him.[28]

Kennedy Family Believed in Conspiracy
Lone-nutters still attempt to deny a conspiracy in JFK's murder by
citing Robert Kennedy's inaction after the assassination. The common cry among the sightless is, "He was Attorney General at the
time. If there really was a conspiracy, he could have uncovered it.
This is proof that the Kennedy family knew there was no conspiracy." The appropriate reply to this nonsense is, the Kennedys knew
almost immediately that JFK had been killed by a domestic right-
wing plot concocted by his many enemies in American intelligence,

government and business. But Bobby knew that, with his brother gone, he no longer had the power that goes with being the top law enforcement officer in the country. After 11/22/63 Hoover and Johnson held all the cards. Any public proclamation by Bobby concerning the truth of how his brother died could have easily been dismissed as the deranged ramblings of a man overcome by grief and bitterness; besides, as Bobby privately acknowledged many times, the truth was not going to bring his brother back, and the only thing left to do was to protect his brother's legacy. JFK's enemies could have countered any move by Bobby with public revelations of JFK's sexual affairs.

With no public avenue of justice to pursue domestically, the Kennedys reached out to Russian officials with their private suspicions about who was really behind the assassination. Bobby and Jackie wanted to assure Moscow that they did not blame the Soviets for Jack's murder, and that Kruschev should continue to advance the peace initiatives he and President Kennedy had undertaken in the year after the Cuban Missile Crisis. It is a cruel irony that the family of the martyred President could only turn to America's Cold War enemy to convey a terrible truth. A little background is necessary to understand why the Kennedys divulged to the Soviets what they could not speak aloud in America after 11/22/63.

During the 1960 presidential campaign, candidate Kennedy's tough-on-communism rhetoric was almost a prerequisite to be elected to the highest office in the world. But his stance towards the Soviets softened even before he was sworn in. As early as December 1960 Kennedy made back-channel overtures to Moscow concerning nuclear disarmament and test-ban negotiations.[29] Once he took office, he was forced, by political pressure and the hawkish generals and intelligence advisors, to maintain a public anti-Soviet posture, but his fear of global nuclear war always informed his deep desire for détente with the Russians. However, his mistake of assenting to the disastrous Bay of Pigs mission undercut any early attempts of dialing back Cold War tensions. Moscow became suspicious of Kennedy's real intentions, and an era of renewed superpower aggression began. Kruschev used the Cuban fiasco to bully Kennedy at their Vienna summit in 1961. Kennedy was stunned by Kruschev's willingness to exacerbate animosities and risk armed confrontation. Tensions culminated in the Missile Crisis of 1962. Two weeks of staring into the nuclear abyss changed the two leaders. Kennedy and Kruschev decided to back away from it all.

For the next year, they forged a tentative but very real alliance in the pursuit of peace and disarmament. It was a sometimes rocky road, what with both men forced by internal war-eager factions to avoid the appearance of weakness, but both Kennedy and Kruschev made great strides in moving towards a peaceful resolution to the Cold War. Kennedy went public with his revolutionary vision on June 10, 1963. His speech at American University that day still reverberates across the decades as the most visionary and courageous of the entire Cold War. In it he praised the Russian people and commiserated with the suffering they endured as our allies in World War II. He proposed that America consider the possibility of peaceful coexistence with our avowed enemies. He lyrically reminded us that, in the end, we shared the same fragile planet with them, they breathed the same air we did, and we both cherished our children's future. Details of that speech were published in Soviet newspapers, and the reaction from the Kremlin was positive. The dawn of a new era in Soviet-American relations had been set in motion. A nuclear test ban treaty was signed by the superpowers two months later. As part of this process, Jack and Bobby Kennedy nurtured friendly back-channel contacts with Russian officials.

But JFK's murder, and the news that his accused assassin had indisputable Soviet ties, threatened to undo all of the progress that Kennedy and Kruschev had made in forging a new superpower paradigm. Indeed, this was a critical aspiration of the plotters. Kennedy's enemies killed him, in large part, because they were angered and terrified by peaceful coexistence with the Soviets. Massive military weapons stockpiles and the domestic contractors who made enormous profits from the manufacture of these weapons were threatened with obsolescence. The CIA feared its usefulness, maybe its very existence, would be extraneous in a world without a Cold War. The right-wing fringe would be deprived of its hot war with the communists. Dallas was their remedy. The framing of Oswald as a Soviet stooge was their attempt to undo all that Kennedy and Kruschev had done.

In early December 1963 the Kennedy family sent a personal emissary, William Walton, to speak with Georgi Bolshakov, a Russian diplomat. Bolshakov had met with Bobby Kennedy countless times before, and during the Cuban Missile Crisis the men had come to trust one another as useful conduits for Soviet-American peacekeeping negotiations. Bolshakov was assured by Walton that the Kennedy family was convinced that Oswald did not act alone. Walton's explicit message contradicted the Kennedys' subsequent public support of the Warren Commission findings. Walton told the Soviets that pro-fascist reactionaries who despised the President and his policies, and who were "...dissatisfied with...improving relations with the Soviet Union..." had organized the plot; these included, among others, oilmen H.L. Hunt and Clint Murchison.[30]

Notably absent from the Kennedys' identification of the plotters were Lyndon Johnson and the CIA. Bobby Kennedy initially suspected both, but he was likely dissuaded by intelligence sources who may have been trying to divert blame away from themselves. John McCone, CIA Director at the time, denied intelligence involvement and swore to the Attorney General that he would have known if the CIA had been involved. But it was Richard Helms, the Allen Dulles protégé, who was really running the CIA, and he would have kept McCone in the dark.[31] And McCone would not have been privy to the machinations of Allen Dulles's CIA-in-exile. In later years Bobby reportedly directly confronted Johnson with his knowledge of Johnson's involvement.

But never did the Kennedys, in any public forum, accuse Johnson and Dulles of engineering the assassination. And Bobby's reticence to come forward with what he really knew was used by the plotters as a means by which they could exonerate themselves. The reasoning was that if JFK's own brother believed Oswald acted alone, there was no reason to believe in a conspiracy. LBJ's surrogates gave their boss cover this way. One of Johnson' aides, a college professor named John P. Roche, wrote a letter to a newspaper denouncing assassination researchers as "paranoids," and cited the Kennedy family's support of the Warren Commission as proof that there was no conspiracy.[32]

The CIA used the same tactic. In a memo distributed to agency assets at major media outlets, it listed several arguments that CIA-friendly journalists could use to counter Warren Commission critics. Included in the list was the reminder that "Bobby Kennedy... would be the last man to overlook or conceal any conspiracy."[33]

In private, however, Bobby quietly sought out the truth of Dallas. He knew quite well who his brothers' dire enemies were, and he directed his close associates to find out what they could. Behind closed doors he engaged in conversations with trusted advisers about assassination scenarios that implicated the CIA, the Mafia, the Joint Chiefs and Texas oilmen. He listened to what they had to say, but remained largely silent. He knew he would not have the power to bring the killers to justice until he himself ascended to the presidency.[34]

Shortly before his death, Bobby momentarily let his guard down on a campaign trip and revealed to a stunned audience that he knew the Warren Commission was a fraud. On March 25, 1968, at a rally in southern California, he was asked by someone in the audience if he planned to reopen the investigation into his brother's death if he were elected president. Bobby paused and measured his words. "I haven't answered this question before, but there would be nobody that would be more interested in all of these matters as to who was responsible for the...death of President Kennedy than I would."[35]

Johnson Goes to Work

While Bobby Kennedy was mourning the loss of his brother in late November of 1963, Lyndon Johnson was hard at work covering his tracks. His first order of business was to make sure that the congressional hearings into his criminal past were stymied. On the plane back from Dallas Johnson called his old friend Abe Fortas to inform him that he was no longer the lead attorney in the government's case against Bobby Baker; instead, Fortas was assigned the task of heading off the Senate investigations into the Baker/LBJ kickback/bribery/ blackmail schemes.[36] With Johnson newly installed in the Oval Office the investigation petered out; Congress had no appetite for bringing down Kennedy's successor. The country and its public servants, having just lost one president, had no desire to indict another. Journalists felt the same way. *Life* magazine's attempt to expose the corruption of LBJ and Baker simply faded away.[37] That is until August of 1964 when a startling expose of Johnson appeared in *Life*. The article pulls no punches in regards to LBJ's voracious ruthlessness; it anonymously quotes a decades-long, Texas acquaintance of Johnson as saying, "LBJ wants it all...All there is of everything...all the respect, all the admiration, and all the love there is...[and] all the votes there are."[38] *Life* was, of course, owned by Henry Luce, a close friend and collaborator of Allen Dulles. So it is somewhat perplexing that a CIA-approved publication would print such a depiction of Johnson. Perhaps Dulles was subtly reminding Johnson that the powers of the presidency were limited, and that LBJ could be driven from office, if necessary, by the same forces that devised the plot of 11/22/63. LBJ knew that he owed his presidency to these forces.

After quashing the Baker investigation, Johnson went about covering his bloody trail from Dallas to the White House. He induced

and coerced Kennedy's cabinet to stay and serve in the new LBJ
administration. It wouldn't have looked good for the new President
to be shunned by the martyred President's aides, especially since the
murder had occurred in the new President's backyard. Johnson met
with his Joint Chiefs, and, with the Honolulu traitors already having gutted NSAM 263, he assured his generals that Kennedy's
planned withdrawal from Vietnam was no longer America's policy.

Johnson also tried to control the chaotic aftermath in Dallas. He
ordered Cliff Carter, one of his lackeys, to keep in constant contact
with the Dallas District Attorney Henry Wade and the Texas Attorney General Waggoner Carr and instruct them to look no further
than Oswald to find JFK's murderer; Johnson himself delivered the
same message to Will Fritz, Dallas PD Chief of Homicide. When
Oswald was rushed to Parkland after being shot by Ruby, Johnson
telephoned Parkland and asked to speak to the attending doctors.
Dr. Crenshaw took the call and said that Johnson demanded he get
a deathbed confession from Oswald.[39]

At the same time, Johnson directed the Secret Service to completely refurbish the death car, presidential limousine SX-100. It
was transported to Detroit where the body was replaced and, thus,
evidence—including bullet holes in the windshield and traces of
blood, skull and brain matter—was destroyed.[40]

On November 25, 1963, the very day that JFK was buried, Johnson started his PR campaign devoted to the importance of proving
Oswald's guilt. As Bobby Kennedy was attending his brother's
funeral, Johnson's acting attorney general, Nicholas Katzenbach,
wrote a memo to a Johnson aide outlining the new administration's
urgency that no assassination conspiracy should see the light of day.
Katzenbach's letter insisted that "the public must be satisfied that
Oswald was the assassin, that he did not have confederates who are
still at large...[that] speculation about Oswald's motives be cut
off...[and there was a need to] head off [investigations or congressional hearings] *of the wrong sort* (emphasis added)."[41]

Then Johnson, in his manic/euphoric condition, went about usurping proposed Texas and congressional investigations into the assassination by appointing the Warren Commission—a collection of anti-Kennedy men who gave the artificial appearance of being nonpartisan—a mix of southern Democrats and northern Republicans (conservatives all). Some were blackmailed; some were co-opted; others were chosen for appearances' sake only, without the expectation that they would attend the hearings or take the sham investigation seriously. Earl Warren was enlisted to run the commission, but only as a figurehead. He attended few meetings and hearings; his appointment was merely political. Johnson knew that the name Warren carried a cache of integrity and judicial fairness, but Warren was a reluctant participant in the sham. Johnson twisted Warren's arm with the threat of nuclear war should Oswald be proven to have Soviet or Cuban connections. Warren felt obliged to serve, but he knew that the real purpose of the commission was to cover up the truth not expose it. He admitted as much to reporters when he told them that the American people, in their lifetimes, would likely never get the truth of the assassination.[42]

While not admitting it publicly, Johnson implied Soviet involvement in the assassination in order to manipulate politicians, reporters, investigators, military chiefs and cabinet members into keep their mouths shut about Dallas. Johnson invoked the threat of having hundreds of millions of lives lost in a nuclear encounter with Russia if the truth of the assassination ever saw the light of day. But as early as 2 p.m. on 11/22/63 Johnson knew there was no Soviet involvement. Aboard AF1 he placed a call to National Security Advisor Bundy who reassured Johnson that there was "no evidence of any Soviet movement [and] there was no evidence that [the assassination] was part of an international conspiracy"; back in Washington Johnson was again told by advisors that there was no foreign plot and that the Soviets seemed as shocked as anyone at what had happened in Dallas.[43]

Meanwhile, Johnson knew when he appointed Allen Dulles to the Warren Commission that Dulles would take charge of it. In a case of the criminal investigating the crime, Dulles attended more Warren Commission hearings than any other member, and his favorite lawyer, Arlen Specter, performed yeoman's work in covering up the truth. In addition to inventing the magic-bullet trick, Specter bullied and badgered witnesses. He belittled crucial eyewitness Jean Hill and criticized her private life instead of accepting her testimony at face value.[44] It was Specter who tried to change the Dallas doctors' accounts of a frontal bullet strike. It was Specter who lied about being prohibited from viewing the autopsy photos and x-rays; Secret Service officer Robert Bouck told the HSCA that Warren Commission members *did* view the medical photographic record.[45] An accessory after the fact, Specter demolished the truth and suborned justice. His reward? A seat in the U.S. Senate as a Republican from Pennsylvania. The young, ruthlessly ambitious attorney was just one of many who built a career on the corpse of JFK.

From the beginning, the Warren Commission's purpose was laid out by Dulles: to allay public concerns about a conspiracy, and, more importantly, to cover his own tracks. While he ostensibly did not choose the members, he certainly was in a position to make recommendations. Dulles would have had access to CIA profiles of all potential Commission members; the agency was very astute at making predictions about politicians' tendencies and proclivities. Together Johnson and Dulles made certain no members would be in a position to have motivation or means to "rock the boat." (See chapter 5 for further discussion of the Warren Commission selection process.) According to Phillip Nelson, Johnson carefully selected Commission members for their unique vulnerabilities; i.e., Hoover's FBI had dossiers on Richard Russell's and Gerald Ford's sexual indiscretions.[46] John McCloy was likely brought aboard by Allen Dulles who knew him as the "establishment's fixer" and "chairman of the American establishment."

McCloy had served the OSS and its corporate partners well in WWII by refusing to bomb the railways leading to the death camps, thus ensuring that Xyklon B, sold by U.S. corporate interests to The Third Reich, would arrive to its buyers. After the war, McCloy served as German High Commissioner for the U.S. and effectively covered up war crimes by the Nazis recruited into the U.S. government by the CIA. As chairman of Chase Manhattan Bank, McCloy had business interest with Texas oilmen Clint Murchison and Sid Richardson.[47] In 1953 he was appointed head of the Council on Foreign Relations, where he interacted with the titans of American industry, media, government and intelligence. Other CFR members were the Rockefellers, the Dulleses, Arthur Sulzberger (New York Times publisher), Murchison, the Bundys (McGeorge and William), CIA Directors Richard Helms and William Colby, and many others who despised Kennedy and would not have grieved over his death.

A brief digression to elucidate the origins and offshoots of the Council on Foreign Relations is appropriate here, for it may clarify the monolithic power structure aligned against Kennedy and provide a viable list of suspects in his murder. The CFR began as a cabal of the richest and most influential Americans in the early 20th century, a confluence of businessmen, politicians, government officials and military advisors who met to solve world problems in the wake of World War I. Funded mostly by right-wing money from the Ford and Rockefeller Foundations, its purpose was to maintain America's military and economic dominance over the world. From the beginning it was an anti-communist reactionary organization. At the end of the Second World War it evolved from a detached think tank to an active policy-making group whose members served in presidential cabinets and government agencies. They were intelligence elites, bankers, oilmen and conservative ideologues. Local chapters of the CFR, known as Councils on World Affairs, were established in cities across the country. One of these was begun in Dallas in 1951 by Bush-family intimate Neil Mallon. At first glance, a dusty, cowboy outpost such as 1950s Dallas may seem like an odd location for an organization composed of Eastern elitists, but at the time Dallas was a burgeoning post-war center for the military-industrial-oil complex. By 1946 America's oil resources had been depleted by World War II, and genuine fear that another hot war would leave America "energy-vulnerable" made Texas, specifically the oil barons of Dallas, the focus of CFR endeavors. Titans of oil and industry joined with kings of Eastern intelligence and politics. They hitched themselves onto the Eisenhower wagon in 1952, and suddenly they were at the center of power. Allen Dulles himself came to visit the Dallas Council in 1953.[48]

Since then, CFR members have served in the cabinets of every president elected, including Kennedy's. The influence they have exerted has been enormous. Close partners of the CIA, they have started wars, toppled heads of state (including their own), affected global economics, and determined presidential elections. The Iranian hostage crisis is one example of the power they have wielded.

In 1979 CFR members David Rockefeller, Henry Kissinger and John McCloy pressured President Jimmy Carter to permit the ousted Shah of Iran safe passage to the U.S. This precipitated a furious backlash by outraged Iranians who had suffered under the Shah's tyrannical rule for decades. Iranian militants attacked our embassy and took Americans hostage. The crisis lasted 444 days and, in essence, got Ronald Reagan elected in a landslide over Carter in 1980. When it was revealed that George Bush had made a clandestine deal with the Iranians to hold the hostages until after the election, Gary Sick, a Carter national security advisor, called the CFR-affiliated action a "coup d'etat."[49] Americans, whipped into a lynch-mob fury over the hostage crisis, lost sight of the fact (mainly because the media completely ignored it) that Allen Dulles's CIA had installed the Shah in the first place in the 1953 overthrow of

Iran's leader Mossadegh because Mossadegh nationalized the oil industry and thus threatened to reduce America's overseas oil supplies. In a very real way, then, America itself was to blame for the Iranian hostage crisis. CFR members used the crisis to their advantage to get a Republican president and his CIA-connected vice-president George H.W. Bush elected. But all this was overlooked in the hysteria of yet another American disaster which could be laid at the feet of the powerful cabal in control of the country.

Delving deeply into the history of the CFR is a book unto itself better left to others. Nevertheless, those curious enough to explore the hidden history of the United States should be alarmed that: 1) Our destiny as a nation is controlled, in large part, by a few power-brokers who meet in secret and arrange outcomes that defy the basic tenet of democracy: rule by the people; 2) The CFR would have provided convenient cover for plotters who wanted to meet privately to plan the assassination of President Kennedy; 3) It is unlikely that an event on the scale of the assassination could have been executed and covered up without the knowledge and assent of the CFR; and 4) America's history is replete with these sorts of secret machinations engineered by CFR power brokers. The Warren Commission, dominated by CFR members Dulles and McCloy, was no exception.

The power insiders who were placed on the Warren Commission closely monitored the other members and staff attorneys for their thoughts and behaviors. There is evidence that some were wire-tapped. Louisiana Congressman Hale Boggs, a commission member who had the courage to publicly express doubts about Oswald's guilt, became so incensed by the FBI's illegal bugging of his phones that he took to the House floor to loudly denounce Hoover and his "Gestapo tactics. [Boggs] called on Hoover to resign and the FBI to be gutted."[50] It was widely known that Hoover had used wiretaps, intelligence contacts and dirty tricks to gather damaging information on his political enemies. Boggs was merely giving voice to what everyone in Washington already knew. Still, Boggs was excoriated by Republicans and Democrats alike. Hoover, who was not one to passively endure such attacks, denied wiretapping him or any other member of Congress. And a private phone conversation between Richard Nixon (President at the time) and Congressman Gerald Ford, gave voice to the fear and outrage Boggs stirred in the Washington establishment. Perhaps, then, it is no coincidence that Boggs died in a mysterious plane crash a year later.

In October 1972 Boggs was on a political trip to Alaska to campaign for his friend and fellow Congressman Nick Begich. They were flying in a twin-engine Cessna between Anchorage and Juneau when the plane simply vanished without a trace. No wreckage or bodies were ever found despite an extensive search. Boggs and Begich were eventually declared dead, but the mystery of their disappearance has never been solved.

Was Boggs' demise related to his doubts about the Warren Commission's conclusions? Was he being surveilled by Hoover at the behest of the plotters who engineered JFK's murder? In the 1960s and early '70s the FBI wiretapped people whom it considered domestic subversives and political enemies. While a Democrat, Boggs was hardly a left-wing rabble-rouser. He was from the Deep South, and his views reflected moderate stances in line with one who knew his constituents would not countenance a wild-eyed liberal. What, then, was it about Boggs that so frightened Hoover and his pals? According to Representative Begich's son, Dr. Nick Begich, Boggs was a threat to the establishment because "he wanted to re-open the Warren Commission...he wasn't willing to lay down."[51] Confirmation of this came from a congressional aide to Boggs who told authors Bernard Fensterwald and Michael Ewing of Boggs' certainty that, "Hoover lied his eyes out to the commission—on Oswald, on Ruby...the bullets, the guns, you name it."[52] At the time of his death, Boggs, depending on the results of the November 1972 congressional elections, was in line to become Speaker of the

House, third in succession to the presidency. This was months after the Watergate break-in, the burglary which would eventually bring down Nixon. If Nixon and Vice-President Spiro Agnew (who resigned in 1973 because of a corruption scandal) had been removed from office at the same time, Boggs, a Warren Commission critic, would have become President of the United States, an intolerable threat to the plotters who pulled off the coup of 11/22/63. Still, despite several theories that Boggs and Begich were killed by a bomb which was placed aboard their plane, there is no definitive proof that the flight was intentionally sabotaged.

Chapter 8

When They Killed Kennedy, They Killed America

"John Kennedy decided to end the war in Vietnam, and after dismantling the CIA he intended to create an intelligence agency...that would gather information and neither conduct operations or make policy...[the CIA] terrified that its dark secrets might become public knowledge and its leaders prosecuted...[devised] a plan to assassinate the President."[1]

—Mark Lane

To grasp the full mechanisms and meanings of the plot that took Jack Kennedy's life, it is necessary to view the assassination as a comprehensive covert operation, one with many moving parts but one that aspired to leave nothing to chance. Once Kennedy was lured to Dallas, the fix was in. The plotters controlled the parade route, the bodyguards, the police, the kill zone, the gunmen's positions, the patsy, the photographs and films, the body, the autopsy, the media and the investigation. Along the way they planted false evidence, used body doubles, and employed phony suspects. After the fact, they silenced anyone who threatened to expose them. It was an elaborate coup d'etat that took meticulous planning; as with any such plot of this size, mistakes were made and improvisation was unavoidable. But in the end, the plotters held all the power. The men who stood to gain the most from the assassination—Lyndon Johnson, Allen Dulles and their co-conspirators—were untouchable after JFK was out of the way. Against such power, uncovering the truth has been a long, arduous endeavor. One that may never end.

On 11/22/63 the American people lost a young and charismatic President who engendered hope and optimism for a new era of peace and social justice. It's a matter of faith among true believers that JFK's America would have been a far different place than LBJ's America. Robert Kennedy gave us a glimpse of what a full, two-term JFK presidency might have looked like. While campaigning for a Senate seat in New York in September 1964, he made some remarkable comments about his vision for America and the world, a vision inspired by his brother. When asked about war with the Russians, Bobby declared that America's military might was pointless in defeating communism. Each side had the nuclear arsenal to wipe out the other. Only through "progressive practical programs which [eradicate] the poverty, misery and discontent on which [communism] thrives" would we see the end of communism. He endorsed the United Nations. He lambasted racial inequality. He urged the country to abolish poverty. He decried the obscenity of millions living in squalor in a nation of outrageous wealth.[2] He spoke for those who were not invited to America's banquet. Eventually he spoke out against the war which arose from the ashes of Dallas. Johnson's war. The CIA's war. The war by which JFK's killers profited handsomely. This marked out Bobby for assassination also. He could not be allowed to return to the White House and avenge his brother's murder.

With both Kennedys out of the way, the America that Allen Dulles had always dreamed of—controlled by landed gentry, secretly run for their own enrichment, inaccessible to the masses, and brutally anti-democratic—came to pass. Johnson had his throne and his war; unaware that it would devour him and all that was left of the shining city on the hill.

The more lasting tragedy of 11/22/63 is that it began an era, an era that has no end in sight, of massive distrust of the government.

Before Dallas, America trusted its leaders. That quaint notion now seems as silly and obsolete as hula hoops. We now expect the worst. We think of our legislative bodies as bombastic bordellos, full of corrupt hacks willing to sell their souls to the highest bidders. "The good of the people" is way down the list of priorities when laws are written and policy enacted. Everywhere one looks, there is corruption and perfidy. Those who have money and power—corporations, special interests and the super-wealthy—control the ministers of government and make the lives of the masses more dangerous, difficult, unhealthy and poverty-stricken. We have become inured to bloody wars for profit. We have accepted the fact that liberty and justice for all are empty words. "Ask what you can do for your country" has been replaced by "greed is good." The home of the brave is now the land of cynical self-interest.

Admittedly, there is nothing really new about this. There has always been a strain of craven opportunism in America. Hucksters, scam artists, for-profit schemers and crooked politicians have always been with us. It's just that today they have prevailed over our better angels. The rise of right-wing radio (Rush Limbaugh and his ilk) and TV (FOX News) has brainwashed those who lack the education and intellect to resist. Progressivism has been demonized. Media, once the only thing that stood between us and fascism, has been neutered by corporate takeover. Trump and other tyrants urge us now to turn our backs on the truth. Lies are given equal time and presented as legitimate counterbalances under the guise of fairness. While the planet slowly burns and oceans rise, climate change deniers, funded by fossil-fuel polluters, are actually granted air time as if they have a legitimate argument to make. Fact and fiction get blurred; truth becomes a subjective guess until there is no truth left. In this environment, all manner of distortion and deception is possible; it was inevitable that a narcissistic con artist and pathological liar, like Trump, would eventually make it to the White House. An unbalanced egomaniac, elevated in the age of lies, now has his finger on the button. One shudders to think what would have happened if Trump had been in charge during the Cuban Missile Crisis.

If we look closely at the history of America, its one lasting and irrevocable legacy is mendacity. The country was even founded on a lie. Columbus did not discover what we now know as the United States. Our leaders lied to the natives who originally dwelled here, stealing their land and slaughtering their people. Industrial barons and corporate giants, and the government they bought and paid for, have owned the country ever since. Their lies help them maintain their power. We are told that we live in a land of equal opportunity, but we know it is a rigged system in favor of the wealthy, and becoming more so every day. Our leaders claim they are doing our bidding when, in truth, they are nothing more than paid agents of the most powerful interests in the country. Government of the people has been replaced by government of the one percent. This dreary reality was facilitated by historical lies. Lies that overwhelm us and, in the end, turn us into helpless children in a land of tyrannical powerbrokers. When did we lose sight of the promise of America as a land where righteousness and justice were at the heart of the great experiment called democracy? It is the argument here that on November 22, 1963, we veered off into an alternate universe, a quasi-fascist state where the power of government and corporations, with the help of the military-intelligence monolith, has merged, and the slow destruction of true democracy has eaten away whatever freedom we have left.

Lies are at the heart of it.

Why hasn't the murder of President Kennedy been solved, and why have the media and the government been so lax in their duties to find the truth? Because the truth was hidden from us by ruthless and amoral men in the first days, months and years following the crime. And since then, the official lie has become so deeply embedded in the establishment's ethos that it has become as prevalent and as ridiculous as the myth of the Easter bunny. It takes no courage to passively regurgitate the nonsense that Oswald alone killed Kennedy, and lack of courage is almost a prerequisite to excel in government and media today. To understand this sorry state of affairs, one must trace the origins of the lie to its sources—Lyndon Johnson and Allen Dulles.

After November 22, 1963, these two men regained the immense influence they had lost when Kennedy became President. Once the Warren Commission had delivered its sham report in September 1964, and Johnson was elected president in a landslide less than two months later, the fate of the truth was sealed. It might as well have been buried with Kennedy. Dulles's CIA-in-exile group controlled media assets in most major metropolitan areas; Johnson cut off all other avenues to the truth. Dulles went on a propaganda tour in defense of the Warren Report; with Robert Kennedy's power abolished, Johnson and Hoover neutralized the Justice Department. Johnson diverted the nation's attention away from Dallas by moving progressive civil rights bills through Congress and by waging a full-fledged war in southeast Asia. Soon, no major network, newspaper, magazine or government agency would dare go near a legitimate investigation of Dallas. In the wake of JFK's murder, the "CEOs" of the plot rewrote history just as all winners do. It is a false history that still haunts us today.

This false history has been promulgated by a small army of disinformationists, derisively referred to in this text as "lone-nutters" because they have perpetrated the abominable lie of Oswald's lone guilt. Rather than dismissing these liars as kooks and opportunists, it is vital to ask: what is their true motivation? Why would anyone feel the burning desire to defend a deeply compromised and flawed commission like the one commandeered by Allen Dulles? It's not as if Dulles was a paragon of principle and morality; on the contrary, he was one of the most evil, depraved and insidious public servants of the 20th century. As head of the CIA, he caused untold harm to millions around the globe. He certainly doesn't merit an ardent defense from lone-nutters. Is their motivation larger than protecting Dulles? Are they indignant that skeptics would impugn such sacred institutions as the CIA, Lyndon Johnson, the Joint Chiefs, the FBI and American businessmen? As we now know, these institutions, and the people who ran them, were rapacious and ruthless, devoid of any compassion, willing to destroy anyone who got in the way of their lusts for power and riches. Certainly honest cynics can examine these men and their connections to 11/22/63; after all, we are talking about the assassination of a sitting U.S. president. All avenues should be explored; all coincidences checked out; all suspects scrutinized, no matter who they are. Yet, lone-nutters viciously denigrate all who have the audacity to question their omniscience. Maybe that's the answer. Lone-nutters are stricken with God complexes and fragile egos. Heavily invested in their anti-conspiracy stance, they can never admit they are wrong. They view themselves as spokespersons for the establishment, those who determine for everyone else what the truth is, and they seek the benediction and riches that come with that service. Why else do they turn away a thousand bits of conspiratorial evidence? Why do they twist logic and go to great lengths to explain away suspicious circumstances and coincidences? Are they just stupid? Not likely.

There is more at work here. Avoidance of all paths that lead to conspiracy requires a more personal animus. A seething resentment of Kennedy, writhing just below the surface, snarls through lone-nut literature. Anti-conspiracy authors like Gerald Posner, Vincent Bugliosi and Max Holland are heavily invested in reducing JFK's presidency to a historical asterisk. By constructing the elaborate lie that Oswald was just a lucky lunatic, they assassinate Kennedy all over again. This is because the portrayal of Oswald as a lone wolf is intrinsically inseparable from the argument that the thousand days of JFK were no more than a footnote. For if Oswald is not linked to the CIA, then any supposed CIA motive for the assassination can be dismissed, and the agency can be absolved despite the fact that

Dulles, Hunt, Lansdale, Harvey, Phillips and others in the agency hated Kennedy and wanted him dead.

Lone-nutters must also bend over backwards to disprove various other facts that would support a conspiracy. Like the fact that JFK was going to drop Lyndon Johnson from the Democratic presidential ticket in 1964. Like the fact that JFK intended to completely withdraw all American personnel from Vietnam by 1965. Like the fact that JFK wanted to end the Cold War and pursue peaceful détente with the Soviet Union. Like the fact that JFK indicated that he would dismantle and reconstruct his national security apparatus, including the all-powerful CIA, in his second term. In other words, lone-nutters must deny that there was any motive for the military-industrial-intelligence monolith and the Vice-President to kill their Commander-in-Chief, and in this process they deprive JFK's presidency of its rightful place in history as the momentous, paradigm-shifting, revolutionary term that it was. The latter assertion is predicated upon the former; the rationales are linked. To indict Oswald, lone-nutters must remove all other suspects and motives, and to do this they must nullify JFK's importance in our history.

The lone-nutters themselves would, and have, adamantly denied an anti-Kennedy bias. I don't believe them. For if their goal is not to diminish Kennedy's legacy, what is it? Surely not a resolute and sincere search for the truth; they ignore, gloss over, or bury a ton of material that would disprove their theses. One example is Posner's book, *Case Closed*. In it Posner skips right over the fact that Oswald was a member of the Louisiana Civil Air Patrol, the organization founded by D.H. Byrd, with the blessing of his pal Curtis LeMay, which employed many CIA-connected operatives who played a role in the assassination. Posner makes no mention that Byrd owned the Texas School Book Depository building, was LBJ's benefactor and friend, and profited from LBJ's handling of the Vietnam War. Instead, Posner supposes that Oswald, by some fantastic coincidence, just happened to work in a building overlooking the President's motorcade route; no matter that the owner of the building just happened to be a Kennedy hater, an LBJ supporter and the facilitator of Oswald's first and last places of employment. On page 262 Posner writes, "Oswald had little time for planning, perhaps not much more than twenty-four hours."[3] Then who was the guy practice-firing at Kennedy on Dallas rifle ranges weeks before the assassination? Posner concedes that, in his lone-nut scenario, Oswald could not have known about JFK passing right under his sixth floor window until just a day or two before the assassination. The correlative question Posner bypasses is, "Why would Oswald prepare weeks in advance for such a momentous event he had no way of knowing would happen"? For such a nondescript loner, he possessed a remarkable skill for predicting the future.

And it is remarkable that, for being such a nobody, Oswald found himself in some historically unlikely places, meeting with Russian and American spies, at the height of the Cold War. Posner makes the absurd claim that Oswald's friendship with DeMohrenschildt was quite innocent, despite the fact that the two men had nothing in common except their CIA connections. Oswald was a ninth-grade dropout who was introverted and poor. DeMohrenschildt was a well-educated, well-traveled oil geologist who fancied himself an aristocrat.

In addition to glossing over the Oswald-DeMohrenschildt relationship, Posner consciously avoids reference to other key players. Excluded from his book are Billie Sol Estes, Bobby Baker, Edward Lansdale, Victor Krulak, Curtis LeMay, Robert Knudsen, Madeleine Brown, David Mantik and countless others. He mentions Allen Dulles just three times, in the most benign way. He consigns what Paul O'Connor and Jerrol Custer saw to a footnote, and he explains away the casket shell game with one sentence: "James Jenkins, a laboratory technician, said that a plain gray coffin, containing the body of an Air Force officer in a body bag arrived at

Bethesda before JFK's coffin."[4] What Air Force officer? There was
no record of any dead Air Force officer at Bethesda on 11/22/63,
and Posner cites no source for the Jenkins' quote. Jenkins did refer
to a rumor that an Air Force colonel or major was kept overnight
in the Bethesda morgue in preparation for burial the next day at
Arlington; however, there were no military burials at Arlington on
November 23, 1963.[5] Jenkins' recollections notwithstanding, there
were many men, other than Jenkins, who recalled a shipping casket
entry into the Bethesda morgue; several of these men witnessed, or
participated in, the removal of JFK's body from this shipping casket. Posner, of course, does not address this.

What Posner does address are Oswald's demeanor and orienta-
tion as a way of convincing us of his motives. He smears Oswald as
a sociopathic, homosexual communist with violent tendencies.
Written in 1993 when homophobia was rampant in America, *Case
Closed* tries to persuade us that gays are more likely to kill presidents
than straights. For this and its other baseless assumptions, *Case
Closed* has been thoroughly discredited since its publication. Even
mainstream historians are alert to Posner's prevarications. Professor
David Wrone called *Case Closed* "theory-driven, rife with speculation, [suffused with] factual errors…[and] stands as one of the stel-
lar instances of irresponsible publishing on this subject."[6]

Bugliosi fares no better despite the fact that his book, *Reclaiming
History*, runs to 1,600 pages. The heft of it, like the Warren Report's
26 volumes, seems to be an attempt to compensate for its lack of
gravity. Like Posner, he fails to mention some of the key assassination figures—Barry Seal, James Bath, James Parrott, Mike Robinson, Aubrey Rike, Dennis David and too many others to name.
What Bugliosi does do is play a sort of con game with phantom
index references to several important players. For instance, D.H.
Byrd merits no mention in the 1,500 pages of text, but he does
appear in the index, where the reader is directed to the footnotes of
pages 513-14. However, readers who turn to pages 513-14 will not

find Byrd's name, in either the footnotes or text. Thus, the man who founded the Civil Air Patrol and owned the TSBD in 1963 is nowhere to be found in *Reclaiming History*. Neither are John Liggett (Bugliosi makes a phantom reference to a "James Melvin Liggett," a non-existent person, in the index) nor Charles Rogers (phantom reference in index) included in the text. With these omissions, Bugliosi all but eliminates the significance of the Civil Air Patrol as a recruiting ground for CIA operatives (including Oswald). Even though the index stipulates references to the CAP on 837n, 892n, 897n and 902n there are no mentions of the CAP on those pages. One who reads no other book on the assassination other than Bugliosi's would know nothing of the head-spinning circumstances which link Byrd and Oswald; I guess that was just too much of a coincidence for even Bugliosi, the king of coincidence theorists, to explain away. In a brief moment of boldness, Bugliosi does have the temerity to admit that Oswald and David Ferrie are photographed together in a 1955 CAP meeting. But he then makes the ludicrous assertion that the two men did not know one another.

At a loss for a way to undermine David Lifton's stunning findings about the casket switch and body alteration, Bugliosi resorts to name calling. Lifton is reduced to a charlatan and a madman; all the while Bugliosi provides no satisfactory resolution to the crucial discrepancy between the Parkland and Bethesda descriptions of the wounds. Conveniently Bugliosi ignores what Paul O'Connor, Thomas Robinson and James Jenkins saw at Bethesda: definitive proof of a casket shell game and alteration of the President's wounds between Dallas and Washington. Bugliosi writes: "Paul K. O'Connor and James Curtis Jenkins...lift the body out of the bronze casket...[and it was] wrapped in sheets."[7] As stated previously in this work, O'Connor and Jenkins unequivocally stated that they removed the President's body, encased in a body bag, from a cheap shipping casket, not from the expensive bronze Dallas casket. Bugliosi also plays tricks with the timeline because he knows that early entry of the casket would prove conspiracy. He claims that O'Connor and Jenkins opened the casket at Bethesda at 6:35 p.m. central time, which would have been 7:35 p.m. eastern time. This is an absolute lie. O'Connor and Jenkins were certain that the body arrived at Bethesda at 6:35 p.m. eastern, while the bronze ceremonial casket was still on its way to Bethesda from Andrews AFB. Bugliosi also ignores technician Jerrol Custer's statement that he processed x-rays of the dead President before the Dallas casket arrived at Bethesda. Bugliosi knows that acknowledging Custer's earth-shattering recollections of 11/22/63 would shred the no-conspiracy scenario. Perhaps that is why Bugliosi employs his phantom-reference tactics on Custer too. Custer's name appears in the index of *Reclaiming History*, with references to 248n-249n, 562n, and 615n, but he is not mentioned on any of those pages' footnotes. How to explain this? Bugliosi is either completely oblivious to multiple casket entries at Bethesda or he chooses to ignore them; either way, he shoots a hole in his credibility with his neglect of this matter.

Other phantom references in Bugliosi's book include Jim Braden, Lois Liggett and Restland Funeral Home. Since I could not muddle through all 1,600 pages, I failed to catch all of Bugliosi's omissions, but undoubtedly there are numerous more. I lost faith in the sincerity of his work when he failed to disclose that Ruth Paine, Oswald's "employment agent," turned down more lucrative offers from other companies so that she could "place him" with the job at the TSBD in Ocotober 1963. Bugliosi, in fact, finds nothing suspicious in Paine's behavior or her family's long and obvious links to Allen Dulles and the CIA.

Unlike lone-nutters, honest investigators would admit there is much that is unexplained, many questions unresolved, many coincidences unexplored, and many nefarious connections indicating conspiracy. By not acknowledging any reservations or doubts, lone-nutters discredit their own works as nothing more than fanciful flights of imagination.

This leaves, in my view, three possible explanations for lone-nutters' motivation: 1) they are intentionally lying to aid and abet the plotters; this is not far-fetched because the CIA has been known to employ an army of disinformationists; 2) they despise Kennedy and seek to denigrate his legacy and reputation by concealing the truth of his presidency and the enemies he made; 3) they are craven opportunists without consciences who know that coming down on the side of the Warren Commission will win them publicity, fame and fortune (after all, the mainstream media rarely accord legitimate conspiracists their due, but instead trot out Posner and Holland and the others whenever they need to mindlessly refute conspiracy evidence.) I tend to think lone-nutters' true sentiments run the gamut between the first and third motivations above. But it is impossible to know for sure, for liars defeat their insidious purposes when they reveal the real reason for their lies.

These lies have been used as cover by those in government who would otherwise have the power and the means by which to solve the JFK case. This is not to say that everyone in officialdom has been ignorant of the truth. Many suspected that something evil was afoot in America, but they were helpless to do anything about it. Some were knowingly complicit in the cover-up despite having the means to do something about it. Earl Warren, when asked whether America would ever know the truth, said, "Not in your lifetime."[8] The implication is that our very way of life and our understanding of who we thought we were as a nation would have been torn asunder. As J. Edgar Hoover once said, "If I told you what I really know…it would be very dangerous to the country. Our whole political system could be disrupted."[9]

Some might ask why it is we can't overthrow the official lie today when most of the people who devised and implemented the plot to kill Kennedy are dead now. I believe the explanation for why the lie lives on in the "fairy tale" version of American history is much more basic. And it is just this: The fake and planted evidence gave a false credibility to lone-nutters like Posner and Bugliosi, whose books, embedded as they are in the zeitgeist, have immensely retarded the search for the truth. The fake and planted evidence has given cover to the CIA and provided enduring justification for why it continues to withhold documents. The fake and planted evidence has given the media an alibi for their lazy dismissal of conspiracy facts. The fake and planted evidence made liars of the Dealey Plaza witnesses and the Dallas doctors. In other words, the plotters' original strategy of using fake and planted evidence has provided the excuse that good men need to do nothing, to resist the urge to pursue courageous investigation, to take safe harbor in a comforting lie, to defend their lack of inquisitiveness, and to remand JFK's death to the dustbin of historical accidents.

But strip away the fake and planted evidence—the altered corpse and the phony bullets and shells—and suddenly the Dallas doctors' testimony and the eyewitness recollections become the best evidence available, for the official medical and ballistic evidence can't be trusted. Most Americans already recognize this, but getting officialdom to admit it is another matter; for all media and government agencies which have perpetuated the lie would have to admit they were wrong, and that is a humiliating proposition for those institutions that pride themselves on being upright and scrupulous. Imagine if the *Washington Post* was forced to print a sheepish contrition for the sins of Katharine Graham and Ben Bradlee, or if CBS News ran a retraction for Walter Cronkite's and Dan Rather's lack of integrity when it came to the Kennedy assassination. Such media giants would be loath to open themselves up to *genuine* jibes of "fake news." And the chances of the CIA, FBI and Secret Service ever acknowledging they were complicit in the crime of the century are, well, don't hold your breath.

Kennedy Legacy

In many ways, America is frozen in time. It's still 1963, at the crossroads of possibility and bloody reality. Some believe all that we were, or ever will be, died 11/22/63 on a Dallas street. The presidency and the country have never been the same. Author Aaron David Miller suggests that presidential greatness died with Kennedy. Since then, he writes, we have been "…lost in a kind of presidential Bermuda Triangle, adrift between the presidents we still want and the ones we can no longer have."[10] Americans, more than a half-century after his death, still idolize JFK. A Gallup poll taken in November 2013 voted him the best president of all who came after him. This despite his shortcomings, of which we have been made well aware in the intervening years.

Why is this? Why do we still cling to a president who has been long gone? I believe there are many reasons. The most salient of which is that he's had little competition. The men who followed him were not just banal and compromised; they were beneficiaries of, and instigators of, some great calamity. They made us suspicious of their motives and stewardship. They were beholden to powers we could not see, but somehow knew were at work. Kennedy, most definitely, was not. Somewhere, deep down where the yearning for democracy resides in all of us, we were confident that Kennedy was trustworthy. He had the unfettered best interests of the greater good uppermost in mind. He resisted the men who represented the corrupt old order of things—a debased America, ruled by a war machine and run for the benefit of a privileged few. We who remember Kennedy like to imagine how he would address today's global and domestic mess; that is the key to unlocking the mystery of why his legacy has lasted. As Larry Sabato, the author of *The Kennedy Half-Century*, writes, "…it is less about Kennedy in his time than about Kennedy in our time."[11] We need a JFK, but there aren't any today.

The murder of Kennedy wasn't just the end of innocence; it was the end of belief. There was nothing of America left to believe in, because beneath the ugly violence of Dallas was the sense that something had changed forever. We knew that the cover story was a lie so monstrous that it made all manner of deceit possible. Before 11/22/63 there were boundaries, rules of acceptable decorum, limits to what a decent, well-meaning civilization would countenance. After Dallas there were no constraints. It was like being awake in a dystopian nightmare, a Disneyland of horrors. We were powerless to do anything about it, because those we had always relied on to do something about it were in on it. To accept the new reality of America was to turn one's back on its principles and presumptions. There was no longer a middle ground to inhabit; the choices were self-deception or an abiding, destructive cynicism. We lost our way for good. Now, what we once thought of as America is dead, replaced by an alternate universe where compulsive liars can become Jack Kennedy's successor; where rampant corruption is met with a shrug and is even broadly expected; where idealism is considered naïve and useless.

All leaders subsequent to 11/22/63 have learned this lesson, and operate under the assumption that they serve only at the will of America's real power: a secret cabal whose founders killed Kennedy. This cabal was protected by the Dulleses—firmly in control of foreign policy and intelligence gathering—who operated their public and private interests for the benefit of their rich clients. Profitability was their priority, not the well-being of democracy. They expected Kennedy, to the manor born just like they, to protect their interests. When he didn't, they revolted. Nelson Rockefeller complained about "losing our property to nationalist movements overseas"; he accused JFK of coddling socialism abroad and demoralizing our allies with his feckless leadership.[12] The *Wall Street Journal* criticized Kennedy's anti-business policy. CIA collaborator Henry Luce used his publications to warn Kennedy that there would be a price to pay for standing up to big corporations.

And just as Eisenhower predicted—the "unwarranted influence" of big business and defense spending infected "every city, every state house and every office of the federal government." It has been so interwoven in the fabric of the country that one can't imagine America without a military-industrial complex. One president, the last one to truly stand up to it, was martyred for his resistance. Since then, we have surrendered all three branches of government and our security agencies to it. That was the real lesson of Dallas. Ever after, we have been at war or under the threat of war. Communism as the common enemy has been replaced by Islamic terrorism. Tomorrow it will be a new threat; anything to keep the monster feeding at the public trough.

Meanwhile, the slow grind of neo-fascism—the merger of corporations with the state's military and intelligence complex—has eaten away at democracy. National security and Wall Street have merged into an unstoppable monolith. They own us. Defense spending now comprises over half the national budget. We are a military economy; the welfare of the people be damned.

Texas-based defense contractors who made enormous profits after Kennedy's assassination included Brown & Root, General Dynamics, Collins Radio, Bell Helicopter and Ling-Temco Vought.[13] Since Dallas, defense spending has mushroomed beyond anything that is reasonable or prudent. Today we spend nearly six of every ten of our tax dollars on defense-related matters. The stated budget for 2016 was nearly $600 billion, but this does not include waste, fraud, cost overruns and tangential costs. Real spending amounts to nearly $1 trillion annually. Almost every major U.S. corporation has a piece of that pie. The obvious ones are Lockheed Martin, Northrop Grumman, Boeing, Bechtel, the Carlyle Group, Exxon, Shell, General Dynamics, KBR (Kellogg, Brown & Root), Halliburton (whose stock LBJ declared he needed to sell on 11/22/63), Rockwell Collins (the descendant of Collins Radio, a CIA contractor in 1963 which employed Tippit-family friend Carl Amos Mather) and Textron (parent company of Bell which employed Michael Paine and Walter Dornberger in 1963). But other beneficiaries of Pentagon largesse are hundreds of organizations one might not expect: Hewlett-Packard, GE, Carnegie-Mellon, Johns Hopkins, IBM, Pfizer, FedEx and MIT among them. Meanwhile, the politicians who are bought by these major corporations will not dare to cut defense spending in any significant way; instead they inveigh against social-welfare recipients, the weakest and most defenseless among us, whose "entitlements" comprise a relatively small portion of the national budget. Corrupt legislators are willing to cut funding for education, infrastructure, childhood welfare, health care and anything else that tangibly benefits people, rather than disrupt the handouts given to the richest and most powerful factions in our country.

What does this have to do with the death of Kennedy? Just this: The powerful interests that Kennedy fought, and who were responsible for what happened in Dallas, have gradually taken over and reshaped America. And each president since Dallas has contributed to the decline of real democracy by failing to stand up to these powerful interests. Some—Johnson, Nixon, Ford—facilitators of the "beast," were devoured by it in the end. Others, like Carter and Clinton, while expressing interest in reforming the CIA and reigning in military adventurism, were, in essence, powerless against the beast. The Bushes thrived by facilitating the beast. Obama promised to extricate us from Afghanistan, but never did. This war now approaches its second decade. Carter's presidency was destroyed by the CIA's historical involvement in Middle East affairs and by Bush's conniving. Clinton, while wily and shrewd, and curious about Dallas, never took the political risks of confronting real historical truth or the power represented by a Republican Congress. Each president since Dallas has owed his office to some ugly, secretive force or deed; unlike Kennedy who was beholden to nothing and no one when he entered the Oval Office. (Some say he owed the Mafia for fiddling with Chicago votes, but, if so, Bobby as attorney general sure didn't act like it.) The malevolent forces which planned and executed Kennedy's death had their hooks into the presidents who followed Kennedy—Johnson's collusion with the CIA and the Pentagon was superseded only by his complete fealty to big oil; Nixon had a long history of plotting with the CIA in the 1950s, and his ties with organized crime (Jack Ruby was once his staff member) are many; Ford was said to be the FBI's best friend on the Warren Commission and the CIA's best friend in Congress; the Bushes' ties to the CIA are numerous and date back to Allen Dulles, who recruited George H.W. and set him on the path to a CIA Directorship.

The gradual erosion of the stateliness and eminence of the office has culminated in an illiterate jackass now occupying it. Compare Kennedy's grace, eloquence and wisdom to the vulgarity and venality of Trump. The American presidency is now a joke; a forum for a barker's shill, and up for sale to domestic and foreign oligarchs.

But it's not just the post-1963 presidents who have gradually transformed America from a democracy to a quasi-fascist plutocracy. It's the people who have surrounded those presidents—military, intelligence and diplomatic advisors—who have had enormous sway in eroding our principles. Fletcher Prouty referred to these men as a Secret Team: "men whose control over military and diplomatic operations are secret...whose actions only [they] are in a position to monitor and understand."[14] It means that the events which have shaped our destiny as a country have secret causes and consequences beyond the comprehension of the common man. People we did not elect have had more power than the ones we did.

Kennedy may have made grave errors when he, like others who followed, surrounded himself with advisors who had their own secret agendas. But Kennedy, unlike other presidents, recognized his error and strove mightily to correct it in his thousand days. In the end, tragically, not even an independent, courageous and peace-minded commander-in-chief was a match for the Secret Team.

Centuries from now when archaeologists and historians unearth the rubble of the 20th century, they will find the remnants of the truth scattered about in books like this one and wonder why the media allowed the truth to evade them, why corporations and defense contractors and oilmen and the CIA were permitted to run roughshod over democracy, why government decayed from the inside out, and why they killed the one commander-in-chief committed to a globe-saving, peaceful disarmament. If they dig a little deeper they will discover that, as in all corrupt civilizations that eventually crumbled, wealth and power, held by a conscienceless and deranged few, brought government by the people to an end. But where were the truth-tellers, they might ask. What about the wondrous gadgets in the technological age—television, the internet and a massive network of social communication—couldn't that spread the truth and root out the evil few? Not when those tools of information were controlled by the powerful few.

In Kennedy's day, the public was unaware of the full extent of the military/intelligence treachery he faced. Only today is the truth slowly emerging. JFK was surrounded by madmen who were willing to blow up the world to destroy the Soviet Union. The Joint Chiefs planned for a nuclear first strike, undeterred by the certainty of Russian retaliation and our own self-extinction. Edward Lansdale, a twentieth century Benedict Arnold who slithered back and forth between the CIA and the Pentagon, spent his days dreaming up weird false flag attacks to drag the country into Armageddon. It was hard to tell who the soldiers and spies hated more—Kennedy or the Soviets. Writer Charles Pierce put it this way: "[T]his criminal lunacy had gone so far up the chain of command that it took the president...to turn it off. Its existence was the best evidence that the defense establishment and the intelligence community was a writhing ball of poisonous snakes during the Kennedy Administration."[15] Kennedy, like the patron saint of his ancestral isle, beat back the snakes for us. Every man, woman and child alive today owes him a debt for that. Political commentator Chris Matthews wrote,

"We had gotten through [the Cold War] alive...thanks to [JFK], I'd say. In the time of our greatest peril...[he] kept us from the brink, saved us really."[16] He gave us a reprieve from self-incineration in the early 1960s and had America on a course towards a permanent peace state when the masters of the permanent war state rubbed him out. And the hope for a better America died with him. When he was buried, there was no one left to resist the snakes. After 11/22/63 the snakes owned everything; not even the men who had been loyal to Kennedy could fight back against the massive forces aligned against them. They had neither the will nor the strength. They gave up.

Even Kennedy intimates O'Donnell and Powers, for their own reasons, never publicly contradicted the Warren Report. Powers suggested that O'Donnell was pressured by Hoover to keep quiet. For his part, O'Donnell ridiculed the Warren Commission findings to family members, and for the rest of his life he was afflicted with the grief and pain of his friend's violent death. According to David Talbot, when Bobby Kennedy was assassinated, O'Donnell uttered just two forlorn words to his son: "It's over."[17] What O'Donnell meant was that the dream of a Kennedy retaking the White House and the opportunity to go after the culprits responsible for Dallas was over. Once and for all. O'Donnell knew, as did the rest of America, that the country had been forever altered. With Bobby and Jack out of the way, the conspirators had the free reign they needed to turn the country away from democracy and towards the era of plutocratic rule. The cabal that decided what was real and what was not had won. In the name of profit and power, truth was dead. The lie of Dallas became the lie of Vietnam, Watergate, Iran/ Contra, Iraq and 9/11. Secrecy and self-interest trampled constitutional restraints. Those who ran the country knew after Dallas they could get away with anything. Lies were their currency in trade. Checks and balances diminished as corruption spread throughout all branches of government. Today an honest public servant is hard to find.

We now live in a country where lies are expected, even accepted. They are told so often, they make our eyes glaze over. Our leaders are three-card Monty hustlers. Every scammer and con artist with a way to sucker us is on the make. The purpose is to make us feel overwhelmed, to make us give up and let them have their way. We lose hope, and this might be the most despicable effect of the proliferation of lies. As one who lived through the age of Kennedy, I can attest to the fact that America was once a hopeful place; where the anticipation of peace, and trust in a president, pulsed through the heart of its citizens. But that died in Dallas, and all that is left is a skeleton of America where caring about one's self is all that matters. Tribal survival in a Republican-dominated landscape, where all men and women must fend for themselves, the greater good be damned, is the state of a once-proud nation.

The truth is now something that is malleable and ephemeral, subject to interpretation and irrelevant in our day-to-day lives. We have forgotten, as the men who engineered Dallas intended, that truth is the cornerstone of democracy; without it, democracy will wither away. The fourth estate was supposed to be the watchdog, the vigilant overseer and protector of the truth. But Allen Dulles changed all that with Operation Mockingbird. Today the legacy of Mockingbird has taken an insidious turn. The media, cowardly corporate lackeys that they are, feign journalistic "integrity" by not taking sides. Rather, under the guise of impartiality, they present both sides, regardless of the validity of either, and this gives rise to a false equivalency of ideas, principles and political candidates. Demagogues and quasi-fascism thrive in a fact-free world. Witness the election of Donald Trump.

Some say Trump supporters voted against the government's half-century of lies, but, if so, they picked the most unrepentant liar of them all. It indicates that Trump voters are neither well-read nor sophisticated enough to know this hard truth—Jack Kennedy's death has gone unsolved because of ignorant people like them who can't be bothered with the time and effort it takes to become a truly informed citizen. Kennedy himself warned against the lazy citizen who can't see through the façade and decide for himself what is true and what is not. He wrote, "It is in your power to perceive deception, to shut off gimmickry, to reward honesty...[the media] can be abused by demigods, by appeals to emotion and prejudice and ignorance..."[18]

How do we know JFK was a great president? Because of the enemies he accrued during his thousand days in office. Enemies whose interests were so threatened that they took the desperate step to eliminate him. No president in our history has ever accumulated such dangerous and powerful enemies.

In His Own Words

In revisiting Kennedy's speeches one can rediscover his allure. This is Kennedy's lasting impact on the American psyche—the eloquence and farsightedness of his words. Sabato writes that JFK had a "... singular style, exceptional substance...that has made his [words] such a touchstone for other politicians, academics, everyday Americans, and people around the world."[19]

Still today, he is often quoted when there are conflicts to address, hypocrisies to decry, and precedents to recall. Yet his rhetoric is also bittersweet because it reminds us of the maddening gap between what might have been and what is.

April 27, 1961: Following the Bay of Pigs, a flawed operation concocted by the CIA to trap the President, Kennedy spoke out against secret organizations: "Secrecy is repugnant in a free and open society. There is a very grave danger that an announced need for increased security will be seized upon by those anxious to expand its meaning...there is a monolithic, ruthless conspiracy that relies primarily on covert means for expanding its sphere of influence." This was a direct shot at the CIA and its culture of secrecy. He also put on notice those organizations whose members had accumulated undue influence over government agencies and, by extension, the American people.

America since then: Two Skull and Bones presidents presided over unnecessary wars which greatly profited their crony defense contractors. The CIA operated clandestinely without oversight in foreign and domestic matters, enriching its corporate sponsors by overthrowing socialist and democratic governments around the globe; subverting the free press; drugging its own citizens; conducting illegal wars; and siding with totalitarian regimes.

May 18, 1963: In a speech at Vanderbilt University, Kennedy warned against those who would "...scoff at intellectuals, cry out against research, [and] seek to limit our educational system. But the educated citizen knows that only an educated and informed people will be a free people; that the ignorance of one voter in a democracy impairs the security of all."

America Today: Intellectuals are regularly denigrated by the right-wing. Public education is devalued and underfunded. Teachers are woefully underpaid and overworked. The uninformed citizens installed a blustering, bullying and ignorant tyrant who thanked the "uneducated" masses for electing him. Because of this our security *is* impaired.

June 10, 1963: In a speech delivered at the American University commencement, JFK declared his intent to end the Cold War, not win it. He advocated for world peace and said, "What kind of peace do I seek? Not a Pax Americana enforced on the world by American weapons of war. Total war makes no sense in an age...when the deadly poisons produced by a nuclear exchange would by wind and water and soil and seeds travel to the far corners of the Earth... every thoughtful citizen who despairs of war and wishes to bring peace should...examine his own attitude towards the possibility of peace with the Soviet Union...Both [the U.S. and USSR] are devoting to weapons mass sums of money which could be better devoted to combating ignorance, poverty and disease…if we cannot now end our differences, at least we can help make the world safe for diversity."

America since then: The Cold War lasted another quarter century, and JFK's vision of world peace never came about. Since November 22, 1963, war and the threat of war have been constants in American life.

September 2, 1963: Speaking with Walter Cronkite about Vietnam, JFK said, "In the final analysis, it's their [the South Vietnamese] war; they're the ones who have to win or lose it." Just weeks later JFK issued National Security Action Memo (NSAM) 263, calling for total American withdrawal from Vietnam in his second term.

America since then: Three days after JFK's death, Lyndon Johnson rescinded NSAM 263 and soon plunged the country into the war which lasted for a decade and cost 58,000 American lives, hundreds of thousands of Vietnamese lives, and billions of American dollars.

October 22, 1963: In a speech praising scientific advancements and research, JFK, in an age where political charlatans were ridiculed for denying or condemning scientific fact, lauded Americans' "…wholehearted understanding of the importance of pure science…" He encouraged scientists to find ways to "…protect land and water, forests and wildlife, to combat exhaustion and erosion, to stop the contamination of water and air by industrial as well as nuclear pollution, and to provide for the steady renewal and expansion of the natural bases for life."

America since then: Scientific research and discoveries are condemned as anti-religion (evolution) and anti-free enterprise (carbon emissions have caused climate change). Politicians and corporations with blatant agendas bully their way into public discourse about climate change, and are not denounced by the media for what they are—regressive, ignorant and greedy.

When they killed Kennedy, they killed his vision for America—peace, progress and an age of enlightenment. Fifty years on, we've seen the America that the plotters wanted—hatred for science, constant war, denigration of social programs for the old and the needy, hatred for minorities, rampant corruption in politics, gerrymandering, voter suppression, wanton and excessive military spending, and protection of the rich and greedy—come to pass.

Today, at the beginning of the 21st century, the battle to expose the truth of Kennedy's presidency is still being fought. The false claim that he would have escalated Vietnam, just as his successor did, lives on in some quarters. It is important for history distortionists to lump Kennedy in with the Cold War militant-presidents who followed him. Never mind that those who knew him best are adamant that he was determined to keep us out of war at almost any cost.

The army of liars now has a new hero. A documentary from Ken Burns, that lauded icon of the establishment, spreads more lies about Kennedy and Vietnam. In a fluff piece promoting his work *The Vietnam War*, Burns and his partner released this statement: "From President Harry Truman to Richard Nixon, our leaders implemented policies and made decisions that sent millions of young Americans...to die."[20] The implication is that all presidents from the 1940s through the 1970s are equally to blame for the war, and this mindset represents a grave injustice to, and a galling ignorance of, the Kennedy presidency.

Sure enough, in the episode which addresses JFK and Vietnam (Episode 2, "Riding The Tiger"), Burns completely avoids discussion of NSAM 263, Kennedy's declaration of total withdrawal from Vietnam, and its reversal by Johnson immediately after Dallas. Thus, any link between the JFK assassination and the escalation of the Vietnam War is eradicated by Burns.[21] Such sloppy and neglectful work should not be tolerated from a high school student's term paper, much less Emmy-award-winning documentarians. As stated elsewhere in this book, Robert McNamara, one of the prime archi-tects of the war, insisted that JFK, had he survived Dallas, would have withdrawn all U.S. personnel from southeast Asia in his sec-ond term. There is no greater expert on this matter than McNa-mara, yet Burns completely ignores his assertion. It is yet another example of establishment-approved "historians" presenting a sani-tized (read false) version of American history. For Burns to focus on NSAM 263 (and Johnson's NSAM 273), you see, would require a frank and dangerous examination of the JFK assassination, and Burns has neither the fortitude nor the insight for that. The bit-tersweet irony is that Burns' rationale for creating the documentary could just as easily describe why it is important to reexamine the Kennedy assassination: "The seeds of many of the troubles that beset us today—alienation, resentment and cynicism; mistrust of our government…and civic institutions—were sewn during the Vietnam War. Until we find a way to come to terms with this…its ghosts will continue to haunt us."[22] Substitute the words "Kennedy assassination" for "Vietnam War" and you have an articulate state-ment about the tragedy and consequences of 11/22/63. But Burns and others like him fail to understand that the two cataclysmic events are intricately and irrevocably linked. None are so blind as those who will not see.

Burns is guided by a more pragmatic and crass concern—money. Funding for his documentary was provided by corporations and individuals opposed to Kennedy and his policies, most notably David Koch. David and Charles Koch, American industrialists with enormous wealth and power, have literally tried to purchase the U.S. government. In a recent election cycle they pledged nearly a billion dollars to Republican candidates for office like Scott Walker, Louis Gohmert, Paul Ryan and Joni Ernst. The Kochs' billions are derived, in large part, from dirty-energy companies that are helping to destroy the planet. They are climate-change deniers, advocates for the abolishment of public health care and Social

Security, anti-unionists, and opponents of fair taxation of the super-rich. More diabolically, they are descended from Fred Koch, one of the founders of the John Birch Society, the Dallas chapter of which paid for the "JFK: Wanted For Treason" ads taken out on the day of the assassination. One would assume, then, that the portrayal of JFK's true intentions regarding American involvement in the war would be distorted by Burns in deference to the man financing the project.

Koch also provided funding for misleading documentaries on the JFK assassination. "Cold Case Kennedy" and "Who Was Lee Harvey Oswald," both concluding that Oswald acted alone in Kennedy's murder, have aired on PBS in conjunction with assassination anniversaries. Koch's influence over public broadcasting doesn't end with financial contributions. He is a trustee of PBS affiliates in New York (WNET) and Boston (WGBH). So much power does he have over editorial content that he was able to kill a documentary about himself. According to Brendan Fischer, in an article he wrote for the Center for Media and Democracy website, "*Citizen Koch*, a documentary about money in politics focused on [David Koch] was shunned by PBS for fear of offending [the] billionaire industrialist who has given $23 million to public television."[23] The irony is, the Kochs and their ilk have for years tried to cut off government funding of PBS programs. When the money dried up, the Kochs stepped in with their vast financial resources to fill the void. But the money came with a catch—they wanted editorial control over the content of political and historical documentaries.

Despite this, the knee-jerk reviews of "The Vietnam War" were positive, especially among conservative columnists like George Will. Will, a Kennedy hater who has always been bitterly mystified by JFK's lasting popularity among Americans, giddily wrote that Kennedy's "obliqueness and evasions greased the slide into a ground war of attrition."[24] Burns' oversights, lazy research, and, perhaps, lack of courage have made it easier for disinformationists to lay the blame for Vietnam at JFK's door and divorce his death from any political context associated with the war. No matter the circumstantial proof that he was killed, in part, for his commitment to abandon southeast Asia.

The business of misrepresenting JFK's thousand days are not confined to Vietnam. Even now there are right-wing denialists who refuse to admit, despite all evidence to the contrary, that Kennedy, alone, kept America from becoming a nuclear wasteland in 1962. Forty years after the fact, JFK aide Ted Sorensen, upon discovering for the first time that the Soviets had ready-to-fire nuclear weapons in Cuba, admitted that, had JFK succumbed to his Joint Chiefs' wishes, "The world would have been reduced to smoking rubble."[25] Kennedy's singularly good judgement saved the world, but it also made him a lot of enemies at the Pentagon, at Langley, at Foggy Bottom, and in Texas where he was viewed as a coward. But this information has been rigorously kept from us, for it provides motive for a conspiratorial plot that lone-nutters say never existed.

Even as new evidence of conspiracy is unearthed, new liars need to rebuffed. Prevaricators, like Posner, Holland and Bugliosi, with their secretive and warped agendas, have bred the next generation of hopeless propagandists. Right-wing blowhard Bill O'Reilly has created a bizarre and macabre assassination franchise. *Killing Kennedy* appeals to a fifth-grader's understanding of the Warren Commission fairy tale. Let's hope his next masterpiece is *Killing Off O'Reilly's Lies*. James L. Swanson is another; his book is called *End of Days*. (It would be more aptly titled "Endless Daze," because it stumbles and bumbles its way from untruth to untruth.)

These lone-nut authors exploit the fact-free times in which we live to distort history and bury it in a way that Allen Dulles and Lyndon Johnson would have relished. Like children who believe in the tooth fairy, lone-nutters take the original myths spun by the Warren Commission and embellish them as if they are somehow uncovering some new Oswald-damning information. Swanson's lack of inquisitiveness is galling. He criticizes Warren Commission critics for their devotion to solving the crime, while at the same time betraying his poor knowledge of the case. He dismisses evidence of conspiracy at every turn; yet he knows far less than the conspiracists he denigrates. His book presumes Oswald's guilt from the very beginning, thus stripping it of the right to be taken seriously. Here's an example of Swanson's narrow view: He freely admits that Oswald, unless he was alerted by fellow plotters, had no idea that "John F. Kennedy would be driving right past the place he worked in three days…it is possible that it was not until November 20…that Oswald learned [it] for the first time…[Kennedy and Oswald] were brought together by a staggering coincidence…[without which] Oswald would have never thought of killing Kennedy."[26] *A staggering coincidence.* Yes it was, and it is only one of a thousand staggering coincidences upon which lone-nutters build their case. That's what the Kennedy assassination comes down to—you must either believe in a thousand staggering coincidences or you must accept that there was an elaborate plot that took JFK's life. And a good murder detective will tell you to never believe in coincidences.

In an interview with *The Oregonian*, Swanson sniveled, "One of the most common misconceptions is that Dallas was a conservative or 'right wing' city of hate that killed President Kennedy. That's absurd. Lee Harvey Oswald was a communist, not a conservative. And he spent more time living in the Soviet Union than he ever did in Dallas."[27] Determined to exonerate the right-wing, he seems to be oblivious of Dallas's temperament and Oswald's place in it in 1963. Contrary to what Swanson asserts, Dallas was not a liberal bastion in 1963; he is apparently unaware that the city leaders were fringe extremists who promoted John Birch Society and KKK dogma to its citizens. Oilmen like Hunt and Murchison, who ran Dallas, hated Kennedy and vowed to "shoot him out of office." Dallas was more right-wing insane and vitriolic than any city in America. Daily radio broadcasts, sponsored by Hunt and listened to by most Dallasites, spewed right-wing hate at JFK constantly. And newspaper publisher Ted Dealey ran an endless stream of negative stories about the President.

As for Oswald's time in the Soviet Union, Swanson is apparently oblivious to the fact that the CIA ran a fake defector program during the Cold War and that Oswald was part of this program. This clandestine twist apparently is too spy-crafty for Swanson's little brain. Imagine if he did any real investigation and found that Oswald's best friends in Dallas—George DeMohrenschildt and Ruth Paine—were CIA. Swanson's tiny cerebral cavity would explode, like JFK's head did when he was shot from the grassy knoll.

Just like anti-abolitionists two centuries ago and flat-earthers of the middle ages, Oswald-did-it historians will be ridiculed and dismissed as charlatans 100 years from now. Future man will ask, "How did pseudo-experts like Swanson get away with their inane fairy tales. Why weren't they challenged by investigative journalists?" The answer is that investigative journalism died in the 20th century.

Burning in Hell

A few scant years after accomplishing his dirtiest covert trick, Allen Dulles went to his grave. He died in January 1969. Four years later, nearly to the day, Lyndon Johnson followed him in death. Both took their evil secrets with them, but Johnson's frail psychic condition near the end of his life gave the others who were involved in the JFK hit cause for concern. A psychiatrist was hired, and according to author Barr McClellan, the shrink was offered $1 million to treat Johnson and protect the secrets his patient divulged.[28] Those records have been sealed away with other incriminating documents from Johnson's political career.

Who first broached the idea of killing Kennedy? Was it Allen Dulles or was it Lyndon Johnson? Was it someone in the military hierarchy, like Curtis LeMay? Was it one of the disaffected Texas oil extremists? We will probably never know for certain, because the decision was finalized at a secret meeting in the deepest sanctum of the treasonous cabal aligned against the 35th president. What we do know is that, at some point, Dulles and Johnson eagerly entered into the conspiracy and desperately needed the cooperation of one another to assure the project's success. Dulles's CIA-in-exile could not have killed a sitting president without the consent of his successor, and Johnson could not have executed the crime without Dulles's vast network of clandestine operatives. Neither man, by himself, would have attempted such a brazen crime. They were tied together by common motives and a shared contempt for Kennedy. From there it was easy to make alliances with Kennedy's enemies—the Joint Chiefs, disgruntled Secret Service agents, Hoover's FBI, anti-Castro Cubans and rabid oil barons—to facilitate the plot. And Dulles's disciples—David Phillips, James Angleton, E. Howard Hunt and Edward Lansdale—men who despised Kennedy and who were fanatically loyal to Dulles, were easily recruited into the scheme.

Our only consolation is the hope that the traitors have been condemned to eternal damnation. One of them spoke of the possibility before he died. Angleton, CIA Counter-Intelligence Chief, told author Joseph Trento that "the founding fathers of U.S. intelligence…Allen Dulles and 60 of his closest friends…were liars… [and] without real accountability, everything turned to shit… Dulles, Richard Helms [and the others] were the grandmasters, people you had to believe would deservedly end up in hell."[29] Angleton was on his deathbed at the time, and in his frail and weakened state he conceded, "I guess I will see them there soon."[30]

And if there is a just God, Lyndon Johnson is burning with them.

Notes and References

Prologue

[1] Prouty, *JFK: The CIA, Vietnam and the Plot to Assassinate John F. Kennedy*, p. xxii

[2] Ibid., pp. xvii–xviii

Chapter 1, The Plotters

[1] Craig, *The Man on the Grassy Knoll*, p. 226

[2] Sullivan, "Democracies end when they are too democratic"

[3] The Papers of Dwight David Eisenhower, vol. XV

[4] Douglass, *JFK And The Unspeakable*, p. 197

[5] Talbot, *The Devil's Chessboard*, p. 15

[6] Kinzer, *The Brothers*, p. 200

[7] Talbot, *The Devil's Chessboard*, p. 491

[8] McClellan, *Blood, Money & Power*, p. 143

[9] Kessler, *Inside The White House*, p. 33

[10] Caro, *Path To Power*, p. 257

[11] Russell, *The Man Who Knew Too Much*, p. 590

[12] Pearson, *The Case Against Congress*, p. 91

[13] Talbot, "Passing The Torch"

[14] Kinzer, *The Brothers*, p. 11

[15] Talbot, *The Devil's Chessboard*, p. 2

[16] Ibid., p. 5

[17]Nelson, *LBJ: From Mastermind to the Colossus*, p. xli

[18]Ibid., p. xl

[19]"LBJ Part I." *American Experience*. Produced by PBS, originally aired 9/30/91.

[20]Shesol, *Mutual Contempt*, p. 7

[21]"LBJ Part I." American Experience. Produced by PBS, originally aired 9/30/91.

[22]Shesol, *Mutual Contempt*, p. 117

[23]Caro, *Path To Power*, p. xv

[24]Ibid., p. xvi

[25]Baker, *Family of Secrets*, p. 132

[26]McClellan, *Blood, Money & Power*, p. 90

[27]Ibid., p. 104

[28]Ibid., p. 105

[29]Ibid., p. 112

[30]Sample, *The Men on the Sixth Floor*, pp. 152–153

[31]Ibid., pp. 150–151

[32]Caddy letter to Stephen Trott, Assistant Attorney General, Criminal Division, U.S. Department of Justice, dated August 9, 1984. Posted 4/20/98 http://home.eartlink.net/~sixthfloor.estes/html

[33]"The Men Who Killed Kennedy, Part 9: The Guilty Men." Written, directed and produced by Nigel Turner. Aired on History Channel, 2003.

[34]Ibid.

[35]Nelson, *LBJ: From Mastermind to the Colossus*, p. 50

[36]Ibid., p. 165

[37]Quinn, "Doris Kearns and Richard Goodwin: A Tale of Hearts and Minds."

[38]Mellen, *Faustian Bargains*, Introduction

[39]Nelson, *LBJ: From Mastermind to the Colossus*, p. 93

Chapter 2, Motive, Means, and Opportunity

[1]Orwell, *1984*, p. 32

[2]Douglass, *JFK And The Unspeakable*, p. 12

[3]Ibid., pp. 12–13

[4]Prouty, *The Secret Team*, p. 2

[5]Ibid., p. 3

[6]Ibid., p. 2

[7]Douglass, *JFK And The Unspeakable*, p. 342

[8]Ibid., p. 343

[9]Kinzer, *The Brothers*, p. 303

[10]Lane, *Plausible Denial*, p. 94

[11]Ibid., p. 94

[12]Ibid., p. 98

[13]Brown, *Treachery In Dallas*, p. 66

[14]Newman, *Oswald And The CIA*, p. 171

[15]Corsi, *Who Really Kennedy?*, p. 251

[16]Warren Report CE 934

[17]Marrs, *Crossfire*, p. 128

[18]Abrams, "How Oswald Knew"

[19]HSCA Report, p. 60

[20]Warren Report, pp. 183–187

[21]Shackelford, "A Celebration of Freedom"

[22]Ibid.

[23]Hurt, *Reasonable Doubt*, p. 226

[24]Baker, *Me & Lee*, Publisher's Foreword by Millegan

[25]Ibid., Foreword by Haslam

[26]Ibid.

[27]Jacobsen, *Operation Paperclip*, p. 11

[28]Ibid.

[29]Ibid, p. 281

[30]Cutter, "Architects of the Cold War," p. 2

[31]Neufeld, *Von Braun*, p. 267

[32]Kinzer, "When a CIA Director Had Scores of Affairs"

[33]Ibid.

[34]Talbot, *The Devil's Chessboard*, p. 537

[35]Ibid., p. 538

[36]Douglass, *JFK And The Unspeakable*, p. 170

[37]Warren Report, pp. 14–15

[38]Douglass, *JFK And The Unspeakable*, p. 171

[39]Armstrong, *Harvey and Lee*, p. 725

[40]Douglass, *JFK And The Unspeakable*, p. 424, note 221

[41]LaMonica, Coalition on Political Assassinations Conference, Oct. 21, 1995. Spartacus Educational Forum, www.spartacuseducational.com

[42]Fonzi, *The Last Investigation*, p. 10

[43]Bryce, *Cronies*, p. 59

[44]Pratt and Castenada, *Builders: Herman and George R. Brown*, p. 158

[45]Stone, *JFK*, p. 111–112

[46]Ibid.

[47]Prouty, Fletcher. "How The CIA Controls President Ford." Topics On The National Security State of America, https://ratical.org/ratville/JFK/index.html (reprinted from *Genesis*, July 1975).

[48]Kelly, "Arthur Young—A Visit At Home With Arthur Young"

[49]Fonzi, *The Last Investigation*, p. 10

Chapter 3, Signs of Intelligence Life

[1]Douglass, *JFK And The Unspeakable*, p. 146

[2]"History of Civil Air Patrol." Civil Air Patrol, United States Air Force Auxiliary. www.gocivilairpatrol.com

[3]*Thirteen Days*. Directed by Roger Donaldson. Produced by Beacon Pictures. Released by New Line Cinema, 2000.

[4]Byrd, *I'm An Endangered Species*, p. 67

[5]Ibid., p. 69

[6]Ibid., p. 70

[7]Ibid., p. 38

[8]Hopsicker, *Barry & The Boys*, p. 37

[9]Ibid., pp. 163–64

[10]Ibid., p. 164

[11]Ibid.

[12]Ibid., p. 165

[13]Smith, *Say Goodbye To America*, p. 167

[14]Douglass, *JFK And The Unspeakable*, pp. 371–72

[15]Ibid., p. 372

[16]Smith, *JFK: The Second Plot*, pp. 269–71

[17]Ibid., pp. 272–73

[18]Ibid.

[19]Hopsicker, *Barry & The Boys*, p. 37

[20]FBI Field Report #105–3711, filed by James F. Morrissey, Dec. 4, 1963.

[21]Ibid.

[22]"Who Was Lee Harvey Oswald?" *PBS Frontline*. Produced by Michael Sullivan and William Cran, Nov. 19, 2013.

[23]Ibid. From interview of Robert Blakey, Chief Counsel of the House Select Committee on Assassinations

[24]Kelly, "Egg Harbor Township Elk of the Year Was Oswald's Bunkmate"

[25]Newman, *Oswald And The CIA*, p. 45

[26]Prouty, *The Secret Team*, p. 378

[27]"Who Was Lee Harvey Oswald?" PBS Frontline. Produced by Michael Sullivan and William Cran, Nov. 19, 2013.

[28]Ibid.

[29]Minutaglio, *Dallas 1963*, p. 14

[30]Craig, *The Man on the Grassy Knoll*, p. 83

[31]"Willem Oltmans Interviewed by Robert Tanenbaum (4th January 1977)." Spartacus Educational Forum. www.spartacus-educational.com

[32]Talbot, *The Devil's Chessboard*, p. 524

[33]Biffle, "Allen Dulles Looks Behind Red Moves"

[34]Warren Commission Report, Vol. VII, pp. 575–76

[35]Trask, *Pictures of the Pain*, p. 59

[36]Ibid., p. 77

[37]Baker, *Family of Secrets*, p. 114

[38]Ibid., p. 116

[39]Bowen, *Immaculate Deception*, p. 31

[40]Ibid.

[41]Baker, *Family of Secrets*, p. 31

[42]Ibid.

[43]Ibid., p. 27

[44]Ibid., p. 29

[45]Ibid., p. 79

[46]Baker, "Bush and the JFK Hit, Part 8," 11/6/13

[47]Trask, *Pictures of the Pain*, p. 309

[48]Interview of Myrna Hauser, 2/21/11

[49]McMillan, *Marina and Lee*, p. 517

[50]Sample, *The Men on the Sixth Floor*, p. 53

[51]Marrs, *Crossfire*, p. 545

[52]Stone, *JFK*, p. 73

[53]Marrs, *Crossfire*, p. 545

[54]Livingston, *High Treason*, pp. 180–81

[55]Hill, *Five Days in November*, p. 92

[56]Ibid.

[57]Simkin, John. Spartacus Educational Forum. "Fabian Escalante, *The Secret War: CIA Covert Operations Against Cuba, 1959–62.* www.spartacus-educational.com

[58]Baker, *Family of Secrets*, p. 117–18

[59]Ibid., p. 121

[60]Weisberg, *Oswald in New Orleans*, pp. 22–23

[61]Baker, *Family of Secrets*, p. 122

[62]Bernstein, "The CIA And The Media"

[63]Ibid.

[64]Trask, *Pictures of the Pain*, p. 107

[65]"A CBS News Inquiry: The Warren Report." CBS News

Production, June 25–28, 1967.

[66]Talbot, *The Devil's Chessboard*, pp. 597–98

[67]McGowan, *Derailing Democracy*, p. 13

[68]The source for this quote is Barbara Honegger, a member of the 1980 Reagan-Bush campaign staff and later a Reagan White House policy analyst. Honegger heard Casey speak these words at a February 1981 White House meeting between President Reagan and his cabinet secretaries and agency heads.

[69]Brinkley, *Cronkite*, p. 287

[70]Ibid., pp. 286–87

[71]Ibid., p. 519

[72]Ibid., p. 520

[73]Rather, *Rather Outspoken*, p. 117

[74]Ibid., p. 118

[75]Davis, *Katharine The Great*, p. 226

[76]Trento, *Secret History of the CIA*, p. 363

[77]Janney, *Mary's Mosaic*, p. 355

[78]DiEugenio, "Ben Bradlee's Not Such a Good Life"

[79]Bradlee, *Conversations With Kennedy*, p. 235

[80]DiEugenio, "Ben Bradlee's Not Such a Good Life"

[81]Dudman, "Oswald Declares He Was Denied Legal Counsel"

[82]Dudman, "Club Operator Charged With Murder Is Held Without Bond"

[83]Dudman, "U.S. Takes Lead In Inquiries Into Kennedy, Oswald Killings"

[84]Dudman, "Uncertainties Remain Despite Police View Of Kennedy Death"

[85]Ibid.

[86]Dudman, "My Neighbor, The International Spy"

[87]Ibid.

[88]Ibid.

[89]Armstrong, *Harvey and Lee*, p. 17

[90]Ibid., p. 9

[91]Ibid., pp. 727–28

[92]Ibid., p. 718

[93]Ibid., p. 781

[94]Douglass, *JFK And The Unspeakable*, pp. 351–55

[95]Weisberg, *Oswald in New Orleans*, pp. 252–54

[96]Summers, *Not in Your Lifetime*, p. 296

[97]Hurt, *Reasonable Doubt*, p. 228

[98]Ibid., p. 229

[99]McMillan, *Marina and Lee*, p. 457

[100]Ibid., p. 458

[101]Ibid., p. 465

[102]Newman, *Oswald And The CIA*, p. 354

[103]"Who Was Lee Harvey Oswald?" PBS *Frontline*. Produced by Michael Sullivan and William Cran, Nov. 19, 2013.

[104]Lane, *Plausible Denial*, p. 82

[105]Hardaway, "A Cruel and Shocking Misinterpretation."

[106]Veciana, *Trained To Kill*, Preface

Chapter 4, Genesis Of The Plot
[1]Palamara, "Main Secret Service Blog"

[2]Associated Press, "Long-Suppressed Report on Bay of Pigs Blames CIA Itself for Failure of Mission"

[3]Bissell, *Reflections of a Cold Warrior*, p. 183

[4]Baker, *Family of Secrets*, p. 35

[5]Douglass, *JFK And The Unspeakable*, p. 136

[6]Galbraith and Purcell, "Did the U.S. Military Plan a Nuclear First Strike for 1963"

[7]Bundy, *Danger and Survival*, p. 354

[8]Talbot, *Brothers*, p. 66

[9]Ibid., pp. 166–67

[10]Ibid., p. 66

[11]Zirbel, *The Texas Connection*, p. 251

[12]Russell, *The Man Who Knew Too Much*, pp. 601–603

[13]Ibid., p. 604

[14]"Indict Two Sons of H.L. Hunt, Two Others in Wiretapping," Mar. 1973

[15]Douglass, *JFK And The Unspeakable*, p. 139

[16]"Steel: The Ides of April," *Fortune* magazine, May 1962, p. 98

[17] Prouty, *The Secret Team*, p. 110

[18]Clark Clifford relayed this message to McNamara in the HBO film "Path To War," Directed by John Frankenheimer, produced by Avenue Pictures, 2002.

[19]"Secretary of Defense Memorandum For The President, 2 Oct., 1963." Papers of President Kennedy: National Security Files, 1/20/1961–11/22/1963.

[20]Galbraith, "Exit Strategy: In 1963 JFK Ordered A Complete Withdrawal From Vietnam"

[21]Prouty, *JFK: The CIA, Vietnam, and the Plot to Assassinate John F. Kennedy*, p. 280

[22]Douglass, *JFK And The Unspeakable*, p.181

[23]Ibid.

[24]Salerian, "A Peace Award for Robert McNamara"

[25]Ibid.

[26]From the motion picture "Path to War," Directed by John Frankenheimer, produced by Avenue Pictures, 2002.

[27]Shesol, *Mutual Contempt*, p. 389

[28]Ibid.

[29]From the documentary "The Fog Of War: Eleven Lessons From the Life of Robert S. McNamara." Directed by Errol Morris. Produced by @radical.media and Senart Films Productions, 2003

[30]Ibid.

[31]Ibid.

[32]Ibid.

[33]McMillan, *Marina and Lee*, p. 425

[34]From the PBS documentary "Who Was Lee Harvey Oswald."

Frontline, produced by Michael Sullivan and William Cran, originally aired Nov. 19, 2013.

[35]Dallek, *An Unfinished Life*, p. 699

[36]Ibid.

[37]Talbot, *The Devil's Chessboard*, p. 7

[38]Appendix to the HSCA Hearings, Volume X, 1979, pp. 37–56

[39]Williams, "Anti-Castro Leader Shot In The Head"

[40]Lane, *Plausible Denial*, pp. 76–86

[41]Nelson, *LBJ: From Mastermind to the Colossus*, p. xli

[42]Ibid., p. 114

[43]A thorough perusal of the August 15, 1963, edition of the *Chicago Tribune* yielded no such photo of Johnson and Dulles at the LBJ ranch. In fact, there exists no such photo in the entire month of August 1963 in either of the two major Chicago dailies.

[44]Bissell, *Reflections Of A Cold Warrior*, p. 157

[45]Stich, *Defrauding America*, p. 316

[46]Ibid., p. 615

[47]Martin, "The mid-20th-century rise of a secret government"

[48]de Burca, "Obit(ch)uary: Zbigniew Brzezinski, a mountain of broken skeletons"

[49]Stich, *Defrauding America*, p. 615

[50]NBC Nightly News report by Connie Chung, Sept. 1, 1983

Chapter 5, Execution Of The Plot

[1]Manchester, *Death of a President*, p. 67

[2]Sloan, *JFK: The Last Dissenting Witness*, p. 113

[3]From the documentary "After Hitler, Part II." Produced by Cineteve. Written by David Korn-Brzoza and Olivier Wieviorka. National Geographic channel, 2016.

[4]"Harry S Truman." National Park Service, U.S. Department of the Interior, Harry S Truman National Historic Site, https://www.nps.gov

[5]Sloan, *JFK: The Last Dissenting Witness*, p. 113

[6]Ibid., p. 112

[7]Marrs, "The Senator Who Suspected a JFK Conspiracy."

[8]Ibid.

[9]Marrs, *Crossfire*, p. 32

[10]Palamara, "The Kennedy Detail Exposed—the real story of the JFK Secret Service."

[11]Andrews, "The Roberts Details."

[12]Bolden, *The Echo From Dealey Plaza*, p. 19

[13]Ibid., p. 50

[14]Ibid., p. 51

[15]Ibid., pp. 51–53

[16]Ibid., p. 72

[17]Warren Commission hearings, vol. V, p. 455

[18]"Tried To Sell Data: Secret Service Agent Gets 6 Years In Jail"

[19]Douglass, *JFK And The Unspeakable*, pp. 271–72

[20]From the documentary "The Day Kennedy Died." Produced by Lorraine McKechnie. Written and directed by Leslie Woodhead. Smithsonian Channel, 2013.

[21]Douglass, *JFK And The Unspeakable*, p. 272

[22]Twyman, *Bloody Treason*, pp. 144–46

[23]Trask, *Pictures of the Pain*, p. 162

[24]Warren Commission Hearings, vol. II, pp. 118–19

[25]Vince Palamara interview of Richard Greer, William Greer's son, on 9/17/91. From Vince Palamara's Main Secret Service blog, http://vincepalamara.blogspot.com

[26]Palamara, *JFK: From Parkland to Bethesda*, p. 97

[27]Newcomb and Adams, *Murder From Within*, pp. 54–55

[28]Ibid., pp. 55–56

[29]Ibid., p. 79

[30]Lopez, "Secret Service also partied before Kennedy assassination"

[31]D'Amato, "Were Secret Service agents too hungover to protect JFK?"

[32]Palamara, Vince. "The Kennedy Detail Exposed—the real story of the JFK Secret Service." November in Dallas Conference, Nov. 20, 2016.

[33]Roberts, *Kill Zone*, p. 131

[34]Canfield and Weberman, *Coup d'etat In America* (New York: The Third Press, 1975, edition), pp. 56–57

[35]Warren Commission Hearings, vol. VII, p. 531

[36]Summers, *Conspiracy*, p. 50

[37]Marrs, *Crossfire*, p. 324

[38]Warren Commission Hearings, vol. VI, p. 312

[39]Marrs, *Crossfire*, p. 321

[40]Golz, "SS Imposters Spotted by JFK Witnesses"

[41]DiEugenio, "The Life & Death of Richard Case Nagell"

[42]Russell, "Oswald and the CIA"

[43]Hancock, *Someone Would Have Talked*, p. 15

[44]Ibid., p. 17

[45]Marrs, *Crossfire*, p. 398

[46]Douglass, *JFK And The Unspeakable*, pp. 244–48

[47]Hancock, *Someone Would Have Talked*, p. 19

[48]Ryan, "Kennedy Assassination Intrigue Swirls in D.C. Federal"

[49]Twyman, *Bloody Treason*, pp. 522–533

[50]Russell, *The Man Who Knew Too Much,* p. 564

[51]Ibid., p. 559

[52]A photo of the note and an explanation as to its origin can be found in *Crossfire*, by Jim Marrs, in between pp. 307–309. Some researchers believe the "Hunt" Oswald addressed was H.L. Hunt, but, since a copy of the note was found in Mexico City where the CIA monitored the comings and goings at the Russian and Cuban embassies, it is more likely that E. Howard Hunt was the recipient.

[53]Lane, *Plausible Denial*, p. 322

[54]Marchetti, "CIA to Admit Hunt Involvement in Kennedy Slaying"

[55]Hunt, *Give Us This Day*, p. 15

[56]Haldeman, *The Ends of Power*, pp. 161–62

[57]From the film *Nixon*. Directed by Oliver Stone. Produced by Cinergi Pictures Entertainment, Hollywood Pictures, and Illusion Entertainment, 1995.

[58]Baker, *Family of Secrets*, p. 181

[59]Haldeman, *The Ends of Power*, p. 146

[60]Ibid., pp. 38–39

[61]Canfield and Weberman, *Coup d'etat in America* (New York: Third Press, 1975 edition), p. 90

[62]Hedegaard, "The Last Confession of E. Howard Hunt"

[63]Ibid.

[64]Lane, *Plausible Denial*, p. 283

[65]Ibid., pp. 295–297

[66]Hedegaard, "The Last Confession of E. Howard Hunt"

[67]Wilkinson, James. "Does this sketch prove that JFK was assassinated by two gunmen? Drawing by fallen president's surgeon in Dallas says bullets came from different directions."

[68]Trask, *Pictures of the Pain*, p. 80

[69]Russell, *The Man Who Knew Too Much*, p. 600

[70]Trask, *Pictures of the Pain*, p. 80

[71]Fetzer, *The Great Zapruder Film Hoax*, p. xiii

[72]Douglas Horne in Appendix C, "The NPIC Report: The Zapruder Film in November 1963," in Fetzer, *The Great Zapruder Film Hoax*, p. 457

[73]Ibid.

[74]Ibid., p. 459

[75]Ibid., p. 458

[76]Horne, *Inside The Assassinations Records Review Board*, vol. IV, pp. 1226–27

[77]Ibid.

[78]David Healy, "Technical Aspects of Film Alterations," in Fetzer, *The Great Zapruder Film Hoax*, p. 118

[79]David Lifton, "Pig on a Leash," in Fetzer, *The Great Zapruder Film Hoax*, pp. 405–406

[80]John Costella, Ph. D., "A Scientist's Verdict: The Film is a Fabrication," in Fetzer, *The Great Zapruder Film Hoax*, p. 157

[81]David Lifton, "Pig on a Leash," in Fetzer, *The Great Zapruder Film Hoax*, p. 352

[82]Ibid., p. 408

[83]Simkin, "David Sanchez Morales"

[84]Fonzi, *The Last Investigation*, p. 390

[85]Douglass, *JFK And The Unspeakable*, p. 273

[86]Twyman, *Bloody Treason*, p. 712

[87]Interview of James Powell by Timothy A. Wray, ARRB testimony, April 12, 1996.

[88]Excerpt of a letter from Victor Krulak to Fletcher Prouty, found in Appendix D of "Understanding Special Operations And Their Impact On The Vietnam War Era: 1989 interview of L. Fletcher Prouty by David T. Ratcliffe, https://ratical.org/JFK/USO

[89]Hedegaard, "The Last Confession of E. Howard Hunt"

[90]Canfield and Weberman, *Coup d'etat in America* (New York: Third Press, 1975 edition), p. 72

[91]Simkin, "Chauncey Holt"

[92]Kamran, "How The CIA Used Refugees To Create War in Vietnam"

[93]Talbot, *The Devil's Chessboard*, pp. 558–59

[94]Kamran, "How The CIA Used Refugees To Create War in Vietnam"

[95]Kinzer, *The Brothers*, p. 192

[96]Douglass, *JFK And The Unspeakable*, p. 186

[97]Talbot, *Brothers*, p. 98

[98]Jack White, "Mysteries of the JFK Assassination: The Photographic Evidence From A to Z," in Fetzer, *The Great Zapruder Film Hoax*, p. 65.

[99]Weiner, "Lucein Conein, 79, Legendary Cold War Spy"

[100]Douglass, *JFK And The Unspeakable*, p. 152

[101]Ibid., p. 200

[102]Ibid., p. 201

[103]Parmet, *JFK: The Presidency of John F. Kennedy*, p. 335

[104]Starnes, "Spooks Make Life Miserable for Ambassador Lodge: Arrogant CIA Disobeys Orders in Viet Nam."

[105]Krock, "Intra-Administration War in Vietnam," p. 34

[106]Sheehan, *A Bright, Shining Lie: John Paul Vann and America in Vietnam*, p. 9

[107]Sample and Collom, *The Men on the Sixth Floor*, p. 209

[108]Mellen, *Faustian Bargains*, p. 162

[109]Sample and Collom, *The Men on the Sixth Floor*, p. 188

[110]Russell, *The Man Who Knew Too Much*, p. 561

[111]Ibid., p. 562

[112]Noyes, *Legacy of Doubt*, p. 34

[113]Ibid., pp. 34–38

[114]Ibid., p. 218

[115]Marrs, *Crossfire*, p. 339

[116]Inkol, "Jack Lawrence Responds"

[117]Shaw and Harris, *Cover-Up*, p. 90

[118]Livingstone and Groden, *High Treason*, p. 16

[119]Summers, *Not in Your Lifetime*, pp. 25–26

[120]Douglass, *JFK And The Unspeakable*, pp. 262–64

[121]Ibid., pp. 264–65

[122]Marrs, *Crossfire*, p. 320

[123]Sloan, *JFK: The Last Dissenting Witness*, p. 23

[124]Ibid., p. 24

[125]Ibid., p. 26

[126]Smith, *JFK: The Second Plot*, p. 146

[127]Ibid., p. 149

[128]Sloan, *JFK: The Last Dissenting Witness*, pp. 24–34

[129]Ibid., pp. 61–72

[130]Ibid., p. 56

[131]Ibid., pp. 75–85

[132]Trask, *Pictures of the Pain*, p. 162

[133]"Rush To Judgment" video of the Mark Lane book by the same title. Interview of J.C. Price, 1965.

[134]Marrs, *Crossfire*, p. 58

[135]Ibid.

[136]Lifton, *Best Evidence*, p. 17n

[137]From the documentary "The Day Kennedy Died." Produced by Lorraine McKechnie, Directed and written by Leslie Woodhead, aired on the Smithsonian Channel, 2013.

[138]Marrs, *Crossfire*, p. 72

[139]Lifton, *Best Evidence*, p. 17n

[140]From the documentary "JFK: The Smoking Gun." Produced by Jesse Prupas, directed by Malcolm McDonald. A Muse Entertainment/Cordell Jigsaw Production. The quote is from Colleen Lorenze, daughter of nationally known ballistics expert Howard Donahue.

[141]Ibid.

[142]Summers, *Not In Your Lifetime*, p. 56

[143]Ibid.

[144]From the documentary "JFK: The Smoking Gun." Produced by Jesse Prupas, directed by Malcolm McDonald. A Muse Entertainment/Cordell Jigsaw Production.

[145]Sample and Collom, *The Men on the Sixth Floor*, pp. 186–87

[146]Livingstone and Groden, *High Treason*, p. 121

[147]Ibid.

[148]Mellen, *Faustian Bargains*, p. 76

[149]Ibid., p. 93

[150]Sample and Collom, *The Men on the Sixth Floor*, p. 75

[151]Ibid., pp. 56–65

[152]Bishop, *The Day Kennedy Was Shot*, p. 255

[153]Smith, *JFK: The Second Plot*, p. 41

154 Russell, *The Man Who Knew Too Much*, pp. 568–69

155 Smith, *JFK: The Second Plot*, p. 41

156 O'Toole, *The Assassination Tapes*, pp. 204–06

157 From the documentary "The Day Kennedy Died." Produced by Lorraine McKechnie, written and directed by Leslie Woodhead. Aired on the Smithsonian Channel, 2013.

158 O'Toole, *The Assassination Tapes*, p. 125

159 Ibid., pp. 127–28

160 Sample and Collom, *The Men on the Sixth Floor*, p. 66

161 Armstrong, "Harvey and Lee Depart the TSBD"

162 From the documentary "Frame 313: The JFK Assassination Theories." Sundown Entertainment, Inc., production in association with Thunderball Films, LLC, 2008.

163 Belzer, *Hit List*, p. 7

164 Marrs, *Crossfire*, p. 347

165 Ernest, *The Girl On The Stairs*, pp. 90–91

166 Belzer, *Hit List*, pp. 7–8

167 Armstrong, "Harvey and Lee: November 22, 1963"

168 Belzer, *Hit List*, p. 11

169 Hurt, *Reasonable Doubt*, pp. 152–53

170 Ernest, *The Girl On The Stairs*, p. 340

171 FBI report dated 1/10/64, Warren Commission Exhibit 2098

172 Marrs, *Crossfire*, p. 20

173 Ibid., p. 26

174 Summers, *Not In Your Lifetime*, p. 39

175 Ibid., p. 38

176 Corsi, *Who Really Killed Kennedy?*, p. 145

177 Marrs, *Crossfire*, p. 329

178 Trask, *That Day in Dallas*, pp. 87–90

179 Armstrong, "Harvey and Lee Depart the TSBD"

180 Douglass, *JFK And The Unspeakable*, p. 274

181 From the documentary "Frame 313: The JFK Assassination Theories." Sundown Entertainment, Inc., production in

association with Thunderball Films, LLC, 2008.

[182]Marrs, *Crossfire*, p. 332

[183]Corsi, *Who Really Killed Kennedy?*, p. 118

[184]Ibid., p. 117

[185]Marrs, *Crossfire*, p. 347

[186]Corsi, *Who Really Killed Kennedy?*, p. 118

[187]Marrs, *Crossfire*, p. 341

[188]Ibid., p. 342

[189]Livingstone and Groden, *High Treason*, p. 123

[190]Brown, *Treachery in Dallas*, pp. 188–91

[191]Nelson, *LBJ: From Mastermind to the Colossus*, p. 267

[192]Brown, *Treachery in Dallas*, pp. 188–91

[193]Nelson, *LBJ: From Mastermind to the Colossus*, pp. 266–67

[194]Ibid., p. 267

[195]Douglass, *JFK And The Unspeakable*, p. 292

[196]Ibid., p. 291

[197]Ibid., p. 293

[198]Johnston and Roe, *Flight From Dallas*, pp. 24–29

[199]Ibid., p. 24–25

[200]Talbot, *The Devil's Chessboard*, p. 546

[201]Ibid., p. 547

[202]Johnston and Roe, *Flight From Dallas*, pp. 26–29

[203]Douglass, *JFK And The Unspeakable*, pp. 294–97

[204]HSCA Report, March 1979, "Oswald–Tippit Associates: The Wise Allegation," Section X, pp. 37–41

[205]Douglass, *JFK And The Unspeakable*, pp. 295–97

[206]HSCA report, "Oswald-Tippit Associates," section X, p. 40

[207]Morley, "Ex-Flame Says Jack Ruby 'had no choice' but to kill Oswald"

[208]Twyman, *Bloody Treason*, p. 275

[209]Ibid., p. 271

[210]Warren Commission Hearings, vol. XIV, 7/18/64, p. 567

[211]Huffaker et al, *When The News Went Live: Dallas 1963*, p. 125

[212]Warren Commission Hearings, vol. V, 6/7/64, pp. 211–212

[213]Huffaker et al, *When The News Went Live: Dallas 1963*, p. 51

[214]Kirk, "Living History: Boyd describes his role at JFK assassination"

[215]Twyman, *Bloody Treason*, p. 278

[216]Huffaker et al, *When The News Went Live: Dallas 1963*, pp. 157–60

[217]Ibid., pp. 47–48

[218]Curry, *JFK Assassination File*, p. 133

[219]Ernest, *The Girl On The Stairs*, p. 332–33

[220]Fry, "Dallas detective: Oswald shot JFK to gain fame"

[221]From the documentary "Frame 313: The JFK Assassination Theories." Sundown Entertainment, Inc., production in association with Thunderball Films, LLC, 2008.

[222]Livingstone and Groden, *High Treason*, p. 122

[223]Hilts, "Louis J. West, Psychiatrist Who Studied Extremes, Dies"

[224]Proctor, "The Phone Call That Never Was"

[225]Douglass, *JFK And The Unspeakable*, p. 366

[226]Proctor, "The Raleigh Call and the Fingerprints of Intelligence"

[227]Baker, *Family of Secrets*, p. 56

[228]Ibid., pp. 53–54

[229]Acoca, "Documents: Bush Blew Whistle on Rival in JFK Slaying"

[230]Baker, *Family of Secrets*, p. 47

[231]Ibid., p. 268

[232]Ibid., pp. 269–70

[233]Ibid., p. 278

[234]Ibid.

[235]Freund, "Nixon Predicts JFK May Drop Johnson"

[236]"A Current Affair," interview with Madeleine Brown, Feb. 24, 1992, produced by Twentieth-Century Fox.

[237]Canfield and Weberman, *Coup d'Etat in America* (New York: Third Press, 1975 edition), p. 85

[238]Lane, *Plausible Denial*, p. 296

[239]Prouty, "People and the Pursuit of the Truth, June, 1978"

[240]McKnight, *Breach of Trust*, p. 283

[241]HSCA exhibit F-20

[242]"Ford Made Key Change in Kennedy Death Report," Associated Press

[243]Sample and Collom, *The Men on the Sixth Floor*, p. 196

Chapter 6, From Washington to Dallas and Back Again

[1]Byrd, *I'm An Endangered Species*, p. 84

[2]Ashman, *Connally: The Adventures Of Big Bad John*, pp. 70–71

[3]Bruno, *Advance Man*, p. 86

[4]O'Neill, *Man Of The House*, p. 96

[5]Bruno, *Advance Man*, p. 87

[6]Ibid., p.89

[7]Ibid., p. 92

[8]Zirbel, *The Texas Connection*, p. 189

[9]Ibid., p. 188

[10]O'Neill, *Man Of The House*, p. 177

[11]Shesol, *Mutual Contempt*, p. 137

[12]Thompson, "Is Deception the Best Way to Serve One's Country?"

[13]Ibid.

[14]Undated You Tube video of unknown origin

[15]Zirbel, *The Texas Connection*, pp. 190–91

[16]Marrs, *Crossfire*, p. 13

[17]Ibid., p.12

[18]Crenshaw, Trauma Room One, pp. 25–26

[19]Horne, *Inside The Assassination Records Review Board*, vol. II, p. 645

[20]Dudman, "Secret Service"

[21]Horne, *Inside The Assassination Records Review Board*, vol. II, p. 651

[22]Ibid., p. 652

[23]Lifton, *Best Evidence*, pp. 192–93

[24]Ibid., p. 705

[25]Ibid., p. 61

[26]Herbers, "Connally Gains, Doctors Report"

[27]Herbers, "Kennedy Hit By Two Bullets"

[28]Palamara, *JFK: From Parkland To Bethesda*, p. 9

[29]Crenshaw, *Trauma Room One*, p. 13

[30]Lifton, *Best Evidence*, p. 42n

[29]Crenshaw, *Trauma Room One*, p. 13

[30]Ibid., p. 17

[31]Palamara, *JFK: From Parkland To Bethesda*, pp. 3–7

[32]Livingstone and Groden, *High Treason*, p. 121

[33]Lifton, *Best Evidence*, p. 271

[34]Summers, *Conspiracy*, p. 52

[35]Marrs, *Crossfire*, p. 38

[36]"Rush To Judgment" video of the Mark Lane book by the same title. Interview of S.M. Holland, 1965.

[37]"The Men Who Killed Kennedy, Part 2: The Forces of Darkness." Produced by Nigel Turner. Arts & Entertainment Network, 1991–2003.

[38]Summers, *Conspiracy*, p. 53

[39]O'Neill, *Man Of The House*, p. 178

[40]Trask, *Pictures Of The Pain*, p. 181

[41]HSCA Report, vol. 7, p. 38

[42]Lifton, *Best Evidence*, p. 172

[43]Ibid., p. 200

[44]Ibid., pp. 200–01

[45]Lane, *Plausible Denial*, p. 79

[46]HSCA (RG 233) Affidavit I, Jan. 1978 interview of Dr. Burkley by Mark Flanagan and Donald Purdy.

[47]Craig, *The Man On The Grassy Knoll*, p. 123

[48]Associated Press, "Long-Suppressed Report on Bay of Pigs

Blames CIA Itself for Failure of Mission"
49Craig, *The Man On The Grassy Knoll*, p. 196
50Ibid., pp. 146–56
51Ibid., p. 172
52Ibid., pp. 8–10
53Mapes, *Truth And Duty*, pp. 59–62
54Brewton, *The Mafia, CIA & George Bush*, p. 218
55Ibid, pp. 218–19
56Mapes, *Truth And Duty*, p. 138
57Unger, "Mystery Man," Apr. 27, 2004
58"The Men Who Killed Kennedy, Part 7: The Smoking Guns."
    Written, produced and directed by Nigel Turner. Aired on
    History Channel, 2003.
59Estes, *Billie Sol Estes—A Texas Legend*, p. 156
60Palamara, *JFK: From Parkland To Bethesda*, p. 94
61Horne, *Inside The Assassination Records Review Board*, vol. IV,
    pp. 1153–54
62Palamara, *JFK: From Parkland To Bethesda*, p. 95
63Lifton, *Best Evidence*, p. 674
64Ibid.
65Palamara, *JFK: From Parkland To Bethesda*, p. 35
66Ibid., p. 46
67Ibid, pp. 45–47, 96–97
68HSCA Memo, Interview with Nathan Pool, 1/12/77
69Manchester, *The Death of a President*, p. 175
70Crenshaw, *Trauma Room One*, p. 60
71Ibid., p. 64
72Hornberger, "The Kennedy Casket Conspiracy"
73Lifton, *Best Evidence*, p. 582
74Manchester, *The Death of a President*, p. 299
75Lifton, *Best Evidence*, p. 674
76Manchester, *The Death of a President*, p. 300
77Ibid.

[78]Ibid., p. 306

[79]Ibid., p. 296

[80]Ibid., p. 296–98

[81]Ibid., p. 312

[82]Hornberger, "The Kennedy Casket Conspiracy"

[83]The Boyajian Report, 26 November 1963, from Sergeant R.E. Boyajian, to Commanding Officer, Marine Corps Institute Company.

[84]Hornberger, "The Kennedy Casket Conspiracy"

[85]Lifton, *Best Evidence*, p. 666

[86]Brown, *Treachery in Dallas*, p. 55

[87]Lifton, *Best Evidence*, p. 679

[88]Manchester, *The Death of a President*, p. 307

[89]Jones, "John F. Kennedy Assassination Flight"

[90]Gillon, *The Kennedy Assassination: 24 Hours After*, pp. 72–73

[91]Jones, "John F. Kennedy Assassination Flight"

[92]Manchester, *The Death of a President*, p. 316

[93]Gillon, *The Kennedy Assassination: 24 Hours After*, pp. 89–90

[94]O'Donnell, *Johnny We Hardly Knew Ye*, p. 32

[95]Gillon, *The Kennedy Assassination: 24 Hours After*, p. 123

[96]Ibid., p. 91

[97]O'Donnell, *Johnny We Hardly Knew Ye*, p. 37

[98]Jones, "John F. Kennedy Assassination Flight"

[99]Ibid.

[100]Nelson, *LBJ: From Mastermind to the Colossus*, p. xxv

[101]Nelson, *LBJ: The Mastermind of the JFK Assassination*, p. 299

[102]Gillon, *The Kennedy Assassination: 24 Hours After*, pp. 117–18

[103]Ibid., p. 128

[104]Jones, "John F. Kennedy Assassination Flight"

[105]Ibid.

[106]Shesol, *Mutual Contempt*, p. 118

[107]Ibid.

[108]Kendall-Bell, "Controversy Still Swirls Around Rifle Used in

JFK Assassination." Dallas Sheriff's Deputy Gene Boone
discovered a 7.65 Mauser on the TSBD's sixth floor on
11/22/63. He stated this in a report submitted to Dallas
County Sheriff Bill Decker.

[109]Horne, Inside *The Assassination Records Review Board*, vol. I,
pp. 155–56

[110]Ibid.

[111]Lifton, *Best Evidence*, p. 690

[112]Ibid., p. 681

[113]Ibid., p. 689

[114]Warren Commission Hearings, vol. II, p. 357

[115]Lifton, *Best Evidence*, p. 478n

[116]Horne, *Inside The Assassination Records Review Board*, p. 596

[117]Lifton, *Best Evidence*, p. 664

[118]Horne, *Inside The Assassination Records Review Board*, p. 599

[119]Ibid., p. 630

[120]Livingstone and Groden, *High Treason*, p. 49

[121]Lifton, *Best Evidence*, p. 283

[122]Ibid., p. 284n

[123]Ibid., p. 250

[124]Nelson, *LBJ: From Mastermind to the Colossus*, p. 42

[125]Lifton, *Best Evidence*, p. 203

[126]ARRB Medical Testimony deposition of James J. Humes, p. 60,
2/13/96

[127]"The Smoking Gun." Documentary produced by Jesse Prupas,
Muse Entertainment/Cordell Jigsaw Productions, aired on the
REELZ Channel, Nov. 2013.

[128]Horne, *Inside The Assassination Records Review Board*, p. 611

[129]Warren Commission Hearings, vol. II, p. 351, Mar. 16, 1964

[130]ARRB Medical testimony of Jerrol Custer, p. 144, 10/28/97

[131]Horne, *Inside The Assassinations Record Review Board*, p. 540

[132]Mantik, David W., M.D., Ph. D. "The Silence of the
Historians." From Assassination Research, vol. 1, Number 1,

2002. http://assassinationresearch.com

[133] Ibid.

[134] Reibe ARRB Medical testimony, p. 40, 5/7/97

[135] Lifton, *Best Evidence*, p. 516

[136] Horne, *Inside The Assassination Records Review Board*, pp. 251–53

[137] Morris, "Shooting The President"

[138] Horne, *Inside The Assassination Records Review Board*, p. 85

[139] Ibid., p. 488

[140] Ibid., p. 487

[141] Ibid., p. 109

[142] Ibid., p. 108

[143] Lifton, *Best Evidence*, p. 601

[144] Mantik and Wecht "Paradoxes of the JFK Assassination: The Brain Enigma," in *The Assassinations*, p. 253

[145] Livingstone and Groden, *High Treason*, p. 407

[146] Horne, *Inside The Assassination Records Review Board*, pp. 44–45

[147] Livingstone and Groden, *High Treason*, p. 405

[148] Warren Commission Hearings, vol. II, pp. 355–60

[149] Newcomb and Adams, *Murder From Within*, p. 186

[150] Lifton, *Best Evidence*, p. 644

[151] Horne, *Inside The Assassination Records Review Board*, p. 314

[152] Ibid., p. 315

[153] Ibid., p. 322

[154] DiEugenio, "Douglas Horne, *Inside The ARRB*"

[155] From the documentary "The Men Who Killed Kennedy, Part 7: The Smoking Guns." Written, produced and directed by Nigel Turner. Aired on The History Channel, 2003.

[156] Warren Commission Hearings, vol. VI, pp. 284–288

[157] Brown, "The Lee Bowers Letter: The One That Got Away." *JFK/Deep Politics Quarterly*, January 1996.

[158] Sloan, *JFK: The Last Dissenting Witness*, p. 187

[159] "America Declassified: JFK 50th." Hosted by Mike Baker. Aired

on the Travel Channel, Nov. 2013

[160]"Man Questioned in Hammer Beating," Mar. 27, 1974
[161]Stich, *Defrauding America*, p. 439
[162]Hardin, "Deputy kills prisoner in break for freedom."
[163]Wagoner, "The Body Alteration Theory and Parkland Hospital"
[164]Ibid.
[165]Ibid.
[166]Ibid.

Chapter 7, The Cover-Up Then and Now

[1]Lifton, *Best Evidence*, pp. 354–356n
[2]Twyman, *Bloody Treason*, pp. 664–65
[3]Ryan, "Kennedy Assassination Intrigue Swirls In D.C. Federal."
[4]Trask, *Pictures of the Pain*, p. 197
[5]Ibid., pp. 194–95
[6]Trask, *Pictures of the Pain*, p. 174
[7]Smith, *JFK: The Second Plot*, p. 132
[8]Marrs, *Crossfire*, p. 36
[9]Brown, *Treachery in Dallas*, pp. 191–94
[10]Marrs, *Crossfire*, p. 37
[11]Trask, *Pictures of the Pain*, p. 614
[12]Marrs *Crossfire*, p. 78
[13]Ibid.
[14]"The Men Who Killed Kennedy, Part 2: The Forces of Darkness." Produced by Nigel Turner. Arts & Entertainment Network, 1991–2003.
[15]Marrs, *Crossfire*, p. 320
[16]Ibid., p. 75
[17]Trask, *Pictures of the Pain*, p. 275
[18]Ibid., p. 295
[19]Ibid., pp. 345–46
[20]"A Current Affair," produced by Twentieth-Century Fox. Episode which aired Feb. 25, 1992.

[21]Trask, *Pictures of the Pain*, pp. 339–40

[22]Canfield and Weberman, *Coup d'Etat in America* (vol. 3 NY: Independent Research Associate edition), pp. 351–53

[23]Lazzaro, "JFK Assassination: First JFK Conspiracy Theory Was Paid For By The CIA"

[24]"Frame 313: The JFK Assassination Theories." Sundown Entertainment, Inc., Production in association with Thunderball Films, LLC, 2008

[25]Lazzaro, "JFK Assassination: First JFK Conspiracy Theory Was Paid For By The CIA"

[26]Rockwood, "Interview: G. Robert Blakey"

[27]Lazzaro, "JFK Assassination: First JFK Conspiracy Theory Was Paid For By The CIA"

[28]Ibid.

[29]Fursenko and Naftali, *One Hell Of A Gamble*, p. 81

[30]Ibid., pp. 344–48

[31]Bender and Swidey, "Robert F. Kennedy Saw Conspiracy in JFK's Assassination"

[32]Talbot, *Brothers*, p. 307

[33]Ibid.

[34]Ibid., p. 306

[35]Bender and Swidey, "Robert F. Kennedy Saw Conspiracy in JFK's Assassination"

[36]Nelson, *LBJ: From Mastermind to the Colossus*, p. 87

[37]Corsi, *Who Really Killed Kennedy?*, p. 297

[38]Lambert and Wheeler, "How LBJ's Family Amassed Its Fortune"

[39]"The Men Who Killed Kennedy, Part 9: The Guilty Men." Written, directed and produced by Nigel Turner. Aired on History Channel, 2003.

[40]Marrs, *Crossfire*, pp. 296–97

[41]Lane, *Plausible Denial*, pp. 51–52

[42]Ibid., p. 53

[43]From the documentary "The Kennedy Assassination: 24 Hours After." Produced, written, and directed by Anthony Giacchino, 2013. Broadcast on the History Channel, 4/25/17.

[44]Sloan, *JFK: The Last Dissenting Witness*, pp. 101–104

[45]DiEugenio, "Douglas Horne, *Inside The ARRB*"

[46]Nelson, *LBJ: From Mastermind to the Colossus*, p. 478

[47]Talbot, *The Devil's Chessboard*, p. 573

[48]Baker, *Family of Secrets*, p. 30

[49]Ibid., p. 311

[50]Hunter, "Boggs Demands That Hoover Quit."

[51]July 2, 2011, interview of Dr. Nick Begich on *Blue State Radio*

[52]Fensterwald and Ewing, *Coincidence or Conspiracy?*, p. 96

Chapter 8, When They Killed Kennedy, They Killed America

[1]Lane, *Last Word: My Indictment of the CIA In the Murder of JFK*, p. 282

[2]Talbot, *Brothers*, p. 297

[3]Posner, *Case Closed*, p. 262

[4]Ibid., p. 300n

[5]Lifton, *Best Evidence*, pp. 643–44

[6]Wrone, "*Case Closed: Lee Harvey Oswald and the Assassination of JFK*, by Gerald Posner"

[7]Bugliosi, *Reclaiming History*, p. 149

[8]Summers, *Not In Your Lifetime*, p. xii

[9]Hancock, *Someone Would Have Talked*, inside cover

[10]Miller, *The End of Greatness*, p. 13

[11]Sabato, *The Kennedy Half-Century*, p. 5

[12]Talbot, *The Devil's Chessboard*, p. 559

[13]Sample, *The Men on the Sixth Floor*, p. 172

[14]Prouty, *The Secret Team*, p. 2

[15]Pierce, "I May Be an Enemy of the People, But at Least I'm No Longer Sick"

[16]Matthews, *Jack Kennedy: Elusive Hero*, p. 406

¹⁷Talbot, *Brothers*, pp. 294–95

¹⁸"JFK's Warnings About Television, Money and Politics Ring True Today." NCC Staff. National Constitution Center, Nov. 14, 2016. https://www.yahoo.com/news/jfk-warnings-television-money-politics-ring-true-today-115013865.html

¹⁹Sabato, *The Kennedy Half-Century*, p. 3

²⁰"Ken Burns and Co-Director Lynn Novick on the Lessons in Their Latest Documentary, *The Vietnam War*." Parade magazine, Aug. 20, 2017, www.Parade.com/vietnam.

²¹From the PBS documentary "The Vietnam War, Episode 2: Riding The Tiger." Produced and directed by Ken Burns and Lynn Novick. Written by Geoffrey C. Ward. Original air date 9/18/17.

²²"Ken Burns and Co-Director Lynn Novick on the Lessons in Their Latest Documentary, *The Vietnam War*." Parade magazine, Aug. 20, 2017, www.Parade.com/vietnam.

²³Fischer, "PBS Killed Wisconsin Uprising Documentary 'Citizen Koch' To Appease Koch Brothers."

²⁴Will, "*The Vietnam War* is a Masterpiece—and a Model for Assessing Our History."

²⁵Talbot, *Brothers*, p. 167

²⁶Swanson, *End of Days*, pp. 68–70

²⁷Baker, "JFK assassination author: evidence proves Oswald did it, conspiracies are a distraction."

²⁸From the documentary "The Men Who Killed Kennedy, Part 9: The Guilty Men." Written, directed and produced by Nigel Turner. Aired on The History Channel, 2003.

²⁹Trento, *The Secret History of the CIA*, pp. 478–79

³⁰Mellen, *A Farewell to Justice*, p. 370

Selected Bibliography

Abrams, Malcolm. "How Oswald Knew Secret Route on Assassination Day." *Midnight*, volume 23, number 43: 12 April, 1977.

Acoca, Miguel. "Documents: Bush Blew Whistle on Rival in JFK Slaying." *San Francisco Examiner*, Aug. 25. 1988.

Andrews, Chris. "The Roberts Details." *Dome* magazine, April 15, 2011.

Armstrong, John. *Harvey and Lee: How The CIA Framed Oswald.* Arlington, TX: Quasar, Ltd., 2003.

_____. "Harvey and Lee Depart the TSBD." http:// harveyandlee.net, undated article.

_____. "Harvey and Lee: November 22, 1963." http:// harveyandlee.net, undated article.

Ashman, Charles. *Connally: The Adventures Of Big Bad John.* New York: William Morrow & Company, 1974.

Associated Press. "Long-Suppressed Report on Bay of Pigs Blames CIA Itself for Failure of Mission." *St. Louis Post-Dispatch*, Feb. 22, 1998.

Baker, Jeff. "JFK assassination author: evidence proves Oswald did it, conspiracies are a distraction." *The Oregonian*, Dec. 6, 2013. www.oregonianlive.com.

Baker, Judyth Vary. *Me & Lee: How I Came to Know, Love and*

Lose Lee Harvey Oswald. Waterville, OR: Trine Day Press, 2010.

Baker, Russ. "Bush and the JFK Hit: Part 8, Prepping a Patsy?" WhoWhatWhy.org, Nov. 6, 2013.

_____. *Family of Secrets: The Bush Dynasty, America's Invisible Government, and The Hidden History of The Last Fifty Years.* New York: Bloomsbury Press, 2009.

Belzer, Richard. *Hit List*. New York: Skyhorse Publishing, 2013.

Bender, Bryan and Swidey, Neil. "Robert F. Kennedy Saw Conspiracy in JFK's Assassination." *Boston Globe*, Nov. 24, 2013.

Bernstein, Carl. "The CIA And The Media: How America's Most Powerful News Media Worked Hand in Glove with the Central Intelligence Agency and Why the Church Committee Covered It Up." *Rolling Stone* magazine, Oct. 20, 1977.

Biffle, Kent. "Allen Dulles Looks Behind Red Moves." *Dallas Morning News*, October 28, 1963.

Bishop, Jim. *The Day Kennedy Was Shot*. New York: Funk & Wagnalls, 1968.

Bissell, Richard M. *Reflections of a Cold Warrior: From Yalta to the Bay of Pigs*. New Haven, CT: Yale University Press, 1996.

Bolden, Abraham. *The Echo From Dealey Plaza*. New York: Harmony Books, 2008.

Bowen, Russell. *The Immaculate Deception: Bush Crime Family Exposed*. Carson City: America West Publishers, 2000.

Bradlee, Benjamin C. *Conversations With Kennedy*. New York: W.W, Norton, 1975.

Brewton, Pete. *The Mafia, CIA & George Bush: The Untold Story of America's Greatest Financial Debacle*. New York: SPI Books/ Shupolsky Books, 1992.

Brinkley, Douglas. *Cronkite*. New York: HarperCollins Publishing, 2012.

Brown, Walt. *Treachery In Dallas*. New York: Carroll & Graf

Publishers, 1995.

_____. "The Lee Bowers Letter: The One That Got Away." *JFK/Deep Politics Quarterly*, January 1996.

Bruno, Jerry and Greenfield, Jeff. *The Advance Man*. New York: William Morrow & Company, 1971.

Bryce, Robert. *Cronies: Oil, The Bushes, and The Rise of Texas*. New York: Public Affairs, Perseus Books, 2004.

Bugliosi, Vincent. *Reclaiming History: The Assassination of President John F. Kennedy*. New York: W.W. Norton & Company, 2007.

Bundy, McGeorge. *Danger and Survival: Choices About the Bomb in the First Fifty Years*. New York: Random House, 1988.

Byrd, David Harold. *I'm An Endangered Species*. Houston: Pacesetter Press, 1978.

Canfield, Michael and Weberman, Alan J. *Coup D'Etat in America, the CIA and the Assassination of John F. Kennedy*. New York: Third Press, 1975.

_____. *Coup D'Etat in America, the CIA and the Assassination of John F. Kennedy, Volume 3*. New York: Independent Research Associate, 2017.

Caro, Robert. *The Years of Lyndon Johnson: The Path to Power*. New York: Random House Vintage Books, 1990.

Corsi, Jerome R. *Who Really Killed Kennedy?* Washington, DC: WND Books, 2013.

Craig, John R. and Rogers, Philip A. *The Man On The Grassy Knoll*. New York: Avon Books, 1992.

Crenshaw, Charles A., MD. *Trauma Room One: The JFK Medical Cover-Up Exposed*. New York: Paraview Press, 2001.

Curry, Jesse, Retired Dallas Police Chief. *JFK Assassination File*. Privately Printed: 1969.

Cutter, Professor Paul S. "Architects of the Cold War: Allen Welsh Dulles." Wikileaks.org, 2006.

Dallek, Robert. *An Unfinished Life*. Boston: Little, Brown and

Company, 2003.

D'Amato, Pete. "Were Secret Service agents too hungover to protect JFK?" DailyMail.com, Oct. 20, 2014, http://www.dailymail.co.uk/news

Davis, Deborah. *Katharine The Great: Katharine Graham and Her Washington Post Empire.* New York: Harcourt Brace, 1979.

de Burca, Joseph. "Obit(ch)uary: Zbigniew Brzezinski, a mountain of broken skeletons." *Village: Ireland's political and cultural magazine*, Aug. 25, 2017, https://villagemagazine.ie/index

DiEugenio, James. "Ben Bradlee's Not Such A Good Life." Consortiumnews.com, March 10, 2015.

_____. "Douglas Horne, *Inside The ARRB.*" Oct. 16, 2010, https://kennedysandking.com.

_____ and Pease, Lisa. *The Assassinations.* Port Townsend, WA: Feral House, 2003.

_____. "The Life & Death of Richard Case Nagell." *Probe* magazine, Nov.–Dec. 1995, vol. 3 no.1.

Douglass, James W. *JFK And The Unspeakable: Why He Died & Why It Matters.* Maryknoll, NY: Orbis Books, 2008.

Dudman, Richard. "Oswald Declares He Was Denied Legal Counsel." *St. Louis Post-Dispatch*, Nov. 23, 1963.

_____. "Club Operator Charged With Murder Is Held Without Bond." *St. Louis Post-Dispatch*, Nov. 25, 1963.

_____. "U.S. Takes Lead In Inquiries Into Kennedy, Oswald Killings." *St. Louis Post-Dispatch*, Nov. 27, 1963.

_____. "Uncertainties Remain Despite Police View Of Kennedy Death." *St. Louis Post-Dispatch*, Dec. 1, 1963.

_____. "Secret Service Gets Revision On Kennedy Wound." *St. Louis Post-Dispatch*, Dec. 18, 1963

_____. "My Neighbor, The International Spy." *St. Louis Post-Dispatch*, Aug. 4, 1996.

Ernest, Barry. *The Girl On The Stairs: My Search For A Missing Witness To The Assassination Of John F. Kennedy*. Self-published, 2010.

Estes, Billie Sol. *Billie Sol Estes—A Texas Legend*. Oklahoma City: BS Productions, 2004.

Fensterwald, Bernard and Ewing, Michael. *Coincidence or Conspiracy?* New York: Kensington Pub Corp, 1977.

Fetzer, James. *The Great Zapruder Film Hoax*. Chicago: Catfeet Press, 2003.

Fischer, Brendan. "PBS Killed Wisconsin Uprising Documentary 'Citizen Koch' To Appease Koch Brothers." *The Center for Media and Democracy's PR Watch*, May 20, 2013, https://www.prwatch.org.

Fonzi, Gaeton. *The Last Investigation*. New York: Skyhorse Publishing, 2016.

Freund, Carl. "Nixon Predicts JFK May Drop Johnson." *Dallas Morning News*, Nov. 22, 1963.

"Ford Made Key Change in Kennedy Death Report." Associated Press. *New York Times*, July 3, 1997.

Fry, Steve. "Dallas detective: Oswald shot JFK to gain fame." *Topeka Capital-Journal*, 24 Apr. 2013. http://cjonline.com.

Fursenko, Aleksandr and Naftali, Timothy. *"One Hell Of A Gamble": Kruschev, Castro & Kennedy, 1958–1964*. New York: W.W. Norton & Company, 1997.

Galbraith, James K. and Purcell, Heather A. "Did the U.S. Military Plan a Nuclear First Strike for 1963," published on the Mary Ferrell Foundation website, http://www.maryferrell.org

Galbraith, James K. "Exit Strategy: In 1963 JFK Ordered A Complete Withdrawal From Vietnam." *Boston Review*, Sept. 1, 2003.

Gillon, Steven M. *The Kennedy Assassination: 24 Hours After*. New York: Basic Books, 2009.

Golz, Earl. "SS Imposters Spotted by JFK Witnesses." *Dallas*

Morning News, Aug. 27, 1978, p. 1A.

Haldeman, H.R. *The Ends Of Power*. New York: New York Times Books, 1978.

Hancock, Larry. *Someone Would Have Talked*. Southlake, TX: JFK Lancer Productions & Publications, 2011.

Hardaway, Dan. "A Cruel and Shocking Misinterpretation." From the Assassinations Archive and Research Center, http://aarclibrary.org, 2015.

Hardin, Jim. "Deputy kills prisoner in break for freedom." *Dallas Times-Herald*, Feb. 15, 1975, p. 1B.

"Harry S Truman." National Park Service, U.S. Department of the Interior, Harry S Truman National Historic Site, https://www.nps.gov

Hedegaard, Erik. "The Last Confession of E. Howard Hunt." *Rolling Stone* magazine, April 5, 2007.

Herbers, John. "Connally Gains, Doctors Report." *New York Times*, Nov. 24, 1963.

_____. "Kennedy Hit By Two Bullets." *New York Times*, Nov. 27, 1963

Hill, Clint and McCubbin, Lisa. *Five Days In November*. New York: Gallery Books, 2013.

Hilts, Philip. "Louis J. West, Psychiatrist Who Studied Extremes, Dies." *New York Times*, Jan. 9. 1999.

Hopsicker, Daniel. *Barry & The Boys: The CIA, The Mob, and America's Secret History*. Waterville, OR: Trine Day, 2001.

Hornberger, Jacob G. "The Kennedy Casket Conspiracy." Nov. 22, 2010. The Future of Freedom Foundation, http://www.fff.org

Horne, Douglas. *Inside The Assassination Records Review Board: The U.S. Government's Final Attempt to Reconcile the Conflicting Medical Evidence in the Assassination of JFK, Volumes I–V*. Self-published, 2009.

House Select Committee on Assassinations Internal Memo.

"Untaped Telephone Interview Of Jan. 10, 1977 with Nathan Pool." Jan. 12, 1977.

House Select Committee on Assassinations Report. "Section X. Oswald-Tippit Associates: The Wise Allegation," pp. 37–40, March 1979.

Huffaker, Bob; Mercer, Bill; Phenix, George; Wise, Wes. *When The News Went Live: Dallas 1963*. Lanham, MD: Taylor Trade Publishing, 2004.

Hunt, Howard. *Give Us This Day*. New Rochelle, NY: Arlington House, 1973.

Hunter, Marjorie. "Boggs Demands That Hoover Quit." *New York Times*, Apr. 6, 1971.

Hurt, Henry. *Reasonable Doubt*. New York: Holt, Rineholt & Winston, 1985.

"Indict Two Sons of H.L. Hunt, Two Others in Wiretapping." *Chicago Tribune*, Mar. 2, 1973; *Associated Press*, Mar. 1, 1973.

Inkol, Sheldon. "Jack Lawrence Responds." *The Third Decade*, vol. 8, issue 6, Sept. 1992, http://www.maryferrell.org

Jacobsen, Annie. *Operation Paperclip: The Secret Intelligence Program That Brought Nazi Scientists To America*. New York: Little, Brown and Company, 2014.

Janney, Peter. *Mary's Mosaic: The CIA Conspiracy to Murder John F. Kennedy, Mary Meyer and Their Vision For World Peace*. New York: Skyhorse Publishing, 2012.

Johnston, James P., and Roe, Jon. *Flight From Dallas*. Victoria, BC: Trafford Publishing, 2005.

Jones, Christopher. "John F. Kennedy Assassination Flight: What Happened On The Flight From Dallas." *Esquire* magazine, October, 2013. http://www.esquire.com/news- politics

Jovich, John Burke. "The Ordeal of Vernon Oneal: The Story of President Kennedy's First Casket." Nov.16, 2013, http://ezinearticles.com.

Kamran, Dr. Syed. "How The CIA Used Refugees To Create War

in Vietnam." *Daily Pakistan Global*, March 6, 2017.

Kelly, William E., Jr. "Arthur Young—A Visit At Home With Arthur Young." JFK Countercoup, Dec. 20, 2009. www.jfkcountercoup.blogspot.com

_____. "Egg Harbor Township Elk of the Year Was Oswald's Bunkmate." The Education Forum, July 27, 2006.

"Ken Burns and Co-Director Lynn Novick on the Lessons in Their Latest Documentary, *The Vietnam War*." *Parade* magazine, Aug. 20, 2017, www.Parade.com/vietnam.

Kendall-Bell, Greg. "Controversy Still Swirls Around Rifle Used in JFK Assassination." *Abilene Reporter-News*, 11/22/11, pg. 8A

_____. "With Oswald At Atsugi." JFK Assassination Debate Online Forum, Feb. 2011. www.educationforumipbhost.com

Kessler, Ronald. *Inside the White House.* New York: Pocket Books, 1995.

Kinzer, Stephen. *The Brothers: John Foster Dulles, Allen Dulles, and Their Secret World War.* New York: Henry Holt and Company, 2013.

_____. "When a CIA Director Had Scores of Affairs." New York Times Opinion Pages: Nov. 10, 2012.

Kirk, Deanna. "Living History: Boyd describes his role at JFK assassination." *Corsicana Daily Sun*, Aug. 18, 2017, www.corsicanadailysun.com/news.

Krock, Arthur. "Intra-Administration War in Vietnam." *New York Times*, Oct. 3, 1963, p. 34.

Lambert, William and Wheeler, Keith. "How LBJ's Family Amassed Its Fortune." *Life* magazine, Aug. 21, 1964, pp. 62–63.

Lane, Mark. *Plausible Denial: Was the CIA Involved In The Assassination Of JFK?* New York: Thunder's Mouth Press, 1991.

_____. *Last Word: My Indictment of the CIA In the Murder of JFK.* New York: Skyhorse Publishing, 2012.

Lazzaro, Joseph. "JFK Assassination: First JFK Conspiracy Theory Was Paid For By The CIA." *International Business Times*, Dec. 5, 2013.

Lifton, David. *Best Evidence: Disguise and Deception In The Assassination of John F. Kennedy*. New York: Carroll & Graf Publishers, 1980.

Livingstone, Harrison and Groden, Robert. *High Treason: The Assassination of JFK & the Case for Conspiracy*. New York: Carroll & Graf Publishers, 1998.

"Long-suppressed report on Bay of Pigs blames CIA itself for failure of mission." Associated Press. *St. Louis Post-Dispatch*, Feb. 22, 1998.

Lopez, Rebecca. "Secret Service also partied before Kennedy assassination." WFAA.com, Apr. 20, 2012.

Manchester, William. *The Death Of A President*. New York: Harper & Row, 1967.

Mantik, David and Wecht, Cyril. "Paradoxes of the JFK Assassination: The Brain Enigma." *The Assassinations: Probe Magazine on JFK, MLK, RFK and Malcolm X.*, edited by James DiEugenio and Lisa Pease. Port Townsend, WA: Feral House, 2003.

"Man Questioned in Hammer Beating." *Dallas Times-Herald*, Mar. 27, 1974, p. 8B.

Mapes, Mary. *Truth and Duty: The Press, the President and the Privilege of Power*. New York: St. Martin's Press, 2005.

Marchetti, Victor. "CIA to Admit Hunt Involvement in Kennedy Slaying." *Spotlight* magazine, Aug. 14, 1978.

Marrs, Jim. *Crossfire: The Plot That Killed Kennedy*. New York: Carroll & Graf Publishers, 1989.

_____. "The Senator Who Suspected a JFK Conspiracy." http://jfktruth.org

Martin, Joe. "The mid-20th-century rise of a secret government." Streetrootsnews.org, Dec. 20, 2016.

McClellan, Barr. *Blood, Money & Power: How LBJ Killed JFK.* New York: Hanover Press, 2003.

McGowan, David. *Derailing Democracy.* Monroe, ME: Common Courage Press, 2002.

McKnight, Gerald D. *Breach of Trust: How the Warren Commission Failed the Nation and Why.* Lawrence, KS: University of Kansas Press, 2005.

McMillan, Priscilla Johnson. *Marina And Lee: The Tormented Love and Fatal Obsession Behind Lee Harvey Oswald's Assassination of John F. Kennedy.* Hanover, NH: Steerforth Press, 2013.

Miller, Aaron David. *The End of Greatness: Why America Can't Have (and Doesn't Want) Another Great President.* New York: St. Martin's Press, 2014.

Mellen, Joan. *A Farewell to Justice: Jim Garrison, JFK's Assassination, and the Case That Should Have Changed History.* New York: Skyhorse Publishing, 2013.

_____. *Faustian Bargains: Lyndon Johnson and Mac Wallace in the Robber Baron Culture of Texas.* New York: Bloomsbury Publishing, 2016.

Minutaglio, Bill and Davis, Steven L. *Dallas 1963.* New York: Hachette Book Group, 2013.

Morley, Jefferson. "Ex-Flame Says Jack Ruby 'had no choice' But to Kill Oswald." 14 Aug. 2016, http://jfkfacts.org.

Morris, John G. "Shooting The President." *Popular Photography,* August 1977.

Nelson, Philip F. *LBJ: The Mastermind Of The JFK Assassination.* New York, Skyhorse Publishing, 2013.

_____. *LBJ: From Mastermind To The Colossus.* New York: Skyhorse Publishing, 2014.

Neufeld, Michael A. *Von Braun: Dreamer Of Space, Engineer Of War.* New York: Vintage Books, 2008.

Newcomb, Fred T. and Adams, Perry. *Murder From Within: Lyndon Johnson's Plot Against President Kennedy.* Bloomington,

IN: Author House, 2011.

Newman, John. *Oswald and the CIA*. New York: Carroll & Graf Publishers, 1995.

Noyes, Peter. *Legacy of Doubt*. New York: Pinnacle Books, 1973.

O'Donnell, Kenneth, and Powers, David. *Johnny We Hardly Knew Ye*. New York: Little, Brown & Co., 1972

O'Neill, Thomas P., Jr. *Man Of The House: The Life And Political Times of Speaker Tip O'Neill*. New York: Random House, 1987.

Orwell, George. *1984*. New York: Signet Classic, 1950.

O'Toole, George. *The Assassination Tapes*. New York: Penthouse Press, Ltd., 1975.

Palamara, Vince. *JFK: From Parkland To Bethesda: The Ultimate Kennedy Assassination Compendium*. Waterville, OR: Trine Day LLC, 2015.

_____. "Main Secret Service Blog: JFK, The Kennedy Detail, and More." http://vincepalamara.blogspot.com

_____. "The Kennedy Detail Exposed—the real story of the JFK Secret Service." November in Dallas Conference, Nov. 20, 2016.

Parmet, Herbert S. *JFK: The Presidency of John F. Kennedy*. New York: Dial Press, 1983.

Pearson, Drew, and Anderson, Jack. *The Case Against Congress: A Compelling Indictment of Corruption On Capitol Hill*. New York: Simon & Schuster, 1968.

Pierce, Charles. "I May Be an Enemy of the People, But at Least I'm No Longer Sick." Feb. 17, 2017, http://esquire.com/news-politics.

Posner, Gerald. *Case Closed: Lee Harvey Oswald and the Assassination of JFK*. New York: Anchor Books, 1993.

Pratt, Joseph A. and Castenada, Christopher A. *Builders: Herman and George R. Brown*. College Station, TX: Texas A&M University Press, 2002.

Proctor, Grover. "The Phone Call That Never Was." *Raleigh*

Spectator, July 17, 1980.

_____. "The Raleigh Call and the Fingerprints of Intelligence." Nov. 23, 2014, http://groverproctor.us/jfk.

Prouty, Fletcher. "People and the Pursuit of the Truth." June, 1978, www.prouty.org/nixon.html

_____. *JFK: The CIA, Vietnam, and the Plot to Assassinate John F. Kennedy*. New York: Citadel, 1996.

_____. *The Secret Team: The CIA and Its Allies In Control Of The United States and The World*. Englewood Cliffs, NJ: Prentice-Hall, Inc., 1973.

Quinn, Sally. "Doris Kearns and Richard Goodwin: A Tale of Hearts and Minds." *Washington Post*, Aug. 24, 1975.

Rather, Dan. *Rather Outspoken*. New York: Grand Central Publishing, 2012.

Report of the President's Commission on the Assassination of President John F. Kennedy, and 26 accompanying volumes of Hearings and Exhibits, 1964; published by U.S. Government Printing Office and Doubleday, McGraw-Hill, Bantam and Associated Press, 1964.

Report of the Select Committee on Assassinations, U.S. House of Representatives, and 12 accompanying volumes of Hearings and Appendices, 1979; published by U.S. Government Printing Office and *Report* only by Bantam, New York, 1979, under the title *The Final Assassinations Report*.

Roberts, Craig. *Kill Zone*. CreateSpace Publishing Platform, 6th ed., 2014.

Rockwood, Bill. "Interview: G. Robert Blakey." *Frontline*, Nov. 19, 2013, www.pbs.org.

Russell, Dick. *The Man Who Knew Too Much*. New York: Carroll & Graf, 1992.

_____. "Oswald and the CIA." *Electronic Assassinations Newsletter*, Issue #2, http://whokilledjfk.net

Ryan, Tim. "Kennedy Assassination Intrigue Swirls in D.C.

Federal." Courthouse News Service, Apr. 4, 2017.

Sabato, Larry. *The Kennedy Half-Century: The Presidency, Assassination, and Lasting Legacy of John F. Kennedy.* New York: Bloomsbury Press, 2014.

Salerian, Alen. "A Peace Award for Robert McNamara." *OpEd News*, Nov. 13, 2009. www.opednews.com

Sample, Glen and Collom, Mark. *The Men on the Sixth Floor.* Garden Grove, CA: Sample Graphics, 2011.

Shackelford, Martin. "A Celebration of Freedom: Latest Research and Secrets from the Files." Electronic Assassination Newsletter: Issue #2: New Discoveries in the Recently Released Assassination Files, 1996.

Shaw, Gary, and Harris, Larry Ray. *Cover-Up: The Governmental Conspiracy to Conceal the Facts About the Public Execution of John Kennedy.* Austin, TX: Thomas Investigative Publications, 1992.

Sheehan, Neil. *A Bright Shining Lie: John Paul Vann and America in Vietnam.* New York: Random House, 1988.

Shesol, Jeff. *Mutual Contempt: Lyndon Johnson, Robert Kennedy, and the Feud that Defined a Decade.* New York: W.W. Norton & Company, 1997.

Simkin, John. "David Sanchez Morales," *Spartacus Educational,* June 2017, www.spartacus-educational.com.

_____. "Chauncey Holt," *Spartacus Educational,* August 2014, www.spartacus- educational.com

Sloan, Bill with Jean Hill. *JFK: The Last Dissenting Witness.* Gretna, LA: Pelican Publishing, 1992.

Smith, Matthew. *JFK: The Second Plot.* Edinburgh: Mainstream Publishing, 1992.

_____. *Say Goodbye To America: The Sensational and Untold Story Behind The Assassination of John F. Kennedy.* Edinburgh: Mainstream Publishing, 2001.

Starnes, Richard. "Spooks Make Life Miserable for Ambassador

Lodge: Arrogant CIA Disobeys Orders in Viet Nam."
Washington Daily News, October 2, 1963.

"Steel: The Ides of April." *Fortune* magazine, May 1962.

Stich, Rodney. *Defrauding America*. Alamo, CA: Diablo Western
Press, 1994.

Stone, Oliver and Sklar, Zachary. *JFK: The Documented
Screenplay*. Applause Books, 1992.

Sullivan, Andrew. "Democracies end when they are too
democratic." *New York* magazine, May 2-15, 2016, pp. 32-104.

Summers, Anthony. *Conspiracy*. New York: McGraw-Hill Book
Company, 1980.

_____. *Not In Your Lifetime*. New York: Open
Road, Integrated Media, 2013.

Swanson, James. *End of Days: The Assassination of John F. Kennedy*.
New York: William Morrow, 2013.

Talbot, David. *Brothers: The Hidden History of the Kennedy Years*.
New York: Free Press, 2007.

_____. "Passing The Torch: An International Symposium
on the 50th Anniversary of the Assassination of President John
F. Kennedy." Duquesne University, November, 2013.

_____. *The Devil's Chessboard: Allen Dulles, the CIA, and
the Rise of America's Secret Government*. New York:
HarperCollins, 2015.

The Assassination Records Review Board, Final Report, 1998.

The Papers of Dwight David Eisenhower, Volume XV—the
Presidency: The Middle Way, Part VI, Crises Abroad, Party
Problems at Home; September 1954 to November 1954.

Thompson, Doug. "Is deception the best way to serve one's
country?" *Capitol Hill Blue*, Mar. 29, 2006, http://rense.com/
general70/connol.htm

Trask, Richard. *Pictures Of The Pain*. Danvers, MA: Yeoman Press,
1994.

_____. *That Day In Dallas*. Danvers, MA: Yeoman Press, 1998.

Trento, Joseph. *The Secret History of The CIA*. Roseville, CA: Prima, 2001.

"Tried To Sell Data: Secret Service Agent Gets 6 Years In Jail." Associated Press. *Tuscaloosa News*, Aug. 13, 1964, p. 2.

Twyman, Noel. *Bloody Treason*. Rancho Santa Fe, CA: Laurel Publishing, 1997.

Unger, Craig. "Mystery Man." *Salon* magazine, Apr. 28, 2004.

Veciana, Antonio and Harrison, Carlos. *Trained To Kill: The Inside Story of CIA Plots Against Castro, Kennedy, and Che*. New York: Skyhorse Publishing, 2017.

Wagoner, Joel. "The Body Alteration Theory and Parkland Hospital." *The Third Decade*, vol. 8, issue 2-3, Jan.-Mar. 1992, http://www.maryferrell.org.

Warren Commission Hearings and Exhibits, Volumes I to XXVI.

Weiner, Tim. "Lucein Conein, 79, Legendary Cold War Spy." *New York Times*, June 7, 1998.

Weisberg, Harold. *Oswald In New Orleans*. New York: Skyhorse Publishing, 2013.

Wilkinson, James. "Does this sketch prove that JFK was assassinated by two gunmen?: Drawing by fallen president's surgeon in Dallas says bullets came from different directions." DailyMail.com, June 23, 2017.

Will, George. "*The Vietnam War* is a Masterpiece—and a Model for Assessing Our History." *The Washington Post*, Sept. 15, 2017.

Williams, Dan. "Anti-Castro Leader Shot In The Head." *Miami Herald*, Sept. 22, 1979.

Wrone, David. "*Case Closed: Lee Harvey Oswald and the Assassination of JFK*, by Gerald Posner." Journal of Southern History 61, February 1995, p. 186.

Zirbel, Craig I. *The Texas Connection: The Assassination Of John F. Kennedy*. Scottsdale, AZ: The Texas Connection Company Publishers, Inc., 1992.

Review Requested:
If you loved this book, would you please provide a review at
Amazon.com?

CPSIA information can be obtained
at www.ICGtesting.com
Printed in the USA
LVOW10s0917210518
577925LV00002B/80/P